BONFIRES AND BELLS

'England's Great Joy and Gratitude' (detail), from a broadside of the 1690s, Firth A3. Item 123, Bodleian Library, Oxford

BONFIRES AND BELLS

National Memory and the Protestant Calendar in Elizabethan and Stuart England

David Cressy

University of California Press
Berkeley and Los Angeles

Copyright © David Cressy, 1989

First published in Great Britain by
George Weidenfeld and Nicolson Ltd
91 Clapham High Street, London SW4 7TA

First U.S. edition published 1989 by
University of California Press
Berkeley and Los Angeles

Photoset by Deltatype Limited, Ellesmere Port
Printed and bound in Great Britain by
Butler & Tanner Ltd, Frome and London

Library of Congress Catalog Card Number: 89–51387
ISBN 0–520–06940–4
1 2 3 4 5 6 7 8 9

CONTENTS

PREFACE

I am grateful to the National Endowment for the Humanities and to the Research Committee at California State University, Long Beach, for summer stipends. A visiting fellowship at the Humanities Research Centre, Australian National University, enabled me to complete this book.

Parts of this study were first presented to the British history seminar at the Huntington Library, California, and at the North American Conference on British Studies. The work has been further refined through criticism at seminars at the universities of Durham, Oxford, and Sussex, and at Adelaide, La Trobe, Sydney and Western Australia. Among many who have helped, I would also like to thank Dorothy Abrahamse, Robert Bucholz, Barbara Donagan, Juliet Gardiner, Barry Reay, Lorena Walsh, Retha Warnicke, and Steven Zwicker for their written comments. Kevin Sharpe read the entire first draft, and offered challenging suggestions. Valerie Cressy accompanied me during research and writing on three continents, and helped keep me sane and cheerful.

All dates are given 'old style', following the usage in Tudor and Stuart England, except that the year is considered to have begun on 1 January. Spelling and punctuation have been modernized.

'The news, Rogero? Nothing but bonfires.'
A Winter's Tale, Act V, Scene 2

INTRODUCTION

Under Elizabeth and the early Stuarts the English developed a relationship to time – current time within the cycle of the year, and historical time with reference to the past – that set them apart from the rest of early modern Europe. In many ways the calendar of seventeenth-century England had less in common with Renaissance France or Spain, and more with twentieth-century America or Australia. It was based on, and gave expression to, a mythic and patriotic sense of national identity. Though founded on Christianity, purged of the excesses of late-medieval Catholicism, the guiding landmarks were taken from recent incidents in English history. The calendar became an important instrument for declaring and disseminating a distinctively Protestant national culture. It served, sometimes, as a unifying force, binding the nation to the ruling dynasty and securing it through an inspiring providential interpretation of English history. But mounting tension and trouble made the calendar increasingly politicized as the seventeenth century wore on.

Several calendrical schemes operated together in Elizabethan and Stuart England, combining economic, ecclesiastical, dynastic and patriotic seasons and dates. Considerable controversy attached to some of these cycles, but the intensity of concern varied with the perceived moral, political or religious dangers of the moment. Sketched simply, the scheme and the sequence seem to have been as follows:

In the early sixteenth century the English celebrated a round of religious festivals, holy days and saints' days, many of which charted the annual Christological cycle, alongside others that masked, with varying opacity, apparently pre-Christian seasonal observances. May day and midsummer, for example, were loosely tied to the Christian year by naming them respectively the feasts of Saints Philip and James, and St John. The national religious calendar shared its rhythms with the rest of Roman Christendom, while at the same time accommodating a host of local devotions and cultic preferences associated with the patron saints of particular guilds and parishes. The year was also sprinkled with royal and civic occasions, such as entries, triumphs and pageants, but these had an ad hoc quality and enjoyed no fixed periodicity and little significance outside of the town or city where they happened. Royal anniversaries passed unnoticed, and there was no special celebration of dates from English history. Under Henry VIII, for example, there was no Agincourt day, and no particular fuss made of the year-day of the king's accession.

In the second half of the sixteenth century, in the wake of the Reformation, the number of religious celebratory occasions was reduced, and the calendar was, to some extent, de-festivalized. The Book of Common Prayer established a national devotional frame-work for the passage of the seasons, firmly centred on commemoration of the life of Christ, with a severe reduction in the number of holy days. Whether reform had gone far enough, or had gone too far, was a recurrent issue. Disputes on this subject helped to sensitize people to the politics of the calendar, and may have aided in the adoption of new anniversaries commemorating the emergence and safety of the English Protestant regime.

Beginning in the last quarter of the sixteenth century, there was added to this prayer-book calendar a new national, secular and dynastic calendar centering on the anniversaries of the Protestant monarch. There had been, for sure, a court calendar in earlier times, involving gift-giving at new year and chivalric deeds on St George's day, and this continued. But the Elizabethan development was distinctly different. Beginning around 1570, and developing into a national cult a few years later, the annual ringing of church bells, and the festive observances of 'the queen's holy day' on 17 November, linked parishes throughout England in an annual symphony of loyal celebration. National observance of the royal accession day, which was a novelty in the mid-Elizabethan period, became an established custom in the seventeenth century. Local festivity – at the least bellringing, and often health-drinking, feasting, illuminations, and bonfires too – greeted the birthdays and accession days of each succeeding monarch, and sometimes the birthdays of their wives and children.

Overlapping this royal calendar, and sometimes competing with it, was the developing calendar of English Protestant thankfulness, watchfulness, and commemoration. A new set of national anniversaries flourished in the seventeenth century as distinctive reference points in the English Protestant year, tying together God's calendar, the king's calendar, and the calendar of the Protestant nation. The crucial dates were 5 and 17 November, the anniversaries respectively of the Gunpowder Treason and the accession of Queen Elizabeth.

The new English calendar became thicker and more crowded as the seventeenth century progressed, with a cumulative accretion of religious and dynastic anniversaries. Just as Elizabeth's accession was celebrated under her Stuart successors, and the Gunpowder Plot against James I created a calendrical occasion of enduring significance, so too did the traumatic events of the revolution, with special reverence reserved in the later Stuart period for 30 January (a day of prayer and fasting), and Royal Oak day, 29 May (a day of prayer and frolic). By the end of the seventeenth century it could be said that the spring belonged to the Tories and the autumn belonged to the Whigs.

During the seventeenth century the English paid increasing attention to the symbolic anniversaries of their own recent history. And since that history involved disputes, with winners and losers as well as struggles that continued or revived, it is not surprising to find the calendar operating as an annual mnemonic, occasioning celebration or recrimination. This is not to argue that the country at large was torn by cultural or religious disputes, or even overly concerned by them, but simply to note divisions among religious and political activists. Recurrent opportunities to excite these divisions were provided by the cycle of the ecclesiastical year and by the calendar of Protestant deliverances. Even if there was agreement on a date, such as 5 November which was enshrined by act of parliament, there could be disputes about what exactly was being commemorated, and about the behaviour appropriate to it.

Momentous episodes involving Queen Elizabeth and the Spanish Armada, the Gunpowder Plot and the fortunes of the Stuart kings, were memorialized and commemorated as signs of God's interest in his Protestant nation. They formed landmarks in the development of the English Protestant calendar, and cumulative elements of the national memory. The anniversary of each monarch's accession and the recollection of famous 'deliverances' shaped a calendar unique for its patriotism and its contentiousness. The anniversaries of these deliverances were celebrated with bonfires and bells, though not always with sweetness and light.

These crucial celebrated moments have been studied extensively in the mainstream political history of England, but very little attention has been paid to how they were registered in the experience of local communities. This has not been the traditional territory of the social historian. Yet considered from an ethnographic perspective, as well as from the standpoint of high politics and religion, these episodes may teach us about the English view of themselves and their history, and about the forces of social and cultural cohesion. By studying social activity on the major public occasions, patriotic festivals, homecomings, deliverances, and anniversaries of early modern England we may discover how people experienced special events, and how they remembered them. One of our purposes is to examine how these occasions touched popular consciousness while they were happening or soon after, and how they became memorialized (and sometimes mutated) in subsequent generations.

A recurrent issue here is the orchestration of festivity, and the degree to which popular responses were prompted in the interests of established power or partisan position. It is clear that the common people who participated in anniversary festivities, and gave their stamp to them, were not the originators of the new calendar customs. Crownation day, Gunpowder Treason day, Royal Oak day, and the host of ad hoc observances, had their origin in the high politics of Whitehall and Westminster, and reached the local community through sermons, precepts, proclamations, and unwritten instructions. The direction descended through a matrix of command involving Privy Councillors, city fathers, ministers and churchwardens. Social superiors and political masters prompted or activated the local celebrations, even if ordinary villagers and townsfolk joined in and made them their own.

If the political aspects of politicized festivals were of most interest to members of the political nation, it may not be unfair to suggest that others were only there for the beer. This is not to diminish popular culture, or to rob the English people of their spontaneity or cultural independence. Rather it is to show once more the interaction of elite and popular culture, in which the elite was often dominant. Though generally a matter of custom and convenience in Elizabethan and Stuart England, calendrical rhythms and commemorative activities also precipitated a cycle of cultural and political collisions. As activities on Gunpowder Treason day often demonstrated, festive traditions and political concerns intersected, and sometimes rubbed each other the wrong way. Older calendrical occasions, most notably Shrovetide, Maytide, Midsummer and Christmas, had enduring popular dimensions. They, too, enjoyed civic, courtly, and ecclesiastical patronage, but it seems that here the dominant impulse came from below, or, at least, from outside the arena of politics. These were the festivals most likely to involve rites of inversion and misrule. On these occasions the authorities were more likely to be found constraining or criticizing popular excesses than reminding people to celebrate.

1
PATTERNS OF TIME – THE TUDOR CALENDAR

Every society has its calendar. Whether shaped and paced by the circling of the heavens or the seasons of the soil, or structured and punctuated by anniversaries of religious or secular signficance, every human community finds regularity and periodicity in the unbroken passage of time. Early modern England had a calendar of layers as well as passages. At the core lay the natural calendar, the cycle of the seasons that existed from time immemorial. Tied to this, or superimposed upon it, were the agrarian calendar of the harvest year, the Christian calendar of seasonally focused worship, the medieval scatter of saints' days, the law calendar, the civic calendar of mayoral years, and the developing repertory of regnal, political and religious anniversaries of Tudor and Stuart England. The calendar was a lesson in history and a reminder of duties, both secular and sacred. It was a convenience and a constraint, linking the lowliest subject and the highest powers, and providing a framework for the flowering of a national political culture.

Pre-Reformation England followed a calendar that drew on celestial, pagan and ecclesiastical elements. Each year matched a cycle of birth, death and re-birth, following the rise and declination of the sun, the waxing and waning of the moon, the lengthening and shadowing of days, and the warming and cooling of the earth. To the solar calendar of solstice and equinox was grafted the agrarian rhythm of cultivation, harrowing, planting, and harvest. In pastoral and stock regions this was further modified by the cycles of lambing and calving, droving and herding, and the autumn slaughter of animals that would not be fed through the winter. In other communities the passage of time was marked by the seasonal business of herring fishing or hop picking, fairs and markets. Every activity had its time.

The close inter-phasing of astronomy and agriculture stretched back to the neolithic revolution. Ancient Britons, whether men of Wessex of the age of Stonehenge or iron-age tribesmen following Druids, acknowledged the power that governed the cycling of the year. The evidence is slender, of course, for pre-history, but the solar

1

alignments of megalithic remains and the traces of the Celtic calendar that have survived the Romans and Saxons testify to the importance of ancient seasonal rhythms in both economic and ritual activities.

The record-keeping societies of Egypt and the ancient Mediterranean developed names and calculations for the reckoning of time which have persisted into the modern era. The Roman Julian calendar, developed in the first century BC, provided the basic system that is still in use. (The Gregorian calendar of the sixteenth century, belatedly adopted in England in the eighteenth, was essentially a technical modification.) The year contains twelve months, approximating a dozen lunar cycles, and the sequence repeats appropriately in the month named after Janus, the Roman gatekeeper God of beginnings. So too in early Anglo-Saxon England the year began and ended in the midwinter month of 'Giuli', which is presumably the basis of the attenuated 'Yuletide' that was still recognized a thousand years later.

To the natural calendar of the seasons and the economic calendar of agriculture was added the ceremonial calendar of the Christian year. The story of the New Testament, prefigured in the Old, could be told in an annual yearly cycle embracing Advent, Christmas, Epiphany, Lent, Easter and Ascension. The liturgical round made these mystical events a common accompaniment to everyday life. The Christian story of birth, death and resurrection provided a dramatic narrative that was roughly accommodated to the older cycle of the solar year. Quarterly Ember days were ordained as times of fasting and prayer at the corners of the four seasons. To the Christological calendar the medieval church attached a series of holy days dedicated to particular saints. Some of these saints were contemporaries of Christ – his apostles and followers and members of his family – but others were men and women of a later era whose holiness or suffering merited sanctification, canonization, and perpetual memory. The saints provided intercessionary avenues to heaven, and their days were distributed comfortingly throughout the year. In England, and throughout Christian Europe, the calendar became cluttered with holy days of varying local, national or international significance.

It is well known, and was known in the sixteenth century, that many of the festivals of the Christian year were based on earlier pagan observances. Renaissance antiquarians understood that Druidic, Roman, or Nordic festivals underlay many of the popular festivities and religious occasions of medieval and early modern Europe. Ancient fire and fertility ceremonies lingered in Christian garb. It was no accident that Christian feasts on 1 November, 1 February, 1 May, and 1 August fell on the same days as the old pagan festivals of Samhain, Imbolc, Beltaine and Lughnasa. 'Long before October 31

2

became Hallowe'en, the Eve of All Saints' day, it was Winter Eve, when the *nod-fyr* ("needfire") was kindled to provide hope of the rebirth of the light after the winter darkness to come . . . Between Christmas and Epiphany the medieval feast of fools was often held, where a ritual return to chaos was enacted in the form of licentious revelling; this was essentially a winter solstice rite signifying the beginning of a new year and a new life. The Roman Saturnalia of December 17–24 was such a cosmic renewal rite; the birth of Mithra occurred on December 25, that of Osiris on January 6, later the Christian Epiphany.'[1]

By no means did all of the holy days of the Christian church originate from pagan customs, but there was sufficient congruity to scandalize some Protestants. New Year's day, once marked by an ancient masquerading hunting rite, (and as late as the nineteenth century the occasion for hunting the cutty wren) became the feast of Circumcision. The first day of February, an ancient fire festival, was overlain by the Eve of Candlemas and the Purification of the Virgin. May day was tamed and renamed to honour Saints Philip and James, although it never shed its associations with the Roman fertility festival of the Floralia or the northern renewal rites of the Maypole and the 'green man'. The midsummer festivity was turned into the feast of St John the Baptist, but it too retained some of its character as the climax of the fire and fertility rites celebrating the triumph of the sun and renewal of summer vegetation. Joshua Stopford, a north-country divine, believed that the midsummer bonfires derived from ancient rituals designed to drive away dragons.[2]

It is virtually impossible to determine what hold these ancient rites had on the people of early modern England. The dates in the calendar may have had pagan origins, but by the sixteenth century they were most likely innocent of conscious pagan associations. There may have been an underlying folk memory of older fire festivals and rites of renewal, masked by Christian practice, and there is certainly evidence that Protestant reformers worried that their church was tainted by the pagan elements that had been taken over uncritically from the church of Rome. But most people observed Christmas as the feast of the birth of the saviour Jesus without knowing or caring that it might formerly have celebrated the birth of Mithra or the Anglo-Saxon Yule. The piety and devotion of late-medieval saints' days was patently Christian, even if it derived from pre-Christian origins and accommodated people with little grasp of Christian theology. Did it matter, then, whether such holidays as Christmas or Easter retained remnants of Judaism, paganism, and the practices of ancient Rome? Opinions on this subject were marshalled on behalf of a larger debate over

3

worship, ritual and authority, and they placed people on opposing sides of an increasingly bitter division.

*

The layers and passages of the old medieval calendar presented several problems to Protestant reformers. The first concerned Romish remnants, in particular the plethora of saints' days; the second struck at the structure of the Christian year and its superstitious or pagan associations. And reformers of manners perennially inveighed against the licentiousness that was associated with popular festivity.[3]

Early reformers of the sixteenth century were less concerned with the pagan origins and structure of the calendar than with the odious proliferation of saints' days. The medieval calendar was heavy with holy days and religious festivals, and their number was expanding in the pious world of the early sixteenth century. There were many more saints than days in the year to honour them. In the view of some reformers under Henry VIII, 'the number of holy-days is so excessively grown, and yet daily more and more, by men's devotion, yea, rather superstition, was like further to increase'.[4] The first phase of the Reformation in England saw an assault on the proliferation of saints' days, but no damage to the underlying structure of the Christian calendar. The emergent Church of England adopted a liturgical routine that would have been familiar to medieval Catholics, and which, in outline, survives to the present. It was driven, however, by a Protestant theology that found no scriptural authority for the intercessionary power of saints. English Protestants could commemorate certain saints, but would be careful not to pray to them. Honouring the saints was simply another way of honouring God. Moderate Elizabethan Protestants might agree to 'keep' certain ceremonies and calendrical observances, but understood them to be 'devised by man', not mandated by God.[5]

Acting as supreme head of the Church of England, Henry VIII in 1536 forced Convocation to agree to injunctions severely limiting the observance of holy days and reducing them to a manageable number. The stated reason was primarily secular, to preserve the moral and economic order. The proliferation of saints' days was deemed 'not only prejudicial to the common weal, by reason that it is occasion as well of much sloth and idleness, the very nurse of thieves, vagabonds, and divers other unthriftiness and inconveniences, as of decay of good mysteries [i.e. crafts] and arts profitable and necessary for the commonwealth, and loss of man's food (many times being clean destroyed through the superstitious observance of the said holy-days, in not taking the opportunity of good and serene weather offered upon the same in time of harvest), but also pernicious to the souls of many men, who, being enticed by the licentious vacation and liberty of those holy days, do upon the same commonly use and practice more excess, riot, and superfluity, than upon any other days'.[6] This was calendar reform in the interest of seemly manners and social discipline, reform which differentiated England from the corrupted church of Rome.

Local parish dedication feasts, which had hitherto been scattered around the calendar, were henceforth to be kept on a standard day, the first Sunday in October. Patron saints' days, 'called commonly the church holy day', might still be recognized, but no religious observance was to interrupt the rhythms of labour. Work also took precedence over worship during the critical harvest period, defined here as 1 July to 29 September. Any saint whose day happened to fall during that period would have to be content with a mere token observance. The clergy might sing their services, but the rest of the community would continue to work in the fields. In this purged religious calendar only the feasts of the Apostles, the Blessed Virgin, St George, the Nativity, Easter day, St John the Baptist, and St Michael the Archangel would be preserved as high holy days or days of general offering. Ascension day, All Hallows day, and Candlemas day were also preserved as days to 'be kept holy and solemnly of every man, as in time past hath been accustomed'.[7]

Purging the calendar was easier to proclaim than to enforce. As the reformers charged, the holy days were often marked by jollity, idleness, and superfluity, and that, of course, was why so many people looked forward to them. Saints' days may have interrupted the labour of harvest, and may have interfered with artisan production, but they stimulated other parts of the economy. Pedlars appeared, fairs were staged, and the wheels of commerce were lubricated with ale. Many communities were fondly attached to their patron saints, and the rhythm of the year was still marked by traditional religious holidays. Saints who were locally renowned for their prayers, cures and comfort could probably withstand most ordinances from Canterbury or Westminster. The government of Henry VIII degraded Thomas Becket from saint to upstart priest, and saw to the destruction of his shrine; but the cult of St Thomas was much harder to eradicate from popular memory. At Canterbury, the seat of the martyr, the pageant of St Thomas was halted in 1536, revived under Mary, and continued with some ambivalence under Elizabeth until 1564. A vestigial recognition of St Thomas continued, and the eighty parish churches dedicated to the English martyr perpetuated the veneration of his name.[8]

Official observance of the feasts of Saints Luke, Mark, and Mary

Magdalene crept back into the calendar in 1541, while other traditional holy days lived on without state encouragement. It was not insignificant that the Cornish rebellion in 1549 took root in the Whit Sunday and Whit Monday assemblies, while Ket's rebellion in Norfolk emerged from the celebration at Wymondham of the presumably illegal feast of St Thomas the Martyr in the same year. Concern for local saints had been an issue in the Pilgrimage of Grace of 1536, and would rise again in the northern rebellion of 1569.[9]

In 1552 the parliament of Edward VI passed 'an act for the keeping of holy days and fasting days'. This legislation stressed that religious holidays existed only for the honouring of God and the edification of his congregations. Certain days were 'sanctified and hallowed, that is to say, separated from all profane uses, and dedicated and appointed not unto any saint or creature, but only unto God and his true worship'. Strict Protestants found no authority for the church calendar in scripture, and regarded all days as 'of like holiness'. They acknowledged the power of custom, however, and were willing to authorize an expanded list of holidays provided it was understood that these days drew their special potency from 'the discretion of the rulers and ministers' rather than the timeless will of God. They also made it clear that harvest workers and other workmen could go about their labours on holy days, 'when necessity shall require'.[10] The framers of this legislation seem to have been salving their consciences and meeting some of the theological advances of the Reformation while at the same time conceding that the Henrician cut-back of holidays had been too harsh.

The approved holy days, 'and none other', were all Sundays in the year, the Mondays and Tuesdays in Easter week and Whitsun week, and the days of the following feasts:

Circumcision of our Lord Jesus Christ	(1 January, New Year)
Epiphany	(6 January, Twelfth day)
Purification of the Blessed Virgin	(2 February)
St Matthias the Apostle	(24 February)
Annunciation of the Blessed Virgin	(25 March, Lady day)
St Mark the Evangelist	(25 April)
SS Philip and James the Apostles	(1 May, May day)
Ascension of our Lord Jesus Christ	(movable)
Nativity of St John the Baptist	(24 June, Midsummer day)
St Peter the Apostle	(29 June)
St James the Apostle	(25 July)
St Bartholomew the Apostle	(24 August)
St Matthew the Apostle	(21 September)

St Michael the Archangel	(29 September, Michaelmas)
St Luke the Evangelist	(18 October)
SS Simon and Jude the Apostles	(28 October)
All Saints	(1 November)
St Andrew the Apostle	(30 November)
St Thomas the Apostle	(21 December)
Nativity of our Lord	(25 December)
St Stephen the Martyr	(26 December)
St John the Evangelist	(27 December)
Holy Innocents	(28 December, Childermas)

These twenty-seven holy days, plus fifty-two Sundays, made a total of seventy-nine days in the year when 'lawful bodily labour' could be set aside for prayer and worship. Furthermore, in an attempt to limit and control traditional religious observances, the legislation authorized certain days of fasting the 'even' or day before 'the feast of the Nativity of our Lord, of Easter, of the Ascension of our Lord, Pentecost, of the Purification and the Annunciation of the aforesaid blessed Virgin, of All Saints, and of all the feasts of the Apostles, other than of Saints John the Evangelist, and Philip and Jacob'. The two days exempt from these provisions – May eve or the eve of Saints Philip and Jacob, and midsummer eve or the eve of St John were traditional occasions for night-time revels and watches that could barely be justified in terms of Christian belief. The legislation of 1552 also gave special permission for the Knights of the Garter to observe St George's day as the feast of their order, but it lent no authority to the honouring of such popular English saints as Hugh of Lincoln or Thomas of Canterbury, or saints like Valentine, Swithin and Cecilia who mattered more in popular folklore than in religious ceremonial observance.

The Edwardian calendar governed the official Christian year under Elizabeth and her successors. The 1559 prayer book featured a calendar which printed the authorized holy days in red letters. The Conversion of St Paul (25 January) and the feasts of St George (23 April) and St Barnabas the Apostle (11 June) were initially included in this list of honour, but they lost their red letters in later editions. When 'the new calendar' was published in 1561 it had exactly the same holy days as the legislation of 1552. Everyone was supposed to attend church on holy days as well as Sundays, and the churchwardens were authorized to collect fines of one shilling for each absence.[11]

The 'Elizabethan settlement', of course, settled nothing. Religious conservatives continued to observe such abrogated days as Corpus Christi, All Souls', and St Thomas of Canterbury, while radicals sought further reform. William Harrison, the Elizabethan commentator, compared the new regime to the old. 'Our holy and festival days are very well reduced also unto a less number; for whereas, not long since, we had under the Pope four score and fifteen called festival, and thirty *profesti*, beside the Sundays, they are all brought unto seven and twenty; and with them the superfluous numbers of idle wakes, guilds, fraternities, church ales, help ales, and soul ales, called also dirge ales, with the heathenish rioting at bride ales, are well diminished and laid aside.' Harrison said this with some satisfaction, noting a significant advance from the days of error. But the work of reformation had not gone far enough. 'And no great matter were it if the feasts of all our apostles, evangelists, and martyrs, with that of All Saints', were brought to the holy days that follow upon Christmas, Easter, and Whitsuntide, and those of the Virgin Mary with the rest utterly removed from the calendars as neither necessary nor commendable in a reformed church.'[12]

Harrison was by no means alone in his criticism of the semi-reformed calendar. Barnaby Googe, one of Elizabeth's gentlemen-pensioners, inveighed against the seasonal rituals of feasts and holidays as vile and heathenlike idolatries spawned by the popish Antichrist. William Keth, preaching in Dorset, imagined God rebuking the papists (and, by implication, the remaining popish practices in England): 'I never commanded . . . your candles at Candlemas, your popish penance on Ash Wednesday, your eggs and bacon on Good Friday, your gospels at superstitious crosses decked like idols, your fires at Midsummer, and your ringing at Hallowtide for all Christian souls.'[13] The authors of the 1572 'Admonition to the Parliament' called the Book of Common Prayer 'an unperfect book, culled and picked out of that popish dunghill, the Mass Book full of abominations'. Among the many 'popish abuses yet remaining in the English church' they cited the ecclesiastical calendar. 'Days are ascribed unto saints and kept holy with fasts on their evens and prescript services appointed for them, which beside that they are of many superstitiously kept and observed are also contrary to the commandment of God. Six days shalt thou labour, and therefore we for the superstition that is put in them dare not subscribe to allow them.' The Bristol preacher John Northbrooke shared this view, regarding the festival days as popish inventions designed 'to train up the people in ignorance and idleness . . . restraining men from their handy labours and occupations'.[14]

The calendar laid down in the Book of Common Prayer established a national devotional framework for the passage of the year, and this was augmented by a host of local emphases, additions and preferences. Puritan critics attacked the official ecclesiastical calendar for its continuity with papism, and reserved even more outrage for the licentiousness of its associated popular customs. For puritans the calendar was more than a notation for the passage of the year; it was a highly charged symbol of the unresolved business of the Reformation. The doctrinal dispute between Canterbury and Rome was often interpreted as a battle between godliness and superstition and a struggle between the social forces of decency and licence, order and disorder. Arguments from theology merged with righteous demands for the reformation of manners. Each year the cycle of holidays, even those approved by law, provoked petty collisions between traditionalists and reformers. In some places the old festivities flourished, elsewhere they succumbed to godly pressure. Episcopal authorities attempted a balanced enforcement of the offical holidays, punishing both those who ignored them and those who augmented them. Sometimes the discipline was left to God. William Vaughan recalled an incident in 1589 when 'an ale wife, making no exception of days, would needs brew upon St Mark's day; but lo, the marvellous works of God! While she was thus labouring, the top of the chimney took fire, and before it could be quenched her house was quite burnt. Surely a gentle warning to them that violate and profane forbidden days.'[15]

Advanced Protestants found fault with the Christian feast days but their push for reform had little immediate effect. Festive emphasis remained a local option. Parish dedication days were not forgotten, nor were the more famous saints of medieval England. Local devotional activities were often reminiscent of customs that were supposed to have been suppressed at the Reformation. In 1586 it was recorded in north Devon that 'on St Luke's day this year there was a trental of sermons at Pilton so that divers as well men and women rode and went thither. They called it an exercise or holy fast, and there some offered (money) as they did when they went on pilgrimage. And the like was kept at Shirwell, to the admiration of all Protestants.'[16] Elizabethan bishops repeatedly asked at their visitations, 'whether any holy days or fasting days heretofore abrogated . . . be superstitiously observed', or whether there be any 'superfluous ringing on All Saints' day at night, or on the day following, of old superstitiously called All Souls' day'. Villagers in Hampshire and Norfolk, they discovered, continued to ring bells on the night of All Saints' (the eve of All Souls'), and to light bonfires on the feast of St James.[17]

Writing at the end of the Elizabethan period Richard Carew observed, 'of late times many ministers have by their earnest invectives both condemned these saints' feasts as superstitious and suppressed the church ales as licentious'. By the time of Charles I, according to the west-country antiquarian Thomas Westcote, the old holiday 'exercises', with their wrestling, leaping, dancing, and music, were 'by zeal discommended and discountenanced, and so utterly out of use'. Moderate opinion allowed the traditional feasts to continue so long as they did not degenerate into disorder. But in many parts of the country similar 'exercises' continued to fuel disputes and heighten animosities, especially after the republication of the king's 'Book of Sports' in the 1630s.[18]

★

Even without a plethora of saints' days, the year was still shaped by ritual observances. The law terms, when the Westminster courts were sitting and when official legal business could be conducted, were marked by ancient religious festival days, some movable and some fixed. To clarify matters, the 1536 Injunctions explained the basis for the dates of the law terms. 'Easter term beginneth always the eighteenth day after Easter day, reckoning Easter day for one, and endeth the Monday next following Ascension day. Trinity term beginneth always the Wednesday next after the Octaves of Trinity Sunday, and endeth the eleventh or twelfth day of July. Michaelmas term beginneth the ninth or tenth day of October, and endeth the twenty-eighth or twenty-ninth day of November. Hilary term beginneth the twenty-third or twenty-fourth day of January, and endeth the twelfth or thirteenth day of February.' (Hilary term took its name from St Hilary, a fourth-century bishop, whose feast fell on 13 January.) A similar 'brief declaration of when every term beginneth and endeth' was included in the Elizabethan prayer book.[19]

Knowledge of this legal calendar was vital for anyone involved in suits and causes. These dates were also important for the settling of obligations and debts. John Stow gave an expanded account of the times of the law terms in his *Summary of the Chronicles of England*, which William Harrison repeated in his *Description of England*. Law dictionaries gave the dates and declared the rest of the year to be 'vacation'.[20] Popular almanacs kept track of these various days and cycles, and so kept in mind memories of saints' days that the reformers would rather have seen suppressed.

The church courts, which held sway over a wide range of probate and testamentary matters, moral offences, and other matters of 'ecclesiastical cognizance', had their own legal calendar, which blithely ignored the purging of saints' days in the Reformation. So did the Admiralty, and all other courts which operated by civil rather than common law. Law days and appearance days in their legal terms were framed as follows:[21]

10

Hilary Term

St Hilary (13 January)
St Woldstan (19 January)
Conversion of St Paul (25 January)
St Blaise (3 February)
St Scolastica (10 February)
St Valentine (14 February)
Ash Wednesday (movable)
St Matthias (24 February)
St Chad (2 March)
Perpetua and Felicitas (7 March)
St Gregory (12 March)
Annunciation of Our Lady (25 March)

Easter Term

Fifteenth day after Easter (movable)
St Alphege (19 April)
St Mark (25 April)
Invention of the Cross (3 May)
Gordian (10 May)
St Dunstan (19 May)
Ascension day (movable)

Trinity Term

Trinity Sunday (movable)
Corpus Christi (movable)
Bishop Boniface (5 June)
St Barnaby (11 June)
St Botolph (17 June)
St John (24 June)
St Paul (30 June)
Translation of Thomas (7 July)
St Swithin (15 July)
St Margaret (20 July)
St Ann (26 July)

Michaelmas Term

St Faith (6 October)
St Edward (13 October)
St Luke (18 October)
SS Simon and Jude (28 October)
All Souls (2 November)
St Martin (11 November)
St Edmund (16 November)
St Katherine (25 November)
St Andrew (30 November)
Conception of the Virgin Mary (8 December)

It was ironic that the ecclesiastical courts, whose tasks included enforcing the discipline of the reformed religion, should adhere to the pre-Reformation calendar and perpetuate the memory of saints whose days had ceased to be festivals. This irony was not lost on observers like Harrison who expressed his sorrow 'that the use of the popish calendar is so much retained in the same and not the usual days of the month placed in their rooms . . . Howbeit, some of our infected lawyers will not let them go away so easily, pretending facility and custom of usage but meaning peradventure inwardly to keep a commemoration of those dead men whose names are there remembered.' Trinity term, in Harrison's account, was punctuated by 'the idolatrous and papistical feast called Corpus Christi', a movable feast of dubious respectability which complicated an already difficult legal calendar.[22]

If the church and civil-law courts kept alive some saints' days that had vanished from the liturgical calendar, it was no wonder that many of these days continued to attract local enthusiasm. Popular almanacs, which were notoriously conservative publications, kept the unofficial saints' days in view alongside the sanctioned red-letter festival days because they were useful markers of time. Later editions of the calendar in the Elizabethan prayer book printed them in discreet black letters. And Catholics still had access to such publications as *A Manuall of Praiers* which featured the traditional monthly array of saints.[23]

2
THE RHYTHM OF THE YEAR
IN EARLY MODERN ENGLAND

The year was paced by a combination of astronomical, agricultural, pagan, Christian, legal, dynastic, and customary seasons and dates. Attached to the rituals and observances of the prayer book and almanac were popular customs of unfathomable antiquity. These have attracted the interest of folklorists from the seventeenth century to the present, who have sometimes inflated their importance and dressed them with unverifiable explanations. Conventional accounts of English calendar customs mingle citations from ancient authors and observations from recent generations to suggest that certain practices existed from time out of mind. But without firm evidence from the intervening period these are untrustworthy indications of community life in Tudor and Stuart England.[1] In this discussion the evidence is drawn mostly from sixteenth- and seventeeth-century sources.

It is possible, indeed likely, that many of the country practices memorialized by eighteenth-century antiquarians were not as ancient as they supposed, but rather were rustic creations or adaptations of the Tudor or Stuart period. As will be shown in such activities as St George's day and midsummer processions, and later in the seventeenth-century commemorations of the Gunpowder Plot, the shading between survival, revival and invention was problematic and complex. Folk practices could be mutable and intermittent as well as timeless and enduring. Civic and ecclesiastical authorities worked to suppress some observances and sponsor others. Even within a brief period, local festive practices could change with the arrival or departure of a reforming or tradition-minded minister, or changes in economic or political conditions.

The rhythmic pattern of the year did not just reside in the almanacs and the prayer book, nor was it only a matter of religious polemic. Calendrical consciousness permeated people's lives, and can be traced in their private reckonings and community observances. Winter and summer, planting and harvest, Christmas and Easter, Lady day and Michaelmas, were the pivots of the year and the standard points of reference for a wide range of activities across time. Activities and tidings would be associated with their season or tide – Christ-tide, Shrovetide, Hocktide, and so on. Writers assumed that everyone knew when certain seasons and holidays befell. The Bristol chronicler, for example, described the hot plague 'about St James tide' in 1575, and observed that 'between St James tide and Paul's tide [25 July to 25 January] there died about 2,000 persons'. Elias Ashmole reported being sick 'about Candlemas' in 1634. A correspondent of John Cosin wrote, 'it may be I shall see you before Shrovetide . . . After Easter I purpose to be at Windsor.' John Chamberlain discussed plans for a marriage 'toward Whitsuntide'. Oliver Naylor wrote, 'I think I come not to London till towards Michaelmas.' John Pory expected the calling of a parliament 'before All Hallow-tide' in 1626.[2] And so on.

Examples like these could be multiplied by reference to dozens of diaries and collections of correspondence. One did not have to be a religious conservative to use the old notations of the Christian year, nor did this conventional calendrical usage necessarily imply devotion to particular feasts or holidays. Robert Woodford, for example, steward of Northampton and a man of strong puritan sympathies, made special note of certain days in his diary between 1637 and 1641. Woodford's year encompassed New Year's day, Twelfth day, Candlemas, Easter day and Lady day (which in 1638 happened to coincide), King Charles's accession day on 27 March, Woodford's own birthday on 3 April, St George's fair day, St Mark's day, Ascension day, St James's day, Bartholomew day, Michaelmas, Powder Treason day, St Hugh's fair day, and Christmas. Some of these days were important for legal or civic business, while others were occasions to hear sermons. Even though some of these dates were sensitive or controversial for puritans of the 1630s, Woodford's calendrical notation was largely conventional and uncontroversial, a convenient and traditional scheme for organizing and recording the passage of time.[3] But it was difficult to treat the year as a neutral grid when so many of its days and seasons had religious or historical significance.

The calendar was layered and structured, but experience of the year varied according to status and situation. A grain-growing yeoman knew rhythms different from those experienced by an upland herdsman. Landlords and tenants had complementary roles in the cycle of duties and payments, attendance and hospitality, and the cycle itself varied according to local custom. Civic officials, country lawyers, Whitehall courtiers, and ceremonial clergymen each had a different perspective on time and a different involvement in its rhythms. For Alderman Samuel Newton of Cambridge the year was a sequence of civic observances, mayoral dinners, scarlet robings, leet courts, quarter sessions, anniversary sermons, audit dinners, and fairs. For the reverend Ralph Josselin, his contemporary in an adjacent county, the year turned around agricultural and ecclesiastical observances. And both experienced the year in a different way than their London contemporary, Samuel Pepys, whose life was paced by the activities of the metropolis and the court.[4] Activities and observances varied with setting, activity, and belief, yet all were embraced within the framework of the English Christian year.

The agricultural calendar was especially conservative, entwining religious holidays with seasonal chores. Thomas Tusser, the Elizabethan expert on husbandry, advised, 'at Philip and Jacob, away with thy lambs/that thinkest to have any milk of their dams'. Henry Best, a seventeenth-century farmer in Yorkshire, 'knew that lambs conceived at Michaelmas would be born before Candlemas; that the ploughing should be over by Andrewmas; that ewes should go to tup at St Luke; that servants were hired at Martinmas; and that hay-fields should not be grazed for more than a fortnight after Lady day', which was a traditional day for the payment of rent. John Aubrey recorded the Wiltshire wisdom, 'if drops do hang on the hedges on Candlemas day it will be a good pease year'. Aubrey also knew from his Wiltshire boyhood early in Charles I's reign that *'non obstante* the change of religion, the plough boys and also the schoolboys will keep up and retain their old ceremonies and privileges'.[5] In many areas the fiscal benefits of ceremonies outweighed (and outlasted) their religious connotations. Opportunities for local fund-raising and redistribution, bounty and largesse, rooted the traditional holidays in the soil of the local economy.[6]

The old saints' days were fondly preserved in the popular memory, governing traditional farming practices and days of markets and fairs. As Keith Thomas observes, 'it was the value of such festivals for marking the days for paying rent, or carrying out other secular activities, which explained why the Elizabethan church calendar remained so liberally splattered with black-letter saints' days, even though they were not otherwise celebrated as holidays'.[7] St Lawrence's and St Denis's fairs were held in Cornwall, alongside a host of local observances commemorating saints who were not recognized in London (or even Rome). St Hugh's fair was held each November at Northampton even though memory of the medieval bishop had been erased from the official ecclesiastical calendar. At Banbury the borough charter of 1608 permitted two annual fairs, 'one of them on the vigil, on the feast, and on the day after the feast of the Annunciation of the Blessed Virgin Mary (25 March); and the other on the first Thursday which shall happen next before the feast of St Nicholas the Bishop (6 December) and on the even and the day after the same day every year forever'.[8] Northampton and Banbury were noted puritan centres in the early seventeenth century, but parts of their civic and economic life still adhered to pre-Reformation patterns.

A catalogue of fairs in 1661 shows the tenacity of the traditional calendar that linked ceremonial and economic cycles. The compiler listed fifty-six towns, from Abbington to Wigmore, with fairs on 25 July (St James's day). Midsummer fairs were held in forty-one towns on 24 June (St John's day), and in another forty-one on 29 June (St Peter's day). The following table shows the most popular fair days, with most of them in the warmer half of the year from springtime to harvest. In addition there were dozens of fairs tied to the movable holidays of Ascension day and Corpus Christi in May and June.[9]

Fair Days and Saints' Days in English Towns

23 April	(St George)	28
1 May	(SS Philip and James)	33
24 June	(St John)	41
29 June	(St Peter)	41
25 July	(St James)	56
1 August	(Lammas)	28
10 August	(St Lawrence)	33
8 September	(Nativity of the Virgin)	29
21 September	(St Matthew)	29
29 September	(St Michael)	39
18 October	(St Luke)	28
30 November	(St Andrew)	30

The calendar began with 1 January, New Year's day, when Christians commemorated 'the Circumcision of our Lord Jesus Christ'. In many parishes the new year was rung in with peals of bells. The year, however, did not change with the passage of this New Year's day, for the year-date remained unaltered until Lady day in March. At the royal court and elsewhere 1 January was the annual day for exchanging gifts, in remembrance of the biblical gift-giving at Epiphany. Boroughs and cities presented new year gifts to their patrons. Individuals made gifts to their masters and friends.[10]

In some parts of the country New Year's eve was an occasion to pass the Wassail bowl, a day of promenades, inebriation, and ritualized begging. In others it was a day for excursions and ritualized hunting. The Christmas season was still in swing, closing with Twelfth night and Twelfth day, the feast of the Epiphany on 6 January. Twelfth night, of course, was a traditional time for masques and plays at court. The days of Christmas were spent with mummeries, disguising, stage plays, dancing, and generous provision of food and drink. The Wassail bowls came out again on Twelfth day amidst a variety of local celebratory customs. In Gloucestershire, Herefordshire and some other areas the end of Christmas was marked with bonfires, a practice still seen in the eighteenth century that is presumed to antedate the Reformation.[11]

Over and above its religious significance, the Christmas season was firmly implanted in most people's experience as a time of warmth and cheer during the coldest part of winter, unless it was chilled by puritan displeasure. In some areas Twelfth day was followed by the mixed piety and blasphemy (depending on viewpoint) of Plough Monday, the ceremonial blessing of ploughs in readiness for the opening of the earth and the resumption of the working agricultural year. Plough Monday festivities were banned in 1548 but continued irregularly in the Elizabethan period. At Wigtoft, Lincolnshire, for example, Plough Monday offerings in 1575 raised twenty shillings for the parish accounts.[12]

Next of the official holy days was 2 February, the feast of the Purification of the Blessed Virgin, generally known as Candlemas. In pre-Reformation practice this day was hallowed by candlelit processions in church, and in some places these continued, or were revived, under traditional or ceremonially inclined ministers. The Candlemas procession was one of the many small battlegrounds of the Reformation, and provided a calendrical occasion for measuring the momentum of reform. On the first Candlemas of Edward VI's reign Archbishop Cranmer forbade the carrying of candles, and it was noteworthy that the procession was omitted throughout the City of London. Elizabethan puritans attacked Candlemas candles as bribes to God. In 1628 the Arminian prebend of Durham, John Cosin, scandalized more austere Protestants by flooding the cathedral with Candlemas candles, tapers and torches.[13]

St Valentine's day (14 February), though not officially sanctioned, was widely observed in the seventeenth century as it is today. It seems to have enjoyed particular favour among anglican ceremonialists. The anti-Calvinist Richard Montagu dated a letter on 'St Valentine's day' 1625, and wrote to John Cosin that his daughter 'chose you for her Valentine last night and would have none else'. The royalist Elias Ashmole, courting Lady Manwaring in 1647, associated his advance in her affections to the power of 'Valentine's day'. Samuel Pepys and his family exchanged Valentine favours in the 1660s.[14] St Valentine's day was for lovers, as St Cecilia's (22 November) was famous for musical performances. Some people believed that birds chose their nesting mates on St Valentine's day.

Spring would be dominated by the movable feasts and observances tied to the date of Easter – Shrovetide and Shrove Tuesday, Ash Wednesday, the forty days of Lent, Palm Sunday, Maundy Thursday, Good Friday, Easter Sunday, Easter Monday and Tuesday, and so on. The complicated calculations were designed to ensure that Easter day always fell on a Sunday, but its date could range from 22 March to 25 April. In consequence, this most sacred season was out of synchronization with the annual climatic and economic routine, some years preceding Lady day, approaching May-tide in others.

The season began before Lent with the festivities of Shrove Tuesday, or, in some northern areas, Collop Monday. At Liverpool the mayor and burgesses chose Shrovetide eve or 'Merry Monday' for their annual perambulation.[15] England had no public carnival, as was common on the Continent, but that did not stand in the way of eating, drinking, and behavioural excess. The popular customs at this time of year had little to do with the original pious purpose of shriving or confession in preparation for the austerities of Lent. It is not necessary to invoke terms like hierarchical inversion, theatrical mimesis, reaffirmative reintegration, liminal transgression, or latent control, to demonstrate that Shrovetide was a time for letting off steam.[16]

Shrove Tuesday was Pancake day, and is still so called in some parts of England. Festivities began with the mid-morning ringing of a church bell, sometimes in defiance of a strict or reforming parson. Descriptions of this practice survive from as far apart as Newcastle and London. According to *Pasquil's Palinodia*, a popular poem of the early seventeenth century:

> It was the day whereon both rich and poor
> Are chiefly feasted from the self-same dish,
> When every paunch, till it can hold no more,
> Is fritter-filled, as well as heart can wish.[17]

In some urban areas Shrovetide was a time when benign commensality degenerated into half-licensed disorder, with apprentices taking the law into their own hands. London apprentices were notorious for their riotous behaviour at Shrovetide, which usually took the form of harrassment of presumed prostitutes and attacks against the Bankside brothels. John Chamberlain noted in 1611, 'our 'prentices were very unruly on Shrove Tuesday and pulled down a house or two of good fellowship'. A few years later the London youth gangs went further and broke into Drury Lane theatre, freed prisoners from Finsbury prison, and brawled with the city officers.[18] The day was made a holiday or half holiday, despite the lack of mandate from church or state.

Shrovetide betokened wrestling matches, football, stoolball contests, and cock fights. Thomas Crosfield, a fellow of the Queen's College, noted 'frittering, throwing at cocks, playing at stoolball in the city by women and football by men' at Shrovetide at Oxford in 1633. At Knotting, Bedfordshire, in the mid-1630s the minister and congregation enjoyed Shrovetide cockfights *inside* the church, to the scandal of both Laudians and puritans. The sport of throwing sticks at tethered cocks was also a common Shrove Tuesday observance. In some parts of rural Middlesex in the seventeenth century the proceeds from the Shrovetide cock-throwing were applied in aid of the poor rates. The church reckonings of Winterslow, Wiltshire, are among those which include payments and receipts for 'throwing at the cock'. Puritans might cluck like the unfortunate battered chickens but they could not eradicate the practice. Thomas Tusser's Shrovetide injunction, 'go thresh the fat hen', could have sexual as well as customary connotations.[19]

Lent, after all this, was an anti-climax. Ministers reminded their congregations that Lent was upon them, and urged appropriate denials. Lenten lore was widely known, and there was probably less consumption of meat. Lenten fasting, according to Cranmer, was 'a mere positive law', made by man rather than God, permitting all who needed to 'moderately eat all kind of meats without grudge or scruple of conscience'. Elizabethan couples still generally observed the prohibition on marriages during Lent, although the observance became attentuated in the seventeenth century. In general the Lenten period passed quietly until high-church reformers made a controversial issue of it in the 1620s.[20]

Easter was the highest holiday of the Christian year, commemorating the triumph over death. In Protestant England it was marked by sermons on the passion and the resurrection. Easter Sunday was the favoured time for holy communion. People who rarely took communion might take the eucharist on Easter day. In the seafaring town of Great Yarmouth, for example, the communicants consumed twenty quarts of muscadine at Easter 1624, several times more than the normal requirements.[21] Certain older customs lingered – Paschal fires, Easter cakes, egg dishes, Easter doles, even creeping to the cross – but these were ridiculed or attacked by reformers. More acceptable was the dole to the poor on Good Friday recorded, for example, in the churchwardens' records of Clifton, Bedfordshire in 1602.[22]

The ancient thanksgiving customs of Hocktide on the Monday or

Tuesday a fortnight after Easter involved the collecting of money for charitable purposes. Men and women competed to see which sex could raise the most. Hock day was supposedly an ancient commemoration of the expulsion of the Danes from England, but it may in fact have a later medieval origin. This was a matter for antiquarians, not for the ordinary parishioners who performed their duties as a matter of annual routine. Hocktide customs had a dwindling following after the Reformation, disappearing in some parishes in the 1570s. But their memory was not entirely obliterated. Some places continued their festive fund-raising on Hock Monday and Tuesday intermittently through much of the seventeenth century, and there were self-conscious revivals of the practice in London in the 1660s.[23]

One crucial fixed date was 25 March, the Annunciation of the Blessed Virgin, popularly known as Lady day. Since the Annunciation initiated the Christological cycle it was reasonable to consider this day as the beginning of the year. The 'new calendar' of 1561 explained, 'the year of our Lord beginneth the 25 day of March, the same day supposed to be the first day upon which the world was created, and the day when Christ was conceived in the womb of the Virgin Mary'.[24] The presence of *two* new year's days – 1 January and 25 March – testifies to the complexity and ambiguity of the early modern calendar. The Lady-day date did not quite fit the solar calendar of the vernal equinox but was often overlain by the holy days of Easter. This was the day when many rents and contracts fell due, and it was the date when the year changed. Agricultural leases were often renewed on Lady day, especially in champion country where fields lay fallow at this time.

Many boroughs and parishes conducted their business on an annual cycle that turned on Lady day rather than Michaelmas. Lady day eve had special connotations in the reign of James I, since the anniversary of the king's accession fell on 24 March. Several parishes rang their bells to honour the king, recording payments to the ringers 'on our Lady day even'.[25]

St George's day fell on 23 April. Although there was scant evidence that England's patron saint ever existed, and none that he performed his heroic deeds against the dragon, the chivalric cult of St George ensured him popular recognition. Before the Reformation parish actors would perform brave plays about St George. The reformed Church of England reserved no official feast for St George, but the bells were often rung on his day along with other community recognition. Puritan critics denigrated St George while traditionalists came to his rescue. The Knights of the Garter traditionally convened on 23 April in St George's chapel at Windsor, and St George's day fairs were held in at least twenty-eight towns. The Jacobean court marked St George's day with tilts and challenges, as well as the chivalric and heraldic business of the Order of the Garter. St George's feast was an annual part of the calendar at court under Charles I, but it was not always held on St George's day.[26]

At York the annual procession and play of St George was suspended in 1558. But at Norwich, England's second-largest city, the annual processions and pageants organized by the Guild of St George survived the Reformation in a temporarily reduced form. The pageant figures of St George and his companion the Lady Margaret were eliminated in 1559, but 'for pastime' the mayor allowed 'the dragon to come in and show himself as in other years'. This pageant on St George's day formed part of the Norwich civic calendar throughout the Elizabethan period, and the gilded figure of St George himself returned to delight the crowd in the reign of James I. Jacobean Chester also observed St George's day with races and processions.[27]

All of these activities sustained St George's day as an occasion of secular and patriotic significance, despite being abrogated as an official holiday. Like most calendrical observances, St George's day was muted during the revolution and interregnum, but revived after the Restoration to occupy a special place in later-Stuart folk life and patriotism. St George's day became the favoured day of coronation of later Stuart monarchs Charles II, James II, and Anne.[28] As the anniversary of England's saint, and a day special to her king, St George's feast took its place in the Restoration springtime that ran from Easter to Royal Oak day.

The feast of St Mark the evangelist on 25 April was the next official holy day. This day, like other saints' days, attracted a mixture of devotion and indifference, ecclesiastical ceremony and popular practices. Scattered references can be found to late-night watching and private divination on St Mark's even despite prohibition of such superstitious observances.[29]

May day was a fixed springtime holiday that helped give regularity and structure to the year. The church sanctioned festivities on 1 May in association with the feast of Saints Philip and James. In practice, however, all veneration for the saints was submerged in a welter of secular and pagan activities. May day was one of the ancient spring fertility festivals, marked with fires and flowers. The ancients knew it as Floralia, and this was well known to seventeenth-century scholars. The early Tudor court had made much of Mayings, with floral masquerades and entertainments. May day was notorious for sexual licence, although perhaps more notorious in puritan polemic than in general social conduct. Historical demographers have shown that springtime was the peak period for conceptions, but there was no surge of pregnancies, legitimate or illegitimate, associated with the May day feast.[30]

Maypoles and May games provided easy targets for reformers of manners, who decried these springtime merriments as 'heathenish vanity . . . abused to superstition and wickedness'. But a vigorous tradition of May revels survived the Reformation and withstood the hostility of puritan critics. May games, May bowers, May fairs and maypoles enjoyed a popular vigour, sometimes encouraged and at other times frowned upon by local authorities. Churchwardens' records of the Elizabethan period sometimes include payments for maypoles or morris men, although such entries became rare after the 1570s. In some parts of south-west England the May traditions declined or were suppressed in the late Elizabethan and Jacobean periods, only to revive with encouragement from the Book of Sports. Elsewhere they needed no such stimulation.[31] The geography of popular festivity still needs to be worked out on a national as well as regional level; there are indications that East Anglia and the south-east shed traditions that still flourished in the midlands and north-west, although there were myriad exceptions to the pattern.

Throughout the country, in the century following the Reformation, disputes over May customs agitated the friction between competing cultural traditions. Maypoles could easily become a source of trouble and a provocation pitting 'zealous brothers' against 'harmless mirth'. In many country villages, much to the distress of reformers, parishioners besotted themselves with Maytide pleasure. In Gloucestershire in 1610, 'there was a Maypole set up near unto the parish church of Bisley, and piping and dancing at the same pole by the youth of the parish'. Scandalizing 'the honest and religious disposed people of the same parish', this merriment took place 'at the appointment of Mr Christopher Windle, the vicar there'. In the same year the corporation of Woodstock, Oxfordshire, provided 'music at the bringing home of the elm from Coombe on May day'.[32] Maypoles were often a source of community pride in Elizabethan and Stuart England, and it was not unusual for them to be encouraged by local officials and sponsored by parish funds. London had its great maypole in Cornhill, 'before the parish church of St Andrew, therefore called Undershaft'. This maypole was a community focus, temporarily overshadowing the church, until it was ordered cut down in 1644.[33]

The royal orders of 1617 and 1633, known as the Book of Sports, authorized 'May Games, Whitsun Ales, Morris Dances, and the setting up of Maypoles' so long as they did not interfere with divine services. The puritan Henry Burton was outraged by this officially sponsored setback to reform: 'The drum is struck up, the pieces discharged, the musicians play, and the rout fall a dancing till the evening.' Bonfires, maypoles or summer poles, pipers, morris dancers, football matches, and unauthorized bell ringing added to the festive atmosphere of this frenetic seasonal merry-making.[34]

The government of Charles I sometimes sent mixed signals regarding traditional May festivity. Officialdom permitted, or even encouraged, the raising of maypoles but took offence when villagers went foraging for them in the royal forest. At the Northampton Quarter Sessions in 1637, 'when men were fined for cutting down Maypoles in the forest, it was told them by one for the king's part that they were not fined for having Maypoles but for cutting them down in the forest'.[35] The annual fuss about maypoles came to a head in the Parliamentary Ordinance of 1644 demanding their permanent suppression. Of course, with the Restoration in 1660 the maypoles came back with a vengeance, perhaps more antic and phallic than ever.[36]

Rogation week, before Ascension day or Holy Thursday, was another calendrical occasion tied to the movable Easter cycle. Rogationtide often overlapped with Maytide, or came later in the month of May, affording a further occasion for springtime revels. At Oxford in 1598, 'the inhabitants assembled on the two Sundays before Ascension day, and on that day, with drum and shot and other weapons, and men attired in women's apparel, brought into the town a woman bedecked with garlands and flowers, named by them the queen of May. They also had morris dances and other disordered and unseemly sports, and intended the next Sunday to continue the same abuses.'[37] The reporter was evidently offended by the carnivalesque elements of cross-dressing, and the disordered travesty of the marching watch and triumphal entry.

Rogation was the time of parish perambulations, conducted, according to Bishop Bickley of Chichester in 1586, 'for the better knowing and retaining of the circuit of your parish, and for the obtaining of God's blessings upon the fruits of the ground'. The secular purpose was to assert and recall the rights and liberties of the parish. The Rogation perambulation could take on the air of an outdoor springtime frolic, although it was supposed to be a solemn occasion with litanies and psalms. William Keth called it 'roguing' week on this score. In some areas the Rogation days were known as 'gang days'. Schoolboys and children were expected to take part in the beating of the bounds, and of course they sometimes got out of hand.[38]

Rogation processions, like so many other activities tied to the old calendar, provided another point of friction between traditionalists

23

and reformers. Strict bishops instructed that only the approved psalms and homilies be used on these occasions. At Canterbury, in the Elizabethan and Jacobean periods, a marching watch on Ascension eve at the end of Rogation week replaced the old St Thomas eve processions. This observance was not fuelled by popular affection, however, and by 1618 it had degenerated into an annual supper for the mayor and constables. In 1652 the Canterbury chamberlain paid for beer and tobacco 'at the setting of the Lammas watch on Ascension even as hath been used'. Sermons sponsored by the corporation on the Monday and Tuesday of Rogation week were part of the civic calendar of seventeenth-century Norwich.[39] By these means the rowdiness of Rogationtide was somewhat tamed, and the ceremony made respectable and select.

Rogation perambulations fell out of use in some parishes, particularly where enclosure defaced traditional boundaries. Elsewhere the Rogationtide treat of bread and beer remained a calendrical fixture through most of the seventeenth century. Churchwardens' records include regular payments for refreshments at the Rogation or Ascension outings. At St Martin in the Fields they disbursed twenty-four shillings and tenpence in 1605, 'for the diet of the inhabitants at the time of the perambulation according to an ancient custom'. Most London parishes conducted a formal perambulation of their crowded streets and alleys. Community leaders distributed doles to the poor and then retired for a Rogationtide or Ascension day dinner. At St Matthew Friday Street, in the City of London, the churchwardens distributed raisins and almonds to the parish children in the course of their Ascension day processions in the 1620s.[40] The rector there was Henry Burton, soon to become a puritan hero, but at this time he was not hostile to harmless seasonal rituals.

Two weeks later came Whitsuntide, a major episode in the Christian year commemorating the mystery of Pentecost and the descent of the Holy Ghost. Whit Sunday, alongside Easter and Christmas, was a favoured occasion for taking communion. For theologians and churchmen, of course, this was a solemn occasion, but in many English parishes Whitsun provided another time for celebration and frolic. Whitsun was the common time for church ales, money-making fetes distinguished by abundance of alcohol and merry-making. In some villages the practice was in decline during James's reign, as church rates took over from church ales, but elsewhere these 'revel feasts' continued to flourish. Whitsun ales caused disputes and divisions in some parishes, with the energetic puritans forming a noisy minority. The defenders of these traditional practices justified them as orderly and venerable 'feasts of charity'.[41]

Also tied to the movement of Easter were Trinity Sunday and Corpus Christi day, the Thursday following. Corpus Christi, the feast of the blessed sacrament of the body of Christ, had been a major festival in the pre-Reformation calendar. It was celebrated with processions and flowers, pageants, dramatic entertainments, and bells. Corpus Christi day was dropped from the Protestant ecclesiastical calendar because it reeked of the rejected doctrine of transubstantiation, but it was harder to eliminate from popular culture. Urban guilds had organized their fraternal and devotional activities around Corpus Christi. Corpus Christi plays were suppressed or suspended in many parts of England, although the tradition lingered for at least a generation after the Reformation.

At York the Corpus Christi plays were suspended in 1558, along with the plays of St George. But within three years they returned, shorn of some elements that Protestants found most offensive. In 1561 the corporation 'agreed that Corpus Christi play shall be played this year with good players as accustomed, except only the pageants of the dying, assumption and coronation of our Lady'. At the same time they authorized the traditional martial parade on horseback on Corpus Christi day, 'as hath been laudibly accustomed'. Two of the sheriffs who had been expected to take part in this procession pleaded 'sundry impediments and disabilities' to excuse themselves, most likely a cover for religious reservations. For the next few years reformist and traditionalist groups at York struggled to preserve or displace Corpus Christi in the civic calendar. As late as 1580, 'the commons did earnestly request of my Lord Mayor that Corpus Christi play might be played this year, whereupon my Lord Mayor answered that he and his brethren would consider of their request'. In the years that followed the Corpus Christi observances fell out of use at York, and the martial parade was confined to the celebration of midsummer. At Little Baddow, Essex, the Corpus Christi celebration was abandoned after 1574. But Sherborne, Dorset, performed its Corpus Christi play annually until 1588 and perhaps beyond.[42] Even after the abrogation of Corpus Christi religious festivities the day continued as a movable complication in the calendar of the law terms.

Midsummer day, 24 June, was observed by many ancient agrarian societies, and still has ritual significance in some traditional parts of the world today. The day celebrated the summer solstice and the cycle of the seasons but was venerated in the church calendar as the Nativity of St John the Baptist. Most commentators recognize St John's day as a pagan solar festival in Christian guise, and some go so far as to discern Druidic origins. Certainly the holiday had little to do with St John.[43] Similar midsummer observances attached to the feast of St Peter on 29 June.

Until the middle of the sixteenth century, Midsummer day was marked with bonfires, including some sponsored by the crown. Henry VII regularly paid ten shillings from his privy purse towards the midsummer bonfire on 23 or 24 June, but the custom disappeared under his successors.[44] Barnaby Googe in 1570 was among those who attacked the St John's day bonfires and floral garlands of midsummer as popish relics. Suppressing them was part of the task of reformist bishops. John Stow's *Survey of London* included reminiscences of floral decorations and bonfires in the streets in the mid-Tudor period, but the midsummer bonfire tradition seems to have died out except in the most remote rural areas. The churchwardens' accounts for Northill, Bedfordshire, include payments for a bonfire at midsummer 1563, but not in subsequent years. If it continued it did so without official patronage. St Peter's eve once rivalled the eve of St John's for its pageants and morris dances in London, but these too were barely a memory by the end of Elizabeth's reign.[45] At Sandhill, Northumberland, the practice was described as 'ancient' when a St Peter's bonfire was lit in 1575.

More than a century later John Aubrey recorded, 'in Herefordshire and also in Somersetshire on Midsummer eve they make fires in the fields and in the ways, to bless the apples. I have seen the same custom in Somersetshire in 1685, but there they do it only for the custom's sake; but I do guess that this custom is derived from the Gentiles who did it in remembrance of Ceres . . . and the people might think that by this honour done to the goddess of husbandry that their corn, etc., might prosper the better.' As late as the nineteenth century midsummer bonfires were lit in the cider counties 'to bless the apples'.[46] Although the ashes cooled on these solstitial occasions, bonfires were too eloquent, and too much fun, to abandon altogether. As will be seen later, they remained a vital part of the English vocabulary of celebration.

Several Elizabethan towns and cities held midsummer pageants and parades featuring artificial giants, dragons and hobby horses that barely coexisted with the Christian tradition. These pageants occurred at London, Oxford and Coventry, and were still seen at Chester in the 1590s. George Puttenham, reputed author of *The Arte of English Poesie* (1589), recalled the midsummer pageants in London with 'great and ugly giants marching as if they were alive' but which were in fact crude creations stuffed with brown paper.[47]

At Chester the traditional pageant came to a dramatic end in 1599 when the mayor, 'a godly zealous man', 'caused the giants which use to go at midsummer to be broken up'. He also destroyed the figures of devils and dragons which belonged to the customary entertainment, and substituted the staid figure of a man on horseback in white armour. For this, not surprisingly, 'he got ill will among the commons for putting down the ancient orders'. The content of the pageant was transformed at Chester, but a midsummer show of sorts continued with the offensive and unruly elements removed. At York, home of St Peter's church, the midsummer pageant and show of armour occupied St Peter's eve until the end of Elizabeth's reign. At Burford, Oxfordshire, the parade of giants and dragons continued until well into the seventeenth century.[48]

Midsummer in London was also celebrated with a marching watch and vigil on the eve of St John's day. This involved an elaborate martial display that continued annually until late in the reign of Henry VIII. It was suppressed in 1539, probably for security reasons, and was temporarily revived in 1548, since when, according to John Stow, 'the like marching watch in this city hath not been used, though some attempts have been made thereto, as in the year 1585'. Canterbury held a midsummer watch, with trumpets, guns and beer, that warranted payments in the city chamberlain's accounts at least until early in Elizabeth's reign. The borough annals for Plymouth record in 1567, 'in this year the watch on midsummer's night was renewed, which had not been used in twenty years before that time'.[49]

Elizabethan Nottingham held marching watches on both Midsummer eve and St Peter's eve, with the aldermen paying for powder and match for the gunners. By 1607, however, it was reported that the seasonal watch 'hath been slenderly performed . . . to the encouragement of divers which are obstinate'. It appears that the Nottingham watch had fallen into disorder rather than decay, and the remedy, 'for the undergoing of this business peacefully in an even and equal course', was to confine it to only one of the midsummer evenings. In reduced form the midsummer watch at Nottingham continued until the civil war.[50]

Midsummer activities of this sort required organization and expenditure under the control of civic officials. When the corporations turned against them, when their sponsors withdraw their support, the customs usually died. It appears that the great outdoor festivity of midsummer generally came to an end in the later decades of the sixteenth century, but attentuated and alternative celebrations continued. Pageants with dragons gave way to processions in armour, and these yielded to innocuous civic dinners.

Midsummer observances varied from parish to parish, region to region. At Winsley, Wiltshire, in 1602 the curate complained of the midsummer feasting, singing and dancing. At Downham, Lancashire, the diarist Nicholas Assheton attended a foot race on

Midsummer day in 1617. St John's day at Great Yarmouth, Norfolk, became 'quest' day, the borough's inquest of liberties and offences, with helpings of bread, butter and beer in a hall seasonally adorned with boughs, rushes and herbs. The London parish of St Botolph without Bishopsgate was still treating its officers to a midsummer dinner in the middle of the seventeenth century.[51] Parish clerks and others in receipt of quarterly wages could look forward to payments and treats at Midsummer as well as at Michaelmas, Christmas and Lady day.

St James's day (25 July), the feast of Saints Simon and Jude (28 October), and St Andrew's day (30 November) were officially observed for the sake of honouring the complete set of holy apostles, along with the feast of St Matthew (21 September) and St Luke the Evangelist (18 October). In some towns these were traditional fair days, but generally they had little calendrical significance and attracted few controversial activities. St Bartholomew's day (24 August) was notable only for its famous London fair and for the memory of the massacre in France.[52] These saints' days, and others that had been dropped from the official calendar, might nonetheless have limited followings associated with local traditions, foundations, and guilds. The parish of Bruen Stapleford in Cheshire held its annual wake on St Andrew's day, much to the distress of the puritan gentry who found it frivolous and irreligious. In some places St James's day was a popular summer fair day. At Whalley, Lancashire, on St James's day 1617, Nicholas Assheton noted 'a rushbearing, but much less solemnity than formerly'. Assheton also heard sermons on the feasts of Saints John, Peter, Katherine and Andrew. Lady Margaret Hoby recorded on 21 September 1603, 'this day being the remembrance of St Matthew, Mr Philips came and preached at Winteringham [Yorks]'.[53]

It was surely no coincidence that James Stuart arranged to be crowned on 25 July, St James's day, thereby associating the majesty of the apostle with the majesty of the king. Some churches rang their bells on St James' day in the early seventeenth century as a compliment to King James. A London merchant endowed an annual feast and sermon on St James's day in the parish of St Pancras, Soper Lane, beginning in the 1620s. Fifty years later this was still observed as 'the anniversary dinner' or 'the churchwardens' feast'.[54]

St Swithin, a ninth-century Bishop of Winchester, had no official festival but everyone knew that if it rained on St Swithin's day (15 July) the summer and harvest would be troubled by rain. Ralph Josselin noted on 15 July 1662, 'this night with us being St Swithin's day, at night it rained, the old saying is it rains forty days after this'.[55]

The next significant day was 1 August, known as Lammas. This was a curious occasion of obscure and controversial origin. Lammas was not recognized by the ecclesiastical calendar, but it was invariably noted in the almanacs, and was a popular day for fairs. Most people in early modern England would have know when Lammas occurred. A diocesan official wrote in 1625, 'you have in rent for the rectory of Mapleton, annexed to your archdeaconry, of twenty-two pounds per annum, payable at Lammas and Candlemas, or within certain days. I remember Lammas last is paid.' Lammas and Candlemas were lesser days for the paying of rents and turning of accounts, secondary to the fiscal reckonings of Lady day and Michaelmas. Lammas land (as at Cambridge) was land that was privately held until Lammas day, but thereafter open for common grazing until the spring. At Coventry it was recorded, 'on the 1st day of August 1628, being Lammas day, certain of our poor commons rose, and pulled down the hedges of a piece of ground at Whitley . . . which in former times was taken out of the commons there'.[56] This challenge to the enclosure of the commons took place on the day when the calendar announced that Lammas rights were due.

The feast of St Michael the Archangel, otherwise Michaelmas (29 September), was a crucial date in the secular calendar. It stood at the opposite side of the year from Lady day, and was most important of the annual, half-yearly or quarterly days for the payment of rents and dues. Farm leases fell due at Michaelmas, at the end of the agrarian year. A seventeenth-century verse on Michaelmas quipped, 'The careful client has his harvest done/And now the lawyer's reaping is begun.' Michaelmas was also the usual day of elections in local government, the day for choosing aldermen, mayors and church-wardens. Many parishes and corporations followed a Michaelmas-to-Michaelmas calendar for their official business, and some marked St Michael's day with a formal dinner and sermon. At Banbury the bailiffs, justices, town clerks, sergeants of mace, auditors, constables, tithingmen, ale tasters, searchers, sealers, toll gatherers and chamberlains held office from Michaelmas to Michaelmas. Michaelmas at Bristol saw the ceremonies for the induction of the new mayor, with contingent feasts for the guild masters and other civic officials on the days immediately following.[57] Though observed as an ecclesiastical festival, Michaelmas mattered more in the secular cycle of the economy and government than in the liturgical cycle of the church. With business completed it was time for the corporation or tenants to tuck in to their Michaelmas goose.

All Saints' day, 1 November, and its preceding vigil on All Hallows' Eve, had limited importance in the ceremonial or customary calendar of Protestant England. The Church of England had only a

29

residual interest in the collective day of saints, and none at all in the suffering souls in purgatory. Halloween had traditionally been observed with bellringing, but this fell out of favour with the Reformation. Some villagers in Hampshire and Norfolk still set lights or rang bells on the eve of All Souls' in the 1560s, but strict Protestants would have nothing to do with such practices. The parishioners of Halesowen, Worcestershire, had to explain themselves before the bishop's court in 1578, 'about ringing on All Halloween day at night'.[58] Crypto-papists and others with a yearning for the old customs drew criticism for any hint or suggestion of prayers for the dead. All Souls day, 2 November, sometimes saw the distribution of 'soul cakes', and even the lighting of bonfires in some northern parishes, but the practice was mostly in decay by the time gentlemen-folklorists paid attention to it in the eighteenth century.[59]

Despite the post-Reformation reduction in the sacred significance of All Hallows', particular towns and parishes still reserved this date for their civic or parochial ceremonies. The leading citizens of Bristol, for example, were accustomed to an All Hallows' dinner 'with spiced cakebread and sundry wines'. In the London parish of St Andrew by the Wardrobe, All Saints' day was the occasion for an annual dole of firewood to the poor, which was no doubt most welcome as winter approached.[60] The calendar carried a reminder of charitable as well as spiritual obligations.

The feast of Martinmas (St Martin's day, 11 November) also dwindled in significance, although it might still be a feature of some local calendars as a fair day or parish dedication. St Hugh's day (17 November) did not officially survive the Reformation but communities within the orbit of Lincoln were especially supportive of the memory of their famous local saint. Payments to the bellringers 'on St Hugh's day' appeared regularly in the churchwardens' account of March, Cambridgeshire, down to the beginning of the seventeenth century. St Hugh still ruled the calendar at Northampton where Robert Woodford noted on 17 November 1638, 'St Hugh's fair kept here today.'[61] National acknowledgment of Bishop Hugh of Lincoln on 17 November might have completely disappeared had not St Hugh's day coincided with the accession day of Queen Elizabeth. Celebrations on that day, which will be examined later, belonged to the new providential-commemorative calendar of Protestant England rather than the older ecclesiastical routine.

Late autumn brought the feasts of St Clement and St Katherine on 23 and 25 November. These were once festive occasions in Bristol, when the weavers and merchants celebrated the annual shipping of cloth to Bordeaux. The ceremony declined in the 1540s, as changes in local employment patterns coincided with the Reformation assault on the saints. Similar observances in London were revived under Mary, but did not survive into Elizabeth's reign. The late autumn feasts of Saints Clement and Katherine ceased to be holy days, although their dates were still noted in the almanacs and calendars.[62] By this time the year itself was in decline, with little to mark the passage of time until the great festivity of Christmas. Such ceremonies as remained were of a local and vestigial nature.

The winter solstice on 21 December, Christianized as the feast of St Thomas the Apostle, generally passed without incident or comment. Organized outdoor revelry was limited by the English climate. Festive energy was stored for the Christmas celebrations that lasted from Christmas Eve to Twelfth Night. At York, however, 'a very rude and barbarous custom' was followed on St Thomas's day until it was suppressed in the 1570s. 'Yearly upon St Thomas's day before Christmas two disguised persons called Yule and Yule's wife should ride through the city, very undecently and uncomely, drawing great concourses of people after them.' Apologists claimed that the shouts of 'Yule, Yule' were Hebrew for 'a babe is born'. The parade occasioned profanities, took people away from their dutiful attendance at church, and could no longer be countenanced as part of the civic or Christian calendar. Royal commissioners pressured the city to abolish the disorderly custom, and in 1572 the aldermen of York agreed to its suppression.[63] Other communities marked St Thomas's day with more than the customary service, but in ways that reformers might approve. A parish bequest at St Martin in the Fields provided for the distribution of firewood to the poor on St Thomas's day, and the gift was recorded in the reigns of James I and Charles I. In some years, however, the dole was delayed until Christmas, perhaps to avoid privileging the saint's day.[64]

The Reformation had little immediate impact on the English observance of Christmas. At court, in town, and country, it was the great winter festival honouring the nativity of Christ, with its attendant 'twelve days madness'. The noun became a verb, as in 'the court is like to Christmas at Windsor'. The season was associated with fellowship, food, drink, games, warmth, and hospitality. The devout attended communion, distributed alms, and engaged in prayer. Landlords met their tenants and neighbours 'with great mirth and ceremony'.[65] Everyone was expected to have fun. Depending on one's point of view, the Christmas revels could be as wicked or as pleasurable as those of Maytime, with the difference that in winter most of the celebration was conducted indoors and therefore attracted less attention.

31

Most churches were decorated with evergreens and illuminated with candles. Pagan holly and ivy mingled with the accoutrements of anglican worship. Even at centres of reformed godliness, like St Stephen Coleman Street, London, where the puritan John Davenport presided, the sum of four shillings was expended in 1628 on 'holly, ivy, rosemary and bays at Christ-tide.[66] Seasonal decorations like these were common in the churches of Elizabethan and Stuart England. Only a minority of puritans attacked the Christmas holiday as unnecessary, unholy and even blasphemous. Attitudes hardened during the reign of Charles I. Some reformers developed a hostility towards Christmas, as much for its gluttony and merry-making as for its evident pagan origins, and when they gained power in the 1650s they pressed for its suppression.[67] However, the attack was short-lived and never popular, and Christmas emerged triumphant along with the rest of the traditional anglican calendar after the Restoration.

★

The Elizabethan year continued to hold sway in the seventeenth and eighteenth centuries. The sun still shone and the earth still turned. The year retained its agrarian rhythm, and was still paced by the secular cycle of law days, markets, and fairs. Easter and Christmas continued as major religious seasons and ceremonial occasions. In many places May day was as vital as ever, despite the conversion of some maypoles into parish ladders.[68] But the observance of saints' days became generally attenuated, with parishioners ignoring all but the most popular feasts. Seasonal wakes and vigils survived on the margin, still performed on their appointed days, but with a diminishing involvement of parish notables. Inhabitants refused to contribute to the cost of activities which they did not approve. Some community observances were abandoned; others went indoors, becoming less rowdy and more select. Open parish feasts were becoming private anniversary dinners, at the same time as public theatres gave way to indoor masques. The classes and cultures of seventeenth-century England were drawing apart, and the calendar provided periodic occasions to express their divisions.

By way of compensation a new set of national anniversaries emerged as distinctive reference points in the English Protestant year. While not forsaking the sacred calendar of an earlier era the English paid increasing attention to the symbolic anniversaries of their own recent history. Gunpowder Treason day and its companions rallied people to a king or a cause in ways comparable to the older religious festivals. Sometimes they were just as controversial. Discussion of this new and developing calendar and the memories enshrined in it will be reserved for subsequent chapters.

3
THE POLITICS OF THE
CALENDAR, 1600–1660

The new English calendar originated in the controversies of the Reformation. After weathering a burst of puritan criticism in the 1570s it emerged by the end of the Elizabethan era as the venerable and customary framework for the anglican year. Usage and regularity established its rhythms. The gospel calendar based on the life of Christ was firmly entrenched, and the red-letter rubric of saints' days appeared popular and secure. Although there were challenges to some of these festivals – against their remains of papism and their sometimes rowdy celebrants – the intensity of criticism was muted during the Jacobean period. Only the most militant puritans continued to press for change. During the laissez-faire regime of Toby Matthew as Archbishop of York (1606–28) and George Abbot as Archbishop of Canterbury (1611–33, but suspended 1627) the Church of England revealed its latitudinarian genius by permitting a wide range of local emphases and practice. Ecclesiastical records of this period reveal a background flutter of disturbances over maypoles and holy days, within a general climate of complaisance and compliance. Most disputes belonged neither to a puritan campaign for reform nor to an episcopal drive for conformity, but rather to local issues of piety, personality and interest.

This moderate consensus cracked in the 1620s, and turned to contention during the 1630s. Protestant anxiety was already heightened by the successes of Catholic forces in Europe after 1618 and by the apparent penetration of Catholic elements into the English realm. James I's pro-Spanish diplomacy and Charles's proposed match with a Catholic princess signalled the alarm. Protestant zealots became alert for signs of Popish remnants and intrusions, and had little difficulty finding them. Existing concerns sharpened when a shift in control of the church led to a reconsideration of the Elizabethan programme of reform.

The accession of Charles I advanced a newly ascendant group of Arminians, Laudians and high churchmen who luxuriated in the traditional Christian calendar and insisted on a disciplined observance of all the holy days and seasons of the year. More alarming, from the point of view of some puritans, the regime that was so strict in regard to saints' days and sacred times was permissive and indulgent of profane sports and entertainments at traditional holiday seasons. While upholding the strictest ecclesiastical calendar, the Caroline regime also gave encouragement to activities that puritans knew to be pagan in origin and licentious in practice, offending the godly on both moral and theological grounds. The king's Book of Sports, promulgated but only lethargically promoted by James I, was reissued by Charles I in 1633 as part of a national programme. Archbishop Laud ordered its distribution to every parish. 'May games, Whitsun ales, and Morris dances, and the setting up of Maypoles' were among the 'lawful recreations' permitted (and, by implication, encouraged) after Sunday services.[1]

Not surprisingly, the Laudian ascendancy provoked resistance and reaction. The calendar, an issue of moderate accommodation in the mid-Jacobean period, became a heated topic in the Caroline politics of religion. While a powerful minority of high ceremonialists insisted on strict and elaborate observances, another minority of godly precisians sought to safeguard the advances of the Reformation, and then to take them further. Disputes about holidays and seasonal observances spilled over into the civil war and revolution, and were not exhausted at the Restoration.

★

Anglican apologists saw the Christological cycle, with its judicious admixture of feasts, fasts and holy days, as one of the distinctive beauties of the English church. To Richard Hooker, writing in the 1590s, 'the sanctification of days and times is a token of that thankfulness, and a pattern of that public honour which we owe to God for admirable benefits . . . The days which are chosen out to serve as public memorials of such his mercies ought to be clothed with those outward robes of holiness whereby their difference from other days may be made sensible.'[2] Many churchmen of the early Stuart period agreed with Hooker that the hallowing of festival days was a dutiful, thankful, reverential, and commemorative action, designed to be pleasing to the Lord.

John Day, an Oxford preacher, quoted approvingly from Hooker on the sanctification of days and times. Day's Easter sermon of 1613 listed with pride the principal celebrations of the English Christian year. 'First, the Annunciation of [Christ's] birth by angelical embassage, commonly called our Lady day. Secondly, his blessed Nativity itself, commonly called Christmas (though there are that will not so speak for fear of I wot not fear) . . . Thirdly, the ministry of his legal

Circumcision, commonly called New Year's day. Fourthly, the testification of his true Incarnation by the Purification of her which brought him into the world, commonly called Candlemas day. Fifthly, his Resurrection. Sixthly, his Ascension. Seventhly, the admirable sending down of his spirit, commonly called Whitsunday.' Other days also warranted special attention, including Epiphany, Holy Innocent's day, St Michael's day and All Saints' day.[3]

Lancelot Andrewes similarly saw structure and meaning as well as beauty in the liturgical progression of the English year. In his seasonal sermons before King James, Andrewes offered 'sermons of the Nativity, preached upon Christmas day; sermons of repentance and fasting, preached upon Ash Wednesday; sermons preached in Lent; sermons of the Passion, preached upon Good Friday; sermons of the Resurrection, preached upon Easter day; sermons of the sending of the Holy Ghost, preached upon Whit Sunday'. When Bishop Andrewes's collected sermons were first published in 1629 it seemed natural to arrange them in accordance with the liturgical calendar.[4]

Preaching at court on Ash Wednesday 1619, Andrewes explained and justified the annual cycle: 'For once a year, all things turn . . . Now at this time is the turning of the year. In heaven, the sun in his equinoctial line, the zodiac, and all the constellations in it, do now turn about to the first point. The earth and all her plants, after a dead winter, return to the first and best season of the year. The creatures, the fowls of the air, the swallow and the turtle and the crane and the stork, know their seasons and make their just return at this time every year. Everything [is] now turning, that we also would make it our time to turn to God.'[5] Andrewes was aware that some members of the church disapproved of some aspects of its annual calendar, but through most of the Jacobean period the matter was not hotly contested. The bishop spoke with an assurance bordering complacency that was gauged to disarm or deflect puritan criticism. For every season in the ecclesiastical calendar, he argued, there was a due observance; every stage in the unfolding of the year called for appropriate devotion. For 'though it never be out of season to speak of Christ, yet even Christ hath his season'.[6]

Christmas commemorated Christ's human incarnation. 'Therefore meet we thus, every year, in a holy assembly, even for a solemn memorial that he hath, as this day bestowed upon us a dignity.' Christmas was 'the very Kalends of Christianity, from whence we begin our era, or Christian computation'; of all days it was '*in altissimus*, the highest of all'.[7] The church enjoined Lent 'not only by way of regiment to keep the body low, that it may be a less mellow soil for the sins of the flesh . . . so to prevent sin to come, but . . . as a chastisement for sin already past'. The forty days of Lent formed 'no physical, philosophical, [or] political, but a prophetical, yea, an evangelical fast'.[8]

The due keeping of Easter, according to Andrewes, was justified both by ancient usage and scriptural authority. Good Friday commemorated Christ's death for our sins, and Easter Sunday marked his resurrection for our salvation. 'The common sort look to Easter day no further than Easter day fare and Easter day apparell, and other use they have none of it. The true Christian enquireth further, what is the *agendum* of the feast, what is the proper Act of Easter day?' Andrewes answered that it was an occasion of solemnity and joy. So too was Whit Sunday. 'This day hold we holy to the Holy Ghost, by whom all holy days, persons and things are made holy.' The cycle was completed, for 'sure it is that all the rest, all the feasts hitherto in the return of the year, from [Christ's] incarnation to the very last of his Ascension, though all of them be great and worthy of all honour in themselves, yet, to us, they are as nothing, any of them or all of them, even all the feasts in the calendar, without this day, the feast which now we hold holy to the sending forth of the Holy Ghost'.[9]

Andrewes also preached on the anniversaries of the Gowrie Conspiracy and the Gunpowder Plot, on accession and coronation days, and at the opening of parliaments. How this adjunct cycle of dynastic and historical observances became a distinctive feature of seventeenth-century English Protestantism will be discussed in detail in later chapters.

Like Hooker and Andrewes, the dominant coterie under Charles I believed that the Church of England was beautifully and sufficiently reformed, and was the true successor to the pristine church of the early Christians. One did not have to be an Arminian to believe this, but the churchmen brushed with Arminianism insisted most on pressing the matter. For John Cosin, an Arminian associate of Laud, Neile and Montagu, the old calendrical observances touched closely on 'the honour of God and his church' and necessitated 'the laudable solemnities and religious ceremonies thereunto belonging', including ostentatious observances of Candlemas and Lent.[10] The arrogance with which the ceremonialists advanced their position, as well as its departure from Calvinism, antagonized some moderate ministers and helped to ignite a revived puritan movement.

Henry Mason was another who thought the Reformation had gone too far. Mason was an Arminian minister in London, and his *Christian Humiliation*, published in 1625, was sure to raise the hackles of his puritan neighbours. 'It were a commendable zeal if men would purge the ancient fasting days of the church and carry out the superstitions with which popery hath defiled them . . . But as it had been too much violence to pull down the Temple for the uncleanness' sake that was in it, so it is too much violence now to abolish all times of fasting and humiliation for the superstition that some men have placed in them.' Mason developed a comprehensive justification for calendrical observances, particularly those requiring fasting (i.e. abstinence from meat). In particular, he urged 'that the old discipline of Lent might be restored again', and he offered elaborate arguments to support this provocative position.[11]

Lent, from Mason's viewpoint, provided the occasion for an annual spiritual audit. It was instituted, 'that the people of God might have a solemn and special time of the year wherein they might in a more special and more exact and devouter manner take account of their lives, and reckon with their souls for the year past'. It was especially appropriate that Lent occurred in the spring. 'Now is the seed-time of the world,' wrote Mason. 'Men plough and harrow and break the clods of the ground, that it may be fit to receive seed and bring forth a plentiful increase; and so men, being admonished by the course of nature, should now take occasion to ransack their consciences and humble their souls and chasten the whole man, that they may be more fit to receive the seeds of grace and to bring forth the fruits of righteousness.' Mason conceded that Lent may not have been 'of divine or apostolical institution' but it was an ancient observance, followed by the church fathers from whom the Church of England was said to be descended.[12]

Clerics like Mason were concerned to demonstrate the authority and antiquity of the Church of England and pointed with pride to their adherence to the ancient Christian calendar, now freed from the corruptions of Rome. Others, however, might see this insistence on Lenten fasting as evidence of resurgent papism. Puritans in particular took exception to the implication that Christians' lives should not be under perpetual scrutiny, and that they should not be engaged perennially in devout living. Strict Calvinists might also recoil from the Arminian notion that reckoning with one's soul, a kind of spiritual book-keeping, could influence one's prospect of salvation. It might be but a small leap from here to the traditional Catholic Lenten preparation of shriving.

John Cosin set the fuse to an explosive discussion of the calendar through the publication of his *Collection of Private Devotions*. This went through five editions between 1627 and 1638, and praised the English liturgical rhythm as a thing of utility, holiness and beauty. 'The calendar of the church is as full of benefit as delight, unto such as are given to the serious study and due contemplation thereof. For besides the admirable order and disposition of times, which are necessary for the better transacting of all ecclesiastical and secular affairs, it hath in it a very beautiful distinction of the days and seasons, whereof some are chosen out and sanctified, and others put among the days of the week to number.' As in the ancient church, so in Caroline England, argued Cosin, the Christian calendar was intended 'to preserve a solemn memory' of God's benefits. The days commemorating saints and martyrs should be observed 'as sacred memorials of God's mercy towards us.' As an aid to this devotion Cosin printed a supplementary calendar of saints' days commemorating Hilary, Valentine, David, Gregory, Benedict, George, Dunstan, Swithin, Cyprian, Martin, and Hugh – dubious or discredited saints who had been purged from the English calendar in the reign of Henry VIII. Cosin further recommended a reverent observance of All Saints' day, a day that the puritan clergy were inclined to ignore.[13] To Protestant stalwarts this handbook, prominently endorsed by the Bishop of London, was a betrayal of the spirit of the Reformation.

Cosin put his predilections into practice in 1628 at Durham, where he became a prebend under Bishop Neile. Protected by powerful ecclesiastical patrons, Cosin restored images, vestments, music, bowing to the altar, and a rich calendrical ceremony. This was not without local opposition. The senior prebend, a Jacobean veteran named Peter Smart, preached against Cosin's innovations, and published his sermon, *The Vanitie & Downefall of Superstitious Popish Ceremonies*, from the relative safety of Scotland. According to Smart, 'on Candlemas day last past, Mr Cosin in renewing that popish ceremony of burning candles to the honour of our lady, busied himself from two of the clock in the afternoon till four, in climbing long ladders to stick up wax candles in the said cathedral church. The number of all the candles burnt that evening was 220, besides 16 torches'. While Cosin saw the beauty of holiness, Smart saw only the promotion of 'superstitious vanities' in the service of 'speculative and theorical popery'.[14]

As the ceremonialists and Arminians gained increasing control over the church they began to enforce their discipline. They insisted on strict conformity to the Book of Common Prayer, including the ritual and calendrical observances that many moderate puritans had dropped. Whereas Elizabethan and Jacobean bishops, faced with residual Catholicism, had attempted to *limit* religious observances to the authorized holy days, the new ceremonialists insisted that all those holy days be meticulously observed 'with their eves'. Matthew Wren, Bishop of Norwich, even required observance of the Conversion of St Paul (25 January) and St Barnabas's day (11 June), feasts which had been dropped from the Elizabethan calendar. Visitation articles reminded the clergy to follow the canons exactly, to declare 'to the people what holy days and fasting days they are to observe the week following', and to pay strict attention to the rules prohibiting matrimony in the holy periods of Advent, Lent and the Rogations. The officials uncovered negligence, like that at Terling, Essex, where in 1632 'they had neither divine service nor sermon in their church on Easter day last, nor on Low Sunday nor on most of the holy days of the year last past'.[15]

Corrective muscle was applied by the Court of High Commission. In 1634, for example, High Commission proceeded against nonconformists like Anthony Lapthorne, rector of Tretire, Herefordshire, who 'never observed any holy days or fasting days except Christmas, Easter, and Whitsuntide', and Francis Abbott, vicar of Poslingford, Suffolk, who 'preached to his parishioners that they who observed holidays did as ill as they who worshipped images'. Actions before High Commission damaged their victims' careers, served as a warning to others, and signalled that the government was serious in its drive for ecclesiastical discipline. Yet it could be argued that the much maligned High Commission, driven by zeal rather than venom, was more concerned to restore harmony to divided parishes than to persecute puritan offenders. In Francis Abbot's case, for example, where part of the problem lay in a personality clash between the minister and leading parishioners, the court removed Abbot from Poslingford, but gave him liberty to exercise his ministry anywhere else, despite his incorrigible indiscipline.[16]

The Laudian ascendancy produced more bluster than effective reform. Visitations were sometimes energetic but the harvest of offenders was slight. One difficulty was that the Arminians and ceremonialists never controlled every diocese, and even where they had power they were often frustrated by incompetent or uncooperative officials. The Government lacked the machinery to enforce a nationwide calendar of devotion and festivity, and could do little more than remonstrate to that end. Nor were Laud, Wren, Montagu, Cosin, and the rest of that circle of ceremonialists single-minded in their application. Nonetheless, the policies pursued by Laud and his associates created an anxious climate in which the godly feared further ills.

The shift in the religious climate can be traced in the various editions of Daniel Featly's *Ancilla Pietatis: or, the Hand-Maid to Private Devotion* published between 1626 and 1639. Featly was not an Arminian, indeed he argued strongly against the Arminians' theological innovations. Nor was he any kind of puritan. Rather he was an anglican Calvinist, and he loved the traditional customs and ceremonies of the English church. The first edition of *Ancilla Pietatis* commended the 'customs of the ancient church and the present practice of the Church of England' regarding feasts and fasts. But apart from a mild rebuke to those who neglected the traditional feast days it did not engage in debate.[17] By the time of the sixth edition in 1639 the ecclesiastical calendar was hotly controversial and Featly felt compelled to argue the virtues of the liturgical year. Both tone and content had changed over a dozen years.

Featly observed, in this later edition, that some of his colleagues and contemporaries 'make scruple to observe public feasts prescribed by the church. They hold it superstitious to place holiness in times and seasons; Judaism to keep strictly set days, especially of Easter and Pentecost; Popery to honour saints with festivals.' These were the puritans who had grown in recalcitrance and vigour under the stimulus of the Laudian regime. In rebuttal, Featly quoted Hooker to the effect that 'feasts are the splendour and outward dignity of our religion'. He argued that the customary feasts were 'dedicated as well to charity as piety', asserted that there was nothing Jewish or heathen about the church holy days despite their historical similarities, and claimed that the ecclesiastical festivities found warrants in scripture and precedents 'in the pure and first ages of the church'. The entire festive calendar was performed to the honour of God. Saints' days involved 'no religious devotion or worship . . . to the creature whose name the day carrieth, but to their and our Lord . . . On such days we sanctify God, we deify not saints.' This apology for the old festive calendar satisfied neither Laud nor the puritans. The puritans kept up their complaints against the abuses and solemnities of holy days, while Featly himself was disciplined by his archbishop for doubting the historicity of St George.[18]

How this new climate affected everyday life is indicated in his diary by Robert Woodford, who had trouble conducting his business in London on Thursday, 23 May, 1639, Ascension day. 'I went this day to a stationer's to buy parchment to make writs, where I used to buy; but the master desired me to forebear for he durst not sell me any. I told him he need not so scruple it for it was no sabbath day; he said no, were it sabbath day he might do it without danger, but if today he should be called in question.' Woodford commented, 'Oh Lord, I pray thee, establish and countenance thy sabbaths amongst us, and so order that we may have liberty to work the six days. Lord, reform whatever is amiss amongst us, for the Lord's sake.'[19] Most puritans shared these concerns, fearing the weekly rhythm of godly sabbatarianism was swamped by the red-letter tide of the Laudian liturgical year.

★

Resurgent ceremonialism sparked a puritan reaction which flared occasionally into hot dispute. While Cosin and his kind gave more weight to the ecclesiastical calendar than at any time since the Reformation, a reinvigorated puritanism sought to divest the church of a liturgical cycle and ceremonial observances that reminded them too strongly of Rome. For each side the calendar provided a symbolic encapsulation of their other disputes. Puritans stressed the weekly cycle of the Lord's day over the annual cycle of feasts and festivals. Godly preachers perceived calendrical ceremony as an offensive anachronism supported by dubious scriptural authority.

The anti-Laudians drew on a strong Elizabethan tradition. Forward Protestants had long argued that the Bible contained no clear command to keep Christmas and Easter, and most of them knew that the festive seasons rested on pagan foundations. In puritan eyes the rest of the calendar had even less justification. Indeed, it was pernicious because the multitude of saints' days encouraged idolatry and thoughts of purgatory, and obscured the solitary splendour of Christ. And many regarded the traditional calendar with its Christmas cheer and Whitsun ales as a source of traditional abuses – licentiousness, superstition and sin.[20]

Henry Burton, the energetic rector of St Matthew Friday Street, London (who had permitted such seemingly innocuous traditions as Rogationtide sweets and Christmas greenery) was among those provoked into militancy. Burton fanned the flames with *A Tryall of Private Devotion* (1628), a stinging attack on Cosin and all he represented. Burton charged Cosin with making 'strange alteration' in the practice of English religion. Cosin had tampered with the prayer book, Burton claimed, and was bent on restoring the cult of the saints. In his 'tedious' calendar of saints' days Cosin 'would have red letters put for the black, and so to canonize more holidays for you to observe'. The strict liturgical calendar with its restrictions on marriage at sacred times of the year – the calendar that Cosin and Mason thought so beautiful – had, according to Burton, 'lurked among some rubbish of Romish relics, and so escaped the shipping away with other of Rome's trinkets'.[21]

Like his Elizabethan predecessors, whose language he borrowed, Burton insisted that 'every day to a true Christian is a day of sobriety, and all his life a Lent, while all along his life is seasoned and sanctified with a conscionable keeping of the Lord's day'. Cosin and his kind offended against this by making a 'difference between the times sacred and common'. Even worse was the behaviour that contaminated these sacred times, when Christmas became a season of 'mad gambols and revels', to be followed by hypocritical 'Lent relentings' with their suggestions of Catholic absolution. Cosin, according to Burton, would allow 'all kind of festivity and jollity and joviality, such as he terms necessary recreations; for example, rush-bearings, Whitsun ales, Morris dances, setting up of Maypoles, hearing of a play or seeing or a masque, or dicing and carding, or bowling or boozing, or whatsoever other gloss the carnal vulgar may make of this unlimited joyful festivity or necessary recreation'.[22]

In attacking Cosin, Burton was challenging Cosin's friends and backers, a circle that extended from episcopal palaces to the heart of the court. The dispute could be seen as a squabble between extremists, but it had implications for the conduct of religious life throughout the kingdom. Backed by the crown, armed with the Book of Sports, the ceremonialists could be seen as leading the church back to the errors and superstitions of Rome with a calendar that encouraged licentiousness and depravity. Unlike the Tudor kings, who had lent their authority to the reformation of manners and the attack on superstition, the Caroline regime appeared to be supporting the other side.

This theme was at the heart of William Prynne's contentious *Histrio-Mastix* (1633). It was written, he said, 'in the midst of all our fears at home and the miserable desolations of God's church abroad'. Prynne used the precepts of early Christian councils to argue that the calendrical ceremonies of Caroline England were rooted in offensive heathen abominations. The Council of Africa, for example, had forbidden Christians to make feasts on the anniversaries of martyrs. Saints Ambrose and Augustine had condemned the New Year's observances as pagan relics. 'Unruly Christmas keeping . . . sprang from the pagan Saturnalia, from whence popery hath borrowed and transmitted it unto us at the second hand.' Likewise, Prynne pontificated, the feast of the Circumcision was the ancient Kalends of January; the Candlemas feast of the Purification of the Virgin Mary masked the pagan rites of Februa, mother of May, who was formerly honoured with burning tapers; and All Saints' day was simply the Roman Pantheon festival in modern guise. The proper Christian alternative, in Prynne's opinion, emphasized the weekly recurrence of the Lord's day, with modest observance of Easter, Pentecost and the fifth of November.[23]

Prynne used his learning to build the case against calendrical ritual, and he struck provocatively at the customs his opponents held dear. Among his targets were Cosin with his candles at Durham and, obliquely, the royal family with its masquing at court. This was antiquarianism with a vengeance, laced with venomous observations about the present. 'Alas, into what atheistical heathenish times are we now relapsed, into what a stupendous height of more than pagan impiety are we now degenerated?' asked Prynne. Christmas in particular he saw as a travesty of seemly Christian observance, with its 'drinking, roaring, healthing, dicing, carding, dancing, masques and stage plays'. As William Lamont has observed, 'Prynne had a Corvo-like appetite for quarrels.'[24] *Histrio-Mastix* led him into a notorious collision with Archbishop Laud which cost him his liberty and a portion of his ears.

English religious life became increasingly polarized in the 1630s. In church courts and parsonages from Durham to London the cere-monial observance of the calendar became a matter of acrimonious dispute. In London, the west country, East Anglia, and parts of the north there were local versions of the collision between Burton and Cosin. Controversy over Christmas and holy days, which had smouldered unregarded for over a generation, flared up like a beacon whenever puritans or Laudians forced the issue and provoked a debate. Disputes followed the Somerset springtime revels, the annual Floral feast at Norwich, and the enforcement of holy days in London.[25] In many communities, of course, there was silence and peace. Charles I's quieter subjects lived, as did ordinary people in most periods, with a mixture of custom, accommodation, and indifference. Only the most committed or most fearless plunged into the contro-versy, and not all would have recognized or acknowledged the labels – 'puritan', 'Arminian', etc. – that their enemies (and modern historians) attached to them.

*

The situation was transformed in 1640 by the emergency of the Scottish invasion and the opportunities of the Long Parliament. Aggressive puritans pushed an agenda for godly reform, but they were not able to implement it until later. The Root and Branch petition of December 1640 listed 'the strict observance of saints' days' among the corruptions of the Caroline church. Examples of calendri-cal ceremonialism supplied ammunition for the attack on Laud and episcopacy, and contributed to the atmosphere of indignation and panic. *A Faithful Remonstrance* by William Hinde, published in 1641, blasted 'these festival solemnities for the anniversary commemoration and celebration of saints and martyrs, and dedication of churches, which savour rank of the cask and smell hugely of the vessels of Judaism, paganism and papism, whence they were first drawn and arrived'.[26] Hinde's work memorialized the life of an early puritan notable in Cheshire, but his observations had fresh piquancy in the turmoil of 1641.

The House of Commons issued orders in 1641 'for the abolishing of

superstition and innovation in the regulating of church affairs', orders
that had no force and that were widely ignored. As polemic gave way
to violence, areas under parliamentary control faced the suppression
of their traditional holidays while royalist areas continued to
encourage them. The parliamentary preachers emphasized the
sabbath and substituted a cycle of monthly fasts for the old calendar of
holy days. This caused some confusion, as on 28 December 1642 when
a fast was held on the day of feast of the Holy Innocents, and in 1644
when parliament's monthly fast fell on Christmas day. Another public
thanksgiving was set for 24 June 1644, a day one scrupulous
parliamentary observer noted, 'we used to call Midsummer day'.[27] A
London schoolboy verse of that year took note of the curtailing of play
days and the loss of the red-letter days from the almanac:

> Since mis-called holy days, profanely spent,
> Are justly now cashiered by parliament;
> For that the scarlet garment that they wore,
> Was but a rubric'd badge o' th' Roman whore.

In the same year the young royalist theologian Edward Fisher,
attending the king at Oxford, charged the 'sectaries' with reviving
'those old, rotten errors of the Petrobrusians, affirming that
Christians ought not to keep or observe feasts'. Fisher asserted the
propriety of traditional holy days against the 'rabble of all opinions'.[28]

In direct contradiction the Directory of Public Worship, adopted in
1645, declared that 'festival days, vulgarly called holy days, having no
warrant in the word of God, are not to be continued'. Londoners
adapted to a new progression of time (though not without conflicts),
but a conservative rural populace clung to the customary observances.
The army proved a powerful force for advancing the new
Reformation. Ralph Josselin, engaged as an army chaplain, preached
two sermons at Stamford, Lincolnshire, on 21 September 1645 (St
Matthew's day) and noted in his diary, 'we spoil one of their church
feasts this day. People are still for their old ways'. The tactic of
swamping traditional holidays with solemn religious exercises had
similarly been employed by John Bruen a generation earlier in
Cheshire.[29]

A parliamentary ordinance of June 1647 finally addressed the issue
that some reformers had been pressing since the time of the
Reformation. The episcopal Church of England was dismantled, and
with it went the old Christian calendar. 'Forasmuch as the feasts of the
Nativity of Christ, Easter, and Whitsuntide, and other festivals
commonly called holy days, have been heretofore superstitiously used

and observed, be it ordained by the Lords and Commons in parliament assembled, that the said feasts . . . be no longer observed as festivals or holy days . . . any law, statute, custom, constitution or canon to the contrary in any wise notwithstanding.'[30]

At the same time there were revolutionary enthusiasts who thought that the official suppression of the anglican calendar did not go far enough. A petitioner to parliament in 1648 argued that the very names of the days and the months were of 'paganish' and 'barbarous' origin and therefore were an insult to God. 'The Christian dedication of days and months to the memory of apostles, saints and martyrs you have already by your authority made null. And why should the rest be left undone, an heathenish dedication to the memory and honour of abominable idols?' Already in New England advanced Protestants had taken to referring to days and months by numbers, as a safeguard against pagan pollution, and the practice had some adherents among the godly community in England.[31]

However, as early reformers had found to their chagrin, it was one thing to declare a practice abolished, quite another to drive it out of use. The new austerity imposed from Westminster failed to command popular support. England's official calendar for the next dozen years denied the old festivals of Christmas, etc., but local practice haphazardly kept them alive. People paced their lives, as they had for generations, by the cycle of the Christian year, even if public celebrations were missing or muted. Almanacs of the Cromwellian era continued to list the old festival days, and some still distinguished them with red ink.

The keeping of Christmas was especially controversial, and became a rough test of godliness or malignancy. Strict puritans would have none of the old celebrations, while traditionalists attempted to maintain good cheer. John Taylor found the Christmas of 1645 most strange, with no bellringing and 'no sign or token of any holy day' in the major towns. Shops remained open and men went about their everyday work. Ralph Josselin's idea of a good Christmas was a day spent in Christian discourse and meditation, but he noted on 25 December 1647, 'people hanker after the sports and pastimes they were wonted to enjoy, but they are in many families weaned from them'.[32]

The Christmas of 1647, the first following the parliamentary ordinance, saw violent confrontations in Suffolk and Kent. At Bury St Edmunds 'the people of God' ostentatiously ignored the old festival and kept their shops open; 'the malignant party', led by rowdy apprentices, tried to close them down. At Canterbury there was a more serious incident involving conservative countrymen who invaded the puritan-controlled town. In accordance with parliamentary instruction the mayor proclaimed 'that Christmas day, and all other superstitious festivals, should be put down, and that a market should be kept upon Christmas day'. This apparently caused 'great discontent' and was 'very ill taken by the country'. Very few shops risked staying open, and most were closed down by a mob that cracked bones and broke windows. At the height of the excitement, with the mayor and his officers vanquished, the crowd produced footballs, the symbol of festival sports. One report tells of soldiers joining the spree.[33] Scholars debated 'the lawfulness of the celebration of Christ's birthday', compared the pagan and scriptural origins of the feast, and argued whether or not Christ was actually born in December.[34] This was an arid controversy that had little direct impact on behaviour in most villages. But it showed that the old regime had vocal champions with easy access to the press.

Many parishes continued to follow an abbreviated version of the traditional calendar throughout the period of the interregnum. Christmas might still occasion an annual dole to the poor, even without public services. Rogation or Whitsuntide perambulations, which served social and secular as well as religious functions, were especially tenacious. The parish of St Peter Mancroft, in the heart of puritan Norwich, spent more than five pounds a year in the 1650s 'upon Whitsun Monday for cakes, wine and beer and other diet amongst the parishioners and children'. Similar traditions were maintained in Cambridge and London.[35] There was also near-universal ringing of church bells on 5 November, but that had other resonances which will be examined later.

By the early 1650s a wistfulness set in in some quarters for the beauty and regularity of the Church of England. Former Laudians and cere-monialists could be expected to lament the suppression of their religion, but moderate anglicans shared their hope for a religious restoration. Edward Sparke caught the mood in his verse of 1652: 'Millions of sons their duty still retain,/And at the least, pray for your fair days again.' Sparke's hefty treatise, *Scintillula Altaris. Or, A Pious Reflection on Primitive Devotion* included 'a catalogue of the feasts and fasts' and a thorough account of the antiquity and dignity of the holy days throughout the year. In Sparke's view these 'Christian solemnities' tended 'only to God's honour, his saints' memory, and our edification; without which ('tis too visible) religion will soon languish, and even die away by degrees into profaneness, heresy and atheism'.[36] A dozen verse endorsement from such luminaries as Francis Wortley, Thomas Fuller, Izaak Walton, Peter Vowel and Henry Delaune, testified to the hopeful survival of the anglican religious cause.

Customary observance had not been extinguished, and the official rejection of Christmas was widely unpopular. In 1652 parliament ordered 25 December to be kept as a market day in London and offered protection 'from wrong and violence' to all who would keep their shops open. It would not have been necessary to resolve 'that no observation shall be had of the five and twentieth day of December' if the puritan cultural revolution had been successful. In fact most of the London shops closed down and merrymakers haunted taphouses and taverns. Christmas was kept with 'games and gambols' that same year in the west country, official disapproval notwithstanding. A few years later Hezekiah Woodward raged against the 'tyranny of custom' and 'the multitude that keep holy day into all excess of riot'.[37] Woodward was writing under the godliest of all governments, but his frustration was not unlike that of the Elizabethan puritan preachers at an early stage of the Reformation when the superstitious multitude failed to respond to the call of reform.

London under the Protectorate had a growing number of celebrations and services on Christmas day. The Christmas of 1657 was an especially challenging test to the authority of the Cromwellian regime. Just before Christmas the Council ordered, 'the festivals of Easter, Christmas, and other holy days having been taken away, the Lord Mayor and justices of London and Westminster are to see that the ordinance for taking away festivals is observed, and to prevent the solemnities heretofore used in their celebration'. They would have done as well to stop the tide. The Venetian ambassador observed that 'the people, unable to forget the ancient custom, refused to obey, for no shop is seen open; but all those who went to the churches to perform their devotions were arrested'. A week later some were still in custody 'under suspicion of some plot against the present government to be carried out' on Christmas day.[38]

The old feasts came back with the Restoration, even before the Church of England calendar was officially restored. Thomas Hall, a Worcestershire parson, fought a rearguard action with his *Funebria Florae, The Downfall of May-Games*, but he could not stem the rush of jollity. 'How perilous it is . . . to tolerate those profane pastimes which open the floodgates to so much sin and wickedness.' Like his contemporary Woodward, and like their Elizabethan predecessors, Hall saw himself in a select company of 'godly magistrates, ministers and people, which oppose the rascality and rout in this their open profaneness and heathenish customs'.[39] The time of their dominance was past.

Ralph Josselin noted sadly after preaching on 25 December 1660, 'divers not there and some in their antique postures'. Even in his godly community the old festive habits held sway. Josselin had no hold over the behaviour of his Earls Colne parishioners, but endeavoured to keep a decent Christmas within his own family. On Christmas day 1674 he preached and entertained his tenants 'plentifully, without disorder'. The following year he noted a small congregation in church, 'all shops open; trade goeth; religion sad'.[40] The complaint of the godly now was not that people celebrated an antique Christmas but that they ignored religious exercises altogether.

4
CROWNATION DAY
AND THE ROYAL HONOUR

As if to compensate for the reduction in holy days, and to provide a dynastic rather than ecclesiastical focus to the calendar, the government of Queen Elizabeth encouraged prayer and festivity on 17 November, the anniversary of the queen's accession. This day developed into a nationwide annual celebration, without precedent in early reigns. It was marked by the ringing of church bells, the holding of special services, and by other manifestations of joy and respect. The occasion went by many names, but, significantly, was often referred to as 'the queen's holy day'. At St Botolph without Bishopsgate, London, they rang 'for the reign of her majesty'. Nearby at St Mary Aldermanbury it was 'the day wherein the queen's majesty began her reign'. At St Stephen Coleman Street it was 'the day of remembrance of her highness' coronation'. The churchwardens of Minchin-hampton, Gloucestershire, accounted loyally in 1576 for expenses 'for ringing the day of the queen's majesty's entering unto the crown, whom God long time we beseech to preserve'. There was no standard phrase and no consistency of usage to describe what became a near universal practice. At Sherborne, Dorset, in various years they celebrated 'the beginning of the year of the queen's reign', 'the queen's day', or simply 'when they rang for the queen'. Other parishes rang 'for the queen's year day', 'on the queen's night,' or on what was popularly known as 'crownation day'.[1] This word was a corruption of coronation day, but it referred to the date of accession (and the death of the previous monarch), not to the formal installation on the throne.

Celebrations involved bonfires, bells, candles, services, music, hospitality, beer, and bread, as well as tilts and entertainments at court. Sir John Neale and Sir Roy Strong have shown in detail the growth of the cult of Elizabeth and the observance of 17 November as Eliza's sacred day.[2] The following discussion builds on their work, to describe and explain local recognition of this national and dynastic occasion. The custom continued and expanded under the Stuarts, providing England with a changing calendar of royal anniversaries.

Crownation day was the first annual concert of bells that was not tied to the Christian year. In some parts, however, the festivity was taken to perpetuate the memory of St Hugh of Lincoln whose feast was formerly held on 17 November. The national dynastic observance was conveniently grafted on to a regional custom, and the ringing could simultaneously satisfy conservative religious instincts and honour the Protestant queen. Interpretation was a matter of custom, context, prompts, and inclination. At Bishop's Stortford, Hertfordshire, in 1575 they spend 2s. 8d. on 'bread, drink, and cheese for ringing on St Hugh's day in rejoicing of the queen's prosperous reign'. Repton, Derbyshire, was another parish where the church-wardens sometimes noted the activity on 17 November as 'St Hugh's day' and at other times as 'the coronation day'. At March, Cambridgeshire, only forty miles from Lincoln, they rang for St Hugh's day in 1571, and referred to both the queen and St Hugh when they celebrated 17 November in the 1590s. So too at Northill and Shillington in Bedfordshire, within the diocese of Lincoln, there was some ambivalence over whether the celebration was for the saint or the queen.

Oxford tradition associates the anniversary ringing with the older celebrations for St Hugh of Lincoln. Lincoln College, Oxford, was reputedly a traditionalist stronghold, and annually held a 'gaudy day' on 17 November in honour of its patron, St Hugh. In 1570, it is said, some pro-Catholic members of Lincoln College rang the bells of All Hallows', and were rebuked by the mayor for ringing a dirge for Queen Mary on the anniversary of her death. When told that, to the contrary, the ringing represented joy at the present queen's accession the mayor ordered bells throughout the city to be rung in the queen's honour.[3] The story points to the potential ambiguity of the ringing, and to the overlap of the festivals of St Hugh and Queen Elizabeth, but it does not identify the origins of a national custom. Some parishes had rung on the queen's day before 1570, and many did so afterwards without reference to behaviour at Oxford. Thomas Holland, an Oxford professor preaching at St Paul's in 1599, believed that 'the first public celebrity [of 17 November] was instituted in Oxford' by vice-chancellor Cooper 'about the twelfth year of the reign . . . and not before'. In his view, however, the celebration had nothing to do with 'bishop Hugh's superstitious festivity' which had been 'abrogated at the least twelve years before'. John Howson, preaching at Oxford on 17 November 1602, in a sermon dedicated to the chancellor, took it as point of honour that the queen's day was 'first celebrated, as we take it, in this her most loyal and Christian University of Oxford'.[4]

The Elizabethan annalist William Camden gave an alternative explanation of the origin of the anniversary commemoration. In 1570, 'the twelfth year of the reign of Queen Elizabeth being now happily expired, wherein some credulous papists expected, according to the prediction of certain wizards, their golden days, as they termed it, all good men through England joyfully triumphed, and with thanksgiving, sermons in churches, multiplied prayers, joyful ringing of bells, running at tilt, and festival mirth, began to celebrate the seventeenth day of November, being the anniversary day of the beginning of her reign'.[5] It was, in this view, a spontaneous outpouring of relief after the queen had survived the year of malignant prognostication and the very real emergency of the northern rebellion. Pope Pius V had issued the bull of excommunication against Elizabeth in February 1570, and it was not yet known how the Catholics in England and abroad would respond. The turning of the regnal year on 17 November 1570 provided an occasion to ring in defiance of Rome and in support of England's Protestant queen. The bells were a convenient vehicle for expressing loyal enthusiasm.

Most likely the custom began in the London area in the late 1560s. Lambeth rang its bells on the queen's day as early as 1567. The churchwardens of the City parish of St Botolph without Bishopsgate paid one shilling 'to the ringers that rung for the queen's majesty's entrance of the eleventh year of her grace reign, which was the 17th day of November 1568'. St Peter Cheap also rang in 1568, and other parishes followed suit. The practice was widely adopted in southern England in 1570 or soon after, and spread during the following years to parishes throughout the country. The university towns of Oxford and Cambridge were quick to ring for the queen, but the accession day custom spread more slowly in the north. Yorkshire parishes were 'ringing for the queen's majesty's reign' by the mid-1570s.[6]

By the 1580s the queen's anniversary day was widely established as a customary calendrical occasion. Indeed, 'November's sacred seventeenth day' was, according to Maurice Kyffin, 'more fit to be solemnized than many other days noted in the calendar'.

> Adore November's sacred sev'nteenth day,
> Wherein our second sun began her shine.
> Ring out loud sounding bells; on organs play;
> To music's mirth let all estates incline;
> Sound drums and trumpets, renting air and ground.
> Stringed instruments strike with melodious sound.[7]

The ringing was generally interpreted as a tribute to the queen and as a confounding of her enemies; it was a salute to the Tudor dynasty and an affirmation of loyalty to the Protestant regime. Thomas

Holland enthused about 17 November as 'the day wherein this whole realm giveth thanks to God, by public service, and showeth great signs of joy in each parish and general assemblies for the happy regiment of our queen Elizabeth'. In the words of the London preacher Thomas White, 'every twelve month, let us in thanksgiving remember her, to whom, under God, we owe all our service upon earth'.[8] It was a day of national cohesion and solidarity, an annual occasion for communal celebration expressed through synchronized bellringing. Whether she spent the day at Windsor or Westminster, the queen was made symbolically present in thousands of parishes through the rituals of celebration. This was a distinctively English occasion; for most of the contemporary monarchies of Catholic Europe it would have seemed blasphemous to mark the anniversaries of a king's accession with the observances associated with holy days.

Though never an official public holiday with release from labour, 17 November attracted much of the festive and liturgical energy that had formerly been reserved for saints' days. In 1576 Archbishop Grindal issued 'A form of prayer with thanksgiving, to be used every year, the 17th of November, being the day of the queen's majesty's entry to her reign'. This was followed in 1578 with an enlarged version displaying Elizabeth in the tradition of Old Testament kings.[9] The service books contained a careful selection of prayers and psalms, with inspiring references to the godly triumphs of Jehosaphat and Hezekiah. Payments for their purchase sometimes show up in churchwardens' records. The parish of St Matthew Friday Street, London, nicely balanced the demands of official and popular culture, paying 10d. in 1578 'for two prayer books and a ballad at the commemoration of the queen's majesty on the 17th of November'. The official collection of readings contributed to the cult of Elizabeth and supplied inspiration for the accession day sermons. Edmund Bunny, subdeacon of York, augmented them in 1585 with *Certaine prayers and other godly exercises for the seventeenth of November: wherein we solemnize the blessed reigne of our gracious soveraigne.*[10]

Elizabethan Protestants held that 17 November represented more than the accession day of a monarch. Rather, it signified the turning point in England's religious history, a providential divide between the nightmare of popery and the promise of the development of God's true church. John Foxe established the tone in his dedication to Elizabeth of his *Actes ands Monuments* in 1563. 'What bitter blasts, what smarting storms have been felt in England during the space of certain years, till at last God's pitiful grace sent us your majesty to quench firebrands, to assuage rage, to relieve innocents.'[11]

Preachers elaborated this message in their accession day sermons.

Isaac Colfe, preaching at Lydd, Kent, in 1587, reviewed the benefits that 17 November had brought to England. 'Queen Mary left it vexed with the insolency of the Spanish nation which she brought in, Queen Elizabeth hath eased it; Mary left it in war, Elizabeth hath governed it in peace; Mary left it in debt, Elizabeth hath enriched it; Mary left it weak, Elizabeth hath strengthened it; nay further, wherein the perfection of our present happiness consisteth, Mary banishes true religion, Elizabeth hath restored it; Mary persecuted it, Elizabeth hath defended it; Mary cast it down, Elizabeth hath advanced it.' Thomas Holland of Oxford recalled 17 November 1558 as 'a day registered in all our chronicles to all happy remembrance . . . a day wherein our nation received a new light after a fearful and bloody eclipse'.[12] The standard theme of these sermons involved loyalty, gratitude and joy, to be tempered by godly vigilance.

By the end of Elizabeth's reign crownation day was firmly established in the national calendar, though not without its critics. Preaching on 17 November 1602, the Oxford vice-chancellor John Howson remarked that some puritans scrupled to put 'a difference and distinction' between days, saving the Sabbath, while Catholics criticized the queen's day too, 'as though we preferred it before the feasts of our saviour Christ'.[13]

Individuals towns and villages developed local customs involving pageants, bonfires, or ritual doles to the poor on 17 November, in a subdued secular version of the old religious festivals. Most places rang their bells. At Liverpool the mayor commissioned bonfires in 1576 and led the leading citizenry in a banquet. Happy with sack, white wine and sugar, the councillors stood outdoors in the evening, 'lauding and praising God for the most prosperous reign of our . . . most gracious sovereign'.[14] Maidstone, Ipswich, Coventry and Nottingham were among the towns holding plays or pageants in the streets on 17 November. At Cambridge in 1578 the university added the queen's accession day to the select occasions when doctors should wear their scarlet gowns. Some towns shot their guns in salute or exploded fireworks. Others engaged in feasts. The city of Norwich fired its great ordnance and held torch-lit processions attended by waits and trumpeters 'on the day of alteration of the queen's reign'. In the village of Tilney, Norfolk, the churchwardens spent three shillings on 'a kilderkin of beer upon the day of the coronation' in 1583. Kendal, Westmoreland, added the sound of drumming to the music of the waits and the clanging of the bells.[15] By 1588, the thirtieth anniversary of the queen's accession and the triumphant year of deliverance from the Spanish Armada, all the elements came together in a surge of joy.

Part of the pattern of local observances can be traced in the surviving churchwardens' records. Most parish expenditures relate to the maintenance of the church fabric, with lesser amounts laid out for ancillary sacred business such as washing the minister's surplice and providing communion bread and wine. Parish officials expended their money with caution and took personal responsibility for their annual accounts. The churchwardens also undertook to reward the ringers with money, bread and beer whenever the parish decided to ring the bells on special occasions. Such payments stand out from the routine expenditures on cleaning and mending, and they provide a rough indication of local participation in national and dynastic events. A common expenditure was for candles. Some were used by the ringers to light their chamber; others were used to illuminate the interior of the church. Parishioners normally worked during the day, because 17 November was not an official holiday, so the accession day sermons were commonly delivered after dark. The churchwardens of St Andrew by the Wardrobe, London, regularly purchased a pound or two of candles for use on the night of 17 November. On the queen's night in 1602, while the bells rang out to celebrate the anniversary, the lectern at St Stephen Coleman Street was lit with six pounds of candles. Similarly at Repton, Derbyshire, the church was lit 'at St Hugh's day at night with candles'. The churches must have shone invitingly amidst the late autumn dark. Sometimes the observance stretched over two evenings, like traditional holy days and their eves. In 1587, for example, the churchwardens of St Martin Orgar, London, 'laid out on the coronation eve and the night following for candles, bread and drink for the ringers'. At Mere, Wiltshire, the churchwardens spent 2s. 4d. in 1574 'for the ringers for the queen's day the 17th of November for meat, drink and candles', and this was quite typical. The scale of the observance, and the intensity of the bellringing, can be gauged from the amount spent rewarding the ringers. At St Edmund's, Salisbury, the ringers were paid fourpence or sixpence for their efforts at Christmas, Easter, Ascension and Whitsunday; but they earned eight shillings on 17 November 1587 'for ringing for the queen's majesty' and another five shillings on the queen's birthday.

By the 1580s the custom was firmly established. The queen's day was generally marked by hearty ringing of parish church bells, sustained by payments of beer, bread and cheese to the ringers. At night the church would be lit with candles, possibly evoking some of the associations of candlemas, the festival of lights in honour of the other virgin. There would be a service of thanksgiving following the printed form, and perhaps a patriotic sermon recounting the blessings that befell England under Elizabeth's happy reign, and warning of the ever-present dangers from Rome. At court there were ceremonial tilts and spectacles with speeches honouring the queen. One Elizabethan participant described 17 November as 'a holiday which passed all the pope's holidays' and this competitive element was clearly part of its didactic message.[16]

It is difficult to discover what combination of official prompting and local enthusiasm gave birth to the developing national observance. The ringers operated at the end of a chain of command, the links of which are by no means clear. Just as royal almoners or outriders sometimes ensured that parishes would ring in the royal presence, government or household officers may have coordinated aspects of the annual celebration. The Privy Council was no doubt pleased that parishes throughout the country signalled their affection for the queen by ringing on her anniversary. But the extent to which councillors actually encouraged this demonstration is unknown. Local officials understood it to be their duty to perform the ringing, and hints of this sometimes appear in the local records. Mayors and bailiffs are known to have instructed those beneath them. At Ludlow, Shropshire, for example, in 1572 the churchwardens paid ten shillings 'to the ringers the 17th of this November that rang for the queen, at the appointment of Mr Bailiff's, in money and drink'. (The payments were lower in subsequent years.) The mayor of Liverpool 'caused . . . a great bonfire to be made in the market place, near to the high cross of the town, and another anenst his own door, giving warning that every householder should do the like throughout the town, which was done accordingly'.[17] The mayor of Oxford sent similar instructions for parishes to ring their bells. Ecclesiastical officials also gave hints and directions. At Minchinhampton, Gloucestershire, in 1585 the church-wardens more than doubled their usual expenditure on 17 November (from 12d. to 2s. 5d.) and 'paid for a prayer for the queen's majesty sent hither by the chancellor'.

In most places the anniversary activity acquired the regularity and momentum of custom. The churchwardens at St Christopher's, London, acknowledged this in 1602 when they 'paid the clerk and the sexton for ringing on the queen's majesty's day and night 4s. 4d. allowed them by custom yearly'. At St Mary Aldermanbury a vestry meeting in 1580 agreed 'that 6s. 8d. is also allowed yearly for the charges of ringing for the queen's majesty the 17th day of November'. This regular expenditure continued well into the seventeenth century long after the death of the queen. The pattern is repeated in dozens of churchwardens' books where the experimental ringing of the early 1570s became the annual routine of the later decades of Elizabeth's reign. Not to be caught unprepared, some parishes took to 'mending the bells against the coronation' day. At Swaffham, Norfolk, the churchwardens 'paid to John Brewer for three days' work about the bells at the coronation day' in 1587. Fresh oil, rope, leather, and woodwork was provided for the bells of Holy Trinity, Cambridge, 'against the queen's day' in 1600.

As if honouring the anniversary of the succession and the turning of the regnal year was not enough, some parishes took to observing the queen's birthday on 7 September as well. This was usually a quieter celebration, with a lower intensity or shorter duration of ringing, but it provided a second secular calendrical occasion in the autumn part of the year. At St Martin in the Fields, Middlesex, for example, they spent 12d. 'for bread and beer for the ringers the 7th of September being her majesty's birthday' and 6s. for the ringing on 'the 17th of November at the changing of her majesty's reign'. At St Bartholomew Exchange, London, the churchwardens expended 2s. 6d. on the queen's birthday in 1599, and 4s. 6d. on 17 November. In 1600 the cost of ringing on 7 September was still 2s. 6d. but the celebratory expenditure on 'crownation day' had risen to 6s. 8d.. At Lambeth, Surrey, there was 3s. 4d. worth of ringing on 7 September 1585 and 5s. on 17 November. Many other parishes also observed the queen's birthday as well as the date of her accession, and the practice continued intermittently under her Stuart successors.[18]

*

Elizabeth died and James Stuart succeeded her on 24 March 1603. Bells sounded all over England 'the day the king was proclaimed' and again on St James's day, the not-coincidental day of his coronation. The celebration signified no disrespect for Elizabeth, although some people were relieved she had finally gone. The ringing was, of course, a forward-looking gesture of welcome for the new king. James's accession also shifted the dynastic anniversary festivities from the autumn to the spring. Parishes purchased 'a little prayer book proper for the said 24th of March to be used yearly'. Communities learned a new calendar with festivities on James's crownation day and on other days associated with the safety or happiness of the king. A new pattern was soon established whereby the annual royal ringing of the late sixteenth century expanded to three occasions a year. Most parishes rang for the regnal year on 24 March, on 5 August, a day of personal significance to King James marking his escape from the Gowry conspiracy, and again on 5 November, celebrating his and the nation's deliverance from the Gunpowder Plot. A few parishes rang on the king's birthday, 19 June. Some places still rang on 17 November in honour of the late

Queen Elizabeth and this custom gained new vigour with the anxieties of the 1620s, a topic to which we shall return.

Vestiges of the older ecclesiastical calendar clung to the new cycle of royal anniversaries. James's accession day on 24 March was the day before Lady day, and some parishes recorded ringing for the king 'on our Lady eve'. James's crownation day was still widely called 'the king's holy day'. St Christopher's, London, was one of thousands of parishes that celebrated the accession of James with bonfires and bells in 1603. Thereafter the churchwardens spent four shillings each year for ringing 'on the king's day' but appear to have reduced this amount after 1618. Other parishes routinely spent two to four shillings on candles and bellringing on the anniversary of the royal accession. At St Botolph without Bishopsgate they spent 6s. 8d. for ringing 'on the king's day' at the beginning of James's reign in 1604. Routine payments towards the end of the reign included five shillings 'to the ringers for the crownation' on 24 March, five shillings 'to the ringers for Gowry's conspiracy' and the same sum on 5 November.

Similarly at St Stephen Coleman Street there were regular payments 'to ringers for ringing on certain days as the king's coronation day, the day of his delivery from the treason of Earl Gowry, and the day of the intended Gunpowder Treason'. In this parish the usual payments were 3s. 4d. on 24 March and 2s. 6d. each on 5 August and 5 November. By the 1620s, however, the 5 November payment had risen to match the payment on accession day. The parish of St Bartholomew Exchange spent 6s. 8d 'for ringing on the king's even and day the 23 and 24th of March' in 1604. This was the same sum previously expended on the queen's day. But the festive investment diminished to 1s. 6d. on 24 March 1620 and a mere shilling in 1624, which may reflect a decline in the king's popularity. By the 1620s the parish had revived its ringing on 17 November in memory of Queen Elizabeth.

Away from London there was greater variety of practice. At March, Cambridgeshire, they started the reign with 'eleven barrels of beer for the joy of the king', but celebration of James's special days in following years was erratic. Some parishes made no public acknowledgements of the Jacobean anniversaries, and many were inconsistent. In some years they might record ringing on all three occasions, in others two, one or none. The churchwardens of Sherborne, Dorset, recorded no ringing in 1620, ringing on 24 March and 5 August 1621, on 24 March and 5 November in 1622, and on all three dates in 1623. Hartland, Devon, marked all three anniversaries, giving eight shillings to the ringers each time. Great St Mary's, Cambridge, usually rang on all royal occasions, allowing 2s. or 2s. 6d. to the ringers. By the 1620s the churchwardens routinely expended six shillings, 'for the ringers upon the three several days'. At St Edmund's, Salisbury, they went further and celebrated the king's birthday as well. The annual accounts from 1607 to 1625 specify payments on the 'four usual ringing days for the king'.

★

King Charles came to the throne on 27 March 1625, only three days after the anniversary of his father's accession. The annual ringing for the king's day remained a spring-time observance, the renewal of the reign coinciding with the renewal of the year and the Easter season. Caroline almanacs listed 27 March among the most notable dates of the year, and local officials responded appropriately. Churchwardens expended their sixpences for new books of prayer for the coronation day. The chamberlains of Bristol spent 3s. 2d. in 1628 'for a draught of timber which was used for the bonfire on the king's holy day, and for faggots spent then'.[19] Most places rang their bells. Some parishes rewarded their bellringers with routine payments of a standard sum; others disbursed a discretionary amount that varied from year to year. At St Stephen Coleman Street, London, the churchwardens distinguished between 'ordinary' and 'extraordinary' payments to the ringers. They made 'ordinary' payments for crownation day and 5 November, the minimum standard ringing days, and 'extraordinary' payments on royal birthdays and days of particular good news, such as a prince's christening or a diplomatic success. The Gowry conspiracy day on 5 August was no longer celebrated, since that deliverance was particular to the new king's father, but remote parishes like Gateshead, Durham, were slow to get the message.

The ecclesiastical calendar attached to John Cosin's *Collection of Private Devotions* noted 27 March as 'the day of King Charles his inauguration'. Cosin also printed a form of 'prayer and thanksgiving for every true subject to use upon the anniversary day of the king's reign'. This asked God to 'bless the king with thy favours and crown him with continual honour, granting him a long, prosperous and religious reign over his people, and granting us a true, quiet, humble and obedient subjection under him'.[20] Only with hindsight can we find this ironic.

Charles soon found himself competing with the ghost of Queen Elizabeth. Some parishes had never entirely abandoned the habit of commemorative ringing on 17 November, long after Elizabeth had died, but many more took up the practice in the 1620s. Often they rang more vigorously on the anniversary of the dead queen than the accession day of the living king, at least so it seems if the amount paid to the ringers is taken as an indication of their enthusiasm or the duration of their efforts.

In November 1626 the churchwarden of St Bartholomew Exchange, London, paid two shillings to the ringers 'on Queen Elizabeth's crownation day', which was more than they customarily spent ringing in the regnal year. If this attention to Queen Elizabeth was a slight to the Caroline regime it was quickly corrected. Parish officials learned that Queen Henrietta Maria had her birthday on 16 November, and the king himself had been born on 19 November. Two more days entered the ringers' calendar. The bells continued to announce Queen Elizabeth's anniversary, but the money was now distributed through several ringing sessions and its effect was masked or diluted. The London newswriter Joseph Mead explained how the loyal demonstration was prompted in 1630. 'On Friday, November 19, being his majesty's birthday, my lord mayor, as he sat at dinner, received a check from the lords of the council because he suffered the bells to stand so silent, and a commandment to set them all on work, both in city and suburbs; which was accordingly done, and above a thousand bonfires kindled that night; although his lordship said, when he heard it, that he never knew that ceremony to have been done before. The message may seem to have been occasioned by that universal ringing and flaming of bonfires for Queen Elizabeth's coronation two nights before.'[21]

Most parishes in the London area responded to this kind of orchestration, as did provincial communities connected to the matrix of command. The bells of St Mary Aldermanbury rang on the royal anniversaries in 1630 and 1631, 'according to a precept from the Lords of the Council Table and my Lord Mayor'. St Botolph Billingsgate devoted two shillings to ringing for the Gunpowder Treason and the same for Elizabeth's accession anniversary in 1631, but only 1s. 6d. to Charles's crownation. In the following years, however, the bells spoke loudly for the king. They rang on his birthday as well as his accession day, celebrated his recovery from illness, and announced both the birth and the baptism of the Duke of York.

The entry in the churchwardens' accounts of St Bartholomew Exchange in 1631 is typical: 'For ringing the 16 November being the queen's birthday, 2s. and the 17th being Queen Elizabeth's crownation, 2s. And the 27 March being our king's crownation, 3s.' At St Katherine Coleman Street, where the crownation ringing on 27 March usually cost two shillings, only ninepence was spent 'for ringing the king and queen's birthday' in 1632. In 1635 the parish spent a total of 6s. 6d. to ring the bells on 5, 17 and 19 November. The churchwardens of St Stephen Coleman Street were more evenhanded. In 1636 they allowed 3s. 6d. to each of five anniversary occasions: the king's accession day in March, and Gunpowder Treason day, the queen's birthday, Queen Elizabeth's crownation day, and Charles's birthday in November.

St Botolph without Bishopsgate marked crownation day with a bonfire as well as bells, although this parish, like many others, spent less celebrating the king's day than 5 November. In 1628 the churchwardens laid out 2s. 6d. for 'two dozen of faggots on the king's day' and another five shillings for the ringers. The bells of St Christopher's rang on 16, 17 and 19 November in the 1630s, as well as on 27 March and 5 November. In suburban Middlesex the bells of St Martin in the Fields rang on every royal and commemorative occasion, in 1630 giving equal weight to the king's birthday and coronation day, and to the 5 and 17 November. Within a few years the birthdays of Queen Henrietta Maria and the infant princes and princess were added to the parochial calendar. The politically important parish of St Margaret, Westiminster, also gave full honour to the days that were special to King Charles and his family, and of course to Gunpowder Treason day, but sponsored no ringing in memory of Queen Elizabeth.

Country parishes also marked Charles' crownation day, and sometimes his birthday too, but with varying degrees of expenditure and enthusiasm. Minchinhampton, Gloucestershire, rang dutifully 'on the king's holiday'. So too did Morebath, Devon, on 'the king's ringing day'. Hartland, Devon, however, appears to have made no provision for ringing the regnal year, although the churchwardens paid their ringers generously each 5 November. At Holy Trinity, Dorchester, renowned as a puritan parish, there were three standard ringing days in the early 1630s: 27 March, 5 and 17 November. Usually the ringers earned a shilling between them on each occasion, but in 1634 the balance shifted. In that year the churchwardens paid 1s. 6d. for ringing on the regnal anniversary, 2s. on 5 November, and 2s. 6d. on Queen Elizabeth's day. The rising intensity of the ringing was perhaps intended to remind listeners of the vulnerability of the Protestant cause. The Holy Trinity account books show no further payments to the ringers on 27 March for the rest of the decade, although they never missed 5 and 17 November. In 1641, however, they paid just 6d. 'for ringing the crownation day'. It would be risky to interpret these entries as indications of loyalty or opposition, but they suggest that the Protestant holy days often mattered more than dynastic anniversaries, and that this valuation could be expressed through the bells.

St Edmund's, Salisbury, was another parish with strong puritan associations, but there is little sign of this in the pattern of celebration. It was here in 1630 that the puritan vestryman Henry Sherfield

61

precipitated a collision with Laud by destroying a stained glass window that he took to be superstitious. The case reached Star Chamber in 1633. Perhaps to compensate for this, and to deflect criticism, the parish was ostentatiously loyal and proper in its ringing. Throughout the 1630s the churchwardens of St Edmund's expended 8s. each time for ringing on crownation and Gunpowder Treason day, and another three to five shillings on the king's birthday. Yet St Edmund's was outrung by the neighbouring parish of St Thomas, Salisbury, where expenditures on coronation day ringing rose from 10s. 6d. in 1632 to 18s. in 1639, with a further six shillings'-worth on King Charles's birthday. Neither parish marked Queen Elizabeth's anniversary with official ringing.

Cambridge offered conventional congratulations to the king on the anniversary of his accession, while continuing to commemorate 5 and 17 November. Great St Mary's rang its bells and sponsored bonfires, as befit the university church. Holy Trinity offered bonfires and bells on the coronation day and Gunpowder Treason, bells alone on Queen Elizabeth's day. The churchwardens of St Botolph, Cambridge, spent fourpence on a book of prayers for 27 March and another shilling on a bonfire in 1632.

Crownation day could prompt reflection as well as loyal celebration. On 27 March 1638 the puritan Robert Woodford noted in his diary, 'this day King Charles hath reigned thirteen years complete. Oh Lord, grant him long to reign for thee and the good of thy church and people'.[22] Woodford's words bear comparison to John Cosin's a decade earlier; the puritan layman thought of protection of the church, the ceremonial clergyman of subjection to the monarch. It was against this background that Convocation in 1640 subscribed a new canon 'for the better keeping of the day of his majesty's most happy inauguration'; to which an anonymous puritan responded, 'can this be to the honour of our king when the annual memory of his inauguration is fain to be forced? What canon or constitution is for the continuation of the joyful memory of Queen Elizabeth . . . which yet to this day ceaseth not?'[23]

Most London parishes continued to observe King Charles's anniversaries through the crisis of the early 1640s. The bells of St Mary Aldermanbury rang on 27 March 1642 for 'the memorial of the king's majesty' although his majesty had already left London. At St Bartholomew Exchange they rang the bells on the king's birthday in 1643, a generous gesture from a city at war. St Margaret, Westminster, the parish church of parliament, meticulously observed the king's anniversaries, although after 1642 they no longer rang on the birthday of Queen Henrietta Maria. St Botolph without

Bishopsgate rang on Charles's birthday as late as 1644, although there is no entry for ringing on the anniversary of his accession. Similar entries abound in churchwardens' records from around the country, from royalist and parliamentarian areas alike. Great Yarmouth, Norfolk, and St Peter Mancroft, Norwich, rang on the king's day in 1643 despite being at war with him. Salisbury's bells rang for crownation day and the king's birthday in 1644, but this was not surprising since the king was in the vicinity. The bells of St Thomas, Sarum, rang 'half a day on the king's birthday' in 1647, and were only silenced with his execution.

In 1647, breaking several years of silence, the churchwardens of St Bartholomew's, London, 'paid the ringers the 5th of November, Queen Elizabeth and King Charles's coronation days, 6s.'. Several other parishes chose to ring on 17 November that year in honour of Queen Elizabeth, though they had not been in the habit of marking the anniversary in recent memory. Holy Trinity, Cambridge, sponsored a parish bonfire on 27 March 1647 'upon the king's coronation', although they had paid little attention to that day since the 1630s. The bonfire, like the bells, was a signal and not merely a matter of customary routine. Auditors could put their own interpretation on the ringing, and might hear it as a healing and conservative message in a time of great confusion. Some might hear it as a provocation. The moment was fraught with danger and uncertainty. Traditional government has been purged or suspended; Presbyterians were at odds with sectaries and Independents; the army was in London, but was riven by disagreements; Levellers were pressing their radical *Agreement of the People*. On 11 November the king escaped from custody at Hampton Court, only to come to roost a few days later on the Isle of Wight. On 15 November Oliver Cromwell quelled the abortive mutiny at Corkbush Field. Add to this a poor harvest and rising prices, and it is not surprising to find a surge of royalist nostalgia expressed by the bonfires and bells.

The following year the churchwardens of St Botolph without Bishopsgate drew special attention to the royal anniversary on 27 March. They rang the bells and recorded the payment 'for ringing on King Charles (never to be forgotten) coronation day'. They wrote the words KING CHARLES and CORONATION DAY in an especially bold and firm hand, making them stand out on the page. The phrase 'never to be forgotten' has a defiant ring, as well as an echo of the trumpeting for 5 November which was also 'never to be forgot'. By this time the king had been a prisoner at Carisbrooke Castle for a third of a year, but royalist sentiment was spreading across the country and

63

leading to a second civil war. Great Yarmouth and Norwich spent lavishly on ringing for the king in March 1648, but there, like everywhere else, the bells were silent in 1649. The last royal ringing at St Margaret Westminster was on Charles's birthday in 1648, and on 29 May, the birthday of his heir.

★

During the 1650s most parish bells were muted, except for dutiful ringing on 5 November, but after the Restoration they burst into joyous voice. Under Charles II there was a further adaption and extension of the dynastic calendar, and parishes equipped themselves with special service books for 30 January and 29 May. Strictly, the regnal year began on 30 January, the date of the execution of the previous monarch, but the observance in honour of Charles, king and martyr, was a solemn fast, not a feast, and was marked by sermons rather than by celebratory ringing. The dynastic festivities were reserved for the spring, with Charles II cast as 'the May king'.

Bonfires and bells announced the news of the Restoration. St Bartholemew Exchange, London, was one of thousands of parishes whose bells rang on 8 May 1660, 'the king being then proclaimed', and then each year on 29 May, the date of Charles II's birthday and his formal accession. This day, 29 May, became known as Royal Oak day (in some places called Oak Apple day), in memory of Charles's escape by hiding in an oak tree after the battle of Worcester. Besides its personal significance for Charles II, the day took on extra meaning as a commemoration of the Stuart Restoration and was so marked for the duration of the dynasty. York parishes rang their bells on 29 May 'in memory of the king's majesty's instauration', and thirty years later in the reign of William and Mary they continued to ring for 'King Charles II's nativity and restoration'. Annual observances included the reading of special prayers, firing of bonfires, ringing of bells, and the wearing of sprigs of oak. At Canterbury two barrels of beer were rolled out for the muster companies on the king's birthday in 1661. At St Botolph Bishopsgate, Royal Oak day that year was the occasion for a slap-up parish feast (costing £12. 3s.) as well as a day for ringing.

Much of the rejoicing at this time seems designed to invoke the memory of 'merry England'. Maypoles reappeared and country festivities enjoyed the patronage of the magistrates. Parish bells rang on 23 April, the day of Charles II's coronation and also St George's day, combining respect for the monarch with affection and pride in England's patron saint. St Andrew by the Wardrobe was among the parishes that rang on Queen Catherine's day and 'on the king and queen's birthdays'. Several parishes revived their ringing on Queen Elizabeth's day, and everyone recognized 5 November. In the years after the Restoration, the City of London bells resounded on all these occasions until they were silenced by destruction in the great fire.

Country parishes were spared the conflagration and continued to sing the dynastic anniversaries from their belltowers. At Isleworth, Middlesex, they rang each 29 May, 'It being the king's day' or 'upon the day of the king's birth and return'. Salisbury parishes likewise rang loyally on crownation day. Hartland, Devon, where they seem to have ignored Charles I's accession anniversary, began ringing its bells for the birthday of Charles II. In county Durham the villagers of Darlington set fire to a tar barrel and burned coals to the accompaniment of bells on 29 May and 5 November.

A comprehensive study of parish accounts might show the strands of enthusiasm for the Stuarts and renewed anxiety about the fate of English Protestantism in the 1670s and 1680s. At Cambridge, for example, they read the special prayers for 29 May and rang bells and lit bonfires on Royal Oak day throughout the reign of Charles II. Stimulated by the king's recent visit to the town in 1672, the churchwardens of Great St Mary's paid 4s. 6d. for faggots and sheaves for a bonfire and 2s. 6d. to ring the bells on 29 May. Their neighbours at Holy Trinity showed a waning commitment, allowing only 6d. to the ringers on 29 May 1675 compared to the 3s. 6d. they spent that year on Gunpowder Treason day. What is one to make of the discrepancy, a meagre campanological gesture for the king and a flaming tintinnabulation for Protestantism? In subsequent years the payment to the ringers on Royal Oak day rose to one shilling, and sometimes two shillings, but it never matched the expenditure on 5 November.

Diaries sometimes supplement the laconic fiscal notations of the churchwardens' records to illustrate the observance of crownation day under the later Stuarts. The north-country preacher Oliver Heywood noted in his diary for 29 May 1667, 'the anniversary day of thanksgiving for the king's return, it was a sweet day'. For Alderman Newton of Cambridge 'the day of the king's birth' in 1669 was a day of scarlet robing, civic procession, and prayers at Great St Mary's, topped off by 'a very good dinner' with claret and tobacco. Sir John Reresby and the leading officers and gentlemen of York celebrated King Charles' birthday in 1683 with drinks, dinner and music; the soldiers fired 'the great guns from the tower,' and 'at night the common people had wine and ale at a bonfire which was made before the manor gate'.[24] The occasion provided entertainment for every sector of the community.

5

BONFIRES AND BELLS – THE VOCABULARY OF CELEBRATION

Special days called for special action. The major holidays, anniversaries, and successes of Tudor and Stuart England were marked by festive activities in the streets and villages as well as by events at court and notations in the calendar. People of the sixteenth and seventeenth centuries could draw on a versatile vocabulary of celebration to express or communicate their enthusiasm, or at least to present the face of public joy. By ringing bells, shooting guns, sounding instruments, or raising cheers, they could make a joyful noise unto the Lord. By firing bonfires, lighting candles, or exploding fireworks, they could bring illumination to the gloomiest night. Celebration took a multitude of forms, including religious services, public processions, pageants, banquets, plays, dances, and other social performances. Customary festive behaviour involved commensality, liberality, conviviality, and lavish dispensations of alcohol.

Most of the elements of this vocabulary belonged to the whole of Europe. England was by no means the only home of bonfires and bells. Yet distinctively in England they were harnessed to the needs of the state, to be deployed on its significant moments and anniversaries. Sir Richard Moryson, an advisor to Henry VIII, had tried to persuade the king to adopt 'an annual triumph, with bonfires, feasts and prayers, to act as a perpetual memorial to the good fortune of the English people in their deliverance from the bondage of the Papacy'.[1] This proposal was ignored in the 1540s, but within half a century its principles had become common practice.

Often the various elements combined to create a symphony of symbolic action. Queen Elizabeth's accession day, according to the preacher Isaac Colfe, occasioned 'the cheerfulness of our countenances, the decency of our garments, the songs of our lips, the clapping of our hands, our melody on instruments of music, the making of bonfires, the ringing of bells, the sounding of trumpets, the display of banners, the shooting of guns' and other 'testimonies of rejoicing' on this 'special day ordained of the Lord . . . for the happiness of England'. 'The annual celebrities,' according to Thomas

Holland of Oxford, were notable for their 'triumphs undertaken and performed at court that day, bonfires, ringing of bells, discharging of ordnance at the Tower . . . and other signs of joy then usually and willingly exhibited by the people of our land.'[2] Proper performance involved noise, fire, dress, aspect, mood, individual behaviour and community action, an Elizabethan vocabulary that was adapted to the national Protestant celebrations of the seventeenth century.

If this was a vocabulary, what did it have to say? Thomas Holland, writing at the end of the Elizabethan era, insisted that it all expressed happiness and enthusiasm. But who was saying what to whom? The vocabulary of celebration was certainly expressive but, like other forms of communication, it was susceptible to prompts and crossed meanings. Public celebration entwined the drives of *communitas* and the needs of power. Ordinary people lit bonfires or made merriment for their own purposes, yet traditional practices were hedged with sanctions, approvals and disapprobation. Tradition and custom may have shaped some practices, but others were orchestrated through the matrix of command. If commemorative festivity marked the development of a national political culture, common to the whole of England, its particular expression was often shaped by local issues, customs and tensions. We need to be alert to the subtle cues and overt instructions that brought the various element of the vocabulary into play.

Bonfires and bells were announcements, and who controlled them was often as important as the message they proclaimed. The timing, duration, volume, intensity, and panache of the bellringing often varied with the occasion. It would be useful to discover who paid the ringers, how much, and why. Was there a battle of the belfry on any of these anniversary occasions? There are hints of such incidents in 1582 when the mayor of Bedford complained of 'the intolerable trouble to others' caused by the vicar's bellringing, and again in the 1630s when churchwardens and bellringers fell to dispute over Sunday ringing.[3] Similarly, the number, disposition, combustion, luminosity, danger and excitement of bonfires varied, and bonfires sometimes sparked contention. Who authorized their construction, who tended them, where did the fuel come from, and what did people understand by them? Communities were not necessarily united in these festivities, notwithstanding the unifying and integrative function that is some-times seen in them.[4]

★

Noise was a crucial element in celebrations. Anthropologists report that noisemaking is a standard part of festive rituals throughout the world, and early modern England was no exception. Besides the sound of bells, the air was filled with the sounds of musical instruments, cheers, percussion, fusillades, cannon shot, and the explosions of squibs and crackers. Explosive noise was not always officially sanctioned or controlled. On Twelfth night, 1623, 'the gentlemen of Gray's Inn' borrowed some small cannon from the Tower and fired it 'in the dead time of the night', causing panic and cries of 'treason!'[5]

The annual celebration of Queen Elizabeth's accession called for cheerful symphony:

> Ring out loud sounding bells; on organs play;
> To music's mirth let all estates incline;
> Sound drums and trumpets, renting air and ground.
> Stringed instruments strike with melodious sound.'[6]

Justifying the bells, an Elizabethan minister explained, 'it is natural to the mind of man to be ravished with great joy by the notes and harmony of music, which thing bells well rung commonly effect in men's hearts, first being well tuned by a skilful artisan and experimental practitioner'. National celebrations called for ordered noise as a counterpoint to the ideal of social harmony. Making the wrong noise, or failing to sound the bells as expected, could signify a social or political offence. One thinks of Shakespeare: 'Take but degree away, untune that string, and hark what discord follows!' Ben Jonson called bellringing 'the poetry of steeples'.[7]

Parish bells were ideal instruments for celebration and for demonstrating approbation and respect. None could escape their clamour. Often the bells could be heard at a distance of a mile or more, ringing above the routine noises of urban or village life. They signalled that something special was happening, a service, a festival, an anniversary, or a visit by one of the great. In the middle of the sixteenth century the preacher Hugh Latimer remarked that 'if all the bells in England should be rung together at a certain hour, I think there would be almost no place but some bells might be heard there'.[8] By the end of the century on each crownation day this could be put to the test.

Bells were rung regularly to summon worshippers to service. Traditionally they rang at weddings and funerals (joyous peals at the one, mournful knells at the other), marking individual rites of passage. They sang out too at midsummer and new year, and on the major Christian holy days. At the parish of St John, Ousebridge, York, for example, the ringers rang through the night on Christmas Eve 1606 'until the middle bell-string broke next morning'. When the seventeenth century created a new calendar of secular, dynastic and patriotic anniversaries which overlaid the traditional cycle of the Christian year, the bells marked it accordingly. As informational and celebratory equipment the bells became harnessed to the propaganda requirements of the ruling regime.

Most of the ten thousand or so parish churches had bells which were rung on festive and ceremonial occasions. Some were simple arrangements with one or two bells, others were finely tuned peals of six or eight designed to make a joyful noise. Most bells were sources of local pride which made inroads into parish funds. They earned money too for ringing at funerals (though ringing at weddings was not normally recorded in the parish books). Churchwardens' records are dotted with expenditures on beer and cheese for the bellringers, and payments for hanging, oiling, framing, setting, and repairing the bells. They reveal the centrality of the bells in the calendrical experience of town and village, and indicate those special occasions when the communities were summoned to festive attention.

Celebration and commemoration in the seventeenth century gave bellringers frequent opportunities to practise, and out of this developed the distinctively English art of change ringing. Instead of mere rhythmic clanging the ringers developed patterns and disciplined combinations. Here was more ordered noise, a suitable accompaniment to the beauty of holiness. Modern change ringing became possible when bells were equipped with full wheels, and this transition can sometimes be followed in churchwardens' accounts. In most parishes the ringers formed a tight-knit group, well rewarded for their skills. In some places they were joined by gentle-born exponents, who took to ringing for sport. By 1637 a group of enthusiasts banded together in London to found the Society of College Youths 'for the purpose of practising and promoting the art of ringing'. Significantly, their first meeting was on 5 November, a day when bells throughout England were pressed into service to recall the providential deliverance from the Gunpowder Plot.[9]

Besides signalling events to the listening community the bells were thought to have protective qualities. Medieval bells were holy, and were baptized or sacralized before being hung. They were believed to have a mystic potency, an ability to cleanse the air and to drive away devils. In early modern England it was still a popular belief that the spirit world could be intimidated through noise. The passing bell was said to deter demons hovering about a person who was dying. Bells were likewise employed during thunder storms to drive away the evil spirits that were thought to be clashing in the air. Although scorned by Protestant reformers, such notions lingered beyond the seventeenth century and may not have been dissociated from the Elizabethan and Stuart ringing.

The bells could speak, according to the Latin verse inscribed on one of them:

> *Laudo Deum verum, plebum voco, congrego clerum,*
> *Funera plango, fulgura frango, sabbata pango,*
> *Defunctos ploro, pestum fugo, festa decoro.*

(I praise the true God, call the people, assemble the clergy, toll for funerals, subdue the thunder flash, signal the Sabbath, mourn the dead, drive away plague, and beautify festivals.)[10]

Advanced Protestants might criticize the bells as Romish remnants, but they were too deeply integrated into parish life to be readily jettisoned.

Puritans, indeed, developed an ambivalent attitude to church bells. The pagan and papist associations of bells made them impure, yet bells could usefully be harnessed to activities that puritans held dear. Rung in triumph for the security of Protestantism, the bells were traditional instruments turned to the service of the Lord. In London in the 1630s, 'the tolling of the bells at five in the morning for a whole hour to summon puritans to the lectures at six was a familiar sound in Budge Row, and a source of great vexation to their antipuritan neighbours'. The annual ringing of 5 November was a source of satisfaction to most puritans, even those who scrupled to make distinction of days, and the practice continued throughout the period of civil wars and interregnum. In the revolutionary enthusiasm of 1647 it was proposed 'that the bells in all the churches of the kingdom may be taken down and melted for the service of the state', but most of the bells remained intact.[11] This repeated a similar proposal from the time of the Edwardian reformation, which also came to naught.

In more tranquil times the sound of bells greeted monarchs on processions and progresses. Booming and clanging from the sacred towers dramatized the presence of royalty on the move. Parishes near palaces and places on the routes frequently taken by royal travellers were particularly accustomed to this use of their bells. Queen Elizabeth, in particular, seems to have had music and bells wherever she went. We read in the accounts of London churchwardens that parish bells sounded 'when the queen came to the Tower', 'when the queen came to my Lord Treasurer's', 'when the queen's majesty came to my Lord Chancellor's', and whenever 'the queen's majesty came by'.

Bells rang for Elizabeth's predecessors, but they seem to have had a special fondness for the virgin queen. The story spread that during Mary Tudor's reign popular affection for the then captive Princess

Elizabeth was expressed through the bells. 'Time was, when passing a prisoner from Windsor to Woodstock, the poor people, joyful of her presence, rang the bells in a village or two; whereat her keeper raged and railed upon them as rebels, clapped the ringers in the stocks, and so silenced the bells. But now,' continued an Elizabethan preacher, 'I hope there is not a bell in England that rings not, a tongue in England that prays not, an heart in England that joyeth not in and for the life of their sovereign.'[12]

Harbingers and officials primed the localities and orchestrated the loyal response. City churches received instructions when the monarch was on the move. In June 1563 Queen Elizabeth went by water from Whitehall to Greenwich, serenaded by bells from the riverside parishes. Those who failed to ring found themselves pressed for a fine of 6s. 8d.[13] Similarly remiss in their duty, the churchwardens of Great St Mary's, Cambridge, paid a fine of 2s. 2d. 'to the queen's almoner's servant for not ringing at the queen's coming' in 1566. If they failed to ring they risked having their church doors nailed shut until they paid the fine. Most parishes learned their duty and were quick to lay on effusive tintinnabulation.

Similar greetings honoured the Stuarts. The bells of St Stephen Coleman Street, London, sounded in 1603 'when the king came to the Charterhouse, by a commandment from my Lord Mayor'. At Bere Regis, Dorset, in 1615 the churchwardens laid out 2s. 4d. 'in beer for the ringers when the king came through our town'. Strood, Kent, put on an impressive display of ringing, costing eight shillings, when Charles I came by in June 1631, and paid the ringers two shillings in 1634 on another royal journey. The churchwardens of St Botolph without Bishopgate, London, laid out the substantial sum of 11s. 8d. 'to the ringers when the king and queen were at the countess's' in 1636. The bells of St Mary Aldermanbury joined the chorus in 1641 'at the king and queen's coming through the city'. Even in defeat the king was honoured with bells, though more muted than before. The accounts of Holy Trinity, Cambridge, for 1648 show a lowly sixpence paid 'for ringing the bells when the king was at Childerley', nearby. And as we have seen, there was widespread ringing of bells for Charles I on 27 March 1648, the last crownation day of his life.

The tradition of ringing in the royal presence continued after the Restoration, with bells sounding 'for joy of the king's coming to town'. But London parishes could not keep this up after so many of their churches were destroyed in the great fire of 1666. London must have been strangely silent in those years before the towers were rebuilt and the bells rehung. Charles II was greeted with bells at Dorchester in 1666 and again in 1672 'when the king came through the town'.

Cambridge laid on a spectacle of sound and light with bells and bonfires when Charles visited in 1671. Holy Trinity put 9s. 4d. towards its bonfire and bellringing 'when his majesty was in town'. Not to be outdone, Great St Mary's paid 6s. 8d. that day for bellringing alone, and 11s. 6d. for its welcoming bonfire. The Thames-side parish of Isleworth, Middlesex, paid for the bells to be rung whenever the king's barge went by, and on various occasions when Charles II landed and took water at the church. Later Stuart monarchs, like their Tudor predecessors, expected their movements to be accompanied by the sound of bells.

Nor was this gesture reserved only for kings and queens. Kinsmen of the king and prospective heirs to the throne were always treated with honour. So too were notables, princes, generals, and bishops, who expected the respect that a community could display through sound. The bells of Minchinhampton, Gloucestershire, rang in 1596 'when the Lord Chandos came to the town'. Bells accompanied the thirteen-year-old Prince Charles's visit to Cambridge in 1613. When the king's nephew the Count Palatine arrived in England in 1635 the parish of Strood, Kent, greeted him with bells as he passed by. Salisbury, in royalist hands for most of the civil war, saluted the king and his commanders, but managed to slight Lord Goring 'for not ringing the bells, which he demanded of his fee 10s.' After parliament's triumph the churchwardens very sensibly honoured their new masters, ringing in 1646 'when Sir Thomas Fairfax came through the town with his great guns'. Cambridge bells rang enthusiastically in 1650 'when General Cromwell came to town'. London churches rang in Cromwell's honour in 1653 'when the Lord Protector dined at Grocers' Hall'. The churchwardens of Great St Mary's, Cambridge, laid out seven shillings in 1663 'for ringing one day and next morning when the Duke of Monmouth was here'. Bells rang out 'by precept' when the Duke of York entered London in 1665. Bells greeted William of Orange in 1688 on his way from Torbay to London, and they greeted him when he travelled in his new dignity as king in 1689.

Parish bells welcomed dignitaries of the church. The bells of Strood, Kent, rang regularly when bishops came by on the road to Rochester, Canterbury, or London. Other churchwardens' books commonly report the ringing of bells at visitations or 'as the bishop passed by'. Worcester greeted its bishop with bells in 1594. The parish of Sherborne, Dorset, rang its bells on all the appropriate occasions, including, in 1622, 'at the Dean's coming', and in 1628 'when the judges came to the assizes'.

Laudian bishops insisted on their due reverence and respect, which conventionally found expression through ringing. The London parish of St Christopher was fined 6s. 8d. in 1631 'for not ringing the bells when the lord bishop rode his visitation'. Dorchester rang at various times in the 1630s 'at the coming in of the vicar-general', 'when my lord archbishop came', and 'at the coming of the lord bishop'. Northampton rang 'when the bishop came through the town' and when Laud's commissioners visited in 1637 to inspect the town's restored altars. Bells at Holy Trinity, Cambridge, rang 'morning and evening at the bishop's coming' in 1640, costing the parish one shilling. At Ipswich a very different interpretation was placed on the ringing when church bells summoned a hostile crowd to protest the visit of bishop Matthew Wren.[14] The bells could be eloquent but double-tongued.

In addition to routine ceremonial ringing the bells signalled significant political and religious developments. Alarm bells alerted the population and brought people from the neighbourhood into the streets. Extraordinary pealing informed the community of critical occasions, and involved local inhabitants in national and international affairs. The bonfires that often accompanied the ringing carried the announcement into the night. Church bells had rung in 1381 to call the peasants to rebellion, and it was rumoured that they would be used for a similar purpose in Essex in 1566. Church bells rang in 1569 to raise the north to rebellion, and later warned the rebel Earl of Northumberland to escape. In 1628 Sir William Wittipoll and his company in arms 'marched to Ipswich and there caused all the bells (where they could prevail) to be rung' in the course of a local affray. At Chidlington, Hertfordshire, they rang to summon villagers to a football match. At Norwich they rang for elections. At Coventry in 1642 the ringing of bells added drama to Lord Brooke's seizure of the county magazine for parliament.[15]

★

Parish bells signalled significant developments in political, constitutional and dynastic history. They rang when monarchs were proclaimed and crowned, and again each year on the anniversary of their accession. They rang to celebrate dynastic continuity and the certainty of the succession. Much of England's royal history unfolded to the accompaniment of ringing. The bells of St Michael Cornhill proclaimed Queen Mary in 1553, and rang again in 1555 'when word was brought that the queen was brought to bed' in childbirth. Bells all over London rang prematurely in anticipation that Mary would give England a prince. Bells greeted the accession of Elizabeth, and the greeting was repeated for James. There were bells in 1605 congratulating James I and his queen on the birth of the short-lived princess Mary. London bells rang for the betrothal of the popular princess Elizabeth, and again in 1614 'at the time the Lady Elizabeth was delivered' of a son. Dutiful bellringing greeted the marriage of Charles I and the births of his children. The bells found their tongues in 1630 to celebrate the birth of Prince Charles, an important event that secured the Stuart dynasty. Lord John Poulett wrote to the court from Hinton St George, Somerset, to boast that he was the first in his country to hear the good news, which he quickly communicated to his neigh-bours 'by bells, bonfires, and public thanksgiving'.[16] The bells of St Andrew by the Wardrobe rang out in 1630 'when the prince was born and baptized' and again in 1631 'at the birth of the Lady Mary', in 1633 'at the birth of the Duke of York,' and in 1635 'when the queen was delivered' of the Princess Elizabeth. The ringers were paid two shillings or more at the birth of princes, half that sum for princesses, in a gendered valuation of potential heirs to the throne. Bells in country churches joined the chorus. Dorchester, for example, rang in 1630 'at the news of the birth of the prince'. Norwich too showed its loyalty by celebrating these royal events. London bells rang out again in 1637 in joy 'for the queen's safe deliverance', although this particular infant did not live long. The bells of St Botolph, Cambridge, rang in 1639 'upon the young duke's birthday'.

Royal marriages and births had religious as well as dynastic implications. A Catholic queen, still worse a Catholic succession, threatened the achievements of English Protestantism. The bells provided commentary on these issues, especially amidst the fraught religious politics of the later seventeenth century. In 1677, by order of the town clerk, Cambridge bells were set ringing 'morning and evening at the marriage of the Prince of Orange' and the Princess Mary. Cambridge parishes also sponsored bonfires 'upon the same occasion', expressing hopes for the possibility of a Protestant succes-sion. Significantly, this day was also Prince William's birthday, 4 November, and the eve of the Gunpowder Treason commemoration. Cambridge bells rang again in the crisis of 1688 'on the day of rejoicing for the birth of the young prince' James Stuart, who would presumably be brought up a Catholic, and again in 1689 on the birth of Princess Anne's son, the Duke of Gloucester, who represented the hopes of English Protestantism. The Vicar of Bray was no doubt a ringer.

A compendious chronology of early modern history, of the sort commonly found in Stuart almanacs, can be constructed from the churchwardens' record of celebration. The principal occasions are listed at the end of this chapter. In the mid-sixteenth century the London parish of St Michael Cornhill celebrated the failure of Wyatt's rebellion against Queen Mary by distributing bread and ale to the bellringers. The same bells announced 'the overthrow given to the Turk' at the battle of Lepanto in 1571. Bonfires and bells celebrated the safety of Queen Elizabeth and her religion when a Catholic conspiracy came undone in 1586. The bells of St Christopher's, London, rang out 'when Babington with the other traitors were apprehended and were taken, and also when the queen of Scots was proclaimed conspirator to the queen and our realm,' and they rang again 'on the day of the execution of the Scots queen'. The same occasions stirred the bells across the river at Lambeth, where there was celebratory ringing in 1586 'when the traitors were taken' and 'when the queen of Scots was put to death'. At Norwich, too, the church bells rang in 1586 on 'the day of the deliverance of the queen's majesty from her enemies'.

The bells served to warn of emergencies and to celebrate victories. It was planned to ring the bells in 1588 if the Spanish landed, and, as we shall see later, they were rung on the day of 'triumphing' in 1588 after England's deliverance from the threat of the Armada. At Norwich in 1588 the bells rang out 'on the victory day that the lord gave us over the Spaniards, appointed by the mayor'. In 1596 London parishes lit bonfires and rang bells 'for the good success of our navy at Cadiz'.

All commemorative and triumphant ringing in the Jacobean period was surpassed in October 1623, when parishes throughout England rang to celebrate the return of Prince Charles from Spain. This outpouring of joy that the prince had not married a Spanish Catholic will be discussed later in detail. In 1625 there were bells announcing the new king's marriage to Henrietta Maria, though not as jubilant as the Council would have liked. A few years later Charles's acceptance of the Petition of Right produced a livelier round of celebration. The churchwardens of St Stephen Coleman Street laid out five shillings 'to the ringers the day that the Petition of Right was granted by the king to the parliament,' which was considerably more than they usually spent on royal and religious anniversaries. The parish of St Pancras Soper Lane, which did not have an active tradition of bellringing, made an extraordinary payment 'to the ringers at the time of the agreement of the king and the parliament, 9 July 1628'. The entry in the parish book, as much as the sounds from the bell-tower, signified that this was an especially noteworthy development.

The 1630s offered repeated occasions for rejoicing, despite the discontents of that decade. London rang heartily 'when the peace between Spain and us was proclaimed,' although some parishes were clearly responding to directions from the Council. A year later news of the great Protestant victory of Gustavus Adolphus at Breitenfeld echoed in English parishes. The churchwardens' accounts of Holy Trinity, Dorchester, include payments on 13 October 1631 'to the ringers on that day for the king of Sweashland's [Sweden's] victory'. In this case the prompting most likely came from the puritan vestry. In 1632 the parish of St Botolph Billingsgate offered prayers when King Charles was ill, and responded with bells when he got better. The parish of St Botolph without Bishopsgate went further, spending 2s. 6d. on bellringing and 3s. 9d. on a bonfire 'when we gave thanks for his majesty's recovery'. Parishes in London and Norwich were among those ringing in 1633 'at the king's return from Scotland'.

An echo of the tintinnabulation of 1623, much diminished, greeted King Charles in August 1639 when he again returned to London from Scotland. The parish of St Christopher paid 2s. 6d. 'for ringing by order upon his majesty's return out of the north'. The churchwardens of St. Bartholomew Exchange gave three shillings to the ringers 'when the king came out of Scotland' in 1639 and a generous eight shillings 'when King Charles came from Scotland' yet again in November 1641. Councillors and city officials orchestrated the local response. The bells gave voice to a mixture of duty, respect, anxiety and enthusiasm as the king grappled with the national emergency.

The exceptional constitutional developments of 1641 were greeted with loud bells in London and the provinces, although not every parish joined in. Sherborne and Dorchester, Dorset, rang their bells early in the year 'at the late news concerning the good proceedings of the high court of Parliament'. Norwich bells rang on 18 February to mark 'the public triumph' at Westminster. The churchwardens of St Bartholomew Exchange, London, paid 2s. 6d. to the ringers 'for joy of the triennial parliament'. St Andrew by the Wardrobe rang 'for the parliament' on 15 February and 8 September 1641, announcing the Triennial Act and a general thanksgiving. At Cambridge and York too the good news was signalled by bells. The activist parish of St Botolph without Bishopsgate celebrated by ringing in 1642, 'that night the bishops were put down'.

Parliamentary strongholds rang to celebrate their victories in the civil war, and royalist towns no doubt did likewise. King's Lynn, Norfolk, acknowledged the victories at York and Newcastle in 1644 and at Shrewsbury and Naseby in 1645 by ringing the bells. Holy Trinity, Cambridge, rang 'the 19th of June 1645 for joy of Leicester being taken by the parliament', and 'the 22nd of July 1645 being a day of thanksgiving for a victory in the west'. The principal parish bells of Norwich acknowledged the parliamentary victories of the 1640s, culminating on 31 August 1648 with eight shillings'-worth of ringing 'upon the surrender of Colchester and routing of the Scottish army'. And parishes from Durham to Dorset rang in recognition of parliament's victory at the battle of Worcester in 1651.

Traditional instruments of celebration were not all silenced during the period of the revolution. The bells continued to signal important days. At Great Yarmouth, for example, the bells rang 'by Mr Bailiff's order' on days of thanksgiving, and on 'the day the Lord Protector was proclaimed'. Several parishes rang on the anniversary of the Protectorate as a substitute for ringing on crownation day. The churchwardens of St Peter Mancroft, Norwich, paid 8s. 6d. to ring for the Protectorate of Oliver Cromwell, but only 2s. 6d. in 1658 when his son Richard was proclaimed, an appropriately reduced valuation. Closer to Westminster, St Martin in the Fields provided ten shillings for festive ringing 'that day the Lord Protector was proclaimed', and 3s. 6d. for the proclamation of Tumbledown Dick.

Bells throughout England proclaimed the Stuart Restoration.[17] The steeples rocked as London received Charles II in 1660 with an extravagent pealing of bells. The bellringers of St Matthew Friday Street received 7s. 6d. for their efforts, five times the amount usually expended in that parish for ringing on 5 November. The ringers at Great St Mary's, Cambridge, devoted five days to ringing: 'at the voting in of the king' on 3 May, at his proclamation on 10 May, 'at the thanksgiving of the Lord Monck', 'at the king's coming into England', and on 29 May 'for the king's restoration'.

Bells of triumph continued to ring throughout the later Stuart period as a counterpoint to national and dynastic developments. The bells of many London parishes, like those of St Katherine Coleman Street, resounded in July 1666 'upon the report of the sea victory' against the Dutch. The notation in the churchwardens' book of St Matthew Friday Street, where the bells were rung 'for our victory against the Dutch, by precept,' shows the parishes responding to instructions from the Lord Mayor. The bells of victory resounded in the provinces too, with Sherborne, Dorset, expending five shillings, for the ringers 'on the news of the overthrow of the Dutch'.

Bells played their part in the drama of James II's reign. The southwest was deeply involved, as the heartland of Monmouth's rebellion and the scene of William of Orange's landing, so it is not surprising to find Sherborne ringing 'when Monmouth was routed and taken', 'when the news came that the bishops were released out of the tower', and 'when the Prince of Orange was in town'. Hartland, Devon, rang its bells on the day of the battle of Sedgemoor and again on the execution of Monmouth in 1685. They also rang modestly (paying four shillings) 'at the news of the birth of the prince' in 1688, and with more vigour (paying ten shillings) 'for the deliverance of the bishops'. Communities elsewhere in the country shared the news. Cambridge bells rang in 1685 'for the victory in the west' over

78

Monmouth, announced the change of dynasty in 1689, and then signalled thanks for King William's victories in the 1690s. The news of the Earl of Derby's reinstatement as Lord Lieutenant of Cheshire and Lancashire caused the bells of Preston, Lancashire, to be 'rung most of the day' on 21 October 1688.[18] This was a vigorous tribute to a local patron as well as a comment on national politics.

Parish expenditures at Great St Mary's, Cambridge, provide a good illustration of local response to the developing crisis of 1688–9. On 29 May 1688, Royal Oak day, which had become a routine observance commemorating the Stuart Restoration, the churchwardens expended 7s. 6d. on bonfires and bells. Less than two weeks later on 11 June they paid eight shillings for 'bonfires for [the] Prince of Wales', and 7s. 6d. 'paid then for ringing by Mr Mayor's order'. Prince James had been born the day before, apparently securing the Stuart succession and opening the prospect of a sequence of Roman Catholic kings. Cambridge, along with hundreds of other towns and villages, dutifully rang the bells. This was followed by 'a thanksgiving' on 1 July which cost the parish another thirteen shillings for bonfires and bells. Routine observances continued in the autumn with 8s. 6d. spent on 'ringing and bonfires' for the king's birthday on 14 October, and a modest display on 5 November.

By this time, of course, William of Orange had landed and the government of James II was crumbling. James fled the country on 11 December, to be succeeded on the throne by William and Mary on 13 February 1689. The parish bells immediately rang for the new regime. At Great St Mary's, Cambridge, the churchwardens allocated 8s. 6d. towards bellringing and bonfires 'for the Prince of Orange' on 14 February, and then 13s. 6d. for more on 18 February, the 'proclamation day for the king'. Festive expenditures rose to 18s. 6d. for the parish celebration of the coronation on 11 April. Bonfires and bells on 29 May 1689 cost eight shillings. There was more to celebrate with the birth of the king's nephew and male heir, Prince William, Duke of Gloucester, on 24 July; the bellringers of Great St Mary's earned 12s. for their efforts to mark the event. The bells did their duty again on 7 October when the king came to Cambridge, and this year of Protestant triumph ended when 10s. 6d. was spent on the bonfires and bells on 5 November. In all, the parish spent £2. 9s. 6d. on celebration and commemoration in the last year of James II, and £3. 19s. 6d. in the first year of William III. National and dynastic ringing continued during the 1690s with a greater cost and intensity than in previous reigns. This may have been done in thanks for the turning from Catholicism, to generate loyalty to William and Mary, and perhaps, too, because people enjoyed the sound and the spectacle. The average annual amount spent on bonfires and bells in the parish of Great St Mary's, Cambridge, in the 1690s was £2. 10s. 6d.

Throughout England in the 1690s the bells rang on the traditional dynastic anniversaries of 29 May and 5 November, on the king's coronation day, birthday and accession days (23 April, 4 November and 13 February), with occasional additional ringing to announce and to celebrate William's victories. At Hartland, Devon, for example, the bells sounded in 1690 'at the news of the reducing of Ireland', in 1692 'at the overthrow of the French fleet', and 'at the news of the king's return from Flanders'.

This use of the bells can be further illustrated from the campanological calendar for 1692 at Westminster Abbey. In that year the bells rang out on 14 February to mark the king's accession day, 11 April for the anniversary of his coronation, 30 April for the queen's birthday, 11 May for news of the naval victory off Cape La Hogue, 26 May for confirmation of this glorious event, 29 May for Royal Oak day, 14 July for the Duke of Gloucester's birthday, 19 October for the king's return to England, 20 October for his entry into London, 27 October as a day of special thanksgiving, 4 November for King William's birthday, 5 November on the anniversary of the Gunpowder Plot, and 15 November for the birthday of the Queen Dowager, Catherine of Braganza. Nor was 'Queen Elizabeth of famous memory' forgotten, for the Westminster bells also pealed on 17 November, the anniversary of her accession.[19]

★

Bonfires commonly accompanied bells on major festive occasions, anniversaries, and the receipt of joyful news. Like most of the vehicles of celebration, bonfires conveyed a variety of meanings. Bonfires were dangerous and exciting. They created light in the darkness, warmth in the cold, and a vibrant visual focus for a crowd. Any household or neighbourhood could scrape together the materials for a bonfire, and with planning and community support the fires could be spectacular. Public resources and private donations contributed to their cost. Ordinary firewood and rubbish provided the basic fuel, but large parish bonfires consumed cartloads of faggots and barrels of pitch, sometimes with packets of gunpowder or even sacks of live cats for added effect. Wood was a valuable commodity, sometimes in short supply, but people were willing to burn it for festive and political purposes. Individual households set modest bonfires before their doors, while parishes organized larger fires in public places. A contrast might be drawn between the annual bonfires prepared for anniversary occasions, and the ad hoc fires set at short notice on the receipt of good news.

The accounts of churchwardens and borough chamberlains often record expenditures on combustible materials on important occasions. Newsletters add to the picture. The churchwardens of Lambeth, for example, paid for 'wood to make a bonfire when the traitors were taken' after the collapse of the Babington plot in 1586. The corporation of Carlisle spent three shillings for 'peats and tar barrels to make bonfires' at the proclamation of James I. At Darlington, county Durham, the parish regularly provided 'a tar barrel and a sack of coals' for its 5 November bonfires in the 1630s. Cambridge bonfires were fuelled by faggots and fenland sedge. At Wells Cathedral the Dean and Chapter also paid for bonfires on such 'days of solemnity' as 5 November and the major royal anniversaries. At Durham, where John Cosin became bishop, the cathedral bonfire celebrating victory over the Dutch in 1666 included three pounds of gunpowder as well as 4s. 6d. worth of tar barrels. The boroughs of Northampton spent seven shillings on half a hundred faggots for a bonfire honouring William and Mary in 1689. In London there were bonfires of 'extraordinary great height', the most elaborate reportedly four storeys high.[20] Bonfires were employed less frequently than bells, but they appeared in all parts of England as a dramatic counterpart to the ringing.

Some bonfires were grand affairs enjoying aristocratic or even royal patronage. In earlier days Henry VII had regularly paid ten shilings each summer towards 'the king's bonfire' on midsummer eve. From 1493 to 1508 there were annual payments from the Privy Purse 'to the grooms of the hall for making the king's bonfire in reward'. This tradition of the royal bonfire on St John's eve decayed during Henry VIII's reign, but midsummer bonfires were still lit in some country parishes. The parishioners of Simsbury, Dorset, lit a summer bonfire in 1634, much to the disgust of puritan reformers who blamed it on the king's *Declaration for Sports and Pastimes*.[21]

Suggestions have been made that bonfires were associated with 'expulsion to hell, and surrender to diabolic enemies', and that they descended from ancient druidic fire festivals. Folklorists, in particular, have claimed a pagan ancestry and potent continuity for bonfires, which there is no way of proving. Late medieval bonfires, or bone-fires, were credited with repelling dragons (a quality they shared with bells), and dragons, it is said, 'hated nothing more than the stink of burning bones'. This comes from a tradition of speculative etymology which traces bonfires to 'bone-fires' (a common Tudor spelling), and goes so far as to associate them with human sacrifice. It has been pointed out that bones do not burn very well, and an alternative origin is found in 'bane-fire' or fire of woe.[22]

Much speculative nonsense has been written about the bonfire traditions that developed around the anniversary of the Gunpowder Plot on 5 November. Folklorists, anthropologists and historians have often claimed that Guy Fawkes day is a secular replacement of the ancient Celtic and Nordic fire festivals of Samhain or *nod-fyr* (need-fire). The medieval church absorbed these pagan festivals and transformed them into the Christian holy days of the Eve of All Hallows (Halloween) and All Souls' day. But much of the pre-Christian meaning is said to have lingered in an attenuated form. Besides its nominal religious content the occasion stood out as a harvest festival and a marker of the end of summer, when there might be debris or surplus materials to burn. Bonfires were lit, it is believed, to strengthen the power of the waning sun. With the decay of All Hallows' in England after the Reformation, the argument continues, the people found it convenient to transfer their festivity (and their fires) to the newly appointed Gunpowder Treason day.[23]

The first part of the story is doubtless true. Given the propensity in human culture to adapt existing materials, the claim that an ancient autumn festival lies behind the Christian observances of All Hallows' has strong plausibility. But there is no historical evidence to support the notion that Guy Fawkes' day shares these origins. The choice of 5 November for Gunpowder Treason day comes from the timing of the opening of parliament and the discovery of the Gunpowder Plot, and had nothing to do with the continuing observance of ancient fire festivals. There is barely a flicker of evidence for autumn fire festivals in England at the beginning of the seventeenth century, although eighteenth- and nineteenth-century observers could point to rustic practices involving ritual fires at this time of year. The evidence is unclear as to whether these were survival, revival or invention. It is, of course, possible that the Gunpowder Treason observances triggered a synapse in the English folk memory, and that they may have sounded echoes of a lost or vestigial tradition. But without evidence we cannot support this conclusion. It is more likely that the 5 November bonfires involved the application of an established festive form (the celebratory bonfire) to a new festive occasion sponsored by the state. The burning of effigies (of popes and devils, not Guy Fawkes), was unknown to the first generation of the Stuart era and was rare before the 1670s; it owes nothing to a putative heritage of human sacrifices.

Stripped of their pagan associations, bonfires were understood as expressions of honour and approbation. Their festive meaning is best caught in the German *freudenfeuer* or the French term *feu de joi* (used in the English Channel Islands). Perhaps they were simply 'bon'. For Elizabethan spectators, bonfires may have sparked associations with the flames of hell or the fires of the Protestant martyrs, as well as destruction, cleansing, and regeneration. Some might remember that in January 1555 there had been bonfires at Cheapside and Smithfield to celebrate the restored Catholic religion, followed by the burning of heretics.[24] But usually bonfires indicated gladness and respect.

Thomas Holland, regius professor at Oxford from 1589 to 1612, explained that bonfires 'be used by the people of this land only as significant arguments to express their sincere affections in joy'. One could hardly wish for a more clear understanding of bonfires as an element in a vocabulary. Holland went on to explain that bonfires 'have been reputed tokens of joy' in England for more than a hundred years. The bonfires lit each year on Queen Elizabeth's accession day were part of 'the ancient and daily practice of this honourable realm'. Almost a century later Francis Osborne pointed with similar approval to 'the bonfires and loud acclamations used still by the people upon the day of [Elizabeth's] inauguration'.[25] Shakespeare caught the meaning, at the joyful reunion in *A Winters Tale*: 'The news, Rogero? Nothing but bonfires.'

John Stow recalled the festival bonfires in London in terms that suggest the conditions of 'communitas' and 'liminality' made familiar by cultural anthropologists. 'After the sun setting there were usually made bonfires in the streets, every man bestowing wood or labour towards them. The wealthier sort also before their doors near to the said bonfires would set out tables on the vigils, furnished with sweet bread and good drink, and on the festival days with meats and drinks plentifully, whereunto they would invite their neighbours and passengers also to sit and be merry with them in great familiarity, praising God for his benefits bestowed on them. These were called bonfires as well of good amity amongst neighbours, that being before at controversy were there by the labour of others reconciled, and made of bitter enemies loving friends.' This, of course, is idealized and nostalgic, but it notes some of the features of bonfires in the following century. The collectivity was often involved, with a temporary suspension of the social distances, disputes and discipline of the everyday world. That, as we shall see, was the case in 1623 with the bonfires at Prince Charles's return from Spain. Stow also reminds us that bonfires were used as a protection against plague, 'for the virtue that a great fire hath to purge the infection of the air'.[26]

In the seventeenth century bonfires signalled happiness and good will, although, like bells, they could take on additional meanings. The accession of James I was greeted in Plymouth with 'great triumph with bonfires, games, and ringing of bells'. So too was the accession of Charles. The fires, like the bells, formed an unofficial commentary on public affairs. Bonfires saluted the royal wedding (by proxy) in May 1625, and a month later, when the new queen arrived in London, 'all the streets were full of bonfires'. In Fenchurch Street alone there were 'above thirty'. During the 1630s bonfires expressed delight that the queen was with child, cheered the peace with Spain, flamed on the king's anniversary, and gave thanks for his recovery for illness.[27] Bonfires cheered the calling of parliament in 1640, and burned for both sides when they won victories in the civil wars. Above all, regularly and spectacularly, they burned to celebrate November the fifth.

The orchestrated deployment of bonfires and other elements in the vocabulary of celebration is revealed in the Privy Council's instructions for 'expressions of joy' at the betrothal of Prince Charles and Henrietta Maria in November 1624. Letters were sent to the Lord Mayor of London, the Lieutenant of the Tower, and the Justices of the Peace in Middlesex, requiring them to 'publish' the good news 'by bonfires, fireworks, lights in the windows, and ringing of bells . . . and all the like demonstrations of rejoicing as can be thought on or put in practice thus on the sudden'. The instructions were reinforced with the admonition, 'herein you are to use especial care and diligence as a particular wherein his majesty, if he shall find the same cheerfully and well performed, will receive good content and satisfaction'.[28] The mayor and justices relayed the message further along the matrix of command, and many London parishes responded, but with no more than a meagre display of enthusiasm.

That niceties of protocol were involved in the setting of bonfires, as well as questions of symbolic action and social order, is further illustrated by a discussion at court in December 1630. Peace with Spain was about to be ratified, and Charles I's Master of Ceremonies, Sir John Finet, reported the following:

Some question grew in the afternoon about bonfires to be made or not that night, as the Lord Treasurer and Lord Chamberlain had propounded to his majesty's pleasure. His majesty seemed not much disposed to it, as an innovation, and more than had been done at the publication of the French peace the year before, but after I had assured that the Spanish ambassador (whom I had then come from) had already begun the structure of his fires before his house, his majesty gave me a command to repair to the Lord Mayor to have it done in the city, as it was (though not by many) with ringing of bells, with the mayor's care of appointing a city marshall (though I had before done the like to the constables thereabouts) for setting of a guard and keeping of good order before the ambassador's house among the exceeding multitude of people, flocking thither for a sight of this ambassador's bonfires, and a taste of his wine which was served forth to them plentifully.[29]

It is clear from this, and from other sources, that bonfires belonged to a versatile social vocabulary. One could mount, host or put on a bonfire, rather as one might give a party, in honour of good news or an important anniversary occasion. Their success, however, depended as much on the public mood as on the intentions of the sponsor. The fires could also be put to other uses, as they were in the anti-Catholic pageants of the Exclusion Crisis, to taunt an enemy or vaunt over his collapse.

Bonfires and bells proclaimed London's delight in the king's acceptance of the Petition of Right in 1628. City churchwardens' accounts show many parishes paying for celebratory bonfires, the parish of St Botolph without Bishopsgate spending 4s. 6d. 'for three dozen faggots for the parliament's concordancy'. This time there was little need for prompting. Secretary Conway wrote that he 'never saw a more general joy in all faces than spread itself suddenly, and broke out into ringing of bells and bonfires miraculously'. The letter-writer Joseph Mead observed on this occasion that 'bonfires were kindled, the number whereof at length equalled those at his majesty's coming out of Spain,' the benchmark for pyrotechnic extravaganza. However, he went on, many bonfires 'were made upon a misprision that the Duke [of Buckingham] either was or should be sent to the Tower . . . This misapprehension prevailed so far, that it went down westward and other parts of the country, as to Ware and other places, where bonfires were likewise made upon the like apprehension.'[30] This is a good example of the ambiguity of the festive form. For some people the bonfires expressed satisfaction in the apparent resolution of political and constitutional difficulties; for others they were signals of triumph at the apparent fall of an unpopular royal favourite. And amidst the London crowd there were no doubt many who viewed the bonfires simply as a source of midsummer fun.

Critical events in the crisis of the 1640s were proclaimed with fire and noise. At Lambeth, across the Thames from Westminster, the parish sponsored a bonfire in February 1640 at the announcement of plans for a parliament. A year later there was 'much rejoicing in the City, and very many bonfires' when the king gave his assent to the Triennial Bill. Religious radicals at Chelmsford greeted the news that Parliament had voted down episcopacy in 1642 with 'great rejoicing and lighting of bonfires'. In this case they had the additional pleasure of plundering the fuel from the unpopular Laudian rector's wood yard. Partisans of the other side made use of the same festive form. A few weeks later a royalist rector in Somerset 'made a bonfire upon top of a high hill, for joy of the overthrow of the parliament forces at Edgehill'.[31]

In July 1643 the Earl of Essex ordered his officers at the Tower of London 'to make a bonfire and shoot off all the great guns in token of joy and thankfulness for the great victory of late obtained over Prince Rupert . . . at which time also the cavaliers made two bonfires and shot off some small guns' in the mistaken belief that there had been a parliamentary rout. This competitive fire-making by rival factions is comparable to the bonfire-building by rival parishes. A year later fortunes were reversed, and royalists could celebrate Rupert's victory at Bolton. 'The bells rang and bonfires were made at almost every door for joy of his highness' good success in Lancashire so far.'[32] Similarly there were bonfires at Oxford to celebrate the king's triumphs, and more bonfires in London and Cambridge to cheer his defeat.

Bonfires formed an essential ingredient in the festive extravaganza welcoming Charles II to London in 1660. They flamed in London early in 1660 at 'the roasting of the Rump', and bonfires throughout the country during Maytide celebrated the return of the king. In the Channel Islands there was 'ringing of bells, and feux-de-joie and great rejoicing' at the proclamation of Charles II. Cambridge celebrated the Restoration with 'many bonfires in town, four on the great Market Hill,' and great expressions and acclamations of joy from all sorts'. At Melton Mowbray the bonfires were kept burning for seventy-two hours.[33]

Bonfires also illuminated the popular politics of exclusion and anti-popery later in Charles II's reign, a topic to be addressed in a later chapter. In 1673 a pamphlet publicizing 'the burning of the Whore of Babylon, as it was acted with great applause in the Poultry, London, on Wednesday night, being the fifth of November', made play with the memory of the fires of the Protestant martyrs, the attempted fire of the Gunpowder Treason, suspected papist involvement in the great fire of London, and the traditionalist bonfires of 5 November. 'Bonfires and squibs are the usual trophies that the juvenile fry in England make use of on that day, to testify their joy and gladness for the wonderful preservation of their fore-fathers.' The demonstration climaxed in 'a great bonfire' on which the papal whore was burned in effigy.[34]

Five years later, 'all the city was in bells and bonfires' after the false report spread that the king was resolved to choose a Protestant successor in November 1678. The 5 November bonfires in 1679 were especially fierce. There were more bonfires on 17 November, celebrating the anniversary of Queen Elizabeth, and more again later in the month announcing the arrival in London of the Duke of Monmouth.[35]

As in previous periods, the bonfires could express both criticism and support for the current regime. In 1681 'the rabble in the City' made disorderly bonfires after the grand jury brought in a bill of *ignoramus* against Lord Shaftesbury. Similarly in 1688 there were 'bonfires made by the rabble upon the news of the bishops being found not guilty'.[36] But there were also loyal bonfires on the accession of James II, on his anniversaries, and at the birth of his son. The accession of William and Mary was naturally another occasion for bonfires, as were Williams's victories in Ireland. So too were the accession and triumphs of Queen Anne. Most fires were organized and orchestrated by political leaders – courtiers, officers, Whig or Tory grandees – but the same vocabulary was available to popular activists. Along with parades and protests, the bonfires were a feature of outdoor politics as the seventeenth century gave way to the eighteenth. Linking immediate political circumstances to memories of past traditions, celebration and commemoration, their purpose was to impress, to demonstrate, and to proclaim, as well as to mobilize and to entertain. The tradition was by no means extinguished with the passing of the Stuart dynasty. Bonfires galore greeted the Hanoverian dynasty. In London the disgraced Tory Bolingbroke tried to ingratiate himself with the new king George in 1715 by building the biggest bonfire in the City, alas, to no good effect.[37]

★

Jubilation meant liberation, sometimes quite literally. A tradition developed that on certain festive occasions the king would display his mercy by ordering the release of prisoners. The triumphal passage of James I and VI south from Scotland in 1603 was marked by the formal freeing of felons at the major cities along the way. At Durham the royal warrant ordered the release of 'all prisoners, saving wilful murder, recusancy, and debt'. A similar warrant freed prisoners at Newark 'out of our princely and Christian commiseration'. Prince Charles's remarkable homecoming in 1623, the subject of the next chapter, included the ritual release of condemned prisoners. The baptism of the king's first-born son and heir in 1630 was also the occasion for 'a general pardon and release of many prisoners'.[38]

Several more elements in the vocabulary of celebration also depended on the actions of the authorities. Shooting ordnance, for example, usually required official permission. Gunshots were regarded as salutes of respect, as they are still today. At the cheerful meeting of James I and the king of Denmark in 1606, 'some three or four score great shot [were] discharged, and of these thundering volleys there were between forty and fifty. You would have thought that Jupiter had been invited,' wrote John Pory to Sir Robert Cotton. Similarly, in December 1624 John Chamberlain reported wryly to Dudley Carleton about preparations for Charles I's French marriage, 'the organs in Paul's played on their loudest pipes and so began to the bells, the bells to the bonfires, the bonfires to the great peal of ordnance at the Tower; God grant it may prove worth all this noise.' Echoing this sympathy, when the new queen Henrietta Maria arrived in 1625 the Tower fired its great guns and the ships in the Pool of London discharged their ordnance in salute.[39]

The Restoration, naturally, was accompanied by percussion and cannonades as well as bonfires and bells. At Cambridge the noise-making involved a mingling of the sacred and the profane; soldiers were placed around the top of King's College chapel, 'from whence they gave a volley of shot'. In London 'the shouts of the people were so great that, though all the bells in the City rung, Bow bells could not be heard there'. The volume achieved some sort of catharsis or, as the contemporary historian James Heath saw it, 'atonement' through noise. The volume 'did hereby purify and cleanse the air of London, dispelling those dark mists of the rebellion'.[40] Not far behind this urbane manner was the medieval belief that noisemaking conjured or dispelled the spirits of the air. A generation later at York the proclamation of James II in 1685 was also accompanied by shots and cannonades. And on 14 October 1688, writes Sir John Reresby, 'being the king's birthday, I gave the great guns at Clifford's Tower, and . . . in the castle . . . the company gave several vollies also of small shot.'[41]

Combining ballistic percussion and the rooted flames of bonfires were the agile pyrotechnics of fireworks. Artful concoctions of gunpowder and other ingredients produced sound and light as well as destruction, and were ideally suited for festive events. By the seventeenth century bombardiers and chemists had enough experience with gunpowder to devise dazzling firework displays, and the Stuart taste for masques and pageants led to an elaboration of the pyrotechnician's skills. Fireworks became an essential part of Jacobean court festivity. At the meeting of the kings of England and Denmark on the Thames in 1606 the fireworks 'continued burning and cracking for the space of three quarters of an hour'. Similar set pieces illuminated the investiture of the Prince of Wales in 1610. John Chamberlain commented on the festivities for the marriage of the Princess Elizabeth and the Elector Palatine in 1613, 'the fireworks were reasonably well performed, all save the last castle of fire, which bred most expectation, and had most devices, but when it came to execution had worst success'.[42]

An accident involving fireworks led to their being banned at Norwich in 1612. At the mayor's pageant on Guild day the previous June, 'certain fireworks, as had been usual, were fired off in the evening, some of which breaking frightened the people'. Thirty-three people were killed in the ensuing panic. The parish register of Saints Simon and Jude records the burial of one man and five women on 19 June 1611, noting 'these six and twenty-seven more were all slain at the fireworks in Tombland, Mr Thomas Angwyste then entering his mayorality'. The mayor's court soon voted to ban all fireworks, on pain of a £20 fine. The cities of London and Westminster also attempted to ban fireworks later in the seventeenth century because of their involvement in seasonal disorders.[43]

Arcane knowledge about pyrotechnics became public information with the appearance of handbooks on the subject. Francis Malthus produced *A Treatise of Artificial Fire-Works, both for Warres and Recreation* in 1629. This explained how to make rockets, golden rain, fiery wheels, and 'stars giving great reports'. Nathaniel Nye's *Art of Gunnery*, first published in 1647 and reprinted in 1670, also contained 'a treatise of artificial fireworks'. In 1651 John White published a useful book of recipes and instruction for making rockets, festive explosions, and all manner of set-piece firework displays. It was titled *A Rich Cabinet, with Variety of Inventions . . . Whereunto is added Variety of Recreative Fire-Works, both for Land, Aire, and Water*. Significantly, George Thomason, the London bookseller, collected his copy on 17 November, the anniversary of Queen Elizabeth's accession.[44]

Royal fireworks formed a standard element in the vocabulary of celebration in the late seventeenth century. In 1688, for example, after the birth of Prince James seemed to secure the future of the Stuart dynasty, Sir John Reresby noted 'the finest fireworks, made at the king's charge on occasion of the Prince of Wales, that ever was seen in England'. Almost a decade later the fireworks celebrating the Treaty of Ryswick were said to have cost £10,000.[45] Squibs and crackers were available to everyone, but festive set-piece fireworks were a luxury only the most powerful could afford.

Lesser elements in the vocabulary of celebration also reveal aspects of politicized symbolic action. A study could be made of the outpouring of wine and beer, cakes and sweets, tobacco and brandy, paying attention to who offered what to whom on great occasions. More might be learned from the etiquette of dress, particularly among those groups whose status was displayed by their costume. Aldermen and burgesses were expected to wear their robes on festival days, and could be fined if they neglected proper raiments. So too at the universities 'scarlet days' called for full academic robing. Gunpowder

Treason day was added to the robing calendar, and at towns like Nottingham the 'Scarlet gownmen of the clothing' were supposed to process to church on that day in their scarlet gowns. The 'high and principal festivals' of the later Stuart period were known as 'collardays' after the collars of golden esses worn by the nobility at court.[46]

Flowers also had their place in the vocabulary (as they do today when we 'say it with flowers') although they rarely appear in the documentary record. They were especially appropriate to celebrations in the spring and summer. May day was, notoriously, a floral feast, and flowers graced religious observances at Rogationtide and Whitsun. Puritans disapproved of flowers at Derbyshire well-dressings, and railed against the 'monstrous idolatry' of flowers at funerals. Norwich had its floral feast and pageant in the 1630s, put on by the florists' guild, which was not without its opponents. The common council of Nottingham was divided eight to seven when they voted in 1638, 'the Midsummer even watch to be continued with garlands, as heretofore'.[47] At Great Yarmouth the guildhall was strewn with herbs and rushes each midsummer day in preparation for the St John's day 'quest' or civic inquest. Flowers and branches (for sweetness and delight) were brought into public buildings on high occasions. Green boughs, bays, holly, ivy, and mistletoe were brought into churches at Christmas. In October 1651, as part of the celebration for the victory at Worcester, 'herbs and laurel were strewed in the church' of St Margaret Westminster, and were renewed on the following 5 November. On Royal Oak day in the 1660s the churchwardens of St Peter Mancroft, Norwich, provided greenery and birch 'to dress up the church'.

Flowers were also employed in politically charged situations. Sir John Finet recorded in 1639, on Charles's return from Scotland, 'the country people had all the way spoken their gladness in strewed flowers, boughs, and bonfires'.[48] In another context it might have been hosannas and palms. When Archbishop Laud's victims Burton, Bastwick and Prynne returned triumphantly to London in 1640 their way was adorned with rosemary (for remembrance) and bays (for heroes). The vocabulary had many extensions, and was capable of expressing a multitude of messages.

A Compendious Chronology of Joyful Occasions, 1558–1702

1558   'when the queen's majesty was proclaimed'.
1570   'when word was brought that the Earl of Northumberland was taken' (Thomas Percy).

1571   'for joy of the great victory that Christians hath gotten of the Turk' (Battle of Lepanto).
1585   'when the traitors were taken' (Parry plot).
1586   'for joy that the conspiracy was prevented and the traitors revealed'/'upon triumph for the discovery of the popish treachery' (Babington plot).
1587   'at the beheading of the queen of Scots'.
1588   'on the triumphing day had of the Spaniards'.
1596   'for the good success of our navy at Cadiz'.
1603   'at the proclamation of our king'.
        'upon the coronation of our sovereign King James'.
1614   'at the birth of the Lady Elizabeth's son'.
1618   'for the birth of the Prince Palgrave's child'/'at the time the Lady Elizabeth was delivered'.
1623   'for the prince's arrival in Spain'.
        'for the happy return of our Prince Charles out of Spain into England'.
1625   'at the proclamation of King Charles'.
        'at the solemnizing of the king's marriage'.
1628   'at the declaration for the happy success of the parliament'/ 'when his majesty granted the Petition of Right'.
1629   'at the news of the queen's majesty being with child'.
1630   'upon the birth of Prince Charles'.
        'the day the prince was christened'.
        'when there was proclamation made of the peace with the king of Spain'.
1631   'at the birth of the Lady Mary'.
        'for the king of Sweden's victory'.
1632   'upon the king's recovery to health'.
1633   'at the king's majesty coming home out of Scotland'.
        'at the birth of the Duke of York'.
1636   'upon the birth of the princess'.
1639   'being the time of his majesty's return to Whitehall from the north'.
1640   'for the parliament'.
1641   'at the birth of the Duke of Lancaster'.
        'on the late good news concerning the good proceedings of the high court of parliament'.
        'for joy of the Triennial parliament'.
        'at his majesty's return from Scotland'.
1642   'for peace twixt England and Scotland'.
        'that night the bishops were put down'.
1642–8 (civil war victories).

1651 'upon intelligence of the overthrow of the Scottish army at
       Worcester'/'when the Scots army was routed'.
1653 'that day when the Lord Protector was installed'.
1654 'for victory over the Hollanders'.
1657 'that day the Lord Protector was proclaimed'.
1658 'the day the Lord Richard Cromwell was proclaimed Lord
       Protector'.
1660 'at the free parliament proclaimed'.
       'at the proclamation of the king'.
       'at the king's coming into England'.
       'when the king's arms were set up'.
       'on the coronation of King Charles II'.
1662 'for the queen's first coming to town'.
1666 'on the news of the overthrow of the Dutch'.
1673 'when peace was proclaimed between the Dutch and the
       English'.
1677 'at the marriage of the Prince of Orange'.
1685 'on the day the king was proclaimed'.
       'on the news of Argyll's defeat'.
       'on the news of Monmouth's defeat'/'for the victory in the
       west' (Battle of Sedgemoor).
       'upon the news of his being taken'.
       'upon the confirmation of his being taken and his forces
       routed'.
1686 'on the rejoicing day for taking of Buda'.
1688 'for the queen's being with child'.
       'upon the birth of the Prince of Wales'.
       'for the bishops being released out of the tower'.
       'for their being acquitted'.
1689 'on the thanksgiving day for the Prince of Orange'.
       'when King William and Queen Mary were proclaimed'.
       'at the coronation of King William and Queen Mary'.
       'for the birth of the Duke of Gloucester'.
1690 'at the news of the reducing of Ireland' (Battle of the Boyne).
1692 'victory over the French at Sea' (Battle of La Hogue).
1693 'for his majesty's return out of Holland'.
1695 'the taking of Namur'.
1697 'peace of Ryswick'.
1702 'at the queen's proclaiming'.

6
AFFECTIONATE GLADNESS – THE RETURN OF PRINCE CHARLES

In October 1623 Prince Charles Stuart returned to London after half a year abroad trying to conclude a marriage to the Infanta of Spain. The negotiations were fruitless, frustrating, and humiliating, and the royal party came back to England having failed in its mission. Instead of commiserating, the City of London went wild with joy at the prince's return, with an extravaganza of celebration. Similar festivities were mounted in provincial towns. At no other time in the seventeenth century, with the possible exception of the Restoration, did the people of England greet their prince with such public enthusiasm. At no other time in his life did Charles Stuart enjoy such fervent popular acclaim. For several years the return of Prince Charles was remembered as an event of major national importance, comparable to the deliverance from the Spanish Armada and the discovery of the Gunpowder Plot. By examining this episode in detail we may reach a deeper understanding of the texture and dynamics of celebration in early modern England. Bound up with the lavish outpouring of joy were the ambiguous issues of spontaneity and control, and the haunting question of who was saying what to whom.

The events of October 1623 tie together the religious politics, urban history, and popular culture of early Stuart England. They have been mentioned, briefly, by Charles's biographers, and they occupy a small place in most accounts of the political history of the age.[1] Charles Stuart's welcome can easily be explained in terms of anti-Spanish sentiment and the relief felt by English Protestants that their prince was not to marry a Spanish Catholic. The return of Prince Charles also signified a triumph of certainty (or wishful thinking) over uncertainty, of dynastic continuity instead of a succession crisis, of the security of Protestantism against expanding Catholicism, now that the Stuart heir was safely home. The adulation of Prince Charles may also have elements of a celebration of youth over age, as the young prince prepared to take over from the increasingly senile king.

The festivities of 1623 may also repay investigation from an ethnographic perspective. The reaction to Charles Stuart's homecoming opens a window on popular behaviour, shows more of the orchestration of festivity, and illuminates the workings of the symbolic vocabulary of celebration. The day had elements of carnival, bacchanal, and *son et lumière* as well as religious and political reverberations. An anatomy of this episode indicates how festive traditions developed and how they were manipulated. It shows how people were taught to interpret a remarkable occasion, both at the moment and retrospectively, and how the return of Prince Charles became, at least in the short run, an icon event in English Protestant memory.

Simonds D'Ewes, who was a student at the Middle Temple at the time, gives the following account which sets the scene:

6 October 1623. This day brought Prince Charles in safety to London . . . The post brought the news hither to London about three of the clock this Monday morning to the Lord Mayor, being one Lumley, that so bonfires might be made . . . Upon this the sergeants dispersed themselves into all places, raising up constables and other officers who raised up every household, so that between six and seven the whole city by reason of the thick-placed bonfires, though it were a rainy morning, seemed to be on fire, there wanting not one almost at every door, where there was an inhabitant. . . . I dare be bold to say this, London never before saw so many bonfires at one time, for a taste of other places, there were 335 or thereabouts between Whitehall and Temple Bar. 'Twas pretty to observe the difference between the bonfires made by command after his landing in Spain, being by express order from the Privy Council and between these that were made upon the matter voluntarily, the first being thin and poor, these many and great. The Archbishop of Canterbury, Doctor Abbot, went out about or between four and five of the clock to meet the prince who came to Lambeth first, and there stayed awhile with the archbishop, and then in his barge with the Duke of Buckingham crossed over to York House, the duke's house. There he came about eight of the clock and dined, ere he departed. The news of his arrival there once known, the officers and noblemen flocked thither . . . who all came in at Watergate, for at the fore gate press of people was so great that no man could get in or out, for they were desirous to see him, many not yet believing that he was come, because they had been deceived so often, and this too was the reason that in all places in the kingdom far distant from London, few or no bonfires were made, in regard they had been deluded before, and so believed not now. But here in London all shops were shut, the day was turned to a holiday, with bells ringing and mirth and jollity. Ten or fifteen prisoners ready this morning for execution were all saved and set free. The very bushes on taverns were set on fire, a load or two of faggots being carried in the streets, were all thrown off and set on fire and the cartman glad to save his from pulling in pieces.[2]

D'Ewes evidently thought he was a witness to something quite extraordinary; he had seen something memorable and impressive, and no other entry in his diary warranted so much space. D'Ewes went on to describe the prince's triumphant passage by Charing Cross, the air thick with bonfire smoke, through crowds cheering, 'we have him, we have him!' And he concluded his long account with the observation, 'the only thing to be lamented was the great excess and drunkenness of this day, the two usual fault[s] of Englishmen upon any good hap . . . At night, many bonfires were anew made, to make up a complete celebration of this great miracle of our latter age'.[3]

D'Ewes' last phrase, 'this great miracle of our latter age', with its millennial resonances invoking the unfolding of cosmic drama, also associates the return of Prince Charles with other historic deliverances of Protestant England. To observers of the 1620s the return of Prince Charles possessed an historical importance comparable to the defeat of the Spanish Armada and deliverance from the Gunpowder Plot. For several years almanac writers listed the 1623 homecoming among the most memorable events of history. Sermonists treated the return of the prince as the latest in a sequence of providential happenings. Indeed, while Tilbury Camp in 1588 marked England's escape from the military might of the Duke of Alva, and Gunpowder Treason in 1605 was remembered as proof of Catholic perfidy, the return of Prince Charles signalled deliverance from the no less devastating threat of a Spanish marriage. In all cases, it could be claimed, England emerged stronger from Catholic attempts to undo the Reformation. From putting his head in the mouth of the beast, Prince Charles had returned to England unscathed, except perhaps emotionally. The heir to the throne was still a bachelor, and, more important, he had withstood intense pressures to convert to Rome or to make dangerous concessions to English Catholics.

Preaching at Great Yarmouth on 19 October, while the reverberations of delight were still ringing, Thomas Reeve cast the newly returned Charles Stuart as royal David. 'Oh, how joyful was the safety of Israel's worthy . . . his delivery gracious . . . behold how great exultation, how great congratulation was there for it . . . must not the whole land be much cheered in this his safe return? . . . The woods have not destroyed him, the floods have not devoured him, the air hath not infected him'. Reeve went on to praise Prince Charles for his courage, valour, prudence, and above all 'his constancy to the faith he hath been brought up in . . . If ever there was a time for the timbrel and the dance,' Reeve concluded, 'this is it, the return of our Prince into the Land should be like return of life into a swooning body'.[4] The prince was home safe, in the puritan Stephen Jerome's words, 'both in body and soul, not so much as the least infected dust cleaving to his feet, much less any corrupted Popish air infect[ing] his royal blood'.[5] The homecoming provided an occasion for puritan preachers to vent their anxieties while ostensibly (and ostentatiously) supporting the royal family.

Charles and Buckingham had left England in the spring of 1623 on a risky and foolhardy quest to woo the Spanish princess. The mission was blithely irresponsible, and its conduct was not improved by the travellers' ludicrous and ineffective disguise. Even if Charles had not gone to Spain to do his own wooing, and had relied, as was conventional, on proxies and intermediaries, the policy itself posed grave risks. Two generations of Englishmen had looked upon Spain as England's natural enemy. Many believed that England should still be fighting Spain rather than engaging in sweetheart diplomacy. What would have happened if King James had died while his only surviving son was overseas? Wise counsellors blanched at the thought.[6] The prospect of the heir to the English throne being held hostage abroad was almost too horrible to contemplate. Yet even worse was the nightmare that the prince might be ensnared by Catholicism, as were so many other young Englishmen on their travels abroad.

Popular opinion, in as far as it can be reconstructed, was vehemently, almost pathologically, anti-Spanish. It was no wonder, then, that when news leaked out about Prince Charles's venture those who heard about it were extremely upset. Fears for the prince's safety mingled with apprehensions about the fate of English Protestantism. The militant anti-Catholic Thomas Scott recalled, 'our hearts were filled with astonishment, doubt, despair; we gave them for lost, ourselves with them, and with them and us, our laws, liberties, land, and (what was dearest) our religion.' Londoners responded begrudgingly when ordered to light bonfires on April 1st in recognition of the prince's safe arrival in Madrid. Their meagre effort can be traced in the churchwardens' accounts. John Chamberlain archly commented, 'God send we may praise at parting', and his letters of this period are heavy with anxiety about the Spanish marriage negotiations.[7]

Anxiety grew as the prince's absence lengthened, 'the common people more than mad in their longings to have him make a quick return home'. In John Taylor's words, 'never any loving mother desired, with more longing, to see her hopeful son, whose long absence had filled her with grief, than all the honest inhabitants of this kingdom did hunger and thirst to see or hear from their most hopeful and beloved prince'. London, by all accounts, was swelling with pent-up apprehensions. Nature herself seemed out of joint, 'as if the waters had been out of course'.[8] The sermons and pamphlets of October 1623 deliberately exaggerated the sense of loss during the prince's absence, to contrast with the joy at his return, but, though rich in rhetoric and heavy with hyperbole, they captured a strain of the public mood. The London crowd was fickle, as Stuart monarchs learned to their cost, but in 1623 feelings ran rapturous for Prince Charles. Few people beyond the court had personal knowledge of the young man, but it was enough that he was heir to King James, and brother to the late Prince Henry and to the Protestant heroine Elizabeth of Bohemia.[9]

While the prince and Buckingham were negotiating for a successful match in Spain, a growing number of people in England were patriotically praying for its failure. Buckingham learned in April 'that the marriage had become so unpopular at home that a defeat in Madrid might well produce a triumph in London'.[10] The English party languished in Madrid from the middle of March to the end of August, until all hopes of concluding the match disintegrated. Charles and Buckingham sailed homewards angry and frustrated, soured with humiliation and defeat. Yet England greeted them as heroes! The Triumph, that was hinted in the April despatch, was about to begin.

D'Ewes's diary is by no means the only account of the celebrations. Letters and pamphlets spread news of Charles's homecoming to those not privileged to experience it in London. Robert Tanfield wrote to Lord Montague at Broughton, Northamptonshire, describing 'reports of the Tower ordnance' amidst the glare of bonfires and the sound of bells. 'This morning the streets were so stuffed with fires as that betwixt Whitehall and Temple Bar my man told three hundred and odd, and at Whitehall, Northampton House, York House and Somerset House there is hogsheads of wine set forth into the street'. This news had already reached Northampton, for Lord Montague wrote back, 'I thank you for your good news of the prince's safe arrival, but we had it in the country on Monday. There was never so great cause of joy as his safe return, all things considered. God makes us thankful for it'.[11] Francis Ryves wrote to Dr Ussher, the Bishop of Meath, 'all London rang with bells and flared with bonfires, and resounded all over with such shouts as is not well possible to express'. Secretary Calvert wrote that the bonfires were so numerous that they 'might have hazarded the burning of the streets, had not they been allayed with London liquor'. The lawyer Sir Richard Hutton recorded 'grand joy' at the return of Prince Charles, and noted in his characteristic law French diary, 'bells et bonfires per tout le realm in grand abundance'. William Laud recorded in his diary, 'the greatest expression of joy by all sorts of people that ever I saw'.[12]

John Chamberlain described the festivities in his letters to Dudley Carleton. Despite the weather, 'a very foul and rainy day', Londoners flocked to the streets in festive spirits. 'I have not heard of more demonstrations of public joy then were here and everywhere from the highest to the lowest, such spreading of tables in the streets with all manner of provisions, setting out whole hogsheads of wine and butts of sack, but specially such numbers of bonfires both here and all along as he went . . . as is almost incredible . . . At Blackheath there was fourteen load of wood in one fire, and the people were so mad with excess of joy that if they met with any cart loaden with wood they would take out the horses and set cart and all on fire . . . But above all certain condemned prisoners had the best hap and most cause to rejoice who being on their way to Tyburn were reprieved by the Prince's coming in the very nick'.[13]

Private communications were quickly supplemented by published pamphlets. John Taylor's gushing 'Brittaines Joy, for the happy Arriuall of Prince Charles' was registered at Stationers' Hall on 7 October, while the ashes of the bonfires were still warm, and was printed as *Prince Charles his Welcome from Spaine* soon after.

> The bells proclaimed aloud in every steeple,
> The joyful acclamations of the people;
> The ordnance thundered with so high a strain,
> As if great Mars they meant to entertain.
> The bonfires blazing, infinite almost,
> Gave such a heat as if the world did roast.
> True mirth and gladness was in every face,
> And healths ran bravely round in every place:
> That sure I think, this sixth day of October,
> Ten thousand men will go to bed scarce [sober].
> This was a day all dedicate to mirth,
> As 'twere our royal Charles his second birth.
> And this day is a jewel well return'd,
> For whom this kingdom yesterday so mourn'd.
> God length his days who is the cause of this,
> And make us thankful for so great a bliss.[14]

Taylor went on to describe a day spent 'in mirth, triumphs and thanksgiving, wherein the people of all degrees, from the highest to the lowest, both rich and poor, in London, Westminster, and the suburbs, to their powers expressed their loves'. Every element in the vocabulary of celebration was brought into play. The air 'was filled with the shouts and acclamations of people, with the rejoicing noises

of instruments, ordnance, muskets, bells, drums, and trumpets . . .
The day was commanded to be kept a holiday, so that no shops were
opened, no manner of work was done from morning to night, but
carrying and recarrying wood to make bonfires, ringing, filling, and
emptying of pots, that all seemed as if the world was newly preserved
from some second flood'.[15] Taylor's notion of 'second birth' for the
prince was coupled with England's deliverance from a 'second flood'.
His reference to 'great Mars' suggests that Taylor now expected war
with Spain.

Like other commentators, Taylor was impressed by the extrava-
gance of the bonfires, on which valuable and useful items were
consigned. 'There was one bonfire made at Guildhall in London,
which cost one hundred pound (belike it was some logwood, which
was prohibited and unlawful to be used by dyers, and being forfeited,
was ordained to be burnt in triumph)'. 'Some in Smithfield burnt their
old coaches', while others, he claims, 'committed their whole estate to
fire and faggot'. Combustible household items were added to the fuel
of timber and pitch barrels. There were 108 bonfires 'betwixt Paul's
Church-yard and London Bridge', besides hundreds more which
Taylor reports, 'I saw not'. The night was alight with bonfires, links
and cresset lights, 'and most excellent fireworks, with squibs,
crackers, rackets, which most delightfully flew every way'.[16]

The celebration knew no social bounds. 'And to the intent all estates
should be merry, there were divers noblemen, gentlemen, and others,
that gave store of gold to the poor; some gave vessels of wine in the
streets'. Taylor was inspired by the vast and varied drinking of the
day. 'The very vintners burnt their bushes in Fleet Street, and other
places, and their wine was burnt all over London and Westminster,
into all colours of the rainbow; whole pints, quarts, pottles and
gallons, were made into bonfires of sack and claret, whilst good
fellows, like loving salamanders, swallowed those liquid fires'. And
Taylor, too, noted the reprieve of condemned criminals, 'six men and
two women'.[17]

Finally, we have the anonymous report of *The Ioyfull Returne of the
most illustrious Prince, Charles* which labels the day, 'this English
masterpiece of ours'. Both London and the country fell 'into such
inutterable expressions of affectionate gladness, such unlimitable and
violent inundations of joy, that the people . . . seemed to lose their
own being, and to forget that they were themselves: men, women,
and children made but one consort, and the music of that consort,
sounded nothing but "the prince is come, our Charles is come." From
the nobleman to the artificer, if contention had arose, which of them
was fullest of good wishes, of glad welcomes, of loud-resounding

acclamations for his coming, it had been hard to decide the difference.' This account, too, goes into raptures about the bells and bonfires, and about the release of the condemned criminals. In all, the day was extraordinary, unforgettable. 'It will be a legacy for young men when they grow old, to read (by the fireside) the chronicle of this day to their children', predicted the author of the *Ioyfull returne*.[18]

In a 'solemn service' at St. Paul's 'the singing of a new anthem was specially observed, the 114th Psalm, when Israel came out of Egypt and the house of Jacob from among the barbarous people'. Here, indeed, was the heir of England's Jacob, Jacobus Rex, come home from the barbarous (and bearded) lair of Spain! The service was no doubt officially sponsored, perhaps with Buckingham's support, and it was a clear riposte to the pro-Spanish policies of the king. It recalled other anti-Spanish services at St Paul's, such as the thanksgiving in 1588 when captured Armada ensigns were on display.[19]

Court drama also commented indirectly on the events of 1623. A month after his homecoming, on 5 November of all days, Prince Charles was treated to a private performance of *The Spanish Gypsy* acted by 'the Queen of Bohemia's Company'. For the Christmas season Ben Jonson prepared *Neptune's Triumph for the Return of Albion*, later reset as *The Fortunate Isles*. The following summer saw Middleton's successful anti-Spanish drama, *A Game at Chess* which celebrates the wit and virtue of the prince and the duke.[20] The episode had clearly captured the literary as well as the popular imagination.

*

Chronicles and descriptions tell only part of the story. Behind these heady accounts lie instructions and actions involving central and local government, some of which can be retrieved from the local records. It is important to discover how much of this welcome was a product of Stuart public relations, and how much of it reflected genuine popular concerns. How much of this enthusiasm was filtered through the matrix of command? If some chroniclers are to be believed, joyous acclaim greeted the Stuarts wherever they went, with the same adulation that followed Elizabeth. Princes were supposed to be greeted with enthusiasm, and a genre had developed to describe it. Much of the literature of 1623 belonged to this genre, drawing on previous rapturous accounts of royal entries, and providing a model for subsequent descriptions. King Charles's return from Scotland in 1641, for example, was described in phrases evocative of his earlier homecoming, despite the fact that the London crowd was this time turning against him.[21] Poets and pamphleteers often exaggerated for rhetorical and patriotic effect, so their description of popular reactions might be discounted as conventional puffery. In 1623, however, the decorative and sycophantic literary view of events is bolstered by private descriptions, letters and diaries that were never intended for public view, as well as by the fiscal entries in churchwardens' records. The diarists Laud and D'Ewes concur with the journalists and pamphleteers. All report an outpouring of enthusiasm that was memorable and unprecedented.

Much of the festivity of 1623 appears to be spontaneous, and some of it got out of hand; but other elements were carefully stage-managed. Although the bonfires and bells expressed a heartfelt joy, they were often commanded and paid for by civic or parish officials. London was showing off, and its spectacular display of love and duty may, in part, have been mounted with an eye to future favours. Parish pride may also have been a factor in the celebrations, resulting in locally competitive bellringing and bonfire building. Authenticity and manipulation are not, however, necessarily exclusive. A truly popular celebration can be fuelled or fostered by official prompts and interventions, while a managed occasion may harmonize with the politics of the street.

The October return differed from the traditional pageant entry of kings and queens. It was neither planned nor scheduled, but rather was improvised on the instant, having more in common with a carnival or a charivari than a great state occasion. The king was away at Royston, and neither he nor the council had advance knowledge of the prince's immediate homecoming. There were no emblematic arches, floats, or elaborate set pieces, no verses or speeches written in advance. There was no centrepiece to the celebration, no contrived court ceremony, no triumphant procession.[22] Instead the merrymaking was amorphous and generalized. It was fired by the fact of the prince's return, but was not dependent on his immediate presence. Charles himself was almost invisible, spending a few hours closeted with senior advisors before setting off to join the king. His own participation in the celebration was minimal.

News of the prince's homecoming reached London by way of Lambeth, where the travel-weary royal party rested with Archbishop Abbot before crossing the river. While Charles and Buckingham refreshed themselves, instructions preceded them into the City to ensure a fitting reception. The chain of instruction went from the archbishop to the Lord Mayor, to the councilmen and aldermen, to the sergeants and constables, and finally to every householder. Pressed into action at three in the morning, Mayor Lumley despatched orders to each of the city's wards, 'to cause bonfires to be made and bells to be rung in the parishes within the ward forthwith, for joy of his highness' said safe arrival, whereof fail not'.[23] By the time the prince reached the City the skies were filled with flames and smoke.

Celebration did not come cheap. Parish bonfires were a charge on the parish accounts, despite voluntary contributions; and bellringers needed refreshment and reward no matter how patriotic their sentiments. Payments for the festivities are sprinkled through many churchwardens' account books. At Lambeth, where Prince Charles began his entry to London, the churchwardens disbursed twelve shillings 'for ringing when the prince came from Spain'. So lustily did they ring that another three shillings was soon required 'for mending the baldrick and clapper of the great bell'. Four shillings more went 'for faggots for a bonfire'. In the parish of St Andrew by the Wardrobe, where only a shilling had been spent on bellringing to mark the prince's arrival in Spain in April, two shillings and sixpence was paid out to the ringers at his return. 'Ringing for the prince' cost three shillings at St Stephen Coleman Street, with similar payments elsewhere according to the wealth of the parish and the traditions of its bells.[24]

Nor were the celebrations confined to London. The prince went post haste to join his father at Royston, and bells and bonfires accompanied him most of the way. And throughout England, in parishes remote from the prince's movements, bells were rung and celebrations were staged to mark this glorious event. D'Ewes's observation, that provincial parishes were loth to set bonfires in case the news was false, was soon overtaken. Couriers carried the news, and local communities responded appropriately. At Chester-le-Street the churchwardens paid two shillings and eightpence 'to the ringers at Prince Charles his coming'. At Dorchester, Leicester, Chester, York, Norwich, and elsewhere, there were similar payments 'at the Prince's return home'. At Coventry the townsmen celebrated with a bonfire at Cross Cheaping, the bells rang until four in the morning, and the aldermen regaled themselves with four hours of feasting and drinking in the Mayor's parlour.[25] The news included something for everyone, in virtually every part of the kingdom.

At Cambridge, 'the news came to our Vice-Chancellor Monday forenoon', brought by a speedy messenger from London. 'Our bells rung all that day, and the town made bonfires at night. Tuesday the bells continued ringing; every college had a speech and one dish more at supper, and bonfires and squibs in their courts, the townsmen still continuing to warm their streets in every corner also with bonfires, lest they should not be merry when we were. Wednesday the university assembled; in the forenoon to gratulatory sermon at St Mary's, in the afternoon to a public oration. The close at night was with bonfires, drums, guns, fireworks, till past midnight all the town about'. The next day the senior members of the university presented a celebratory book of verses to the prince and king at Royston.[26]

The churchwardens of Great St Mary's 'paid to John Hall money that he sayeth he spent upon the ringers the 6th, 7th and 8th days of October upon the prince's return from Spain, 4s.', and 'more paid unto him (as he sayeth) money that was commanded to be laid for faggots for a bonfire the same time, 3s. 4d.' Not to be outdone, Holy Trinity at Cambridge, on the other side of the market square, paid 4s. 6d. 'to the ringers at the prince's return', and another 6s. 3d. 'for two bonfires two nights'. Cambridge, like London, celebrated with sound and light, with the parishes vying with each other and the town vying with the university in dutiful solemnity and rowdy abandon.

In Great Yarmouth, too, the bells pealed mightily, 'that so we may make the world ring with our joy, and the sky to resound with our gladsome melody'. Stirred on by the preacher Thomas Reeve, Yarmouth celebrated so magnificently with 'your church-joy, your streets-melody, your instruments of music, your banners displayed, your ordnance roaring, your bonfires flaming', that the town ancients declared, 'such triumphing they never did behold'. The town outdid itself with 'cornets and sackbuts, powder and shot, bonfires and ringing of bells'.[27] In an extraordinary expenditure of parish funds, the churchwardens of Great Yarmouth spent thirteen shillings for ringing 'one day and one night for the happy return of our Prince Charles', and laid out another 10s. 4d. 'for bread, beer and candles for the ringers'.

Norwich, England's second city, had its officially sponsored celebration, involving alcohol, bonfires, and noise. The church-wardens of St Peter Mancroft paid six shillings 'for ringing upon the prince's coming from Spain', and the other parishes rang their own best efforts. The Norwich chamberlain's accounts for 1623 include the large sum of £6. 15s., 'paid to Peter Peke, vintner, for a hogshead of wine which was appointed to be laid out at the market cross and there drank out by the captains of this city and their companies making show of joy and triumph for the safe return of Prince Charles from Spain'.[28] (A hogshead is 63 old wine-gallons.) The free-flowing liquor was just the beginning of the boisterous merry-making at Norwich.

Some of the excitement can be imagined from further entries in the chamberlain's books. 'Prince Charles his return from Spain' occasioned a grand bonfire on Mousehold Heath, burning two pitch barrels (one shilling each) and twenty shillings'-worth of the city's wood. Associated expenses included five shillings for carrying the wood, eightpence 'to a labourer to help up with the wood and make a fire', and 16s. 8d. 'for five dozen of torches then used'. The Norwich festivities were further dignified by drummers and trumpeters, costing another twelve shillings. Finally, since no celebration would be complete without explosions, the city paid three shillings for carrying the guns to Castle Hill, ten shillings 'to Edward Wright for discharging them' – and twenty shillings 'towards the mending of the glass windows that were broken in St Gregory's parish when the wheel-guns were discharged'.[29]

★

Although there were other festive occasions in early Stuart England, none matched the intensity of October 1623. On this magical occasion the ordinary, workaday world stopped, albeit temporarily, and a miraculous new dispensation prevailed. Pent-up longings and fears burst in an outpouring of patriotic enthusiasm. D'Ewes, who called it 'this great miracle of our latter age', was not normally given to hyperbole. Another commentator noted 'such unlimitable and violent inundations of joy, that the people . . . seemed to lose their own being, and to forget that they were themselves'.[30] This does not sound like the usual behaviour of seventeenth-century Englishmen. Something strange was happening, which we might understand better with assistance from anthropology. Some cautious interdisciplinary borrowing may help expand the discussion beyond the traditional historical concern with politics and religion.[31]

The October celebration invoked established traditions of public and popular festivity, and in turn gave new meaning to them. Most of the elements of festivity – fire, noise, alcohol, and crowds – were fully familiar in the Jacobean period, but their combination and intensity was unprecedented. We may achieve a deeper appreciation of the event celebrated by D'Ewes and his contemporaries by recalling their symbolic vocabulary of celebration.

Bonfires, we have seen, were ancient signals of community and joy. By 1623 they were invested with anti-Catholic meaning by their annual association with Gunpowder Treason day. Early Stuart bonfires may also have recalled the beacons that warned of the Spanish Armada, whose defeat, like the prince's homecoming, was a signal of God's favour to Protestant England. What was special about the fires of 1623 was their number, their intensity, and the lavish amounts of fuel consumed on them. Stuart England was suffering a wood shortage, as the forest retreated, yet costly loads of wood were consigned to the flames. The weather was wet and miserable that 6 October, yet in defiance the bonfires were kept burning into the night. The day was marked by flames and light from well before dawn until well beyond midnight. The links, lights and fireworks added to the festive effect.

All the church bells rang, in a symphony of tintinnabulation. Bells, of course, had well established layers of significance, which would have been meaningful to most of their listeners. In October 1623 the bells of hundreds of churches were rung with enthusiasm, for hours on end, in a communal exorcism of the Spanish threat. Parish records contain hundreds of accounts of payments to the ringers and of repairs occasioned by their unaccustomed intensity. The bells, like the fires, can be understood as not only welcoming the prince but as signalling a cleansing, a catharsis, a release through noise.

Other elements in this episode suggest a transformation, a temporary re-ordering of the world. Night became day, dark became light, wet became dry, the rain was dispelled by fire. Cold autumn was remade as warm spring. Conventional respect for property and commodities was inverted, private possessions became public property, wood carts were commandeered, and valuable items were consigned to the flames. In normal circumstances the law gave protection to wood carts but the festive dispensation on 6 October countenanced this illegal activity.[32]

The social hierarchy was simultaneously dissolved and re-established, as at other times of inversion and 'misrule'. An unscheduled carnival took the city by storm. Londoners entered a state of liminality, in which normal routines were suspended and conventional boundaries were set aside. Citizens experienced an interlude of love, harmony, healing, togetherness, bonding, and joy, akin to the *communitas* described by Victor Turner. Gentlemen provided wine and beer, and joined in the streets in the drinking of it. The rich distributed largesse to the poor. Common tables were set up in the streets for a feast of commensality. Taps and barrels were set up in the market place for all to enjoy. Alcoholic beverages were a consistent and essential part of the proceedings, loosening social and behavioural bonds. Civic officials from mayors down to constables, the custodians of order who normally undertook the suppression of unruliness and the maintenance of decorum, were here sponsoring drunken parties in public places. John Hacket recalled when 'bacchanals of drunken riot were kept too much in London and Westminster' in October 1623, and quoted St Augustine, '*Publicum gaudium celebratur per publicum dedecus*'.[33]

If there were two cultures in Stuart England, a culture of licence and a culture of reformation, they achieved temporary harmony. The return of Prince Charles created a moment of fellowship between the respectable and the disreputable, reformers and reprobates, the sober and the debauched. Gentlemen and commoners, rich and poor, prince and people, became temporarily bonded in a moment of rapture. For the prince, and perhaps for the world, this was alleged as a second birth, a renewal. People were said to be besides themselves, or out of themselves, on the brink of frenzy. Finally, and significantly, the condemned were reprieved, prisoners were released, those on their way to death were given life. The 'second birth' of the prince meant a second chance of life for some of his lowliest subjects. Though a conventional gesture, familiar on other royal occasions, this act of mercy was an indispensable part in the improvised ritual of the prince's homecoming.

Behind these activities, and guiding contemporary interpretation of them, may have been a hidden homology with 'the return of the prodigal son' as its operative motif. There are striking parallels between the events of October 1623 and those recited in Luke, chapter fifteen. 'Bring hither the fatted calf, and kill it; and let us eat and be merry,' said the father on the return of the prodigal son. 'It was meet that we should make merry, and be glad: for this thy brother was dead, and is alive again; and was lost, and is found.' Although no preacher is known to have made the comparison to the prince, and perhaps none dared utter it, the parable of the returning prodigal could easily have come to mind. It was a favourite topic in sermons. The official homily 'on the miserie of man', regularly recited in churches since the reign of Elizabeth, and reprinted in London in 1623, invoked the parable of the prodigal son. Plays of *The Prodigal Son* were part of the repertory of early seventeenth-century acting companies. Richard Brathwaite's meditation, *The Prodigals Teares*, was sufficiently popular to have been reprinted in 1619.[34] As in the parable, so in Stuart England, the prodigal's behaviour (Charles's outrageous excursion to Spain) was forgiven and forgotten in the rejoicing at his safe return. In October 1623, as in the parable, the homecoming indicated celebration, revelry, and rebirth.

★

What difference did it make? When the bonfires died down, when the bells were silenced, and when the hangover headaches began to fade, had anything changed? The return of Prince Charles hardly ushered in a new order. The euphoria was transitory. Life went on much as before. Yet the national consensus on foreign affairs which emerged in 1624, with court, city and parliament agreed on an aggressive anti-Spanish policy (the old king dissenting), may have some relation to the events of the previous October.[35] Indeed, the very activity of public celebration may have helped that consensus to take shape in the streets of the City of London and in the country at large. The revelry around the bonfires may have facilitated a coalescing of popular and political opinion, though it was not to last long.

Charles and his people soon had other events to distract and divide them, among them a French Catholic marriage, a coronation, and a new and troubled reign. But the October miracle was not permitted to disappear from memory. Almanac writers and anniversary preachers kept the event in view as a valuable rousing symbol, at least until Charles Stuart ceased to be convincing as an anti-Catholic hero. In Protestant memory the important thing was Charles's homecoming, his coming safe ashore, rather than the joyous celebration. The puritan Nehemiah Wallington recalled, 'great was the enterprise and hazard of our gracious prince into Spain, but greater was God's mercy to guard him back again'.[36] For Wallington, compiling his 'Bundle of Mercies' (probably in the 1640s), October 1623 was a providential moment in the tradition of 1588 and 1605.

The calendar was a store of significant days and sympathetic similarities, providing regular occasions for pious commemoration. In the politicized calendar of the seventeenth century, 5 October never rivalled 5 November as an annual occasion for Protestant-patriotic festivity, yet many commentators of the mid-1620s saw connections between the prince's homecoming and England's deliverance from the Gunpowder Plot. Charles had landed in England on the fifth, to be greeted in London the next day. 'Memorable therefore ever amongst us be the fifth day of October, for our prince his joyful arrival here in England . . . As those two other fifth days stand remarkable to the end of the world; viz. the fifth of August [Gowry Conspiracy], and fifth of November; the first for the particular preservation of our king; the second for the general delivery of our country. Let one red letter more be now added to our calendar, and an anniversary held with thanksgiving to God, and with bells and bonfires, testifying the joy of the people in memory of so inestimable happiness'. Thus from the author of *The Ioyfull Returne*.[37]

In the same vein Stephen Jerome adapted his 5 November sermon in 1623 into a paean for the homecoming of Prince Charles and a plea for its annual commemoration. 'Let the day of our preservation from the Powder Treason, of the coronation of our king, the reduction of the prince, be to us as the Jews' Purim, let them be writ in red letters, inserted in our calendar, but for ever these mercies with their memorials, let them be . . . ingraven . . . in the tablets of our grateful hearts, perpetuated traditionally to our children's children'.[38]

During the next two decades the anniversary of the return from Spain seems to have been honoured as one of King Charles's special

days, rather as the 5 August anniverary of the Gowry conspiracy had
been special for James I. Ringing the bells on that day was a voluntary
matter, not widely performed, but a few prominent parishes made 5
or 6 October part of their local calendar. Great St Mary's, Cambridge,
the university church, rang its bells to the accompaniment of bonfires
on 5 October during the 1630s. St Margaret Westminster, the parish
church of parliament when parliament was sitting, also rang 'for joy of
his majesty's safe return from Spain' more than a dozen years after it
happened. In 1637 the churchwardens paid five shillings 'for ringing
on the sixth of October, being the day that the king's majesty landed in
England at his highness' return from Spain'. Similar payments were
made as late as 1643, with a brief revival during the post-war political
crisis in October 1647.

Almanac makers also took the cue, recalling the events of 1623 well
into the 1640s. The return of Prince Charles warranted two entries in
Jonathan Dove's Cambridge almanac for 1641. Dove's 'chronological
description of many things worthy of memory' recalled that in 1623,
'our noble king Charles (then Prince) having been in Spain, arrived safely
in England on the 5 of October'. And the calendar section of the almanac
dignified October 5 with the red-letter entry, 'K. C. ret. fr. Sp.' Richard
Allestree, in *A New Almanacke and Prognostication, for . . . 1628*, included
'the happy return of King Charles from Spain' among the momentous
historical events commemorated in his 'compendious chronology of
years to this year 1628'. Charles's return from his embarrassing and
unsuccessful attempt to marry the Spanish Infanta was solemnly listed
alongside such other significant moments as, 'since the creation of the
world, 5598 . . . since the destruction of Sodom with fire and brimstone,
3543 . . . since Duke William conquered England, 562 . . . since the
beginning of Blessed Queen Elizabeth's Reign, 70 . . . since the Camp at
Tilbury, 39,' and 'since the Damnable Powder Treason, November 5,
23' years.[39] Other almanacs of the pre-war period similarly placed
Charles Stuart's miraculous homecoming among the more significant
events of human history.

The compendious chronology was not simply padding, nor was it
intended for idle amusement. Like the anniversary bellringing, it
served a solemn didactic function. The table reminded the reader of the
passage of time, of the purposeful working out of providence over the
years and centuries. It allowed the English reader to place his country's
recent political and religious history in a scheme of events stretching
back to the creation of the world and, by implication, looking forward
to its end. As a history text and as a reference guide, the almanac
presented important information, even if the constellation of events
varied among different publications.

From the viewpoint of English Protestants in the 1620s the previous hundred years contained a compacted history of combat between the forces of God and the forces of the devil, between Christ and anti-Christ, light and dark. English history since the Reformation had become foreshortened and crowded with significant moments, as time accelerated towards the present. The accession of Queen Elizabeth marked the deliverance of England from a Catholic monarchy, the end of the dark and fiery days of Queen Mary. The Camp at Tilbury in 1588 symbolized England's resistance to the Spanish Armada, and the triumph of English Protestantism over the powers of the Counter-Reformation. Gunpowder Treason day, vigorously commemorated throughout the seventeenth century, marked the providential deliverance of England and the house of Stuart from the diabolical machinations of Guy Fawkes and the Catholic conspirators. Each of these events was a hinge-point in time, a resolution of critically dangerous uncertainty, a moment when English history was fatefully determined. So with October 1623.

Understanding one's place in time required periodically recalling these crucial events to memory. During the second quarter of the seventeenth century, until overwhelmed by other events, the return of Prince Charles was remembered as one more manifestation of God's providence in delivering England from the twin embrace of Rome and Spain. Charles's homecoming, for those who witnessed it, was extraordinary and uplifting. As an emblem event, it was to be savoured as 'this great miracle of our latter age'.

7
THE SPANISH ARMADA – ANXIETY, DELIVERANCE AND COMMEMORATION

If the return of Prince Charles was a moment of exhilaration that quickly faded, the collapse of the Spanish Armada was the opposite. This was an episode that became magnified with memory, and which took its place, alongside the deliverances of 1558 and 1605, among the pattern of providences and mercies that underlay the Protestant calendar. Celebration was relatively quiet and hesitant in 1588, due to the exigencies of war, but in years to come the deliverance was cheered as a centrepiece of the English national legend. As if to compensate for the belated and tentative nature of the initial rejoicing, 1588 was memorialized by later generations as a providential moment, a signal event, a triumph for English Protestantism, that coloured sermons and historical writing for centuries. Invested with mythic properties, the events of 1588 were taken as confirmation of the special destiny reserved for God's Englishmen.

The 'miraculous deliverance' of 1588 was a reflection on England's vulnerability as well as God's remarkable favour to his Protestant island. Given the balance of forces, especially the weakness of England's domestic defences, it was reasonable to fear that the enemy would prevail. In order to understand the overwhelming sense of relief that swept across England after the failure of the Spanish Armada, we must first assess the fears and apprehensions that gripped the country as the invasion fleet approached. We can then turn to the rejoicing, and its amplification in subsequent years.

In the spring of 1588 it was no secret that Philip II, with papal support, was preparing a mighty sea-borne army to invade England. News of 'la felicissima Armada' circulated throughout Europe, and England braced for its expected onslaught. The Council was busy with instructions to the county lieutenants and their deputies, relaying anxiety about the Spanish invasion from the inner circles of policy and intelligence to the outer reaches of the political nation. The entire matrix of command was stirred and agitated, if not effectively

110

mobilized to action. 'Whereas the Queen is given to understand the continuement of the great preparations of the king of Spain which are thought to be intended towards these parts,' the Council ordered on 2 April 'a survey of all the horsemen and trained men' in each county.[1]

Captains took stock of the local inventories of arms and equipment. Muster masters prepared to ready and stiffen the shire militias. Inevitably there were shortages and difficulties, and the usual bumbling, blundering and recalcitrance of unwilling and unpractised volunteers. Equipment was missing, people were ill prepared. It was difficult for ordinary people in the rural heartland to appreciate the urgency of the international situation, and a state approximating national readiness was only sluggishly obtained.

The Earl of Huntington wrote in April about the inadequacy of the Yorkshire musters and the reluctance of the gentry to commit their purse and persons 'for the defence of the realm against invasion'. Chester and Lancashire were 'ill supplied with munitions'. The county of Southampton, directly exposed to the prospect of attack, was reported 'very rawly furnished' with military equipment. At Dover the troops were in the wrong place, under divided command, and prone to desertion. Walsingham told Burghley on 19 June how sorry he was 'to see so great a danger hanging over the realm so slightly regarded and so carelessly provided for'. That month, in an attempt to inspire more active involvement, the Queen sent a general letter, through the Lord Lieutenants, reminding the gentry of what was at stake: 'country, liberty, wife, children, lands, life, and . . . the profession of the true and reformed religion'.[2]

Despite these efforts England never assembled an army that could counter the forces of the Duke of Parma. The great camp at Tilbury was not in proper order until early August, by which time the Armada had already passed. Later in 1588, after the immediate danger was over, several commentators expressed relief that English defences had not been put to the test. Robert Greene, author of *The Spanish Masquerado*, saw the Armada as a jolt to English complacency, 'to waken us out of our dreams'.[3] Knowledge of the ill-preparation of England's land forces only heightened the subsequent interpretation of 1588 as a miraculous deliverance.

The navy, by contrast, was in fine fighting fettle. English ships were nimbler and better handled than their Spanish counterparts, and quick-firing guns could keep the heavier Spanish galleons at bay. The English navy possessed important tactical and strategic advantages over the Spanish, but these were not clearly apparent at the time. Only with hindsight could naval historians conclude that Drake and

Howard had history on their side. And revisionists have begun to doubt even this proposition.[4]

Intelligence reached the Council at Greenwich on 15 June that 'the king of Spain's navy is already abroad on the seas'. Where it might land and what it might do was a matter of conjecture. Philip's Armada 'may take some course to make some attempt on such part of the realm as shall be thought fit for his purpose, whereby as yet we cannot know any certainly'. The most frightening prospect was that the Armada might sail into the mouth of the Thames, taking the isles of Thanet and Sheppey in Kent as bases from which to attack London. Defensive plans focused on a barricade across the river, with the Tilbury encampment on the north side. If the enemy landed elsewhere he would be virtually unopposed. Leicester lacked the authority to command any troops to repel an invasion in Suffolk or Kent.[5]

Instructions raced from the Privy Council to the county lieutenants to put all their forces on alert. Sir Christopher Hatton, as Lord Lieutenant of Northamptonshire, immediately relayed the order that 'all the gentlemen that are captains and leaders of men in that county' should not leave the shire and should be ready for action 'upon an hour's warning'.[6] Northamptonshire was an inland county, which would be spared the first brunt of any Spanish invasion, but its hastily armed forces would augment Leicester's makeshift army at Tilbury.

Preparations were in hand for a national chain of signal communications to announce the arrival of the Armada. Beacons were set up in coastal and inland counties alike, 'in places accustomed,' on the ridges, hilltops, and church towers that commanded clear lines of sight. Old and decayed beacons were to be repaired; all would be fitted with 'barrels, links and other necessaries' to set them ablaze; watchmen were appointed to attend them 'both day and night,' with constables and justices on hand to guard against false alarms and to secure an orderly response when the dreaded moment came. As a set of signals the beacons were primitive but efficient; as a summons to disciplined action they were found wanting. One observer recalled that 'upon the firing of the beacons (whereby an alarm was given), the country people, forthwith, ran down to the seaside, some with clubs, some with picked staves and pitchforks, all unarmed, and they that were best appointed were but with a bill, a bow, and a sheaf of arrows, no captain or commander appointed to direct, lead or order them'.[7] Heaven help them if they ever came face to face with a Spanish battalion.

Reports reached Plymouth on 19 July that the Armada had been sighted off the Scillies, and when the watchers along the south coast sighted the Armada in the Channel on the morning of 20 July their beacons flamed the message to London and to all strategic points inland. That, at least, is the traditional story. Illustrations made soon after the event show blazing beacons with columns of smoke along the headlands, but some scholars question whether the beacons were ever fired. Accurate news of the approaching Armada was relayed by post-horse.[8]

As invasion loomed closer the English looked to prayer as well as to military preparations. On 23 July the Council ordered all bishops and pastors in the Province of Canterbury 'to move their auditories and parishioners to join in public prayers to almighty God, the giver of victories, to assist us against the malice of our enemies'. A week later the Stationers registered 'A godlie prayer, for the preservation of the quenes maiestie, and for her Armyes both by sea and lande against the Enymies of the Churche and this Realme of England'. Prayers were written for use in all parish churches, on Wednesdays and Fridays, imploring 'deliverance and good success'.[9] These prayers formed a new national litany in the sombre summer of 1588. They served, at one level, to alert and to warn the country and to bring about a pious and determined national consensus. At another level they appear as an attempt to rally God, to fore-guess his purposes, and to argue him into a definitive tilt in favour of England. Given the shambles of England's military preparations, prayer was, perhaps, the most promising line of defence.

Richard Rogers, the godly minister of Wethersfield, Essex, was one who found refuge in prayer and fasting when his parishioners rushed to the coast to face the threatened invasion. On 4 August he confided to his diary, 'the troubles are so great as we are every day and hour fearing them coming upon us'. And on 13 August, perhaps after visiting the camp at Tilbury, he wrote, 'if anything may be fit to stir one up to the continual and earnest meditation of a godly life, this may be it: that we are now in peril of goods, liberty, life, by our enemies the Spaniards, and at home papists in multitudes ready to come upon us unawares'. The only refuge lay with the Lord.[10]

Oliver Pigge, another East Anglian puritan, wrote prayers of sorrow, appealing to God for the safety of England. He desperately wanted to understand God's purposes, to decode the message of events. England's sins, Pigge believed, deserved chastizement, so the Armada could legitimately be seen as an instrument of God's wrath. But England, for all its faults, was the only upholder of God's true church, whereas the Spaniards were obviously God's enemies. In the past God has been generous to England with his 'ancient mercies' and he would not want them wasted. 'Spare this sinful nation' was Pigge's appeal. 'Try us once more, that our magistrates and ministers may in their callings reform whatsoever is amiss.'[11]

The widely used official 'prayer to be delivered from our enemies' moved from an acknowledgment of the country's manifold sins to a reminder of God's previous mercies. Surely there was purpose and pattern in God's 'preserving our most gracious queen, thine hand-maid, so miraculously from so many conspiracies, perils and dangers'. The prayer then developed a plea for further divine intervention. 'And especially, O Lord, let thine enemies know, and make them confess, that thou hast received England (which they, most of all for thy gospel's sake, do malign) into thine own protection. Set, we pray thee, O Lord, a wall about it, and evermore mightily defend it.' Finally, moving easily from sixteenth-century England to ancient Israel, the prayer recalled God's assistance to Abraham, to Joshua, and, most pertinently, to David against Goliath. A prayer of more limited circulation, used in the queen's chapel, argued forcefully for God to show himself on the English side. 'The cause is thine, the enemies thine, the afflicted thine; the honour, victory and triumph shall be thine.' Influenced by the national-Protestant paradigm of Foxe's *Acts and Monuments*, the interpretative schema for England's 'deliverance' was already in place before the events of August 1588.[12]

★

The Armada fight is an oft-told story. How the English under Lord Howard of Effingham harrassed the Spaniards as they sailed down the Channel in crescent formation, how the nimbler handling and the longer-range guns of the English ships reduced the confidence and eroded the cohesion of the Spanish fleet, how a chastened Armada took refuge in Calais Roads, to be scourged there by English fire-ships, and how Drake and the other captains hurled destruction at the floundering Spanish at the battle of Gravelines, this is the stuff of national legend. Remembered, too, is the sudden storm, 'the Protestant wind,' that scattered the invincible Spanish Armada. Of Philip's invasion fleet, consisting of one hundred and thirty vessels, only fifty-three returned to Spain.

We know, in retrospect, that this was victory. The anticipated Spanish invasion was averted. Medina Sidonia's seaborne army never made contact with Parma's forces in the Netherlands. The Spanish fleet was crippled, and the remnant embarked on its perilous course up the North Sea and homeward in disgrace by way of Scotland and Ireland. But military observers of the time could be certain neither that the Armada was destroyed nor that England was saved. The matter was still unresolved, and the Spanish threat was as menacing as ever.

The fight up the Channel had been confused and inconclusive, with much expenditure of shot but few reliable reports of damage. The

English could claim a few prizes, like Drake's *Nuestra Senora del Rosario*, but until the battle of Gravelines they could do little more than pick on Spanish stragglers. Medina Sidonia's fleet was fundamentally intact when it reached the narrows of the Channel off Calais, and the prospect of his fulfilling his mission seemed good. The Duke of Parma's passivity, the flaws in the Spanish command structure, and the serious logistical problems of the Spanish forces, all worked to the English advantage, but no English strategist could appreciate this at the time. A Spanish invasion was still an immediate possibility, and the means to accomplish it had not yet been destroyed.

The Spanish fleet escaped from the fire-ships on the night of 28 July, in considerable disorder it is true, but ready to fight again. The next day, off Gravelines, they fought desperately against the English guns. After a full day of battle, ravaged by English cannon, the Armada re-established its formation and stood away into the North Sea. Though weakened and depleted it was still unvanquished as a fighting force, and was still thought capable of joining up with the Spanish army in Flanders. Historians know that the Armada was severely wounded, and that it would be further shattered by weather on its long way home, but the English did not know this at the time, and would not for several weeks. In his report on the battle of Gravelines, Lord Howard reported only tentative progress, 'their force is wonderful great and strong; and yet we pluck their feathers little and little'. Drake, too, was pleased with the day but expected to have to fight again. A week and a half later the military appraisals were generally pessimistic. Captain Henry Whyte complained to Walsingham on 18 August that, 'our parsimony at home hath bereaved us of the famousest victory that ever our nation had at sea'. Walsingham wrote irritably to Hatton of English dishonour and a job only half done.[13] The Spanish Armada had escaped, and rumours abounded that Parma's invasion was still on. Given the circumstances, it is understandable that the bells did not ring for victory in August 1588, but still tolled solemnly for vigilance and prayer.

When Elizabeth came to Tilbury, then, on 8 and 9 August, it was not to celebrate a triumph but to rally her forces in a continuing campaign. She appeared 'full of princely resolution, and more than feminine courage . . . like some Amazonian Empress . . . full fraught with manly spirit'. Elizabeth's famous speech, the most inspiring and proudly remembered of her reign, placed the queen herself 'in the midst and heat of battle,' and looked forward in defiance to engagement with the might of Spain. This performance took place on 9 August, eleven days after the Armada had departed from Gravelines, but before the realization sunk in that the crisis was past.[14] Rumours still circulated about Spanish landings and an expected invasion in Kent.

Accordingly, the literary propaganda that accompanied these events was martial and blustering, in line with the notion that the country must brace for a siege. 'Regard your duties! Think to your country's good!/And fear not in defence thereof, to spend your dearest blood,' wrote Thomas Deloney. Deloney's 'joyful new ballad declaring the happy obtaining of the great Galleazzo . . . through the mighty power and providence of God was entered at Stationers' Hall on 10 August, together with his poem describing 'the Queen's visiting of the camp at Tilbury'.[15] These seized on tokens of victory, of victory yet to come.

Awareness that England was safe, that deliverance was given, was slow in coming. There was no single moment that signalled victory, no particular day when the Spanish menace lifted. It was only in retrospect that the scale of the deliverance became apparent. By the middle of August the immediate danger was over, with the remnants of the Armada beating their way to the north of Scotland. There would be no invasion, at least for the present. Leicester wrote to Shrewsbury on 15 August that 'God hath also fought mightily for her Majesty', and hoped that the Spanish would be 'too much daunted to follow their pretended enterprise'.[16] The English could breathe with relief and stand down their forces. The Tilbury army dispersed, its patriotic duty done. The Northants militia were allowed to return home on 19 August.

Yet England was still at war, facing the most formidable enemy in Europe. There were still traitors to deal with at home and the massed forces of Antichrist overseas. Even the breaking and scattering of the Armada, however miraculous, might only delay a renewed Spanish onslaught. The failure of the Armada meant respite, not victory. As late as 21 August, when the collapse of the Armada was widely known, the Stationers entered 'Psalmes of invocation upon God to preserve her Maiestie and the people of this Land from the power of her enemies'. In September the Council heard reports that the Armada, by this time off Scotland, was planning to return to the narrow seas; and in October there was intelligence that the Armada was planning to return next spring.[17]

In Oliver Pigge's opinion, 'the hatred and malice of the Spaniards and his partakers is not yet quenched, but rather we may be assured, much more increased, so as they will but wait opportunity to set upon us again'. Anthony Marten's *Exhortation, to stirr up the mindes of all her Maiesties faithfull subjects, to defend their countrey in this dangerous time, from the invasion of enemies* was written, did he know it, *after the*

Armada had collapsed. The danger continued, despite the apparent failure of Spain's enterprise, and the time still called for the English to arm and to strengthen themselves. 'Though the Dragon be driven into his den, yet is his sting and poison still in force. Though they be chased and repelled for a time, yet their malice and fury abideth.' Indeed, one benefit of the Armada crisis, in Marten's eyes, was that 'it hath stirred up our minds to look to ourselves' and to put England on a war footing.[18] With adjustments for image and metaphor, this was a ground upon which puritan preachers and privy councillors could agree.

★

In the summer of 1588 the English prayed for deliverance, and the Lord responded to their prayers. Their request for a sign that God had taken England into his special protection was gloriously granted through his scattering of the Spanish fleet. The God of Abraham, Joshua, and King David had spoken decisively for Elizabeth and England, and his favour would never be forgotten. The victory over the Spanish Armada produced a round of celebration in 1588 and a flood of commemoration and embellishment in the generations that followed.

Public thanksgivings began late in August 1588 and built to a crescendo three months later. The national mood shifted from anxiety to exhilaration as the scale of the deliverance became apparent. Thanksgiving services proclaimed the victory, and explained to the nation at large the deliverance that had befallen. They served, too, to marshall opinion and to interpret God's blessings as an overwhelming endorsement of the Elizabethan regime. All credit for the victory was given to God. The celebrations were not for the triumph of English arms but for the signal mercy shown to England by an anglophile divinity. The Spanish Armada was reputedly invincible, yet Israel's God, through his providence, had prevented its success. God had humbled the Catholics and deflected the force of their enterprise against England.

Dean Alexander Nowell preached at St Paul's on 20 August, giving thanks and praise to God 'for our great victory by him given to our English nation, by the overthrow of the Spanish fleet'. This officially sponsored service was valuable in shaping opinion at a time when news was incomplete and contradictory. On Sunday, 8 September (the day after the queen's birthday), a special service of thanksgiving was held at St Paul's, with visual evidence to support the spoken word. 'Eleven of the Spanish ensigns (the once proud badges of their bravery, but now of their vanity) were hung upon the lower battlements of that church, as palms of praise for England's deliverance'.[19] The following day these same captured Spanish flags were flaunted on London bridge, to the delight of those passing to Southwark fair. In fact, at this time, there was little more to show for the fight in the Channel than a dozen Spanish ensigns. Their display was didactic as well as decorative, with more than a touch of bravado.

Later in the autumn, when the Armada was known definitely to have been destroyed, publications began to appear proclaiming victory. The tone of worried defiance that had marked the summer publications gave way to jubilation in the autumn. The presses now took flight with joyful and celebratory items. A new tone was adopted in such works as 'The late wonderfull dystres whiche the Spanishe Navye sustayned yn the late fight in the Sea, and upon the west coaste of Ireland in this moneth of September 1588'. This told of the further misfortunes of the shattered Armada as the remnants of that fleet attempted to make their way home. On 7 October the Stationers registered 'A Ballad of thankes givinge unto God, for his mercy toward hir maiestie begynnynge *Reiocye England*'. On 3 November appeared 'A ballad of the most happy Victory obtained over the Spaniards and their overthrowe in July last 1588'. On 21 November came 'A newe ballad of Englands Joy and delight, in the back Rebound of the Spanyardes spyght'. James Aske's remarkable *Elizabetha Triumphans* appeared in the Stationers' register on 23 November, to be followed by joyful songs and sonnets relating the queen's triumphant reception by the City of London.[20]

At the end of September the Privy Council summoned the bishops of Salisbury and Lincoln to Westminster to help plan a national thanksgiving. 'Her majesty hath thought it very necessary that certain sermons should be made of thanksgiving to God in the late victory it hath pleased him to give her majesty against the forces of the Spanish king.' By 3 November the Council was ready to order the clergy 'to appoint some special day wherein all the realm might concur in giving public and general thanks unto God, with all devotion and inward affection of heart and humbleness for his gracious favour extended towards us, in our deliverance and defence in the wonderful overthrow [and] destruction showed by his mighty hand on our malicious enemies, the Spaniards, who had sought to invade and make a conquest of the realm'.[21]

It was not until late in November, a quarter of a year after the collapse of the Armada, that the government felt ready to sponsor a major public thanksgiving. Why the festivities came so late in the year is open to question. Perhaps such an event required several months of planning. More likely it was timed to coincide with Elizabeth's accession day in November, the thirtieth anniversary of her reign. It was also affected by the Privy Council's sense of the international situation, and the need to demonstrate the unity of England to observers at home and abroad.

Crownation day on 17 November 1588, inaugurating the thirty-first year of Elizabeth's reign, was, conventionally, 'another day of joy'. Bells rang nationwide, but the queen, though expected, made no appearance at Sunday services at St Paul's. She may have been reserving her energies for the major celebrations later in the week. Antonia de Vega, a Spanish agent in London, reported that 'every year on the 17th November the Queen celebrates the feast of her coronation; and this year on the 19th, which is St Elizabeth's day, she determined to hold another festival, in celebration of the recent events. There was a great public procession, jousts, and great bonfires all over the city.' (Elizabeth of Hungary, though not a saint in the anglican calendar, had virtues that might be associated with the English queen, except that St Elizabeth was renowned as a wife and mother, as well as a monarch.) John Stow records that Tuesday, 19 November 'was this year kept holy day throughout the realm, with sermons, singing of psalms, bonfires, etc., for joy and a thanksgiving unto God for the overthrow of the Spaniards, our enemies on the sea'.[22] It was, in fact, a compound festivity, a victory celebration and a thirty-year jubilee.

The following Sunday, 24 November, Elizabeth rode from Whitehall to St Paul's, 'attended upon by her Privy Council, the nobility, the French ambassador, the judges, the heralds, with noise of trumpets, sitting in a chariot like a throne, made with four pillars, drawn with four white horses'. Her procession dramatically presented the survival and triumph of the Tudor crown and government. This week of general thanksgiving services and triumphal processions in London was echoed in the English provinces. Chester held a special service in the cathedral on 19 November, 'all shops, taverns and tippling houses being shut up all that day lest through any worldly occasion those who were not fully grounded in good heale might withdraw themselves from that most godly action'. At Shrewsbury it was recorded that 'all people that day kept it holy unto the Lord that had given her majesty such victory'.[23]

The impression from local records is that the Armada celebrations in 1588 were more solemn than jubilant, and that the festivities were conducted in a minor key. Churchwardens' accounts, which were quick to show payments for bonfires and bells 'when the traitors were taken', rarely record extra ringing for the Armada deliverance. Many pass 1588 as though nothing unusual had happened. Some borough chamberlains noted joyful observances, but little on the scale one might expect. Most evidence confirms the view that the victory reverberated more in memory than in the bell towers of the time. In the Devonshire parishes of Tavistock and Westbury, where the Armada might be expected to have made a vivid impression, crownation day passed with the usual ringing and drinking but no festivities were noted specifically for deliverance. So too in most parishes throughout the country. At Baldock, Hertfordshire, the bells of St Peter rang in 1588 'for our good success against the Spaniards', but with less charge than the annual ringing on 17 November. At Shillington, Bedfordshire, the churchwardens allowed 5d. 'for drink for the ringers the 19th of November', less than half the sum they spent on crownation day. At Swaffham, Norfolk, they dignified 'the rejoicing day' in 1588 by buying an extra candle.[24]

Major towns did better. Salisbury had ringing on 19 November 'for the great victory against the Spaniards by the mighty hand of God'. In the parish of St Thomas the expenditure on ringing matched that of the crownation day, and surpassed it when the cost of 'the ringers' breakfast' is taken into consideration. At Nottingham there were bonfires and bells in 1588, although whether these were directly related to the Armada is unclear. At Norwich the parish of St Peter Mancroft spent 5s. 4d. for two rounds of ringing 'on the victory day that the Lord gave us over the Spaniards, appointed by her majesty'. Other Norwich parishes rang dutifully 'upon the day of triumph for the Spanish victory'.

Norwich was one of the few places to adopt an annual commemoration of 1588. This was, apparently, a local initiative. Norwich parishes, which already celebrated the anniversary of Ket's rebellion, thenceforth added the Armada to their civic calendar. The mayor appointed 26 September for an annual thanksgiving. Shops were to close while the citizens partook of 'preaching and thanksgiving for so gracious deliverance'. During the 1590s the bells rang and the waits sang 'on the day of thanksgiving for driving away and discomforting the huge and great navy of Spaniards'. In most parishes, however, even in Norwich, the day of triumph over the Spanish Armada became entwined with the 7 September and 17 November celebrations for the queen. 'Triumphing day' in Salisbury served both functions. In 1589 the townsmen of Northampton staged a 'a warlike fight . . . in honour of victory over the Spanish Armada', a commemorative pageant which was not repeated.[25]

★

Deliverance from the Spanish Armada prompted patriotic prayers and sermons. Preachers made it an occasion to reflect on God's mercy, and to turn away from superstition and sin. Sermons mixed appeals to English xenophobia, anti-Catholicism, affection for the monarch, indignation that anyone should lay an attempt against England, and the lurid image of atrocities to follow should any attempt succeed. A much-repeated theme was the parallel of God's favour to England and his earlier favour to the Jews.

Robert Humston, a Norfolk minister, preached on 22 September comparing 'the excellency of this work and mercy of God towards this nation' to God's special treatment of Israel. The deliverance granted to England was comparable to the deliverances in the Bible. In the Armada summer, as Humston saw it, 'our enemies came against us as fierce as the wolves in the evening, or as the eagles greedy of their prey, with purpose, had not the Lord in mercy prevented them, to have taken away and trampled under feet the glorious Gospel of Christ, and to have erected superstition and idolatry in all our land, to have bereft us of our most lawful and loving sovereign, the Lord's annointed queen, and to have turned our inheritance to heathenish strangers, to have invaded our country with Edom's alarm.'[26] God had saved England, so England should turn to God.

Richard Rogers wrote in his diary on 26 October, 'I have been oft times well moved with thinking on our late deliverance from the rage of Spain, as memorable a work of God as ever was in any my remembrance.' As Israel, so us. 'If God had not then been on our side, we had not been here to enjoy his blessings, but had been swallowed up.'[27]

In the same vein were Oliver Pigge's 'meditations concerning thanksgiving', written late in 1588 and printed the following year. Pigge's earlier prayers for England's safety appeared miraculously to have been answered. Like many of his brethren, Pigge held up the Old Testament as a mirror to English history. God's mercy to Protestant England drew to mind a host of Biblical parallels and precedents, from Moses to Mordecai, but this was not a source of unallayed optimism. Had not the Jews ultimately lost God's favour and suffered catastrophe? So might the English, Israel's successor, unless they embraced reformation.[28]

From the queen's printers came *A Psalme and Collect of thanksgiving, not vnmeet for this present time: to be said or sung in Churches*. This was a selection and reordering of extracts from the psalms, sometimes substituting 'England' for Israel and 'our queen' for King David. Strung together they told a story of 'subtle and cruel enemies' whose massed forces were devastated by the Lord. The official 'prayer of thanksgiving' also reminded churchgoers of the fundamental evil of

England's enemies. The Spanish 'came with most cruel intent and purpose to destroy us, our cities, towns, countries, and people; and utterly to root out the memory of our nation from off the earth for ever. And withal wholly to suppress thy holy word and blessed gospel of thy dear Son our Saviour Jesus Christ. Which they being drowned in idolatry and superstition, do hate most deadly.' The image of the Spanish being 'drowned' in idolatry was especially telling, now that news was coming in of the Spanish wrecks off Ireland. The official prayer also cited England's sins and called for 'the amendment of our lives', but without much enthusiasm.[29] It was a delicate matter to use the Armada victory to advance patriotic piety, without lending support to puritan programmes for reform.

The triumph over the Spanish Armada became a constant theme in sermons and histories, not only for the Armada generation but for a hundred years thereafter. The Spanish enterprise, as Anthony Marten saw it, was 'such as, I suppose, in that kind, hath scarcely been heard of or read of, since the beginning of the world, against any nation'. For Maurice Kyffin it was a turning point in English history, 'a miracle of mighty magnitude, done by the dreadful power of God's right hand'. It was a covenant, a sign that England and English Protestantism would prevail.[30] The deliverance of 1588 was forcefully imprinted on the English national memory. It was not institutionalized, there being no 'Armada day', but the horror of the invasion attempt and the miracle of God's judgment were too remarkable to be forgotten.

The 'prayer of thanksgiving' of 1588 promised everlasting gratitude, 'we never forgetting, but bearing in perpetual memory this thy merciful protection and deliverance of us'. Citing Psalm 107, the English promised to 'offer unto [God] the sacrifice of thanksgiving and tell out his works with gladness'. Oliver Pigge hoped that 'continually we may stir up our selves to thankfulness, and to speak of it to our children, and they to their children's children, that so the memory of this thy glorious fact may be continued from generation to generation on even for ever'. In later times just to mention '88 was sufficient to recall and compress all the mercies and providences of that wonderful year. Speaking in parliament in 1593 about 'great imminent perils and dangers', Robert Cecil reviewed 'things past of late years and since eighty-eight'.[31]

Memories of 1588 also served to inflame anti-Catholicism and hatred and fear of the Spaniards. English observations about Spanish cruelty had all the features of a black legend, depicting the enemy as wolves, dragons, and other malicious beasts. The official 'prayer of thanksgiving' cited the malice, force, fraud, and cruelty of our enemies, 'bent on despoliation' and 'the end of our nation'. The psalm of thanksgiving cast the Spaniards as 'cruel enemies, intending nothing but bloodshed and murder', and the English as 'sheep appointed to the shambles and slaughter' were it not for God's intervention. In Thomas Deloney's works 'these devilish tyrants' were bent on 'extreme villainy'. They meant to 'kill and murder' and 'deflower our virgins' as well as to destroy the English crown and religion. Spanish ships were said to be laden with 'strange and most cruel whips' with which they intended 'to whip and torment English men and women'.[32]

The counterpart to this hostile caricature was an idealized picture of Elizabethan England, a blend of Arcadia and the land of Canaan. 'We may each of us sit peaceably under our own vines and fig trees, enjoying our wives, our children, our friends, our liberties, and many other blessings yielded to us in this most fruitful and pleasant land,' wrote Oliver Pigge towards the end of 1588, relieved that his sovereign was secure and his religion intact. England, in Robert Greene's view, 'defended by God, and governed by so virtuous a princess as God hath chosen after his own heart, standeth and withstandeth their forces'. In this favoured and blessed nation 'our cities are full of joy, and our children are seen sporting in the streets; peace and plenty flourisheth in England, and all our land floweth with milk and honey'.[33]

Greene's *The Spanish Masquerado* of 1589 was partly a history of the previous year's triumphs, but mostly a vaunting attack against Spain and Rome. The Armada was the engine of Antichrist, and its demise was a demonstration of the power and the glory of God. England, by contrast, was God's most favoured nation. Another publication of 1589 was a poem ridiculing the Spanish enterprise against England, *A Skeltonicall Salutation/Or condigne gratulation/And iust vexation/of the Spanish Nation,/That in a bravado,/Spent many a Crusado,/In setting forth an Armado/England to invado.*[34]

★

Since there was no 'Armada day', no national calendrical occasion set aside to commemorate the deliverance from the threatened Spanish invasion, there was no annual prompt for reflections on the subject. Stuart almanacs had no place for the Armada in their calendar, although they regularly noted such anniversaries as the accession of Queen Elizabeth and the Gunpowder Plot. Almanacs did serve, however, as a digest of English history, and during the seventeenth century they regularly included the Armada year in their 'compendious chronology' of 'things worthy of memory'. Attention was directed to the year '88 as a whole, rather than a special day. 'Tilbury

Camp' and the overthrow of 'Spain's Armado' were regularly listed among the most significant historical events since the flood.[35]

Seventeenth-century memorialists cherished the deliverance of 1588 as one of the principal icons in the shrine of national memory, and did not need a special day to call it to mind. The memory was kept alive by the repeated need for reassurance about England's special mission. From the accession of James I to the fall of James II, English Protestants could turn to the events of 1588 for comfort, instruction and inspiration. Nehemiah Wallington, for example, listed the defeat of the Spanish Armada at the head of the 'bundle of mercies' bestowed by God on Protestant England, although it was overshadowed by still more remarkable mercies shown to a later generation.[36]

Preaching at the beginning of the seventeenth century, on Queen Elizabeth's accession day in 1601, William Leigh prophesied, 'that *Mirabilis annus* of '88 will never be forgotten, so long as the sun and moon endureth'. Against 'that invincible navy, for preparation, might, and bloody designs, the greatest and most fearful that ever was intended,' stood England's queen and England's prayers. Against such a combination, of course, the Armada stood no chance. Their ships 'were but wood, their tacklings but hemp, their oars but reeds, and their powder but dust'. Though terrifying in its size and fire-power, the invincible Armada collapsed before the greater power of England's God. 'Thus England had the honour of the day, a day like that of Joshua, bright shining from heaven, wherein the black night of our threatened destruction was beaten back by the puissance of our prince praying, our armies fighting, and the creatures of God relieving, to make us glorious by deliverance.'[37] It took less than a dozen years, some might say less than a dozen months, for this vaunting reconstruction of history to enter the mainstream.

Early in the seventeenth century the deliverance of 1588 was confirmed and compounded by the even more remarkable deliverance from the Gunpowder Plot. Events acquired coherence by seeing them in patterns, and historically minded preachers immediately and consistently linked 1588 and 1605 in their account of the providential protection that befell God's English nation. Furthermore, the official annual commemoration of the Powder Treason on 5 November provided a calendrical occasion for recalling the earlier mercy of 1588. Armada commemorations had previously been loosely attached to Queen Elizabeth's accession day; henceforth they could be moved forward a fortnight as part of the national thanksgiving for the discovery of the plot.

In 1606 William Leigh published a meditation on the Gunpowder Treason which connected the recent deliverance to previous popish outrages. As in 1588, 'when the winds, the seas, the rocks and shelves fought for us', so now in Jacobean times God revealed his favour to Protestant England (or Great Britain, as the fashion was under the Stuarts).[38] The same connections were seen by Thomas Chapman, a pious Londoner, who endowed a set of sermons in 1616 including one to be preached 'the tenth or twelveth day of August every year by way of thankfulness unto Almighty God for his mighty and merciful deliverance of the kingdom anno 1588 from the invasion of the Spanish forces and the invincible Armado, as they falsely termed it, which sought to root out the true word of God out of this kingdom, and the truth of his holy gospel'. Chapman's other sermons commemorated the accession of Queen Elizabeth and the deliverance from the Gunpowder Plot; together they marked a powerful pattern of providential intervention in England's affairs.[39]

Michael Sparke, a popular religious writer of the 1620s, also linked 1588 and 1605 in his *Thankfull Remembrances of Gods Wonderful Deliverances of this Land* (entered 1622, 7th ed. by 1628). And, inevitably, he repeated the legend of the Spaniards who came, 'to slay our strong men, to torture our young men, to ravish our wives, and to deflower our virgins'. 'When we were even faint with sorrow, and fear over-ran the land,' then God brought deliverance. Sparke identified 7 August as the day of triumph.[40]

It became useful to invoke the memory of '88 in moments of crisis or tension. Bishop George Carleton celebrated *Octogesimus octavus mirabilis annus* in his *Thankfull Remembrance of Gods Mercy*, published in 1624 amidst calls for renewed war with Spain. 'We are now come to that fateful year, which the astrologers called the marvellous year; some said it was the climacterical year of the world.' This was the year of the cruel Spanish Armada, designed 'utterly to overthrow the church of England and state'. After almost thirty pages reviewing the manpower and firepower of the Armada, its hideous purposes, and its ultimate destruction, Carleton concluded, 'if a man with an unpartial eye look upon these, though he be an enemy, though he be a Jesuit, he must needs confess that God was on our side'. The Psalms pointed a similar message: 'the works of the Lord are great, and ought to be had in remembrance of them that fear him . . . for one generation shall praise thy works to another generation, and declare thy power'.[41] All of this was dedicated to Prince Charles, whose recent return from Spain was generally regarded as another sign of God's providence. Prince Charles, representing the younger generation, was made aware of the Elizabethan heritage that might inspire his people in the impending war. Memories of the Spanish Armada fed into the renewed wave of anti-Spanish hysteria that was sweeping through late-Jacobean and early-Caroline England.

The renewal of war and the apparent ascendancy of Antichrist in Europe in the 1620s revived memories of the sixteenth century. Elizabethan history was recast for present purposes, a tendency to which every age is prone. The radical Thomas Hooker, preaching at Chelmsford on 5 November 1626, warned that the flames of war had already scorched Bohemia, the Palatine, and Denmark, and might sear England next if her people did not return to the Lord. By invoking the memory of former deliverances, Hooker reminded people of their duty as well as their history. God 'reckons up his former mercies', warned Hooker, and he would withdraw his protection from an apostatizing England, as he did when the children of Israel declined from the Lord. Hooker insisted that 'above all other deliverance that in '88 was a great deliverance', which, like the deliverance from the Gunpowder Treason, demanded thankfulness and devout attention.[42]

Henry King, also preaching in 1626, had a more comforting message about 1588, couched in biblical-baroque rhetoric. 'When Spain rose up like a flood . . . and like a dragon in the sea . . . troubled the waters with his fleet; when every ship was ballasted with destruction, and the pregnant sails swelled with fury more than wind . . . [God] smote that multitude, whose pride was higher wrought than the seas that bare them, and by the breath of his rebuke made them fly like dust before the whirl-wind'.[43] Surely this God of deliverances would save England again from the twin scourge of enemies abroad and contagion at home?

For King in 1626, like Anthony Marten in 1588, the Armada was the 'dragon', a sea-monster, the serpent Satan, a beast of the Apocalypse, and also the creature vanquished by St George. Churchgoers in Lincolnshire could see a vivid allegory of this on a painted panel. Beneath a representation of the Armada's crescent formation in the shape of a fiery dragon, with a flag of St George in the foreground, was the inscription:

> Spain's proud Armada with great strength and power,
> Great Britain's state came gaping to devour.
> This dragon's guts like Pharoah's scattered host,
> Lay split and drowned upon the Irish coast.
> For of eight score save two ships sent from Spain,
> But twenty-five scarce sound returned again.[44]

Thomas Gataker, yet another preacher of 1626, thought that

contemporaries paid too little heed to past triumphs, even though the deliverances of 1588 and 1605 were the staple of every pulpit. 'We see too great and general a want, in these our days, of monuments and memorials of that miraculous deliverance which God wrought for this land in '88.' Gataker found his forum in the anniversary sermons at St Pancras in Soper Lane, London, endowed by Thomas Chapman; and he published *An Anniuersarie Memoriall of Englands Delivery from the Spanish Invasion* in 1626, and again in 1637. England should constantly be thankful, argued Gataker, and should keep all past mercies in mind. Memory, especially memory of providential deliverances like that of 1588, was an essential aid to godliness. The refrain, 'let us continue to be God's, that God may continue to be ours', was a commonplace of puritan preaching.[45]

Peace with Spain in 1630 did nothing to dispel the attachment of Protestant patriots to the memory of 1588. 'That year of eighty eight, Oh never spare it/To blaze the praise of that year all thy days', wrote John Vicars in 1631 in his verse panegyric entitled *Englands Hallelu-jah; or, Great Britaines Retribution*. Vicars praised 'English Israelites . . . ingrafted on old Israel's stock'. For them, the work of 'the Lord's strong arm' in defeating the Spanish Armada was a talisman and an emblem, a cause for rejoicing and a promise of greater things to come. John Rhodes, in *The Countrie Mans Comfort* published in 1637, recalled 1588 as 'the year . . . when the Devil, Pope and Spaniard did rage against our late Q[ueen] Elizabeth (never to be forgotten) and this kingdom, to have both killed us and to possess the land, and when God had so miraculously delivered us from that invincible navy (as they termed it)'.[46]

The popular poet John Taylor reduced the miracle to trite verse, but still conveyed the essential memory of providential deliverance in 1588.

This year Spain with a mighty preparation
With twelvescore vessels loadeth Neptune's back,
With thirty thousand men attempts invasion,
Of England's kingdom and Elizae's wrack.
Then many a bragging desperate doughty Don,
Proud of the strength of that great huge Armado,
Went barely off, though they came bravely on,
The power of heaven opposing their bravado.
Our numbers unto theirs inferior far,
Yet were they ta'en, sunk, slain, banged, thumped and battered,
Because the Lord of Hosts the God of war,
He was our trust and aid, our foes he scattered.

His name is over all the world most glorious,
And through his power his church is still victorious.[47]

Reflections on English history took on new significance in the troubled years of the mid-seventeenth century. Several authors drew attention to former glories and past deliverances as a guide to understanding the confusions of the present. Thomas Morton, former bishop of Durham, saw 'the hand of God's providence in the Spanish invasion', and cited it among other deliverances and preservations of biblical and modern times. Thomas Horton, describing *The Pillar and Pattern of Englands Deliverances* in an address to the Lord Mayor and Aldermen of London in 1654, similarly included 'our deliverance from the Spanish invasion in eighty-eight'. By this time the defeat of the Spanish Armada was a staple item of Protestant discourse, and the audience would have been alarmed to find it missing. Spain, in Oliver Cromwell's view, was the 'old and implacable enemy of our religion and country', and it was no surprise to hear '88 mentioned as England once again approached war with Spain.[48]

Nonetheless, some writers hammered on the urgency and importance of holding past events in memory. Writing in October 1657, at a time when even the most confident of Englishmen were troubled by the drift and disappointment of the revolution, Samuel Clarke set down 'a true and full narrative of those two never to be forgotten deliverances, the one from the Spanish invasion in eighty-eight, the other from the hellish powder plot'. This was published as a pocket history book, cheaply produced 'for the information and benefit of each family', and it went through four editions by 1679. Clarke's specific intention was to show, as had been shown many times before, 'the wonderful power and mercy of God to us in this poor nation'. Elizabethan and Jacobean history served to demonstrate this, and Clarke devoted sixty-six pages to the Spanish Armada, and twenty to the events of 1605. His larger purpose, however, was to instil attentiveness to the past as the foundation for godliness in the present and future. Knowing and commemorating England's significant history was a matter of keeping the faith, as well as signalling gratitude to God. Clarke explains, in phrases that encapsulate the historical tradition, 'if there be not such a recognition of former deliverances, we that should be as temples of [God's] praise shall be as graves of his benefits. Our souls indeed are too like filthy ponds, wherein fish die soon and frogs live long. Rotten stuff is remembered, memorable mercies are forgotten; whereas the soul should be an holy Ark, the memory the pot of Manna, preserving holy truths and special mercies'.[49] The store of memories remained for subsequent generations to revise and manipulate as occasion demanded, from the exclusion crisis of the 1670s to the present. As recently as 1988, in post-Falklands Britain and in various parts of the English-speaking world, the story of the Armada has been retold for current cultural purposes, as well as in the interests of historical scholarship.

8
QUEEN ELIZABETH
OF FAMOUS MEMORY

The memory of Queen Elizabeth fascinated and haunted the subjects of her Stuart successors. The mystique of the virgin queen, Protestant saviour and paragon of princely virtues, served as a gloss and counterpoint to the anxious politics of the seventeenth century. In high culture and low, the cult of Elizabeth gained momentum in the decades after her death. Religious reformers and Protestant historians made creative use of her legend; parish bells rang out to celebrate the anniversary of her accession. 'Queen Elizabeth of famous memory' became a rival with whom no living kings could compete. At best they might associate her image with their own; at worst, Elizabeth's memory loomed as a reproach to her less illustrious successors. Some members of the Caroline court affected nostalgia for the Elizabethan era; others sought to recreate its finer attributes. In the later seventeenth century the 'most politick princess' became transformed into Good Queen Bess.[1]

Political memory was invariably selective. As the Elizabethan era receded in time the frustrations, prevarications, and shortcomings of that period were selectively forgotten. One would hardly imagine, from the developing popular history, that Elizabeth's reign experienced plagues, bad harvests, and economic distress, that religious reformers like Grindal and Cartwright were thwarted in their efforts to advance the Reformation, or that the kingdom was mired in an expensive and unproductive war. In life, in her later years, Elizabeth may have been a crotchety old woman presiding over an exhausted kingdom, but in death she assumed all the 'Gloriana' virtues of Deborah, Hester, Judith, Diana, Minerva, and the 'Faerie Queene'.[2]

Renaissance courtly art and literature had depicted Elizabeth in these roles in her lifetime, mixing flattery and propaganda with literary conceit and genuine adulation. Her birthday and accession day had been occasions to celebrate and embellish these heroic queenly qualities. With her death in 1603 it was natural that this flattery should cease, and that royal propaganda should focus on the virtues of her successor. But Elizabeth's image was so potent, her memory so

130

deeply ingrained, that it soon re-emerged with an unsuppressible vigour. Indeed, there were immediate attempts to co-opt the Elizabethan virtues on behalf of the new dynasty. 'Eliza' was dead, gone to the 'Elizian fields' (artfully renamed in her honour), but 'her name revives, which never dying lives eternally,' sang one verse obituary of 1603. England was secure, however, because the new King James was 'a Phoenix from Eliza's ashes bred'.[3]

Christopher Lever, author of the verse memorial, *Queene Elizabeths Teares*, hinted that praise for Elizabeth was not universal. The Jacobean court included 'those who have their tongues dipped in the poison of envy' who 'bite her honourable name'. Whether these were people expressing a genuine relief that the Elizabethan era had at last come to an end, Stuart flatterers who over-praised James by diminishing his predecessor, or Scotsmen who never knew the previous monarch, Lever felt compelled to set the record straight. In doing so he set the tone for much subsequent Elizabethiana. Dedicating his work to Robert Cecil, a councillor who embodied the continuity from Tudor to Stuart, Lever praised 'Queen Elizabeth of blessed memory' as 'a lady beyond example' with 'a reputation that can never die'. In life she was famous for 'her resolute bearing the Christian cross'. She was, in effect, a Protestant saint, 'whom God hath made more glorious than the sun, giving her a place of glory, in fellowship with his holy angels and saints'. Elizabeth's glory redounded to her countrymen and her successors, 'whereby this our little world, the English nation, is made famous to all posterity'.[4]

William Leigh followed in 1612 with *Queene Elizabeth Paraleled in her Princely vertues, with David, Iosua, and Hezekia*. This was the substance of three sermons, first preached on Elizabeth's accession day in the last three years of her reign, and now thought fit to be printed for a Jacobean audience. The work was part chronicle, part inspiration, and part warning against the renewed Catholic menace of the early seventeenth century. The Gunpowder Plot in England and the murder of Henry IV in France were recent examples of the ruthless tenacity of God's enemies, against which was neeeded a new Elizabethan resolve. Leigh dedicated his work to James's daughter, the Princess Elizabeth, on whom some of the qualities of her illustrious namesake were thought to descend.[5]

Queen Elizabeth, in this account, lived a 'sacred life'. She prevailed over threats of treasons at home and invasions from abroad, and 'the Lord still made her glorious by deliverance'. Like King David, she escaped from persecutions by the guiding hand of providence, and triumphed over afflictions in order to build God's church. Like Joshua, she had demonstrated 'her puissance, to protect the Church,' most notably in 1588. And like Hezekia, she had striven 'in her piety, to reform the church'. England was made 'glorious by deliverance' under the leadership of 'this our English Judah'. But God's favour could easily be withdrawn. Leigh ended each sermon with calls to godliness, warning England not to 'beat back the river of God's mercies with the seas of our ingratitude'.[6] The Elizabethan record thus became a stick with which to beat backsliders, as well as a model of puissant Protestant kingship.

Writing in 1618, Samuel Garey, a Norfolk minister, digressed from his treatment of Britain's blessings under King James to review the accomplishments of 'our late deceased sovereign Queen Elizabeth of most famous and blessed memory'. Elizabeth, he maintained, 'could never be persuaded to tolerate popish religion' but rather, 'professed to maintain the truth of the Gospel, and to deface idolatry and superstition, which with singular constancy she continued all the days of her life'. James, as heir to Elizabeth's virtues and responsibilities, would surely continue the struggle.[7] Nobody was foolish enough to suggest that the king was anything but adamant in his defence of the reformed religion; but the image of his predecessor cast long shadows, and sometimes questions, particularly when the government was developing close relationships with Catholic Spain.

Bishop Godfrey Goodman hints that commemoration of Elizabeth grew under James as a displacement of affection from the Stuart regime. 'In disparagement of the Scots and in hate and detestation of them, the Queen [Elizabeth] did seem to revive. Then was her memory much magnified – such ringing of bells, such public joy and sermons in commemoration of her, the picture of her tomb painted in many churches; and in effect, more solemnity and joy in memory of her coronation than was for the coming in of King James.'[8] Unfortunately Goodman does not indicate at what point in James's reign this revival happened – perhaps as early as 1616 – but it seems to have gathered pace in the early 1620s.

In some quarters, especially those brushed by Protestant providentialism, the historical event of Elizabeth's accession took on an importance that transcended the mere facts of the Tudor regime. To Thomas Brightman, writing in the Jacobean period, the accession of Queen Elizabeth signalled the sounding of the seventh trumpet of the Apocalypse, 'for now is the last act begun'. The millennium lay at hand, and the final cosmic drama, the battle of Christ against Antichrist, was unfolding in English history. The precipitant was the beginning of Elizabeth's reign in November 1558.[9]

Without necessarily partaking of Brightman's millenarian enthusiasm, senior churchmen shared the view that the accession of

Queen Elizabeth marked the opening of a new epoch in English history, 'when the gospel began here to flourish'. This was the starting point for George Carleton's *Thankfull Remembrance of Gods Mercy. In an Historical Collection of the great and mercifull Deliverances of the Church and State of England, since the Gospel began here to flourish, from the beginning of Quene Elizabeth*, first published in 1624. Dedicating the work to Prince Charles, Carleton remarked that 'the remembrance of the great works of God is a glass fit for a Prince to look on'. Many others looked there too, and *A Thankfull Remembrance* went through four editions by 1630. Elizabeth, of course, featured prominently. From difficult beginnings Elizabeth was soon 'made strong against her enemies'. Her success 'was a work of God in defence of his church here'. Elizabeth's reign, from this perspective, was a series of tests and challenges, plots and conspiracies, all overcome 'because we see God hath made our enemies his enemies'. In sum, Queen Elizabeth 'yet lived to see all the malicious practices against her defeated and overthrown, the practices themselves ruinated, her people and kingdom defended, God's truth maintained, her service for the truth rewarded, and after all, died quietly in her bed, and hath left a blessed memory behind her'.[10] This was a predecessor to revere, an inspiring model to emulate, but a paragon impossible to match. Thomas Morton, Bishop of Durham, similarly saw 'the hand of God's providence' inextricably involved with the successes of 'Queen Elizabeth of blessed and ever surviving memory'.[11]

Mediated through the history books, the Elizabeth of popular memory was the princess who survived Mary's reign to reinstate English Protestantism, and the warrior queen who stood up to the Spanish Armada. John Taylor's *Memorial of all the English Monarchs*, first published in 1622 and expanded in 1630, was an uncritical encapsulation in which Queen Elizabeth appeared as

> A Deborah, a Judith, a Susanna,
> A Virgin, A Virago, a Diana:
> Courageous, zealous, learned, wise, and chaste,
> With heavenly, earthly gifts, adorn'd and grac'd.

Elizabeth's achievements, in Taylor's presentation, were primarily religious: 'She did repurify this land once more,/From the infection of the Romish whore.' Elizabeth's 'mercy, justice, temperance, fortitude, magnanimity, prudence, learning, and incomparable wisdom would each of them fill a volume,' Taylor added in 1630, 'wherefore I refer the reader to the great volumes of Hollingshed's story, the reverend learned Camden, Master Speed, and others, who have written more largely of her, though all of them are much short of her unimmestable merits'.[12]

By this time readers could turn to several narrative histories, including John Stow's *Chronicles* of England, or John Speed's *Theatre of the Empire of Great Britain*, both periodically reissued and updated. (The 1631 edition of Stow included 180 pages on 'the life and reign of Queen Elizabeth'.) The standard story was told in William Camden's *Annales: The True and Royal History of Elizabeth, Queene of England*, which appeared in Latin in 1615 and in English in 1625, with more editions to follow. When Queen Henrietta Maria visited Oxford in 1636 the university presented her with a copy of Camden's *Elizabeth*, mostly likely the French translation by P. de Bellegent.[13] It is not known whether she was delighted or affronted.

★

England was never so conscious of Elizabeth as in the 1620s and 1630s. The Elizabethan legend grew quietly under James I, but it became loudly amplified with the renewed Spanish threat and the beginning of the reign of King Charles. Symptomatic of this revival were the sermons delivered each 17 November at St Pancras in Soper Lane, London, 'in thankful remembrance of the coronation of that Virgin Queen Elizabeth of famous and never-dying memory'.[14] As the Stuart accomplishments fell short, as the international situation deteriorated, and as war with Spain stirred ancient memories, England seemed in need of another 'deliverance'. In these circumstances the Elizabethan motif gained renewed power.

'Queen Elizabeth of famous memory' became a benchmark and touchstone for commentary on contemporary politics. Sir Edward Coke in 1621 eulogized Elizabeth as 'the flower of queens' as the rose is queen of flowers. John Chamberlain wrote approvingly in 1623 of a preacher at St Paul's who 'gave Queen Elizabeth her due'. Then in 1625, amidst mutterings in parliament about the Catholic entourage of Queen Henrietta Maria, Chamberlain reported, 'some spare not to say there that all goes backward since this connivance in religion came in, both in our wealth, honour, valour, and reputation, and that it is visibly seen God blesses nothing that we take in hand. Whereas, in Queen Elizabeth's time, who stood firm in God's cause, all things did flourish.'[15]

Thomas Gataker, preaching and publishing in 1626, *An Anniuersarie Memoriall of Englands Deliuery from the Spanish Invasion*, thanked God for making Elizabeth 'a mother over his Israel and a nurse over his church'. The accomplishments of the virgin queen were to be recited alongside the litany of mercies shown to England, 'that in succeeding ages fathers may declare unto their children how great things God hath done for us in the old times before them'. Gataker recalled how Elizabeth had brought 'much happiness to our kingdom,' especially 'the establishment of that truth of the Gospel and discipline of the church which we now enjoy under our dread sovereign Lord King Charles'.[16]

Also preaching in 1626 on the popular theme of 'deliverance', Henry King included Elizabeth in a 'catalogue of female wonders'. The queen was ranked with biblical heroines and with the greatest warrior kings of English history. 'Our Elizabeth, that unpatterned mirror of her sex, that only example of masculine heroic virtue, which the latter or indeed any times produced, hath as many pennons, as many streamers hung about her hearse, as many trophies of conquest to adorn her precious memory, as any of those whose names who whilst they lived were wedded to victory, the Edwards or the Henrys.'[17] Beset by plague at home and war abroad, it was a fitting moment to invoke the Elizabethan legend.

Sir John Eliot in 1628 turned praise of Elizabeth into a weapon of criticism, contrasting the glorious past with the unfortunate present. Invoking the memory of Elizabeth, he reminded the House of Commons, 'how she advanced herself, how she advanced this kingdom, how she advanced this nation in glory and state . . . how she enjoyed a full security, and made them then our scorn, who now are made our terror'.[18] Maritime successes under Queen Elizabeth were a standing reproach to the forces of Charles and Buckingham, but the subsequent failures of the Elizabethan navies were discreetly forgotten.

The year 1630 saw the publication of *A Chaine of Pearle. Or A Memoriall of the peerles Graces and Heroick Vertues of Queene Elizabeth of Glorious Memory*, by Diana Primrose. This was a poetic encomium enumerating the virtues of 'Great Eliza, England's brightest sun, the world's renown and everlasting lamp . . . whose name still reigns in all our hearts'. Elizabeth was venerated as the embodiment of feminine virtues – religion, chastity, prudence, temperance, clemency, justice, fortitude, science, patience, and bounty – that set her above the normal human condition. None could take offence at this manifestation of the cult of Elizabeth, unless they contrasted Elizabeth's 'Golden Days' with the cloudier Caroline present.[19] Nothing is known of the author, and it is likely that 'Diana Primrose', a name almost too good to be true, was a pseudonym.

Thomas Heywood's popular history of *Englands Elisabeth*, first published in 1631, told the story of 'her life and troubles during her minority, from the cradle to the crown,' in a tone once reserved for the lives of the saints. Heywood, like others, commemorated 'the prosperous and successful reign of this royal queen and virgin'. Readers were reminded that the close of Mary's reign had seen 'great dearth in the land . . . home troubles, foreign losses'. Then came the miracle of 17 November, and 'the wished sun appeared in our horizon, like a fresh spring after a stormy winter'. Looking back to a balmier time, the English could honour the memory of a queen 'whose never-dying fame even in this our age is so sacred amongst all good men, that it is scarce remembered, at the least uttered, without a devout thanksgiving'.[20]

The lustrous aura of Queen Elizabeth, sustained and polished by histories and sermons, shone forth afresh each year on 17 November. As personal memory faded, the anniversary observances became further detached from the person of the queen, and promoted instead her mythic role as a Protestant deliverer. Celebrating Elizabeth's accession was a pious and patriotic activity, and a safe and discreet way to criticize the current regime. Seventeenth-century almanacs often singled out 17 November for special treatment, a calendrical reminder for bonfires and bells. Usually the entry was printed in red, an honour reserved only for the holiest days or for the anniversaries of the reigning monarch. Most almanacs explained that this red-letter treatment was in honour of the accession of Queen Elizabeth, though sometimes the information was veiled beneath the laconic entry, 'St Hugh'. *Alleyns Almanacke* of 1608 noted both the birthday and the accession day of Queen Elizabeth. Richard Allestree's almanacs marked 17 November in 1628 and 1629 as a red-letter day with the entry 'init. Reg. Eliz.' The year 1628, Allestree noted, was seventy years 'since the beginning of blessed Queen Elizabeth's reign'.[21]

Not surprisingly, the cult of Elizabeth grew directly in proportion to the perceived Catholic menace. In the autumn of 1626, while ladies at court were dallying with the Mass, and while Spanish forces appeared ascendant in Europe, the anniversary of Elizabeth's accession produced a resounding clamour of bells. 'Today these bells rang merrily in remembrance of famous Queen Elizabeth' wrote one London correspondent on 17 November. Similarly in 1630 there was 'universal ringing of bells for Queen Elizabeth's coronation' on 17 November.[22] The pattern is familiar from our previous discussion of the politicized vocabulary of celebration. This anniversary ringing, quite innocent of official prompting, combined elements of reassurance and defiance, as if the commemoration of Elizabeth could somehow restore the virtues of her reign. 'Our Elizabeth' had become the unofficial patron saint of England.

As we have seen, the bells that once expressed joy in Elizabeth's person and government, rang out again in the seventeenth century to celebrate her memory. The queen was summoned to life again by the ringing, just as she was made symbolically present by the anniversary activities on crownation day. Ringing in honour of Queen Elizabeth was a matter of local preference. The cult was strongest in the City and vicinity of London, with an echo in provincial towns. After 1603 there was no pressure from the court to arouse the bells on 17 November, as there was on the birthdays and accession days of the living king, and for most of the Jacobean period Elizabeth's accession day passed without special notice. But as the cult of Elizabeth revived in the 1620s it became more common to hear the bells on her special day in November. The anniversary of Elizabeth's accession day once again became an occasion of popular celebration, with some of the devotion formerly attached to favourite saints.

During Charles's reign Queen Elizabeth's regnal anniversary was dangerously close on the calendar to the king's birthday on 19 November and to Henrietta Maria's birthday on 16 November. Cheerful bells and bonfires on Elizabeth's day compared unfavourably with muted public celebrations for the royal family. The government attempted to remedy the situation by commanding suitable birthday ringings for the king and queen. Pique at the popular affection for the memory of Elizabeth, which seemed to diminish respect for the present king, therefore added extra celebratory days to the seventeenth-century calendar. Mid-November became a busy time for bells and bonfires in the 1630s, since so many anniversaries were clustered together. The news-writer John Pory reported from London in 1631, 'yesterday they rang for the queen's birthday, today for Queen Elizabeth's coronation, and on Saturday for King Charles's birthday'.[23]

Churchwardens' accounts show the different sums of money expended on the various ringing days, which may indicate the different ceremonial weight attached to them. Celebratory ringing on the anniversary of Elizabeth's accession was intermittent in London parishes in the 1620s but by the later 1630s had become a regular feature. At St Stephen Coleman Street, the payment of 3s. 4d. to the ringers on 17 November 1636 was more than the sum spent on the king's birthday, and equal to the expenditure on 5 November. Puritan parishes like St Stephen meticulously observed the royal birthdays and official ringing days of the Caroline calendar, but seem to have celebrated 'Queen Elizabeth's coronation day' with particular relish. Similarly in the puritan parish of St Botolph without Bishopsgate, the official dynastic and patriotic ringing days were scrupulously observed, but by the 1630s the campanological calendar also included ringing on 17 November. The parish accounts show the contrast between perfunctory ringing by order and enthusiastic ringing from the heart. On 16 November 1634, the churchwardens spent three shillings for ringing 'by command from the Lord Mayor' on Henrietta Maria's birthday. But the next day, 17 November, they paid ten shillings without prompting for ringing in memory of Queen Elizabeth. Here the observance of 'Queen Elizabeth's coronation day' continued annually until 1645. So too in the important Middlesex parish of St Martin in the Fields the bells rang 'in remembrance of the late Queen Elizabeth of famous memory' during most of the years of Charles I's reign.

Across the river at Lambeth celebratory ringing was mostly reserved for the Stuart accession days and birthdays, and 17 November was generally ignored. In 1635, however, Lambeth joined many of the City parishes in ringing on Elizabeth's accession day. Lambeth was under the archbishop's eye, being adjacent to his palace though outside his immediate jurisdiction, and it would be interesting to know what Laud thought of this matter. Provincial parishes followed their own discretion in commemorating Elizabeth's accession. At Cambridge, for example, the churchwardens at Holy Trinity expended fourpence 'to the ringers on Queen Elizabeth's day in 1627 and sixpence for the ringers on 17 November the following year, while the university church of St Mary stood silent. Neither Salisbury nor Norwich paid much attention to the Elizabethan anniversary in the 1630s, but Dorchester made 17 November a special day of bellringing.

There were dissenters from the passion for Elizabeth. Some of the dons at Laudian Oxford in the 1630s disdained the annual celebration on 17 November. Thomas Crosfield, fellow of the Queen's College, wrote in his diary in November 1634, 'the discourse at this time by Mr Provost was, touching the celebration of the 17th of November for Queen Elizabeth who was held in great reputation and memory at London, and yet was very sacrilegious, keeping the bishopric of Ely in her hands for twenty-four years'.[24] This was loose talk, simply indicating the cultural distance between Oxford chapels and the streets of London.

★

As the very model of princely behaviour, Elizabeth was made to do duty in the crisis of the 1640s. *Queene Elizabeths Speeche to her last Parliament, 30 Nov. 1601*, the 'golden speech', was twice reprinted, without editorial comment, at critical moments. The book collector George Thomason bought copies from the London bookstalls in

January 1642, after the king's bungled attempt to arrest the five members, and again in March 1648 when Charles was a prisoner in the Isle of Wight. This famous speech, with its appeal to the harmony of crown and people, made Elizabeth the mouthpiece of concord and charity. Sir Robert Naunton contributed to the aura with his *Fragmenta Regalia, or Observations on the late Q. Elizabeth*, published in London in 1641. In other guises Elizabeth was the target of Catholic perfidy, and the holy damsel (or patron saint) of the English Reformation.[25] Fresh stories of Catholic plots at the time of the Scottish and Irish rebellions gained credibility against the well worn narrative of the myriad plots against Elizabeth.

Anniversary sermons gave further currency to the Elizabethan legend. The House of Commons observed a public fast on 17 November 1640, not ostensibly to honour the accession of the virgin queen, but rather to catch its breath and to probe its conscience amidst the impeachment proceedings against Strafford and Laud. The date, however, had a potency of its own. Everyone understood the calendrical resonances when the preacher Stephen Marshall urged the Commons to 'make this another blessed seventeenth of November'. Stephen Burgess also preached before parliament that day and invoked the memory of Elizabeth as if she was a participant in the present proceedings. The 'Root and Branch' petition against episcopacy was then gathering signatures and would soon be presented to the House of Commons. Burgess gave out that Elizabeth, 'that glorious Deborah', would surely have approved. Had she not been hamstrung by history and circumstance, she 'would have thoroughly plucked up popery both root and branch, superfluous ceremonies and all remaining rags of superstition as well as gross idolatry'.[26] This was a wilful and wishful interpretation of Elizabeth's religious position, but it served the moment.

Some members of the Long Parliament saw themselves as historical actors in direct succession from the age of Elizabeth, just as they sometimes saw themselves as the heirs of ancient Israel. Their prevailing view of English history praised Henry VIII for throwing out the pope, with even more applause for Edward VI for throwing out popery. Mary restored both the religion and power of Antichrist, leaving Elizabeth to begin again the task of reformation. Under Elizabeth, according to Matthew Newcomen, 'the Lord caused the work to prosper' but he did not bring it to perfection. Now, after the tribulations of the Laudian period, the godly men assembled in parliament had the chance to bring the Reformation to perfection. The London preacher Nathaniel Hardy adopted a similar historical perspective when he preached at St Paul's in November 1646. 'This month of November is memorable among other for two days, the seventeenth and the fifth; on the one the purity of the gospels broke forth; on the other the treachery of the gospel's enemies brake out: the one the initiation of as gracious a queen, the other the continuation of as wise a king as England ever enjoyed.'[27]

Anniversary ringing broke out again in some London parishes upon 17 November 1647. The bells recalled God's providences, and directed attention to an earlier phase of the Reformation, amidst the political and religious confusion that followed the civil war. Elizabethan values were invoked at the Restoration, notably in Dryden's *Astraea Redux*. Later in the seventeenth century the cult of Elizabeth revived again, most notably on behalf of the exclusion movement. On 17 November 1681 *The Impartial Protestant Mercury* pronounced, 'This being the anniversary of that day that put a period to established popery and bloody Queen Mary's persecution of Protestants in England, and brought the blessed Elizabeth to reign over our happy ancestors, has always since been celebrated; but much more since that damnable, long-exploded idolatry and tyranny of the church of Rome, by cursed plots and sham plots, etc., dares of late perk up its head again and threaten to invade us. To express our universal detestation of which it was thought fit now, as well as some years past, to have a solemn cavalcade representing in emblem, and executing in effigy, those wicked disturbers of our peace, and subverters of our religion.' It was not without significance that the anti-Catholic processions in Charles II's reign culminated around the statue of Elizabeth at Temple Bar. Nor that Queen Anne adopted Elizabeth's motto, *semper eadam*, and attempted to attach the Elizabethan virtues to herself. Nor that the cult of Elizabeth should serve both Whig and Tory propagandists in the early eighteenth century.[28]

9
REMEMBERING THE FIFTH
OF NOVEMBER

Of all the providences engrained in the memory of seventeenth-century English Protestants, the discovery of the Gunpowder Plot on 5 November 1605 was the most enduring. Although the anniversary eventually lost its anti-Catholic venom, and is no longer seen as part of a pattern of national deliverances, Gunpowder Treason still has a place in the English popular calendar. As 'Guy Fawkes day' or 'bonfire night' the date is still observed throughout England with community bonfires and fireworks. The cellars below the Palace of Westminster are still subjected to a ritual search on the eve of the opening of parliament. Everyone knows the verse,

> Remember, remember the Fifth of November,
> The Gunpowder Treason and Plot.
> I see no reason why Gunpowder Treason
> Should ever be forgot.[1]

The story can readily be summarized. Despairing that the political and dynastic process would ever produce a Catholic restoration, and frustrated by the reversal of King James's apparent promise of toleration, a clutch of Catholic gentlemen conspired to kill the king and destroy his government at the opening of parliament on 5 November 1605. Their intended method was an explosion of gunpowder, and the man to set it off was the Catholic adventurer Guy (or Guido) Fawkes. Thirty-six barrels of gunpowder were concealed in a basement below the House of Lords. The gunpowder weighed eighteen hundred pounds. If ignited the explosion would have been spectacular, the damage immense. Fortunately for those attending the opening of parliament, the government got wind of the plot. A search was conducted, and on the evening of 4 November Guy Fawkes was discovered with match and lantern, tending his lethal store. The conspirators were rounded up, tortured, and executed. Church and state thanked God for a miraculous deliverance, and issued orders that the fifth of November should be marked henceforth with annual commemoration.[2]

Like the collapse of the Spanish Armada, the failure of the Gunpowder Treason was attributed to God rather than man. Public thanksgiving downplayed the human frailty and investigative ingenuity that had broken the plot, and focused instead on God's role as the protector of Protestant England. The plot was interpreted as further proof of the relentless evil of Roman Catholicism, and its discovery as a renewal of the promise that God would deliver England from his enemies. The mercy of 1605 confirmed the implied covenant of 1588. Special prayers were printed for distribution to churches throughout the nation, and these were recited annually on Gunpowder Treason day, at least until the civil war. 'O Lord, who didst this day discover the snares of death that were laid for us, and didst wonderfully deliver us from the same, be thou still our mighty protector, and scatter our enemies that delight in blood. Infatuate and defeat their counsels, abate their pride, assuage their malice, and confound their devices. Strengthen the hands of our gracious King James, and all that are put in authority under him, with judgment and justice, to cut off all such works of iniquity, as turn religion into rebellion, and faith into faction.' So spake the *Form of Prayer with Thanksgiving to be used yearly upon the Fifth day of November; For the happy Deliuerance of the King, and the Three Estates of the Realm, from the most Traiterous and bloody intended Massacre by Gun-powder.*[3]

The king himself, the principal target of the Gunpowder Plot, paused every 5 November to hear a sermon on the subject of deliverance. Since the king was present these court sermons also dwelt heavily on the rights of kings, the sacredness of their persons, the divine protection afforded them, and the wickedness of those who rose up against them. Lancelot Andrewes, Bishop of Winchester, preached the first commemorative sermon before the king on 5 November 1606, declaring, 'this day of ours, this fifth of November, a day of God's making; that which was done upon it was the Lord's doing . . . This day is the scripture fulfilled in our ears.' The day was likened to biblical deliverances of the chosen people: 'the destroyer passed over our dwellings this day. It is our Passover, it is our Purim.' Like King David before him, King James was granted deliverance from a murderous plot.[4] Similar sermons were preached in churches and cathedrals around the country, embracing biblical exegesis on the patriotic paradigm of the elect Protestant nation.

While Bishop Andrewes was preaching before the king on 5 November 1606, William Leigh was preaching to his parishioners at Standish, Lancashire, on *Great Britaines Great Deliverance from the Great*

Danger of Popish Powder. This 'meditation upon the late intended treason' was dedicated to Prince Henry, the heir apparent. The intended plot had shaken the Stuart family and the Protestant country they governed. The deliverance of 5 November was understood as a continuation of divine protection from papist subversion, including 1588, 'but of all that ever were, this last device of gunpowder to blow up all was most detestable, devilish, and damnable'.[5]

Several parishes enjoyed endowed sermons on 5 November, the gift of prominent merchants or citizens. St Martin Orgar, London, had a sermon, 'every year on the fifth day of November, which day is kept in remembrance of our miraculous preservation from the horrible and unheard of Gunpowder Treason'. This was established in 1612 by the will of Humphrey Walwyn, citizen and grocer. Nearby at St Pancras Soper Lane, Thomas Chapman left money by his will of 1616 for a sermon 'on the fifth day of November in every year to give due praise and thanks unto the divine majesty for the wonderful and miraculous preservation and deliverance,' and in 1626 Thomas Chapman, Jr confirmed and augmented his father's bequest. Chapman's sermons became a regular fixture at St Pancras in the reign of Charles I.[6] Meanwhile the Lord Mayor and aldermen assembled each 5 November for a sermon at St Paul's, and, if a parliament was sitting, the members heard afternoon and evening sermons at Westminster. Several of these anniversary sermons were printed, and may have been used as models by country preachers.

Popular publications supplemented the official message. John Rhodes produced a verse narrative telling how 'Fawkes at midnight, and by torchlight, there was found/With long matches and devices, underground.' This came from *A Brief Summe of the Treason intended against the King & State, when they should have been assembled in Parliament, November 5. 1605. Fit for to instruct the simple and ignorant heerein: that they be not seduced any longer by Papists.* Rhodes taught that God and his angels protected 'English Britain' from the wicked designs of Rome. Joyful recognition of his mercy called for 'bells and bonfires on this day'.[7]

The physician Francis Herring wrote a wordy Latin poem which became popular in various English translations. There were 113 stanzas of *Popish Pietie, or the first part of the history of that horrible and barbarous conspiracie, commonly called the Powder-treason*, printed in 1610. Herring dedicated his work to Princess Elizabeth, who would have been among those killed had the plot succeeded, and he stressed yet again the importance of memory and commemoration. 'The Powder-treason, that monstrous birth of the Romish harlot, cannot be forgotten without great impiety and injury to ourselves . . . We shall be guilty of horrible ingratitude, the foulest of all vices, if we do not embrace all means of perpetuating the memory of so great, so gracious, and wonderful a preservation.'[8]

Histories, litanies, and sermons helped imprint the memory of the Gunpowder Plot on the English popular consciousness. Annual almanacs sustained and perpetuated the memory. In Edward Pond's *New Almanacke for this Present Yeare of our Lord 1608*, and many more like it, the 'Papists Conspiracy' made 5 November a 'red-letter day'. Henry Alleyn, author of *Alleyns Almanacke, or, a Double diarie & prognostication* for 1608, marked 5 November as the day 'King James preserved'. Richard Allestree's almanacs of the 1620s and 1630s invariably accorded a red-letter entry to 5 November. For the rest of the seventeenth century, almanacs distinguished the Powder Treason day as one of a small number of enduringly significant anniversaries. Other special days, anniversaries and birthdays, varied with the monarch, but 5 November was a constant day for the memory and celebration of England's deliverance. John Booker's *Telescopium Uranicum* for 1665 noted, 'The powder plot was papish, was it not?/ Yea, and an act made ne're to be forgot.' 'Poor Robin's' almanac for 1695 offered similar doggerel:

> Let papists now with blushing cheeks remember,
> What they were practicing this month November;
> When as by powder they did vaunt and vapour,
> To make king, prince and lords, i'th' air to caper.

To which the compiler added, 'What ere's forgot, the memory o' the Powder Plot will hardly die.'[9]

Jacobean diarists often singled out 5 November for historical reflection. Nicholas Assheton, a fox-hunting squire in Lancashire, noted on 5 November 1617, 'Gunpowder Treason, twelve years since, should have been; but God's mercy and goodness delivered us from the snare of devilish invention. To church; parson preached; dined parsonage.' Simonds D'Ewes, studying at the Middle Temple, recorded in his diary on 5 November 1622, 'This is the memorable day upon which the papists had decreed to have blown up the parliament house, but God delivered this land. At night preached Mr Crashaw and made an excellent discourse of it.' The following year he noted, 'Wednesday being the fifth of November, the memorial of that act and shame of popery was celebrated, the Gunpowder [Plot] . . . At night we had a sermon in memory of it.'[10]

★

Even more than by writing, the importance of the Gunpowder anniversary was registered by social action. A day with no pre-existing calendrical connotations, the fifth of November became firmly fixed as an annual reference point, alongside more ancient markers of the year. In the seventeenth century it was indelibly associated with deliverance from Catholic treason, although other festive and secular elements came into play. Each year after 1605 the anniversary was marked by bells, bonfires, services, and a temporary suspension of everyday activity. The day was not a holiday, in the sense that people were excused from work, but it was a special occasion on which to reflect on God's providence and his mercies to England. It was a time for praise and thanksgiving, and for making a joyful noise unto the Lord. And for some it became a day of mischief, an autumn analogue to the rowdiness of Shrovetide and May. The annual commemoration drew on the traditional vocabulary, involving noise, light, action and prayer, though not always with the utmost decorum. Michael Sparke sought to maintain the solemnity of the celebration in the 1620s when he urged, 'Let us and our posterity after us with bonfires, trumpets, shawms and psalms laud and praise thy holy name on the fifth of November yearly and forever.'[11]

Individual parishes rose to the occasion. Ministers read the special prayers authorized by parliament, and sometimes delivered commemorative sermons. The day was graced by special doles, deeds of philanthropy, and actions of honour. Adrian Mott of Braintree, Essex, left one hundred pounds to invest in land, 'the profits to be distributed every November 5th so that Guy Fawkes's treason should never be forgot'. At court it was a day for banquets and promotions as well as devotions. In 1617, for example, Buckingham mounted a 'great feast at Hatton House', and Sir Henry Rich 'received his charge of Captain of the Guard upon the Powder-Treason holiday'.[12]

Churchwardens purchased the books of special prayers for the fifth of November, and committed money each year to the payment of bellringers. At Northill, Bedfordshire, for example, the accounts show 8d. spent on 'the book of thanksgiving for his majesty's delivery' in 1605, and 18d. more in 1607 for 'the books of articles and the brief for the fifth of November'. The churchwardens of St Botolph's, Cambridge, spent 6d. in 1606 'for a book of prayers and thanksgivings for his majesty's deliverance from gunpowder', and bought another one in 1620. Fourpence more would buy the revised 'book for the fifth of November' in 1636, a revision that some puritans protested.[13]

The phrases written in the parish records to explain the anniversary expenditures may throw some light on the question of popular understanding. What did people think this festivity was all about? At

145

St Martin-cum-Gregory, York, they rang in 1606 to give thanks, 'for the preservation of the king's majesty's person from the treacherous treason of these traitorous traitors'. At the other end of the country at Bere Ferrers, Devon, they rang on 5 November 1610, 'in remembrance of the former dangers on that day pretended by traitors at the parliament house'. A distillation of the anniversary sermons found its way into the churchwardens' books, and perhaps into the minds of ordinary parishioners. By the 1620s the key words were 'deliverance' and 'remembrance'. The ringing at St Martin in the Fields on 5 November 1622 was performed, 'in memory of that great deliverance from that hellish Gunpowder Treason which was to have been executed at the parliament house at Westminster, contrived by treacherous papists, and prevented by God's gracious goodness'. Bells rang in York in the 1630s, 'for the deliverance from the traitorous plot of the papists by gunpowder'. To the churchwardens at Swaffham, Norfolk, 5 November was 'a day appointed by the king for our deliverance from the popish conspiracy'. Most places rang 'on Gunpowder Treason day,' or simply recorded ringing 'on 5 November', as if the occasion was obvious. Just to write the word 'gunpowder' was to bring to mind explosive forces; to add the word 'treason' was to imagine the subversion of the state. The phrase 'Gunpowder Treason' implied a horrifying linkage, and to repeat it each year must have induced fearful associations, if only subliminally.

As we have seen, the amount spent on bellringing varied with local resources and traditions, and also changed somewhat from year to year according to the intensity of feeling about the Catholic threat and affection for the present regime. The ringing may have been especially vigorous or purposeful in the puritan parishes of London and the south-east, but it cannot be said that 5 November was a regional occasion. Every area of England joined in. With bellringing in churches from Devon to Durham, the annual celebration was a binding ingredient in the developing mix of a national political culture. Wherever there were bells they rarely failed to ring on this most significant Protestant commemoration.

Payments for bonfires and bells on 5 November became an 'ordinary' expense in many parishes, and Gunpowder Treason day became as firm in the calendar as Christmas. Indeed, during the interregnum, when Christmas and the rest of the holy seasons disappeared from the official calendar, only 5 November remained as a national day of common celebration. Unlike other days of royal or dynastic thanksgiving, when the bells rang 'by precept' or 'by order of Mr Mayor', the ringing on 5 November rarely needed prompting by higher officials. Most parishes found one or two shillings for the ringers each 5 November, to reward them with bread and beer. At St Edmund's, Salisbury, the churchwardens allowed eight shillings for ringing 'the 5th of November, being the day of the Gunpowder Treason'. At Hartland, Devon, the sum ranged from five to ten shillings for twelve ringers to pull their best. Candles illuminated the church in the November night.

Some communities went further and laid on a public beer barrel or supply of wine for all comers, or established a parish commemorative feast. The anniversary became a day of indulgence, of drinking and festivity as well as worship and meditation, even though it was never an official day of absence from work. Hospitality shaded into charity in some places, where 5 November was a day for distributing doles to the poor. Often the day concluded with a bonfire, with flaming tar barrels and bundles of faggots supplied from the parish funds. Great St Mary's, Cambridge, usually allowed 2s. 6d. towards a parish bonfire on 5 November in the 1630s. Not to be outdone, the rival parish of Holy Trinity, Cambridge, laid out 3s. 8d. 'for a pitch barrel and faggots for a bonfire' on 5 November 1635.

These bonfires were not orchestrated from London – indeed their message was sometimes antithetical to that put forward by the court –but they enjoyed the support of parish notables and the discretionary use of community funds. On one occasion the citizens of Norwich staged a highly symbolic bonfire when they burned a collection of leftovers from the days of papism. Until 5 November 1626 the chamberlains' inventory included 'one little chest with an old cope, a surplice, a pax, a crucifix, an altar stone, and one mass book'. These dangerous relics were disposed of, no doubt with much glee and gloating, when they were 'burnt upon a thanksgiving day.'[14] (The custom of burning effigies of the pope, the devil, or his agents, reportedly began in the reign of Charles I, and became more common later during the period of the Exclusion Crisis and the Popish Plot. But the burning of Guy Fawkes in effigy seems to have been a nineteenth-century addition to the tradition.)

In some towns the celebration of 5 November became a civic occasion with much of the festive solemnity that before the Reformation had been reserved for saints' days. At Norwich the waits sang, bells rang, and a shilling each was paid 'to three trumpeters the 5th of November, by command of Mr Mayor'. The soldiers rolled out the wheel-guns at Norwich Castle and fired them each 5 November. In the afternoon the corporation assembled for a sermon in the church of St Peter Mancroft, 'in commemoration of the great delivery of the king and state from the Gunpowder Treason'. The evening was devoted to bonfires, bells, and drinking. Carlisle, too, had its mayoral

147

feast, with wakes, waits, actors, and bellringing on 5 November. At Nottingham 'the scarlet gownmen' of the corporation were ordered to church 'on the fifth of November yearly, decently clad in their scarlet gowns, to give God thanks for the great deliverance from the Powder Treason,' and were liable to a fine of one shilling if they neglected this duty. Similarly at Wells Cathedral the clergy were fined if they missed the formal service on this 'day of solemnity'.[15]

At Canterbury, where the civic calendar once centred on the pageants of St Thomas, the Gunpowder Treason provided a new opportunity for noisemaking, dinners and parades. In 1607 'there was delivered out of the tower in St George's gate . . . to triumph withal upon the 5th of November . . . 106 lb of gunpowder and 14 lb. of match'. This would provide some splendid explosions, and one wonders whether a veiled kind of sympathetic magic was at work here, with festive gunpowder combating the destructive horror of the Gunpowder Plot. In 1610 the aldermen and officers of Canterbury treated themselves and their wives to a slap-up dinner and entertainment on the evening of 5 November. The chamberlain laid out 14s. 7d. for wine, 6s. 8d. for the waits, 5s. for musicians, and another 15s. for gunpowder. The occasion called for a martial parade, in the tradition of the midsummer marching watch, and the accounts for 5 November show another 20s. spent 'for thirty of our soldiers which did show themselves with their muskets there'.[16]

The London parishes developed a variety of traditions. St Botolph without Bishopsgate, a large and crowded parish on the northern edge of the city, mounted the most impressive bonfires. Gunpowder Treason day became the high point of the local calendar, involving fires, lights, bells, noise, charitable doles, outdoor rowdiness, and a dinner at the White Hart for the parish officials. In 1632 the churchwardens accounted for festivities costing a total of 27s. 6d. Comparable observances involving formal church attendance, scarlet robings, civic processions, drinks for the populace and dinner for the dignitaries can be found in dozens of towns and parishes in early Stuart England.

★

It is important to remember that the Gunpowder Plot was no mere assassination attempt, a matter of knives or pistols directed at a single human target. It was altogether a higher enterprise, a more dastardly undertaking. At risk was not just the person of the king, but the entire panoply and personnel of government. The succession to the throne, so recently resolved after the uncertainties of Elizabeth's reign, was dangerously jeopardized. The royal family, the first in London since the reign of Henry VIII, was exposed to violent death. Lords and gentry, bishops and burgesses, all the structures of ranks and authority were imperilled. The very records of parliment and law were at risk. The plot threatened, in the words of the Norfolk preacher Samuel Garey, 'the general martyrdom of the kingdom'. Preacher after preacher invoked the horror of the Gunpowder Plot as an affront to all things English. It was, for Francis Herring, 'the quintessence of Satan's policy, the furthest reach and stain of human malice and cruelty, not to be paralleled among the savage Turks, the barbarous Indians, nor, as I am persuaded, among the more brutish cannibals'.[17]

Writing in 1618, barely a dozen years after the event, Samuel Garey reminded his readers of the enormity of the Gunpowder Plot and the commensurate magnitude of England's 'miraculous preservation'. This was '*Amphitheatrum scelerum*: or the transcendent of treason, the day of a most admirable deliverance of our king, queen, prince, royal progeny, the spiritual and temporal peers and pillars of the church and state, together with the honourable assembly of the representative body of the kingdom in general, from that most horrible and hellish project of Gunpowder Treason'. The Plot, *in quintum Novembris*, comprised 'the quintessence of all impiety and confection of all villainy,' and therefore should always be remembered.[18]

Puritan preachers like Garey felt compelled to stir the memory of former deliverances in a population perpetually prone to complacency and backsliding. The deliverance of 1605, Garey thundered, cannot be 'buried in oblivion'. It was, rather, to be kept as 'a holy feast unto the Lord throughout the generations'. Memory and commemoration were vital instruments in seventeenth-century godliness, and keeping the holy day of 5 November became part of the covenant between God and his Englishmen. 'How unworthy shall we be of future favours, if so unthankful for past blessings? And truly herein the land is faulty in forgetting these benefits.' Immediately after the discovery of the plot the people were aroused to prayer and thankfulness, but, Garey claimed, 'a few years being past, they began to slacken this duty, and are cold in praising God for so blessed a deliverance'. The time was ripe for a return to duty, 'to awaken our slumbering affections to this perpetual service of thankful rejoicing,' and 'to imprint an eternal memento in the calendar of our hearts forever, of the marvellous mercy of God in keeping us from that intended destruction'. One way, beside exhortation, was to recite the historical narrative of the Gunpowder Plot, 'to rouse up and revive the languishing spirits of the land, with the renewed remembrance of so joyful a work'. Garey devoted more than fifty pages to relating the background, progress, and outcome of the Gunpowder Plot.[19]

The ritual re-telling of the story was an integral aspect of commemoration.

There may be some truth to Garey's contention that popular interest in the Gunpowder Plot had diminished in the middle years of James's reign. Annual religious observances, required by law, had kept the memory alive but they could become merely formulaic unless driven by a religious or ideological passion. The urgency and anxiety that had fired the earlier sermons may have become less profound if the domestic Catholic threat appeared to have moderated, and as the overseas Catholic menace receded. By 1618, however, the situation was changing. The outbreak of religious war on the Continent severely jeopardized international Protestantism. England's Princess Elizabeth, married to the Elector Frederick of Palatine, was in danger. King James's diplomatic rapprochement with Spain rang alarm signals for English puritans. A proven way to gird for present crises was to summon memories from the past.

In an atmosphere troubled by renewed fears of Catholicism, war with Spain, and the recurrence of plague in London, the memory of past deliverances excited a remarkable amount of attention. The first few years of Charles I's reign were especially fraught, and produced an outpouring of sermons and pamphlets on the subject of Gunpowder Treason. The plot had been aimed at King James, but his entire family, government, and nation had been threatened; all had been blessed with miraculous preservation. The deliverance was national, not personal like James's earlier escape from the Gowry plot, so the celebration continued under James's successors.

Bishop George Carleton's *Thankfull Remembrance of Gods Mercy*, which went through four editions between 1624 and 1630, reminded a new generation of the implications of the conspiracy of 1605. The illustrated title page carried dense iconographic messages showing the true church as vulnerable but victorious. The earlier deliverance from the Armada (*per aquas*) was matched by the deliverance from the Gunpowder Plot (*per ignem*). Elizabeth and James were shown as Deborah and Solomon, triumphing, with God's help, against the machinations of popes and devils. Carleton's words indicate what was at stake.

Their hellish device was at one blow to root out religion, to destroy the state, the father of our country, the mother of our country, the olive branches the hopeful succession of our king, the reverend clergy, the honourable nobility, the faithful councillors, the grave judges, the greatest part of our knights and gentry, the choices burgesses, the officers of the crown, council, signet, seals, and other seats of judgment, the learned lawyers, with an infinite number of common people, the hall of justice, the houses of parliament, the church used for the coronation of our kings, the monuments of our former princes, all records of parliament, and of every particular man's right, with great number of charters, and other things of this nature, all these things had the devil by his agents devised at one secret blow to destroy.[20]

Only a miracle prevented the English constitution and the propertied society it served from being annihilated at a stroke!

Preaching in 1626, the puritan Thomas Hooker also dwelt on the diabolical comprehensiveness of the Gunpowder Plot. The target, he reminded his Chelmsford listeners, embraced the parliamentary gentry, nobility, and royal family, 'assembled for the glory of God, to enact good laws for this commonwealth. Now these in that place in one hour, in one instant, should all have been miserably blown up and torn in pieces, so that they should not have been found, should not have been known that they might be buried according to their degree. This is that matchless villainy and that unconceivable treachery which the papists had contrived' which should be recorded 'to all posterity.'[21] The radical Hooker agreed with Bishop Carleton that the plot had threatened the entire social and religious order, so that every English subject had a stake in its outcome, and an obligation to its memory.

Other ministers sang variations on the theme. Thomas Gataker, preaching the anniversary sermon at St Pancras in 1626, gave thanks 'for the preservation of our king and state from that damnable powder plot, as yet unparalleled in any age since the world began'. Henry King, preaching at the Spittle in London in the same year, also recalled God's mercy to England in revealing the Gunpowder Plot. 'He snatched us like brands from the mouth of the furnace, and by discovering the bloody trap, delivered us from the snare of those fowlers.'[22] By implication, he might do it again.

Laymen as well as clergymen took up the theme. John Cope, a puritan gentleman, observed that 'if there had been a council called in hell, and a company of devils sent upon earth for the executing of their designs, they could not have found out a more damnable plot, nor with greater resolution have prosecuted it, than they did the Gunpowder Treason'. The notion of a council in hell projecting the use of gunpowder against God's creation was not lost on the young John Milton. The theme of Gunpowder Plot inspired a series of poetic exercises in the mid-1620s, including the suberb Latin verse *In Quintum Novembris* (probably written in 1626). Milton returned to the theme in book six of *Paradise Lost* (written after the Restoration) where Satan, the archetypal conspirator, invents gunpowder as a diabolical counter to God's thunderbolts. The message of the sermons, in which God's grace ultimately triumphed over treason and malice, was echoed in Milton's art.[23]

Lesser poets and ballad-makers joined preachers and historians in revitalizing the memory of the Guy Fawkes conspiracy. One of the publications of 1625 was *A Song or Psalm of thanksgiving in remembrance of our deliverance from the Gunpowder Treason*. The following year John Wilson came out with *A song or story, for the lasting remembrance of divers famous works, which God hath done in our time*. This included 'a short song made upon the powder treason,' with the injunction, 'O England, praise the name of God/That kept thee from this heavy rod.'[24]

The popular poet John Taylor had a verse for every occasion. His commemoration of 1605, published in 1630, ran as follows:

> Now treason plotted in th'infernal den,
> Hell's mischief masterpiece began to work,
> Assisted by unnatural Englishmen,
> And Jesuits, that within this land did lurk.
> These would Saint Peter to saltpetre turn,
> And make our kingdom caper in the air,
> At one blast, prince and peers and commons burn,
> And fill the land with murder and despair.
> No treason e're might be compared to this,
> Such an escape the church had ne're before:
> The glory's God's, the victory is his,
> Not unto us, to him be praise therefore.
> Our church is his, her foes may understand,
> That he defends her with his mighty hand.[25]

Less glib and complacent, was John Vicars's patriotic poem, *Englands hallelu-jah; or, Great Britaines retribution*, published in 1631 with a dozen stanzas on the deliverance of 1605. Here again, God's chosen people were the 'English Israelites . . . ingrafted on old Israel's stock'. But God's favour might be withdrawn if the English did not turn to repentance.[26]

In the 1630s the Gunpowder anniversary began to lose its unifying character. Though still a national day of commemoration, enjoined by statute, the fifth of November took on an increasingly partisan tone. On the one hand puritan preachers used 5 November as an occasion to emphasize the dangers of creeping popery and the necessity of further reformation; on the other, the Caroline regime sought to muffle the commemoration. Anti-Catholic bonfires were distasteful to a

Catholic queen, and to a government building good relations with the Catholic powers. Yet to the outraged puritans the papist presence at court made memory of past deliverances all the more urgent and vital. The popular practice of noisemaking and burning of popish effigies incurred official displeasure. Such conduct, it was said, 'was a mark of a "puritan" and that house must be put into the black book'.[27]

Official Gunpowder anniversary sermons, which had been a regular fixture in the Jacobean court calendar, attracted much less attention under Charles. Archbishop Laud usually preached at Christmas and Easter, and on 27 March, the anniversary of the king's accession, but seems to have ignored 5 November. The day was not lacking in significance, however, as Laud confided to his diary in November 1633, 'about the beginning of this month the Lady [Eleanor] Davis prophesied against me, that I should very few days outlive the fifth of November'. Laud's chaplain Jeremy Taylor preached at Oxford 'upon the anniversary of the Gunpowder Treason' in 1638 but avoided the traditional themes of the day. His was an anniversary sermon without remembrance, about traitors in general rather than Catholics in particular, and more concerned with threats to princes than threats to religion. It represented the 'lukewarmness and apostacy' which drove some puritans to despair.[28]

Puritans, thrown on to the defensive by the rise of Laud and the Arminians, clung to the calendrical occasion of the Gunpowder anniversary, and indeed developed it as a licensed occasion for criticism. Some godly ministers in the 1630s took the opportunity of 5 November to preach against the popish superstition, pollutions, and persecutions which they saw besetting the church of England, while others took comfort in the underlying message of deliverance.[29] Preaching at Ipswich on 5 November 1633, Samuel Ward warned his congregation 'to beware of relapse into popery and superstition'. He preached 'that men began to ring the changes, as in bells and fashions, so in opinions and manners,' and that 'the best way of thankfulness for that deliverance [of 5 November] . . . was a more strict observance of the Ten Commandments'. Though outwardly unexceptional, this was taken as an oblique attack on the leaders of the church, and Ward had to answer for it before the High Commission.[30]

John Goodwin kept the memory fresh in his Gunpowder Treason sermons at St Stephen Coleman Street. This puritan congregation gathered 'to pay the yearly tribute of praise and thanksgiving . . . with the rest of our brethren of this nation'. Goodwin told his people in 1634 that the deliverance was a work of God 'of the first magnitude' which commanded 'this solemn remembrance'. It may be a sign of the times that these sermons were not printed until 1640. Censorship was subtle rather than blatant, and puritan pieces could still go to press. In 1637, however, permission to reprint a Jacobean poem on the subject of the Gunpowder Plot was refused with the words, 'we are not so angry with the papists now as we were twenty years ago'.[31]

More confrontational was Henry Burton who preached two sermons at St Matthew Friday Street, London, on 5 November 1636. He took as his text the verse from Proverbs 24:21, 'My son, fear thou the Lord and the king: and meddle not with them that are given to change.' An observer reported that Burton 'then urged his people to take note of many *changes* of late in books allowed, and in practice, as altars, etc.' Even the official service book for 5 November had been changed the previous year, with alterations that implied, to a sensitive reader like Burton, 'that the religion of papists is the true religion. Thus with altering of a word, they have quite perverted the sense, and so turned the cat in the pan.' And as an aside, Burton noted that the original text had been approved by parliament, but the alterations had not.[32]

Gunpowder Treason day was an especially apt occasion on which to berate the Laudian regime. Burton explained, in the printed version of his sermons, 'I deemed that day, the memorial whereof should cause all loyal subjects forever to detest all innovations tending to reduce us to that religion of Rome, which plotted matchless treason, the most seasonable for this text . . . This is a time of sorrow and humiliation, but this day a day of joy and festivity.' It was time, this 5 November, to recall the true meaning of the deliverance from the Gunpowder Plot, 'a deliverance never to be cancelled out of the calendar, but to be written in every man's heart forever'. God had intervened in 1605, so it seemed, not just to save the royal family and government but to preserve the true Christian religion. The Gunpowder Treason had threatened cataclysmic change, but now 'popery, like a thief, stolen in upon us step by step,' was freshly menacing. Back in 1605, Burton recalled, 'through God's mercy, the change was prevented: the change of a noble kingdom into an anarchy and Babylonian tyranny; a change of Christ's religion into Antichrist's; of tables into altars; of preaching ministers of the gospel into sacrificing mass priests; of light into darkness; of Christ into Belial; of the temple of God into a temple of idols; of fundamental just laws of a kingdom into papal canons; of the liberty of the subjects into the servitude of slaves; of regal edifices and monuments into vast solitude and ruinous heaps.'[33] Such a transparent and provocative characterization of the Laudian programme was bound to cause trouble, and Burton's challenge cost him a portion of his ears.

Puritan polemics had come some distance between Hooker's

154

sermon in 1626 and Burton's a decade later. The providential interpretation of English history, distilled into the observance of Gunpowder Treason day, become one more point of contention between the Caroline government and its critics. Few puritans were as outspoken as Burton, but many found comfort in the gathering of the godly on 5 November. Robert Woodford, the borough steward, was moved to thankfulness after attending Mr Ball's sermon at Northampton on 'Powder Treason day', 1638. 'It was a sermon to stir up God's people to wait on God for deliverance and to live by Faith. Lord prevail with us by it,' Woodford wrote in his diary.[34] Memory and commemoration would become further politicized in the disturbing decades that followed.

10
HISTORY AND PROVIDENCE
IN THE ENGLISH REVOLUTION

That the Gunpowder Plot was not a remote historical event, but rather part of a continuing pattern of danger and deliverance, was particularly clear to the generation of the 1640s. The crisis of the Scottish war, the Irish rebellion, and the disintegration of royal government, directed memories to the past and prayers to heaven. For puritans like Nehemiah Wallington it was manifest 'how Antichrist, even these bloody-hearted papists, doth plot against the poor church of God, as in '88 and that hellish Gunpowder Plot'. Wallington meditated on 'that hellish Gunpowder Treason' of 1605 and included a narrative of the plot in his manuscript 'Bundle of Mercies'.[1] The observance of Gunpowder Treason day provided firm points of reference in the turbulent decades of the 1640s and 1650s.

The London minister John Goodwin explained that 5 November 'was the anniversary remembrance of that great battle fought between Hell and Heaven, about the peace and safety of our nation . . . wherein Hell was overthrown and Heaven and we rejoiced together'. To stir proper remembrance he thought it fit in 1640 to publish some of the Gunpowder Treason sermons he had delivered at St Stephen's Coleman Street, in the preceding years. 'I have not, to my present remembrance, met with anything published of late of any special influence or tendency, to maintain the life and spirit of the solemnity and joy of that day and deliverance. And pity it is that such a plant of paradise should wither, or languish for lack of watering. Such a deliverance may, through the mercy and goodness of God, prove a breeder, and become a joyful mother of many children.'[2] With the Laudian ascendency at an end, Goodwin would not have to wait long for a spate of publications that made pointed reference to the events of 1605.

Anxiety about renewed popish plotting ran high in 1640, and rose to fever pitch in the months preceding the civil war. The routine annual commemoration of the Gunpowder Plot became charged with new significance as fresh conspiracies were feared or uncovered. Some agitators used the Gunpowder Plot to stir up division, but more moderate voices invoked the memory of 1605 in the interest of national unity. The Plot had become all things to all men, a malleable symbol in the face of fragmentation.

That the opening of the Long Parliament coincided with the Gunpowder anniversary was not lost on the assembled members. Addressing the Commons on 5 November 1640, Speaker Lenthall urged particular attention to 'this day's solemnization'.[3] Some people saw the calling of the parliament as part of an historical process which had earlier been marked by the discovery of the Gunpowder Plot. Debate would begin in November amidst the clamour of bells, in an atmosphere tinged with the smoke of bonfires and squibs.

On the healing side, *The Muses Fire-Works Upon the Fifth of November: or, The Protestants Remembrancer of the Bloody Designs of the Papists in the Never-to-be-forgotten Powder Plot*, appeared as a broadside in 1640. Replete with biblical and classical references, this work of wit was obviously directed to an educated audience, including the members assembled in parliament. Its message was benign, from the opening line, 'Hail happy hour, wherein that hellish plot was found,' to its conclusion, 'our nation need not fear/Dark lanterns while God's candlestick is here'. The valediction placed the poem on the side of unity in the current political crisis. 'Christ bless this kingdom from intestine quarrels,/From schism in tubs, and popery in barrels.'[4]

Less accommodating was John Vicars's *The Quintessence of Cruelty, or Master-piece of Treachery, the Popish Powder-Plot*, which appeared in time for November 1641. This was the English verse treatment of Francis Herring's classic Latin poem on the Gunpowder Plot, which had been barred from republication in 1637. It was addressed to 'all loyal-hearted English Protestants which sincerely relish the power and purity of Christ's gospel, and zealously detest the damnable doctrine of Antichrist'. Vicars's work contributed to the heightened anti-Catholicism of 1641 which turned memories of the Gunpowder Plot into attacks on malignants and adversaries wherever they might be found. It was not coincidental that the mob at Chelmsford chose 5 November 1641 to destroy a stained glass window that reminded them of Catholicism. According to a hostile reporter, 'on the fifth of November, in the evening, all the sectaries assemble together and in a riotous manner with long poles and stones beat down and deface the whole window'. This they did in pursuit of a 'thorough reformation', in a mocking reference to the government's policy of 'thorough'.[5]

The same day, in more sedate circumstances, Cornelius Burgess preached before the House of Commons. (Parliament normally heard two sermons on 5 November, if sitting, but in 1641 the members were too busy to hear more than one.) Burgess stressed that the Gunpowder anniversary was no mere antiquarian commemoration, but rather belonged to a significant and unfolding present. 'That great deliverance we now celebrate was not as a dead bush to stop a present gap only, nor a mercy expiring with that hour and occasion; but intended for a living, lasting, breeding mercy, that hath been very fertile ever since.' The lesson of Gunpowder Plot, forcefully reiterated, was *never* to trust or accommodate the Catholics, who even now were 'walking too openly, and boldly . . . pressing too near'. At the same time, Burgess warned, the parliament should guard against the radical furies of sectarianism and schism that undermined prosperity and peace. Zealous violence (such as occurred that evening at Chelmsford) would undermine rather than extend England's claim to further mercies.[6]

By the autumn of 1642 gunpowder had returned to the English scene with a vengeance. With the country at war, puritan preachers took the opportunity of Gunpowder Treason day to arouse both memory and action. In London on 5 November, 'both Houses kept the thanksgiving this forenoon at Saint Margaret's Westminster, before whom preached one Mr Newcomen, and after his sermon they sat again and ordered that thanks should be returned to Mr Newcomen for his sermon, and that he be desired to publish it in print'.[7]

Matthew Newcomen's sermon, like others of the revolutionary period, explored a dynamic tension between past, present and future. The ancient past was declared in the Bible, in particular the Old Testament, where the struggles and deliverances of the Israelites established precedents and parallels for Stuart Englishmen. The more recent past was structured by the English reformation, especially the establishment of Protestantism under Edward and Elizabeth. The book of Nehemiah talked of discouragements and deliverances, and sure enough, 'this day thirty-seven years was this scripture fulfilled in England'. Never was there so destructive a treason, never so marvellous a deliverance! Now, a full generation later, amidst renewed discouragements on the religious, political and military fronts, the situation called for decisive action. Mere commemoration would not be enough. 'Do you in your consciences think that the bare keeping this deliverance in memory, or an acknowledging of it in our assemblies, as at this day, is sufficient retribution of dignity and honour to our great deliverer,' asked Newcomen. No, came his answer. 'Arise, arise . . . ye members of the honourable houses of parliament, act something this day . . . worthy of this day . . . Root out not only popery but all that is popish. Let this day add something towards the perfection of that work.'[8]

Parliament went back to its business, and the same day a committee of the House of Commons took order 'for the demolishing of all the popish ceremonies at Somerset House, and the banishing of the Capuchin Friars out of this kingdom'. The Gunpowder sermon would stiffen the members to deal with the related issues (at least related in activist minds) of Archbishop Laud and the Catholic rising in Ireland. Matthew Newcomen was happy to conform to parliament's order to print his sermon, and *The Craft and Cruelty of the Churches Adversaries* appeared on the bookstalls almost at once. George Thomason had his copy by 22 November 1642. The planning behind this becomes clear when it is learned that Newcomen's sermon for 5 November had been entered at Stationers' Hall as early as 12 October.[9]

Despite the war and the press of extraordinary business, members of parliament usually paused each year on 5 November for collective meditation and thanksgiving. As many as four official sermons would be delivered, one to each house in the morning and the evening. The mayor, aldermen and civic leaders of London would similarly be regaled with a sermon at St Paul's, while diligent preachers in London and the provinces would mark the anniversary of the Gunpowder Plot in their parishes.

A parliamentary newspaper of 1644 reported, 'Tuesday the 5 of November was a day of thanksgiving, as first for our deliverance from the Powder Plot, and it was kept very solemnly; many guns went off, and many fine popish gods were burnt, which to do in the reign of Canterbury [i.e. Archbishop Laud, whose trial was just beginning] was a mark of a puritan'. The celebration also extended to the parliamentary successes at Newbury, Newcastle and Liverpool, which were thereby placed in the tradition of historic mercies and deliverances.[10]

Parliamentary preachers used the anniversary occasions to review recent and historical events, and to comfort or chastize as they saw fit. The four Westminster Gunpowder sermons of 1644 provide a sample of their reasoning and their rhetoric. William Spurstowe, who preached the morning sermon before the Lords on 5 November 1644, saw more darkness than light in the present moment. This was a day to 'tremble in the behalf of poor England' rather than a day of celebration and triumph. The nation had experienced a 'matchless salvation and deliverance' in escaping the Gunpowder Plot, but dangers were in store if the governors and people were 'careless in preserving its memory'. God had bestoweed remarkable gifts, but England had squandered them. 'The truth is,' Spustowe thundered, 'all the ways by which eminent mercies are abused and God provoked, we have practiced'. Memory of 1605 should be a stimulus to personal,

159

family and public reformation. Spurstowe appealed to the parliament to be vigilant against sabbath-breaking, drunkenness and swearing, and to 'be eminent in your zeal against popery'. Spurstowe titled his sermon, *Englands Eminent Judgements Caus'd by the Abuse of Gods Eminent Mercies*, and he expounded on a text from Ezra on the theme of ingratitude, apostasy and sinfulness.[11]

John Strickland, who preached to the Lords in the evening, would probably have agreed with most of his colleague's sermon but he adopted a much more cheerful approach. Strickland's title was *Immanuel, or The Church Triumphing*, and he spoke from Psalm 46, 'the lord of hosts is with us'. The parliamentary successes at Newbury and York belonged to a chain of providences and mercies that promised 'confidence for the future'. So too did the recent adoption of the Solemn League and Covenant, 'a matter of joy' according to Strickland. Just as in the days of the Spanish Armada and the Gunpowder Plot, God had taken our part in recent struggles and had secured us victories. Rather than reformation, Strickland urged praise. 'We should strive to give God perpetual praises, by perpetuating his praises unto posterity, a laying up a stock of seed and praise, that may bring forth a plentiful crop in the generations to come.'[12]

Anthony Burgess, preaching before the Commons, fanned the familiar fears of 'what darkness would have covered the land' had the Gunpowder Plot succeeded. He warned against 'connivance at popery' and, rather redundantly, urged against toleration or 'moderation'. Reflecting on the course of the civil war, Burgess offered thanks for the 'deliverances and victories vouchsafed by God to your armies', adding, 'every time you have a victory it is a deliverance from a Gunpowder Plot'.[13]

Charles Herle, who also preached before the House of Commons on 5 November 1644, spoke as if he was preparing the members for combat. He took his text from the book of Samuel, describing David's battles with the Philistines, and used this as a metaphor for England's present conflicts. Lest anyone associate the biblical monarch with King Charles he was quick to point out that 'David in fighting God's battles is a type of no earthly king, but a type or rather emblem of God's church in all succeeding ages'. David, then, who had previously been linked with Queen Elizabeth and King James, was now recruited as a supporter of the Solemn League and Covenant, and became associated with a partisan view of English history. As for the deliverance of 5 November, Herle told the Commons, 'you must expect to stand in need of more deliverances: the same brood of enemies that then durst venture but an undermining, dare now attempt an open battery'. The Philistine pioneers were tunnelling 'from Oxford, Rome, Hell, to Westminster, and there to blow up, if possible, the better foundations of your houses, their liberties and privileges'. The English David, of course, would triumph. Herle concluded with a vision of Protestant unity and military success in which the English, allied with the Scots, recover Ireland, liberate Germany, and carry the battle to the Catholic heartlands.[14]

Even in royalist areas the commemoration went on, but charged with different resonances and expectations. Royalists, not surprisingly, took exception to the parliament appropriating this national and dynastic symbol. William Sclater, a prebend at Exeter Cathedral, had published his 5 November sermon of 1641 as a rallying cry for the king and the Church of England. This represented Charles, 'the very mirror of Christian princes', as defending the established religion against puritan 'novelty'. Gunpowder Plot was 'treason unheard of' until, by implication, the actions of the present rebels.[15]

A royalist pamphlet on *The Fifth of November*, published at Oxford in 1644, went further in comparing the parliamentary rebellion to the Gunpowder Treason, and likening the London schismatics to Jesuits. Both threatened crown and church, both promised bloodshed. Scandalizing the devout anti-papists at Westminster, the royalists sneered at the similarity of the popish plotters and the 'schismatical rebels'. 'Religion is made the stalking horse to rebellion by both parties. The Jesuited and Anabaptized party row with the same oars, sail by the same wind and compass, though their coats be as far distant as Amsterdam and Rome.' The true custodian of the November commemoration, by implication, was the king, whose very life had been threatened when he was a boy in 1605, not the parliamentarians who were in arms against him.[16]

If puritans and parliamentarians pointed to November as a month of exceptional providences, royalists could respond that November was even more significant for anniversaries affecting the established church and the king. The month began with All Saints' day and All Souls', two days of religious sensitivity. 'The unhappy parliament' had assembled on 3 November; the next day was the birthday of Princess Mary. Everyone knew that 5 November marked 'our delivery from the papists conspiracy', an event of national rather than partisan significance, which is more than could be said for 12 November, the day of the royalist victory at Brentford (in 1642). Queen Henrietta Maria had her birthday on 16 November; 17 November marked the beginning of Queen Elizabeth's reign; and the king had his birthday on 19 November. November was 'red in ink, redder in wine,' declared a royalist broadsheet of 1647, referring to the coloured lettering in the almanacs and to the healths drunk by loyal subjects.[17]

In November 1647 the royalist cause was at a very low ebb (the king himself was a prisoner of the army), but Gunpowder Treason day still prompted thoughts of 'inestimable' mercies, past and yet to come. 'If it shall please God (as who shall doubt it) to stop the issue of blood in this kingdom, and to confound the plots and devices of the enemies thereof, restore the king to his crown, and the languishing subject to his liberty, posterity will undoubtedly set apart the day, whereon to commemorate . . . so universal and unspeakable a deliverance of his majesty, and the whole kingdom, from the most destructive and damnable conspiracies of a mad and bloody parliament.'[18] The author of these hopes would have to wait until 1660 to see them realized.

★

Gunpowder Treason celebrations took on new vigour after the parliamentary victory in the civil war. The bells of the City churches rang forth, and bonfires were lit with abandon. Victory, however, did not mean security, and the triumph over the king could not confidently be called a deliverance. On 5 November 1647 the House of Commons sat down to a challenging sermon, struggled to debate the matter of the king's negative oath, and then retired to watch a pageant of fireworks.[19] William Bridge, sometime fellow of Emmanuel College, Cambridge, and 'now preacher of God's word at Yarmouth,' told the House that sinful England had not *deserved* deliverance either in 1605 or more recently; preservation came about through the mere grace of the Lord. 'Witness the mercy and deliverance of this day. When the Powder Treason was on foot, what a dark night of security had trodden upon the glory of our English day . . . what pride, oppression, court-uncleanness, superstitions, and persecutions of the saints then under the name of puritans? Nevertheless he saved us, and our fathers. And now of late, what bitterness of spirit among professors, what divisions, oppressions, instead of justice? What new-fangled prides? What unwillingness to be reformed?' The discovery of Gunpowder Plot was a great blow to the papists, and a great salvation to England, but the situation called for continual watchfulness. 'I fear the hand of the Jesuit is too much among us at this day. But, Oh England! Oh Parliament! for ever remember the fifth of November: the snare is broken and we are delivered.'[20]

To cap the day a spectacular firework display was presented in Lincoln's Inn Fields 'before the Lords and Commons of Parliament and the militia of London, in commemoration of God's great mercy in delivering this kingdom from the hellish plots of papists, acted in the damnable Gunpowder Treason'. The gunner George Brown applied his skills of military engineering to mount a pyrotechnic extravaganza with a dozen set pieces. Spectators could obtain a printed programme which explained what each tableau 'intimates'. This is worth citing at length for its representation of the Catholic threat to England's king and parliament, its conservative sentiments, and its elaboration of the vocabulary of celebration.

1. Fire-balls burning in the water, and rising out of the water burning, showing the papists' conjuration and consultation with infernal spirits, for the destruction of England's king and parliament.
2. Fire-boxes like meteors, sending forth many dozen rockets out of the water, intimating the popish spirits coming from below to act their treasonous plots against England's king and parliament.
3. Fawkes with his dark lantern, and many fire-boxes, lights, and lamps, ushering the pope into England, intimating the plot to destroy England's king and parliament.
4. Pluto with his fiery club, presenting himself maliciously bent to destroy all that have hindered the pope from destroying England's king and parliament.
5. Hercules with his fiery club, who discomforteth Pluto, and suffers him not, nor any of his infernal spirits to hurt England's king and parliament.
6. Runners on a line, intimating the papists sending to all parts of the world, for subtle cunning and malicious plotters of mischief against England's king and parliament.
7. A fire-wheel, intimating the display of a flag of victory over the enemies that would have destroyed England's king and parliament, in the time of which motion a pair of virginals musically playing of themselves.
8. Rockets in the air, showing the thankfulness of all well-willers to true religion, for the deliverance of England's king and parliament.
9. Balloons breaking in the air, with many streams of fire, showing God's large and bounteous goodness towards England's king and parliament.
10. Chambers of lights, showing England's willingness to cherish the light of the glorious gospel therein to be continued.
11. A great bumber-ball breaking in pieces, and discharging itself of other its lights, holding forth the cruelty of the papists to England's king and parliament.
12. Fire-boxes among the spectators, to warn them to take heed for

the future that they cherish none that are enemies to England's king and parliament.[21]

This was a spectacular display, reminiscent of some of the elaborate masques and entertainments of the Stuart court, though charged with a different message. The royalist newspaper *Mercurius Elencticus* dismissively referred to the show as 'some squirting and squibbling fooleries in Lincoln's Inn Fields'.[22] The performance was accompanied by bonfires and bells.

Most metropolitan parishes made regular annual payments to their bellringers on Gunpowder Treason day in the 1640s and 1650s; only during the later years of the Protectorate was there any sign of hesitation. Saints' days may have been suppressed, and royal anniversaries ignored, but the 5 November celebrations carried on with only slight diminution in vigour. The bells of St Martin in the Fields and St Margaret Westminster, scarcely missed a beat. In some London parishes there was even an intensification of the Gunpowder Treason celebration in the 1640s, associated, no doubt, with the anxieties of war and revolution. On 5 November 1645 the parish of St Martin Orgar spent £1. 4s. on sermons and candles and a further 8s. 8d. to illuminate the church lantern. Bonfires, bells, and exceptional pyrotechnic performances marked 5 November 1647 when the city was full of soldiers. Soldiers and civilians, presbyterians and independents, sectaries and defeated royalists, all had an interest in the anniversary, even if their hopes and expectations were different.[23]

At St Mary Aldermanbury, London, in 1650 five shillings was 'given to the ringers on the 5th of November according to custom,' and the custom continued throughout the decade. Similarly, the ringers at St Andrew by the Wardrobe rang every year. But other parishes, for example St Bartholemew Exchange, recorded no commemorative ringing between 1655 and 1660. Whether this was due to religious scruple, mob intimidation, or defective record keeping is not yet clear.

St Botolph without Bishopsgate, which had a lively tradition of celebration, continued to mark Gunpowder Treason day in the 1650s by ringing the bells and distributing bread to the poor. But there were no more parish bonfires. Instead the commemoration became safer and more select, culminating in an indoor dinner for the elite. In 1658 the parish sponsored a 'Gunpowder Treason dinner' at the Red Lion, incurring £5. 12s. 6d. in expenses, itemized by the churchwardens as follows:

five stone, two pounds of beef	11s. 6d.
two legs of mutton	6s. 6d.
four capons	10s. 0d.
four mince pies	12s. 0d.
a gallon of canary	8s. 0d.
a gallon of claret	3s. 4d.
twenty dozen of bread	£1. 0s. 0d.
for a sermon	10s. 0d.
the porter	4d.
the clerk	1s. 4d.
the sexton	8d.
the maid	1s. 0d.
two ounces of tobacco	2s. 0d.
the house bill of the Red Lion	£1. 5s. 10d.

The varying practices suggest that considerable uncertainty developed about whether the old festivity was appropriate or permissible under the altered conditions of the revolution. In the provinces, as in the capital, the celebrations were partly a matter of custom, partly a measure of the confidence of local community leaders. There are hints in some writings of the 1650s that the Gunpowder anniversary was neglected or faced with suppression. In some places it was marked more by irregular activity – private bonfires and the throwing of squibs and crackers – than by sponsored observances.[24] Urban parishes at Norwich, Derby, and York kept up their ringing, but at Salisbury the tradition faltered. The accounts of St Thomas, Sarum, show no payments for ringing on 5 November during the period of the Protectorate. Holy Trinity, Cambridge, maintained its traditions of bonfires and bells on Gunpowder Treason day into the mid-1650s, but seems to have stopped during the last three years of the Protectorate. Neighbouring Great St Mary's, however, rang the bells on 5 November throughout the period of the civil war and inter-regnum. Great Staughton, Huntingdonshire, was one of the many country parishes with an unbroken record of bellringing throughout the interregnum. But here the amount given to the ringers shrank from 6s. 8d. in 1649 to 2s. 6d. in 1656, before resuming its former level in 1660. At Hartland, Devon, the churchwardens laid out between four shillings and eight shillings for ringing on 5 November every year up to 1656. In that year the expenditure was disallowed by the local justices, and the outgoing churchwarden had to reimburse the parish from his own pocket. That was the end of community-sponsored bellringing at Hartland until the practice was resumed at the Restoration. That bellringing flourished elsewhere during the interregnum, for recreational as well as commemorative purposes, is suggested by the continuation of the Society of College Youths and the further development of the art of change ringing.[25]

*

Burdened with the anxieties and confusions of a dangerous present, it was not surprising that some authors of the 1650s sought comfort in England's past. The accession of Elizabeth, the escape from the Spanish Armada, and the deliverance from Gunpowder Treason still formed a triumphant motif in the chorus English history. The same providential protection that had secured such spectacular historical deliverances was believed, optimistically, to be operating in the present. The record of earlier deliverances, signs of God's mercies to his chosen people, still provided assurance and inspiration. The past century of deliverances gave structure to English history, and allowed a measure of confidence about the future. In this light the old calendar of Protestant anniversaries continued under the revolutionary regime, providing annual occasions to harness the past to present partisan concerns.

Gunpowder Treason sermons continued to touch the pulse of the nation, at least the political mainstream, during the troubled years of the interregnum. Peter Sterry addressed the Rump Parliament on 5 November 1651 on the theme of *England's Deliverance from the Northern Presbytery, Compared with its Deliverance from the Roman Papacy.* The view preached to parliament in 1644, that the Scottish alliance was another of God's mercies and that the Solemn League and Covenant was 'a matter of joy', collapsed amidst the religious and political wrangling in the years that followed. Sterry now argued that the 'zeal plot' of presbytery was more dangerous than the Gunpowder Plot of Catholicism, and warned that 'the same spirit which lay in the polluted bed of papacy may meet them in the perfumed bed of presbytery'.[26]

One did not have to look to the Elizabethan or Jacobean periods to find examples of popish plotting. The devil, the pope and the king of Spain sought tirelessly to ruin England and to subvert true religion, or so it was widely believed. Jeffrey Corbet, a London grocer, catalogued recent examples of Catholic plotting in his remonstrance, *The Protestant's Warning-Piece*, published in 1656. 'The unparalleled mercies which God hath bestowed upon these nations have been hitherto intermixed with dreadful judgments threatening utter destruction.' Corbet made no specific reference to the Gunpowder Plot, but the connection was apparent in the timing and context. George Thomason found Corbet's pamphlet on the London book-stalls on 8 November 1656.[27]

166

Some writers feared that memory of these former mercies was fading. Official sermons still drew attention to the deliverance of 5 November, but there was a falling off in the popular celebration with bonfires and bells. It was as if the revolution induced confusion, indifference or exhaustion, rather than fresh infusions of godly zeal. In 1654 John Turner published *A Commemoration, or a Calling to Minde of the Great and Eminent Deliverance from the Powder-Plot.* This came out in advance of the November anniversary, and was clearly intended to stimulate commemorative observances; George Thomason collected his copy on 10 October. Turner began, 'England alas almost hath quite forgot/The great deliverance from the Powder Plot', and continued in this vein for six pages. He warned of the danger of burying these events in oblivion, and observed, 'The mercies all that now we do enjoy/We owe unto the mercy of that day.' Moved by pious wonder and devout admiration, the English were supposed to keep the deliverance of 1605 for ever in mind, but half a century later, Turner feared, the commemoration was neglected.

> So dealt our good and gracious God with us;
> But he may say, Do you requite me thus?
> Was the mercy I showed you worth no more?
> That you by it do set no greater store?
> Sure we have cause for ever to remember
> The mercy show'd the fifth day of November.[28]

Turner need not have worried that the day might pass unnoticed. Shorn of its royal and dynastic associations, 5 November was generally observed as a Protestant day of thanksgiving throughout the period of the interregnum. The established rhythm of services and sermons continued in most places with little interruption, even if the celebrations were somewhat muted. According to *The Weekly Intelligencer of the Commonwealth*, on Sunday, 5 November 1654, 'Mr Nanton and Mr Vines preached before the parliament, it being a day of commemoration for deliverance from the Gunpowder Treason.' The Lord Mayor and Aldermen of London assembled at St Paul's on 5 November 1654 to hear a sermon by Thomas Horton, Doctor of Divinity and Professor at Gresham College. This was a civic event of some solemnity, and the first Gunpowder day of the Protectorate. The day, being the sabbath, was, of course, the Lord's day; but, Horton remarked, as 5 November 'it is *our* day, the day which God hath marked with an eminent and famous deliverance of this land and nation'. Horton stressed that the Gunpowder deliverance was 'a monument of God's goodness to the nation'. 'It is a deliverance and preservation which is never to be forgotten by us, nor our posterity after us, so long as the sun and moon shall endure in heaven.'[29]

The central feature of Horton's sermon was the importance of memory and commemoration. 'The goodness of God to his people in his deliverances and preservations of them, it is such as even succeeding ages and generations shall take notice of.' *The Pillar and Pattern of Englands Deliverances* should be proclaimed for the glory of God, for the shame of his enemies, and for the comfort of God's church and people. Memory, then, was a weapon as well as a salve and balsam. 'It is our duty to be mindful and talkative of the goodness of God to us in the times and generations which are past . . . As it should be often in our memories and thoughts and meditations and mental reflections, so it should be likewise in our lips and mouths and speeches and daily converse.'[30]

How should these memories be preserved? Horton answered that parents and masters had the duty to transmit the information to successive generations as part of their household instruction. Public commemorations, such as the annual sermon on 5 November, were equally important, for the memories might die out 'were it not for such solemn times as these are, which are set apart on purpose for their commemoration'. Without perpetual attention to past mercies, England could not expect further dispensations of God's goodness in the future. Memory and commemoration was also the theme of Ralph Venning's sermon at St Paul's on 5 November 1656. 'Memory is a slippery thing', he noted, but the Gunpowder Treason should be firmly recalled in our 'catalogues of mercies' and ledgers of debts.[31] The book-keeping image was especially apt for a congregation of merchants.

Horton and Venning were by no means alone in reminding English readers about former deliverances. In 1657 Samuel Clarke, pastor of the City of London church of St Bennet Fink, published a comprehensive account entitled *Englands Remembrancer, Containing a True and Full Narrative of those Two Never to be Forgotten Deliverances: The One from the Spanish Invasion in Eighty Eight; the Other from the Hellish Powder Plot: November 5. 1605*. To this he added the helpful note, 'they that would see further into this work of darkness in the powder plot are desired to look into the sermons of the Reverend Dr Spurstowe, pastor of Hackney, and Mr Matthew Newcomen, pastor of Dedham, both preached before the parliament on the fifth of November. As also Mr Venning's sermon preached at Paul's last fifth of November.'[32] A dozen or more anniversary sermons from previous years were still available in print.

Clarke prepared his historical account to the end 'that all sorts may be stirred up to real thankfulness and transmit the same to their posterity; that their children may know the reason why the fifth of November is celebrated; that God may have glory, and the papists perpetual infamy'. Clarke set forth the story of the plot 'lest the remembrance of so signal a mercy and deliverance, vouchsafed by God both to our church and state, should be buried in oblivion . . . And truly, the remembrance of this great mercy hath the more need to be revived at this time, when some noted persons amongst us begin to lessen and decry it, and wholly to lay aside the observation of that day, though enjoined by Act of Parliament and made conscience of by most of the godly people of the nation.'[33]

A similar memorial, Thomas Spencer's *Englands Warning-Peece: or The History of the Gun-powder Treason*, appeared on the bookstalls towards the end of 1658. This narrative of eighty pages was also intended to reinvigorate what the author feared might be a fading memory. It was written in order that 'the memorial of this most prodigious conspiracy, which never had any fellow, being almost obliterated and forgotten in many places of the land, may be renewed, revived, and presented to succeeding generations'.[34]

Parliamentary and civic preachers of the 1640s and 1650s harped constantly on the theme of memory and commemoration. Like their counterparts in New England, they preached jeremiads on the theme of declension as well as more optimistic sermons of thanksgiving. The calendrical opportunity of 5 November took them to their pulpits, and most of their official sermons were quickly circulated in print. Royalists lay low. Many of the moderate and conforming clergy were dismissed as 'malignants' and their critical voices were suppressed. An alternative press operated vigorously in the 1640s but in the 1650s there were fewer opportunities to distribute dissident views. The Gunpowder Treason anniversary may have stimulated opinions other than those that conformed to the official mainstream, but they are mostly lost to history since so few of them appeared in print.

As the decade came to an end, however, in the last gutterings of the protectorate, the old anniversary took on yet another coloration. Ralph Brownrigg, the deprived bishop of Exeter, preached on 5 November 1659 on the text from Daniel, 'O king, live for ever.' His talk of 'miraculous deliverance' from 'a malicious conspiracy' made explicit reference to Daniel in the lions' pit and to England in 1605, but he clearly had an eye on the possibilities of the present. Brownrigg could not anticipate the Restoration, nor would he live to enjoy it (he died on 7 December 1659), but he believed that England's day of deliverance was heavy with portent. 'If you count it now a day out of date, an old day, and it may be forgotten, take heed a second war does not finish that work that those traitors would have done but could not accomplish.'[35] Whether the traitors were Guy Fawkes and Catesby, or more recent historical actors, was for the reader or listener to decide.

11
THE POLITICS OF MEMORY
IN LATER STUART ENGLAND

Charles II ruled over a divided religious culture and a fractured political nation. The rifts between Protestants and Catholics, anglicans and dissenters, Tories and Whigs, have no doubt been exaggerated, but there were plentiful opportunities in the later seventeenth century for the festering of old wounds and new. It was therefore all the more important that England should have certain common and unifying symbols. The restored Protestant monarchy and its special anniversaries provided a potential framework for reconciliation, but this was only partially achieved. Rationality, scepticism and an urbanity verging on tolerance may have been the hallmarks of some cultural leaders, but the old anxieties were never far from the surface.

The bells that welcomed Charles II in 1660 not only announced the restoration of the anglican ecclesiastical calendar but also fore-shadowed the adoption of new politicized national anniversaries on 30 January and 29 May. Christmas, Easter, and Whitsun again took their place as markers of the Christian year, and as favoured times for taking holy communion. With them came Shrovetide and Maytide, tradi-tional festive seasons that were only loosely connected to the church. Charles II was the May king, born in that month, and re-born to his kingdom, ever to be associated with maypoles and the revelling good fellowship of his father's and grandfather's Book of Sports. Another springtime anniversary, St George's day, took a new significance as Charles II and his successor chose 23 April for their coronations. Court and country saw the promotion of the calendar of 'merry England' as well as a calendar of deliverances.

The Restoration calendar included three special days commemorat-ing the sufferings and successes of the Stuart dynasty of the Church of England. The first was 30 January, the anniversary of the execution of King Charles the royal martyr, which was to be observed with solemn fasts and sermons. 'On this day murthered was King Charles the first/Oh, let king-killers ever be accurst,' sang the *Telescopium Uranicum* almanac for 1662. The second day was 29 May, Royal Oak day, the king's birthday and the day of his restoration. This was to be celebrated as a day of joy for dynastic continuity under Charles II and his successors. 'King Charles the second born, and safe return,/Lets all rejoice, bells ring, and bonfires, burn,' trilled the almanac. The third, of course, was 5 November, an old anniversary that could be observed with enthusiasm by both supporters and critics of the Stuart crown. Gunpowder Treason had long been an anniversary of sensitivity and ambivalence, and was to provide a fresh focus for dissent in the later seventeenth century. The almanac could do no better than this lame verse: 'The Powder Plot was papish, was it not?/Yea, and an act made ne'er to be forgot.'[1] The almanac also remembered Queen Elizabeth's day, 17 November.

By the age of Charles II, England's historic deliverances of the Elizabethan and Jacobean period lay beyond the reach of most living memory, yet they continued to influence religious consciousness and political behaviour. Rather than fading with time, such 'mercies' as the triumphs of Queen Elizabeth and the discovery of the Gunpowder Plot remained in view as highly charged points of reference and commentary. Any danger that they might lapse into oblivion was overcome by their continuing utility for religious polemic and political mobilization. Instead of being drained of meaning they were reinfused with significance in the face of recurrent popish threats. The recollection of historic threats and deliverances served to warn against the ceaseless machinations of popery, and to reassure believers that God would again rescue his Protestant Englishmen from danger. The renewed fear of Catholics in the 1670s, and the volatile religious politics of the period that followed, brought the memory of past providences to the fore and shaped them to the fears and pressures of the moment.

During Charles I's reign the rhetorical temperature of Gunpowder Treason day had been raised by the anxious and inflamatory sermons of puritan ministers. But under Charles II the nonconformist ministry was decimated and lost its voice. Close to one thousand clergymen were ejected from their livings after the Act of Uniformity in 1662. (Significantly, the date of ejection was 24 August, which some dissenters referred to thenceforth as 'our St Bartholomew's day'.) The Conventicle Act of 1664 and the Five Mile Act of 1665 made it difficult for them to meet their former congregations.[2] The dissenters yielded their pulpits to anglican conformists, and most were deprived of the opportunity to interpret the anniversary occasions in public. Gunpowder Treason retained an important meaning for religious radicals of the later seventeenth century, but we have to search for that meaning elsewhere since so few nonconformists sermons survive. Philip Henry, for example, a dissenter in Flintshire, noted 5

November 1670 as 'a day which ought to be remembered forever, but is almost forgotten by these unthankful nations, which bodes ill in my eye; *ingentia beneficia, ingentia flagitia, ingentia supplicia*' (large benefits, large crimes, large punishments).[3]

It would be wrong, however, to assume that the ousting of nonconformists deprived the Restoration church of godly preachers. Many examined their consciences and found it right to continue as priests of the Church of England. Ralph Josselin, for example, though heavy of heart for 'the church's troubles', held his place at Earl's Colne, Essex, and preached regularly on the anniversary occasions.[4]

Royalist apologists linked 5 November to 29 May, celebrating both occasions as deliverances of the Stuart dynasty. Patriotic preachers invoked the litany of divine interventions as endorsements of the established regime. Anglican conservatives recalled the deliverance of a king and his progeny from danger, and emphasized the safeguarding of Protestant episcopacy and the Book of Common Prayer. The history of Gunpowder Plot and its Elizabethan antecedents was, for them, a vindication of the established church. John Evelyn heard such a sermon at Westminster Abbey on 5 November 1664 'concerning obedience to magistrates, against the pontificians and sectaries,' and judged it 'an excellent discourse'. In 1666 the Bishop of Winchester (George Morley) made 'the Gunpowder delivery' before the king, and 'did so pelt the papists and presbyterians with such evangelical broadsides of allegiance as would make the severest schismatic of their persuasions be in love with loyalty'.[5] As always, the anniversary provided a polysemous occasion which could be repoliticized for current purposes.

Though made customary by two generations of tradition, the Gunpowder anniversary was both a divisive and a unifying occasion. It was universally observed but subject to various interpretations. For some it was a day of self-congratulation; for others, a day of anxiety and hope. For apprentices in the London crowd the November bonfires occasioned licensed lawlessness. Samuel Pepys saw 'boys in the street fling their crackers', and found his way home from the theatre obstructed by bonfires. On 5 November 1668 young people threw fireworks into the Spanish ambassador's coach. Mayoral proclamations failed to stop the practice.[6] But despite these excesses, commemorative celebrations of the 1660s were mostly customary and high-spirited observances, not driven by the raging anti-Catholic passion that would come later.

The Gunpowder Treason commemoration continued to be institutionalized and ritualized with sermons, bonfires and bells. Churches throughout the country rang their bells each 5 November, as they had for more than half a century. As in previous decades, the amount expended on ringing varied with local resources and custom. During Charles II's reign the ringers at All Saints', Dorchester, received a mere shilling for their efforts each 5 November. The ringers' reward at Minchinhampton, Gloucester, was two shillings. At Isleworth, Middlesex, they earned five shillings. At Hartland, Devon, the parish expenses on 5 November topped eight shillings. And at All Saints', Derby, the churchwardens paid ten shillings for each set of anniversary ringing. In most places the money was evenly distributed, with the same amount spent on 5 November as on 29 May.

Firing a bonfire on Gunpowder Treason day was still a matter of local preference and custom. The churchwardens of Holy Trinity and Great St Mary's, Cambridge, kept up their anniversary bonfires in the 1670s. At Darlington, county Durham, both 29 May and 5 November were celebrated with flaming coals and tar barrels. Londoners lit bonfires too, but after the great fire in 1666 the authorities were understandably nervous. Increasingly they were seen as sources of disorder, as well as potential damage.

The catastrophe of 1666 brought commemorative bellringing to a halt in the City of London. In parish after parish the ringing was temporarily silenced when the belfries were destroyed in the great fire. It took several years, sometimes decades, to refound the bells and to hang them again and to make them chime. Other forms of noise-making were a poor substitute. London bonfires continued to express local approbation, although on 5 November 1666 Pepys could find 'not one bonfire through the whole town in going round the wall, which is strange, and speaks the melancholy disposition of the City at present, while never more was said of and feared of and done against the papists than just at this time'. Catholics, of course, were blamed for the conflagration.[7]

★

Hostility to Roman Catholics flared up again in the early 1670s after a dozen years of relative calm. Charles II issued the Declaration of Indulgence in March 1672, suspending the penal laws against Catholics and nonconformists. He was forced to withdraw it twelve months later amidst a howl of anglican protest. This unpopular attempt to introduce religious toleration raised fears of creeping popery, and led to the Test Act of 1673. The Test Act required all office holders to subscribe the oaths of supremacy and allegiance and to deny transubstantiation. Protestant dissenters suffered from its provisions, but the Act was widely construed as action towards the suppression of popery.[8] Its passing, therefore, produced a whoop of anglican delight. The Protestant cause was further troubled in September 1673 by the marriage of James, Duke of York, to the Catholic Mary of Modena. By this time James was known to be a Catholic, and his marriage raised the nightmare prospect of a Catholic succession.

In this climate it was not surprising to find a renewal of interest in the history of the Gunpowder Plot, and lively demonstrations on its anniversary. Ralph Josselin preached at Earl's Colne on 5 November 1673, hoping 'God's deliverances . . . will deliver against the fears of popery at present in England, the Duke marrying Modena's daughter'. In 1675 he used his pulpit to give a narrative history of the Gunpowder Plot.[9] November 1673 saw a further split between the polite anniversary observances of the elite and the popular celebration and agitation in the streets. Parliament was in session at this time, so the members were treated to sermons at Westminster, with Peter Gunning, the Bishop of Chichester, preaching to the Lords and Edward Stillingfleet, a royal chaplain, regaling the Commons. Their efforts met with 'universal applause, and the night was solemnized with the usual divertisement of fireworks'.[10]

Meanwhile in the City of London, the apprentices were turning 5 November into a dramatic anti-Catholic fire festival. Some exploded squibs 'to testify their joy and gladness for the wonderful preservation of their forefathers'. The occasion excused their dangerous behaviour, as they stopped coaches and demanded money for alcohol and bonfires. To these standard expressions of celebration the apprentices made 'a new addition', which provided a prototype for the later pope-burning processions. They constructed an effigy of the Whore of Babylon, decked out with 'all the whorish ornaments' of papal crosses, keys, beads and triple crown, and carried it in a torchlight procession to 'a great bonfire' in the Poultry. There the monster was strung up above the street, to dance in the air and to provide a target for pistols, before descending into the flames. The crowd was noisy, rowdy, and inebriated, but the symbolism was specific and controlled.

A printed report that appeared a few days later linked this performance (for performance it was, complete with audience and applause) to the dying words of Hugh Latimer in 1555, that the Marian martyrs would 'light such a fire this day in England as by God's grace the papists shall never be able to quench it'. (Latimer was burned at Oxford, but many of his fellows had gone to the stake at Smithfield, only half a mile from the site of the immolation of the Whore of Babylon.) The author explained that the papists notoriously used fire as a weapon (citing the martyrs' fires in 1555, the planned conflagration of 1605, and current suspicions about 1666), so it was appropriate that fire should now be used against them. The pamphlet promised that there would be no quenching of 'the fire of the Gunpowder Treason in the thoughts of the present generation'.[11]

It was disconcerting, therefore, to be told that the Gunpowder conspiracy was no popish plot at all, but 'Cecil's contrivance', a scheme devised by Sir Robert Cecil to entrap innocent Catholics. Catholic apologists repeated this story early in Charles II's reign, and some Protestant activists felt forced to rebut it. Several publications of the 1670s made use of a Latin account by the French Catholic Jacques Auguste de Thou to discredit the Jesuits and to prove that reasonable Catholics acknowledged the historical truth of the Gunpowder Plot.[12] The Plot had become an indispensable feature of the English political landscape. Scholarly Protestants of the Restoration era were willing to consider the evidence, and to recognize that not all Catholics were conspirators or incendiaries. But there was little room for reasonable detachment in the frenzied atmosphere of the late 1670s.

A series of publications of the 1670s drew fresh attention to Gunpowder Treason in order to make the point that the 'restless mysterious practices' of the papists were as threatening now as ever. Edward Stephens compiled a history of Catholic plots and conspiracies with the assertion 'we are still in danger'. De Thou's account was variously translated as *Popish Policies and Practices* and *A Narration of that Horrible Conspiracy against King James*. Several of the early-Stuart treatises on Gunpowder Plot were reprinted to serve a new readership. Thomas Barlow, Bishop of Lincoln, sponsored the republication of 'an authentic history' of the Gunpowder Treason because parliament in November 1678 'did diligently seek after this book' but 'found it not'. The historical record would show that the conspiracies of 1605 and 1678 were 'hatched and hammered in the same popish forge'.[13]

Anti-Catholic writings abounded, and the bookstalls were laden with 'authentic histories' of popish plotting. *The Gunpowder Treason: with a discourse of its discovery; and a perfect relation of the proceedings against the conspirators*, first published in 1609, was reprinted in 1679 at the height of anxiety about the Popish Plot. A *History of the Gunpowder Treason* by John Williams, Barlow's predecessor at Lincoln between 1621 and 1641, was printed in 1678 and again in 1679. John Wilson's *Song or story for the lasting remembrance of divers famous works which God hath done in our time*, first published in 1626, appeared again in 1680 with its warning of the 'fell and furious rage' of the papists. Samuel Clarke's *Englands Remembrancer, containing a true and full narrative of those two never to be forgotten deliverances: the one from the Spanish invasion in eighty eight: the other from the hellish Powder Plot, November 5. 1605*, written in 1657, appeared in three new editions between 1671 and 1679.[14]

Though written for earlier generations, these reprints ensured that the narrative of 1588 and 1605, and the particular providential interpretation that went with them, would fuel Protestant concerns at the time of the exclusion crisis. Samuel Clarke had worried 'lest the remembrance of so signal a mercy and deliverance vouchsafed by God both to our church and state should be buried in oblivion'. The enterprise of godly printers and the circumstance of revived anti-Catholicism ensured that the memory stayed alive. Playing cards with illustrations of Catholic atrocity and popish plottery were also popular at this time. In 1679 a dealer near Stationers' Hall advertised 'a pack of cards, price one shilling, forming a history of all the popish plots from those in Queen Elizabeth's time . . . with the manner of Sir Edmundbury Godfrey's murder'. Another series traced the history of the Spanish Armada and related the attempted invasion of 1588 to later Catholic attempts against English Protestantism. Publications of 1680 included the verse pamphlet, *Faux's Ghost: or, Advice to Papists. The Domestick Intelligence* of 3–7 November 1681 reported, 'there is lately published the history of the life, bloody reign and death of Queen Mary . . . and other popish cruelties . . . seasonably published for a caution against popery, illustrated with pictures'.[15]

If Duke James's marriage to Mary of Modena alarmed Protestant activists, the marriage of his daughter, Princess Mary, to William of Orange gave them great satisfaction. This Protestant wedding was celebrated on 4 November 1677, and the news 'occasioned great acclamations of joy' on the Gunpowder Treason day that followed. The bonfires and bells expressed hope for a Protestant succession, as well as the usual anti-Catholic commemoration. Effigies of the pope were burned at the Monument, the memorial to the great fire, which had some of the features of an anti-Catholic shrine. Despite fears for the worst, however, the day passed relatively quietly.[16]

Twelve days later, on 17 November, London launched a more elaborate popular celebration. It is best described in a letter Charles Hatton sent from London to his brother in the country: 'Last Saturday the coronation of Queen Elizabeth was solemnized in the city with mighty bonfires and the burning of a most costly pope, carried by four persons in divers habits, and the effigies of two devils whispering in his ears, his belly filled with live cats who squalled most hideously as soon as they felt the fire; the common saying all the while it was the language of the pope and the devil in a dialogue betwixt them. A tierce of claret [42 gallons] was set out before the Temple gate for the common people. Mr Langhorne saith he is very confident the pageantry cost forty pounds.'[17] Though fueled by anxiety about papism, the spectacle bespeaks as much a lark as alarm, and indicates an underlying confidence in the superiority and permanence of English Protestantism.

★

During the later years of Charles II's reign, in an atmosphere poisoned by suspicion of popish plotting and the likelihood of a Catholic succession, the November commemorations again changed in tone and style. Preachers and pamphleteers focused more acutely on the dangers of Catholicism and the revived popish menace. Polite anglican ministers and principled dissenters found themselves swept along with Whig rabble rousers and the London crowd as the November anniversary flared into a storm of anti-Catholic agitation.

The shift of mood can be dated to the revelation of the so-called Popish Plot in September 1678. Titus Oates and Israel Tonge spread tales of a murderous conspiracy aimed at eliminating Charles II and bringing in a Roman Catholic regime under his brother James. Conditioned by memories of a century of popish plotting, people were inclined to believe anything foul tainted by Rome. The mysterious murder of Sir Edmund Berry Godfrey, the London magistrate who had taken Oates's deposition, gave credibility to the story. So too did the discovery that Edward Coleman, a former secretary to the Duke of York, had engaged in treasonable correspondence with Catholics overseas. Religion, the church, the state, and the fabric of law and custom, were seen to be imperilled by popish plotting, just as they had been seventy-three years earlier by the Gunpowder Plot. In the months that followed, a frenzy of accusations and revelations led to the execution of Jesuits and an intensification of popular anti-Catholicism.

Oates eventually ran out of steam, and the lies and inconsistencies of his account became apparent. The panic subsided by 1682, but the hysteria left its mark in a toughening of the Test Act and in the energetic campaigns of the exclusion crisis. Bills were read in parliament in May 1679, November 1680, and March 1681, designed to exclude the Duke of York from the royal succession.[18] Not surprisingly, November's Protestant anniversaries in those years produced lively and violent demonstrations. Parliament was sitting in November 1680, and the second exclusion bill was read against the background of bonfires and demonstrations in the streets. It is significant that this exclusion bill set 5 November as a deadline.

The crisis of 1678–81 pushed leading churchmen to assert their Protestant patriotism while avoiding, if possible, the excesses of zeal and enthusiasm. William Lloyd, a rising star of the anglican establishment, preached at fashionable St Martin in the Fields on 5 November 1678. Custom and circumstance required him to recall the plots against Queen Elizabeth and King James, and to denounce their 'barbarous and horrid and execrable cruelty'. But even as the Popish Plot was raging Lloyd reminded his audience that not all Catholics were guilty of such plotting. The deliverance of 1605 could be represented as essentially dynastic, rather than religious, assuring the safety of 'our prince, the annointed of the Lord, his gracious queen, their hopeful children'. But Lloyd's tone would change as the crisis intensified; his sermon before the House of Lords on 5 November 1680 shows more alarm about 'popery' and even the 'danger of another civil war'.[19]

A sermon by Thomas Wilson, rector of Arrow, Warwickshire, is indicative of the message being delivered from country pulpits. While the calendar brought the congregation to 'our present business of celebrating our deliverance from popish conspiracy,' all attention was focused on the current conspiracy unfolding in London. As in the past 'God hath delivered us, so he will deliver us still, if we hold his truth without corruption.' Holding to his truth required remembrance of past mercies, and an understanding of the difference between Protestantism and Catholicism. The people needed to be reminded of what might befall them if popery came in. 'Popery', according to Wilson, was a religion of lies and luxury, cruelty and rebellion. 'Blessed be God, then, that our religion, which is spiritual, substantial and lively, is not turned into idle and dead ceremony, shows and gazings, crosses, beads and relics.'[20]

While preachers sharpened their attack on popery, agitators took to the streets. London saw ingenious dramatic processions and demonstrations illuminating and ridiculing the popish menace. The burning of the Whore of Babylon in 1673 and the burning of the cat-filled pope in 1677 were but rehearsals for the complex commemorations in the years that followed. The most elaborate parades were in London, which had exceptional resources and audiences for this kind of extravaganza, but there were echoes in provincial towns, such as Salisbury, Taunton and Oxford.[21]

In London, during the period of the Popish Plot and the exclusion struggle, the costumed figures and representational effigies were reminiscent of the parades and pageants of the Elizabethan and Jacobean periods, or the midsummer devil processions of an earlier era. But these were angry and partisan presentations of a decidedly Whiggish cast, living tableaux as political cartoons. Their sponsorship was partisan, not corporate, and they invited bystanders to jeer and to

179

cheer. Printed pamphlets served as programmes, souvenirs and propaganda, explicating the meaning of the various floats, and describing them for people not privileged to be in town. One such was *The manner of the Burning of the Pope in Effigies in London On the 5th of November, 1678. With the manner of carrying him through several Streets, in progression to Temple-Bar, where at length he was decently burned.* To this was usefully appended *A Particular of several Bloody Massacres done by the Papists upon the bodies of English, Irish and French Protestants.* Similar pamphlets and broadsheets repeated or elaborated these descriptions in each of the next three years.[22]

The anti-Catholic pageant season opened with bonfires, bells, and sermons on Gunpowder Treason day, and climaxed with pope-burning processions on 17 November. What had been a novelty earlier in the 1670s rapidly became established as a metropolitan tradition. Artisans and apprentices used their spare time to construct figures and floats, and on Queen Elizabeth's day they strutted and paraded, brawled with popish sympathizers, and ended the festivities with fires. Rich in imagery and symbolic reference, the November demonstrations were controlled and imaginative adaptations of customary forms. 'This yearly trouble and charge' had a serious purpose: to proclaim the identity of the pope as Antichrist, and to 'renew a holy indignation in all true Protestant breasts.' The vocabulary of celebration became a vocabulary of venom, a weapon against political and religious enemies. Under the patronage of Whig politicians, the pope-burning was carefully scripted and choreographed. On the streets but not of the streets, and hovering within the limits of control, it was more like the Lord Mayor's show than a popular protest. The crowd was aroused, but not to the point of insurrection. Members of the Green Ribbon Club paid up to ten pounds apiece to subsidize the November processions. The pageant on 17 November 1679 is said to have cost a total of £2500. Two hundred porters were hired, 'at two shillings a man, to carry lights along with the show'. With money, alcohol and slogans in abundance, the atmosphere was filled with exuberance as much as anger.[23]

Not all Protestant activists approved. Oliver Heywood, a north-country preacher, was unimpressed by 'spectacles, shows, bonfires, squibs in London and other places that are very expensive and not very useful; that papists deride and serious Protestants lament, especially at what sin is there committed; it bodes no good, as appears by what preceded the French massacre'.[24] Heywood and others who were concerned about manners as well as menaces would prefer to work through prayer and ministry than popular demonstrations.

The London processions were designed to impress members of

parliament and to intimidate the court, as well as to gratify the Whigs and to arouse or indulge the mob. They followed an established route, assembling at Moorgate or Whitechapel Bar in the east, pausing at points of political or religious sensitivity, and usually ending at Temple Bar on the western edge of the City. Here was the headquarters of the Green Ribbon Club, the Whig organization; and here too was an oversized statue of Queen Elizabeth, the Protestant protectress, who was decked out with weapons and illuminations for the occasion. In 1679 she carried a representation of Magna Carta, establishing her as the defender of liberties against arbitrary government. Making good use of the symbolic geography of London, the 1681 procession culminated in a 'great bonfire' in Smithfield, the scene of the Marian martyrs' fires and a site used for three-quarters of a century for bonfires on 5 November. St Margaret Westminster, and St Clement Danes were among the churches west of Temple Bar to resume the practice of ringing on 17 November, 'on Queen Elizabeth's birthday [sic]'.[25]

As each November approached there were expectations of lively confrontations. A newswriter reported in 1679, 'great preparations are made for the extraordinary observation of the 5th November, in which the papists will no doubt see much of the temper of England'. Young people paraded diabolic and papal effigies, and called at the houses of eminent persons demanding money. The exchange of coins linked the crowd with the elite, and turned selected merchants and gentlemen into informal sponsors of the processions. Unwilling contributors were booed, and the windows of suspected papists were broken. Travel was unsafe for Catholics and people associated with them. Fights broke out between Protestant apprentices and their antagonists. A newswriter reported that 'several of the French ambassador's servants with some of the rabble attempted to put out the bonfires near Covent Garden, but were quickly forced to betake themselves to their lodgings'. At the same time, fuelling the excitement and hysteria of the evening, 'Sir William Waller burnt in the Palace Yard the popish books, etc. taken by him, and several of the pope's effigies were burnt about the city with great approbation of the people.'[26]

The activities began at three in the morning with the ringing of church bells. Drums, squibs, gunshots and shouts built up the excitement for the evening procession. The parade began with the fall of twilight and lasted until eight or nine at night. Crowds lined the streets, and refreshments flowed freely. In addition to mocking effigies of the Pope and his minions there were floats representing Protestant heroes and popish villains. Current and historical references were intertwined, in celebration of England's Protestant past and its imperilled present. One float in 1679 displayed the body of Sir Edmund Berry Godfrey, whose murder was fresh in mind. Another depicted Sir George Wakeman, the queen's doctor and a suspected plotter, as 'the pope's chief physician with Jesuits' powder in one hand and an urinal in the other'.[27] When the procession reached the final bonfire the popish villains were burned but the Protestant heroes were saved from the flames.

This practice of parading and burning an effigy could be adopted by rival political factions. In 1681, after the failure of the exclusion movement, Tory propagandists turned the device against their Whig opponents. On 5 November, it was reported, 'the scholars in Westminster school, instead of a pope burnt the effigy of Jack Presbyter in Dean's Yard. He had in his right hand a seditious pamphlet called *vox patrie*, in his left hand a scroll of parchment on which was written the Solemn League and Covenant; on his clock was fixed another pamphlet on which was fixed an *ignoramus.*' Here the privileged scholars of Westminster were playing the role of the London apprentices, employing their dramatic political vocabulary but reversing its meaning. The action connects to a long tradition, embracing rough music and ridings, symbolic mockery, and the later American practice of tarring and feathering.[28]

By 1682 the November activities had lost their theatricality and flaunting mockery, and degenerated into rowdy confrontations. Gunpowder Treason day took on a sullen, festering mood with an air more of grievance than celebration. The Popish Plot had unravelled. No parliament was sitting, and the legislative road to exclusion was blocked. In terms of high politics the Whigs had lost their advantage, but anti-Catholic sentiment ran hotter than ever in the streets of London. Popular protest tied to Protestant anniversaries reached fever pitch in November 1682. There were no formal processions, now that the Whigs had crumbled and had their patronage withdrawn, but Gunpowder Treason bonfires abounded. Energies that had been channelled towards ritual performance were now free to spill over into uncontrolled violence. Orchestration gave way to anarchy. In London the trained bands were readied and their numbers strengthened. Orders were issued 'for preventing tumultuous disorders' but with little effect. The 'multitudes of the *mobile* . . . behaved themselves very insolently . . . Captain Bloomer, coming through Newgate Street, was barbarously pulled out of his coach, and knocked down several times by the rabble.' Symbolic violence was directed against such inn signs as *The Pope's Head, Cardinal's Hat* and *His Royal Highness' Head*.[29]

Manuscript newsletters tell more of the story. Since they are little known, and since the account they give is so vivid, it is worth quoting one at length.

Sunday night last being the 5th [November] all true and loyal Protestants in London, to express their horrid dislike of the Gunpowder Treason, put on bonfires to the great dislike of the papists here; who thinking to have their bridle always cast on their necks promised to put out several fires, but were hindered as much as possible by the owners. This working much upon the young men apprentices of the place, they gathered together in a body; and after having soundly beat off these persons that were putting out the fires, obliging them to run to their several holes with beaten bones, they proceeded to go through the streets calling, no York! a Monmouth, a Monmouth . . . By ten o'clock they were increased to a numerous multitude, where marching through the streets they broke down several windows of those they knew to be popish and popishly affected, and those they got into their hands they most soundly beat off. They pulled down a great part of Nathaniel Thomson's house, and did not leave one whole window in Sir John Moore's. From there they marched to Holborn in search of Roger L'Estrange; but not finding him they brought forth chairs, stools, beds, etc. of which they made a great bonfire, and calling for drink drunk rounds of the destruction of Towser [the devil-dog] and the pope., etc. . . . At every bonfire they drank round the king and Duke of Monmouth's good health, the people most willingly giving them drink.[30]

Eventually the trained bands turned out, but they met only drunken defiance. At this point the mayor ordered his officers to open fire, 'but was told by the colonel that he could not be answerable for it, and therefore desired him to desist in regard it might be the commencement of further mischief. Then he ordered them to draw their swords and run amongst them, which they did but were manfully resisted and forced to retire to the Exchange, which they barricaded. Thus they continued all night, and in the morning dismissed. But about eight, some ten or twelve were seized . . . and committed to prison.'[31]

The same extraordinary story was relayed in newsletters to subscribers in various parts of the country. One described the rioters as 'some hundreds of butchers' men and other mean fellows'. All writers were shocked by the occupation of the Exchange, and several described the aftermath, in which the captured rioters were threatened with arraignment 'for levying war against the king'. The trouble allowed the government to clamp down on future festivities. A letter of 11 November reported that the mayor and aldermen had met with the king in council, and were instructed, 'that on the 17 November, being the anniversary of Queen Elizabeth, they order a strong guard of trained bands, and suffer no more bonfires to be made, and neither pope nor other effigies to be burned, to prevent which that the City gates be kept shut in the evening and all assemblies dispersed'. Effigies (described as 'monsters') being prepared for the annual procession were discovered and destroyed before they could be paraded to the flames.[32]

Queen Elizabeth's day was dampened by this official intervention, but its celebration would probably have withered in any case without further Whig support. The recent commemoration of 17 November was a conscious revival, no longer deeply rooted in the popular calendar. Gunpowder Treason day, by contrast, was a statutory occasion recognized by state and church, as well as an enduring popular custom. Inflammatory activities on 5 November always had the potential for trouble, so the establishment sought to contain them by restricting the vocabulary of celebration. The trick was to maintain a solemn Protestant commemoration without inspiring too much anit-Catholic enthusiasm; it was enough that the anniversary should be marked by the decorum of sermons and bells. A proclamation of 1683 outlawed bonfires, squibs and crackers, and this was repeated, though not necessarily observed, in later years. After 5 November passed quietly in London in 1684 the king informed the mayor that he was 'well pleased with the greater care he took in keeping the 5th of November free from all manner of disorders, and desired him and the aldermen to keep those days of jubilee with the same care and they should want no assistance from the court'. A bonfire and firework festival planned for the queen's birthday on 15 November took the spark from any demonstration on 17 November, and harnessed the pyrotechnic spectacular to the interests of the court.[33] By the end of Charles's reign the anti-Catholic hysteria had subsided, and the memory of Gunpowder Treason appeared stronger than belief in the more recent Popish Plot.

★

The accession of a Catholic king in 1685 gave an ironic twist to the observance of anti-Catholic anniversaries, an irony not lost on the diarist John Evelyn. If there were some at court who wished to construe 5 November as a day honouring the crown and the dynasty, there were others who insisted on its sanctity for the Protestant Church of England. The authorities sought to stifle the wilder annual celebrations, but in many parishes there were people prepared to mark the day with the full battery of festive venom. Bells rang as usual, and in 1686 there were formal Gunpowder anniversary sermons at Whitehall, Westminster and St Paul's. These official sermons attempted to be reasonable and accommodating, but in the parishes and pulpits of Protestant London the preaching was 'sharp' and pertinent. John Evelyn 'went to St Martin's in the morning, where Dr Birch preached very boldly against the papists, from John 16:2. In the afternoon I heard Dr Tillotson in Lincoln's Inn chapel, on the same text but more cautiously.'[34]

The City and suburbs saw mild disturbances and demonstrations, despite official attempts to curtail them. The mechanisms of control were tested, the effort of orchestration strained. Acting on orders from the king and council, 'the Lord Mayor forbid bonfires, fireworks, etc., but the boys lighted up a vast number of candles on cross heads and some were carried about streets on cross sticks'. King James expressed his displeasure at this parade of lights, and instructed the city governors 'to take more care for the future and to find out the promoters of such disorders'. The following year the mayor and aldermen issued a precept 'to prevent disorders by bonfires, etc., on the 5th and 17th of this instant November'.[35] Bonfires were welcome on royal occasions, but not on the traditional Protestant anniversaries. The parish of St Andrew by the Wardrobe lit bonfires 'by order of the Lord Mayor' at the accession of James II and at the birth of his son in 1688, but did not resume its tradition of bonfires on 5 November until 1689. Most parishes in town and country kept up their bellringing on 5 November throughout James's reign.

★

November 1688 was a troubled and confusing month in English history. One wonders how many people understood what was happening. Bells rang and congregations prayed on Gunpowder Treason day, but few could have known that they were in the midst of another momentous 'deliverance'. After William's arrival at Torbay, significantly but fortuitously on 5 November, renewed emphasis was given to the pattern of Protestant commemorations. The arrival of William of Orange was ranked among England's most fortunate providences. Beginning in 1689, the new form of service for 5 November thanked God for discovering 'the snares of death that were laid for us' in 1605, 'and likewise upon this day' for bringing King William 'safely into his kingdom, to preserve us from the late attempts of our enemies to bereave us of our religion and laws'. Like previous books of prayer and explanation, this was distributed to parishes throughout the country. The official service was followed by bonfires and bells.[36]

Sermons at Whitehall and Westminster pressed the same message. Bishop William Lloyd addressed William and Mary on Gunpowder Treason day 1689 on the theme of deliverance from 'popery and

185

slavery'. Rather extravagantly, he called this 5 November, 'the day of our resurrection . . . a day that brought us new life from the dead'. Lloyd's colleagues Gilbert Burnet and Samuel Freeman preached the same day, and in the same vein, to the Lords and Commons. Burnet argued that 5 November 1688 was more important than 5 November 1605. Forgetting the claims of his Jacobean predecessor Bishop Carleton, Burnet claimed 'the Gunpowder Treason was a personal thing; but the late conspiracy was national' for it attempted to subjugate us all to France and Rome. A few years later William's armies had made the revolution secure, and such sentiments yielded to a more complacent tone. Archbishop John Sharp told the House of Lords on 5 November 1691 that the 'storm is blown over' and England seemed now 'in a good measure out of the danger of our old inveterate enemy, popery'.[37] To the extent that this was true it would take some of the sting out of the 5 November celebrations.

William and Mary took over the Stuart calendar, as well as other important symbols of dynastic continuity. The commemorative calendar in their reign revolved around the familiar Protestant and dynastic anniversaries. Almanacs of the 1690s still singled out 30 January, 29 May, and 5 and 17 November for special attention. Preachers observed the traditional sacred occasions. Balancing Whig and Tory sensitivities, most churches rang to commemorate Royal Oak day and Gunpowder Treason. A round of ringing in the spring was matched by commemorative festivities in the autumn. The important church of St Margaret Westminster, rang its bells on 29 May, 5 November, as well as crownation day and the king's and queen's birthdays. To this routine was added celebratory ringing for William's naval and military victories. The borough of Northampton lit bonfires each 5 November, and on the days of victory thanksgiving.[38]

Williamite Whigs even took possession of the anniversary of the 'martyrdom' of Charles I. The day was established in the calendar, enshrined in the service book, and venerated by the Tories. Perhaps for these reasons it had to be appropriated by the usurper regime. Bishop Lloyd, now William's lord high almoner, preached on 30 January 1691, explaining that the 'resurrection' achieved in 1660 had been squandered, and that 'a second resurrection' in 1688 passed the mantle of Protestant protector to the present king. In a later anniversary sermon Lloyd again connected the 'deliverance' of the accession of William and Mary to the solemnities of 30 January. 'God brought us two plants united together out of that royal oak that was cut down upon this day,' 30 January. The same talents were employed to harness the 29 May festivities to the new regime. The anniversary commemorated 'the restoration of the royal family; and therewith of our church and religion, our government and laws'. Just as in 1588 and 1605, Lloyd argued, so in 1660 and 1688 England experienced 'an irresistible impulse of God'.[39] By this time the 'impulse of God' and its bearing on English history had been subject to scrutiny for one hundred and fifty years.

★

Eighteenth-century England perpetuated the Stuart calendar of deliverances and dynastic anniversaries, but altered social and political circumstances invested many of the dates with fresh meanings. Protestant providentialism generally gave way to secularized partisanship. Religious concerns shifted. Political issues found new expression in parliament, pulpits, and in the streets.

The court of Queen Anne observed sensitive and significant anniversaries with appropriate sermons, receptions, and entertainments. The year progressed through the royal martyr's day on 30 January, the queen's birthday on 6 February, Prince George's birthday on 28 February, crownation day (lavishly observed) on 8 March, coronation day on 23 April, and restoration day on 29 May. These were all royal and dynastic occasions that were especially satisfying to the Tories. They were followed, some months later, by Gunpowder Plot day on 5 November and Queen Elizabeth's day on 17 November, the late autumn season for the Whigs.

November was a dangerous month, resonant with the symbolism of memory, partisan contest, and intimations of riot. Away from the dull decorum of court, there was agitation and violent spectacle in the City. Bells rang and bonfires blazed in honour of the double deliverance on 5 November 1605 and 1688. The anniversary sported a variety of meanings, on which rabid Whigs and revanchist Tories could feed. The Whigs spoke of liberty, and celebrated deliverance from arbitrary power, Jacobites and France. The Tories remembered God's blessing on the Stuart dynasty, and saw the dangers elsewhere. It was a sermon on Gunpowder Treason day that sparked the Sacheverell riots that rocked pre-Hanoverian London. Henry Sacheverell preached at St Paul's on 5 November 1709, more than a century after the Gunpowder Plot, on the familiar theme of 'the church in danger'. But the danger that Sacheverell saw came not from the traditional enemy at Rome, but rather from local political opponents, dissenters, tolerationists, occasional conformists, and the Whig bishops and grandees.[40]

By 1711 the Whigs had lost control of the government, but Whig sentiments were extravagently represented in processions and demonstrations. Queen Elizabeth's day was chosen for a parade in London, to culminate in the burning of effigies of the devil, the pope, and the pretender. When the government sent a detachment of Grenadier Guards to confiscate the effigies it was marvelled, 'that a popular rejoicing so grateful to this Protestant city, which was never attempted to be quashed but in King James II's reign, should, at this juncture, be interrupted.' The Whigs had to make do with a procession of bag-pipers playing 'Lillibullero', and a makeshift immolation of effigies of the pope and the court of Rome.[41]

A report of celebrations and disturbances on 4 November 1712 contains elements that would be repeated in other combinations throughout the eighteenth century. 'The same day being the anniversary of King William III, great rejoicing were made in the cities of London and Westminster by those who being well-affected to the late revolution and the protestant succession in the house of Hanover, entertain a due respect and veneration for the memory of a prince whom they look upon as the deliverer of these nations from popery and arbitrary power, and the asserter of the liberties of Europe. Among the rest, a considerable number of lords, gentlemen, and citizens met at the "Three Tuns and Rummer" in Gracechurch Street to celebrate that festival, caused a great bonfire to be made before the house, and gave beer to the mob, to pledge the healths they drank on the balcony, or at the windows, to the queen, the house of Hanover, and the memory of King William. A party of men were, it seems, offended at it, and raised an opposite mob, who offered to disturb the rejoicings around the bonfire, a scuffle ensued, in which the aggressors were repulsed with some broken heads and bloody noses; but the trained bands being that day (and the next) under arms, the fray was soon parted, and all was quiet, till the bonfire was consumed, and the company in the tavern retired, when part of that mob that had been worsted, finding no opposition, they revenged themselves on the glass windows of the tavern.'[42]

Bonfires still formed the centrepiece of the celebration, though their sponsorship now came from patrons of a political drinking establishment rather than a borough or parish. Alcohol, of course, was essential to the festivity, and violence was not far behind. The activity was sponsored by social and political leaders (though not of the first rank), and they invited their social inferiors to join in. It was the city's Whig gentry who caused the bonfire to be made, the healths to be drunk, the mob to be aroused; and their opponents retaliated with a mob of their own. The mob, of course, had its own dynamic, which was shown in bloody noses and broken windows.

The Hanoverian succession in 1714 brought Tories and Whigs into new collisions, both symbolic and real. The sequence of bellringing, health drinking, competitive bonfires, and scuffles on the accession day and coronation day of the late Queen Anne, the birthday of the Duke of Ormonde and the pretender's birthday, offset by the Whig anniversaries of 4, 5 and 17 November, was partly responsible for the Riot Act of 1715. And for the next thirty years, perhaps longer, the calendar provided the occasion for the expression of competing political loyalties.[43]

12
THE ENGLISH CALENDAR
IN COLONIAL AMERICA

The English calendar amalgamated astronomical, classical-pagan, and traditional Christian elements. In addition to marking the seasons and pacing the agricultural year, the calendar fixed and proclaimed the major Christian holy days, and registered such secular events as law terms, court days, times of fairs, and anniversaries. Lady day, May day, and Lammas marked the wheeling of the English year, alongside holidays with more specific religious connotations. As we have seen, many of the saints' days of the old Roman Catholic calendar were rejected after the Reformation, but still in the seventeenth century the calendrical cycle of Protestant England was modelled on that of Catholic Europe. The year was shaped by the Christian observances of Lent and Easter, Whitsuntide, and Christmas. (The English refused until 1752 to adopt the Gregorian calendar reforms of the Counter-Reformation, but this only affected the timing of the calendar, not its overall structure.) The English calendar of the seventeenth century also drew attention to red-letter days such as royal accession days and birthdays, and to the anniversaries of English Protestant 'deliverances'. Each of these calendrical layers had meaning in Stuart England, making the passage of time a matter of cultural and political significance.

How much of this complex calendar crossed over to colonial America? What happened to English seasonal patterns and observances in the seventeenth-century English settlements overseas? These questions turn our attention to the seasonal, religious, ceremonial and festive components of the year in New England and Virginia, and to the larger issue of the transfer of culture to the colonies. A study of time and the ritual marking of its passage in colonial America provides an instructive contrast to Elizabethan and Stuart England, and to the experience of the British diaspora elsewhere in the world.

Did the migrants carry over a deeply rooted experience of periodicity and seasonality which was as natural to them as their language? How attached were they to the annual cycle of commemo-

190

rations and observances, and did they attempt to replicate this English pattern in the New World? To what degree did the colonists perpetuate or reject the customary calendar of old England when their political and religious circumstances were transformed? The questions can be more finely focused in terms of religion and agriculture, since some migrants disapproved of the ancient calendar, and others found themselves too busy to follow it. How effective was the puritan effort to discard the old religious routine and to suppress seasonal observances in the godly commonwealth of New England? What was the impact of puritan dominance in Massachusetts and Connecticut, and did it find any echo in the anglican and Catholic settlements of the south? What were the cultural effects of the seasonality of Atlantic shipping, and the different rhythms of tobacco farming, corn growing, and animal husbandry? To what extent did the social and economic rhythms of early America alter the experience of time?

In seventeenth-century England the calendar and its customs were deeply rooted and well recorded, so questions about the experience of time can be addressed without great difficulty. In colonial America, by contrast, there is little documentation of the sort that might illuminate the problem. There is no seventeenth-century American equivalent of the English borough chamberlains' accounts that record civic processions and drinkings, or the parish churchwardens' accounts that indicate when the bells were rung in celebration or when bonfires were lit. The private record is as meagre as the public. Early colonial diarists were few, and little more than hints can be taken from their jottings. How are we to gauge the significance of Lent and Easter, for example, in the religious calendar of New England or Virginia if contemporaries said nothing about it? It becomes a matter of judgment whether silence suggests that an established English custom was observed without mention, or whether it had faded from view.

The evidence is better when calendrical observances were controversial. If one group within the colonial community wished to maintain the old customs and another sought to suppress them the issue was likely to leave traces in court records, diaries, polemic, or correspondence. Such sources are thin by English standards, but they reveal aspects of a struggle over the calendar in colonial New England that echoed disputes in the homeland. The English settlers of seventeenth-century New England and Virginia were inheritors of ancient European traditions and at the same time creators of a new American culture. They brought with them established rhythms of life and ingrained patterns of behaviour, and adapted them, sometimes consciously and at other times unwittingly, to the demands and

191

opportunities of the colonial environment. Agriculture and religion both played a part in the modification of English customs that travelled across the Atlantic. So too did distance and detachment from the cultural sources and context in which the old-world traditions had thrived.

Newcomers from England found the cycle of the seasons familiar enough in America, although the climate was more extreme. (Spring and autumn could be delightful, but winters were severe, especially in New England, and summers were humid and hot, especially in the south.) Health and fortune would be governed by the same sun, the same turning moon, and the same cycling of the constellations. From an astrological point of view the transatlantic world would be quite familiar, even if adjustments had to be made for the lower American latitudes.

Subsistence agriculture followed similar cycles in England and America, but new crops – indian corn in New England, corn and tobacco in Maryland and Virginia – required a new farming calendar as well as new techniques. In New England the wheat crop came in during July, and the Indian corn in September, with corn shucking and husking parties to follow. Harvest was a time for neighbourly festivity and thanksgiving, similar to that observed in England. Many of the days of public thanksgiving prescribed by the puritan magistracy of New England coincided with the completion of the annual harvest, especially during the later decades of the seventeenth century.[1]

In the tobacco regions of Virginia and Maryland, however, planters spoke of cutting but nothing so final as 'harvest'. There was no time for relaxation after the crop was cut in September. Workers moved immediately to curing, stripping, sweating and prizing, and these tasks kept them busy throughout the autumn. October was often the busiest time, but the preparation and packing of the precious weed kept men occupied until the turn of the year. By then it was time to plant again, and the cycle began anew. The packed hogsheads of tobacco lay in warehouses until the ships arrived from England in the late winter or early spring, and the planter might wait another half season before he saw his money. The tobacco regions may have developed a distinctive culture, as T. H. Breen has suggested, but it was one without community festivity and ritual dimensions.[2]

In the colonies to the north and south the lifeline to the old world also tightened and slackened with the passage of the year. English shipping to New England normally left in the spring to catch the most favourable Atlantic weather, and the vessels arrived in Boston harbour about eight weeks later in the early summer. Captains preferred to begin their onward or return voyages with a minimum of delay. The Chesapeake tobacco fleet arrived early in the year to land servants and to collect the previous autumn's crop.

Dependence on the transatlantic economy dictated an economic rhythm unlike anything known in Europe. In Massachusetts the economic year climaxed between May and September. Summer was the prime time for payments, deeds, contracts, and exchange of goods. (This can be verified by a seasonal analysis of colonial economic documents.) The flow of information in the colonies was also paced by the sailing season, with fresh gazettes from England in June and a dearth of news in the winter. Chesapeake rhythms were also paced by the Atlantic traffic, with major tobacco sales and purchases of goods in February or March. If indentured servants counted their term from their arrival in the colony they could look forward to freedom on an equivalent date some years into the future. The employment and tenurial cycle of old England, pivoting on Lady day (25 March) and Michaelmas (29 September), had little relevance in the pioneer colonies, although neither of these terms was forgotten.

The ritual infrastructure of the early colonies was thin and deficient by English standards. Whereas each parish in England followed the liturgical calendar of the established church (in a lavish or subdued manner according to local preference), the institutionalized religious routine was weak in Virginia and non-existent in seventeenth-century New England. Without the discipline of the prayer book and the momentum and tradition of official religion, the sweep of the Christian year narrowed to a succession of Sundays. English towns followed old traditions which, though weakened by reform and reformation, still gave pattern to the urban year, but colonial communities, by contrast, were *ab initio* and slow to develop civic memory. Nor were there craft guilds or other associations with a keen sense of tradition and a developed practice of annual activity. It is hard to keep customs when the mechanisms of support and regulation are undeveloped.

★

The public calendrical cycles in early Virginia were loosely related to English rhythms, which in turn rested on older ecclesiastical foundations. The governor received his quarterly salary 'upon the feast day of St John the Baptist, St Michael the Archangel, the nativity of our Lord God, and the annunciation of the Blessed Virgin Mary' (24 June, 29 September, 25 December, 25 March, approximating the four seasons). Other salaries were paid for a year ending at Lady day.

Vestrymen met for official business 'upon the feast day of St Michael the Archangel, being the 29th day of September'. Land grants were made 'for the term of ten years next ensuing after the feast of St Thomas the Apostle last past'.[3] In choosing these days the southern colonial rulers attempted to replicate the ceremonial cycle of the old country.

Beginning in 1619 Virginia's ministers were supposed to meet as a judicial council with the governor four times a year, 'at the feast of St Michael the Archangel, of the nativity of our saviour, of the Annunciation of the blessed· Virgin, and about midsummer'. These quarterly meetings were soon superseded by the establishment of county courts which were supposed to meet on a similar schedule.[4] In planning dates of meetings, periods of office or terms of agreements it was natural for the early colonists to follow the conventional dating scheme which was familiar to them in England. The old religious holidays were dates that the Virginia settlers would recognize, even if they no longer observed them with festivity or devotion. There were other regularities, too, imposed or encouraged by the colonial assembly. Easter was the time to choose churchwardens as well as being one of the three occasions when adults were supposed to take communion. Ministers and churchwardens were required to attend the 'midsummer quarter courts holden at James city on the first day of June' to register burials, christenings and marriages together with their financial accounts.[5]

These early calendrical attachments are not surprising, given that the society and popular culture of Virginia was an overseas extension from the homeland. The religion of Virginia was based on the English prayer book, (though without the discipline imposed by English bishops). Virginia's population, like England's, contained the devout and the reprobate, and all shades between. Social and demographic conditions were not conducive to a settled parochial liturgical routine, but the leaders of the colony repeatedly asserted their conformity in religion. Alexander Whitaker, one of the first ministers at Jamestown, described in 1614 a religious regime with sabbath observances, monthly communions, and annual fasts that would not have been out of place in Jacobean England. In 1619 the General Assembly agreed that 'all ministers shall duly read divine service, and exercise their ministerial functions, according to the ecclesiastical laws and orders of the Church of England'. In 1624 and again in 1632 the Assembly insisted on 'uniformity in our church as near as may be to the canons in England, both in substance and circumstance', including the ecclesiastical calendar of feasts and fasts.[6]

In practice there was laxity and indifference, illuminated by shafts of zeal. The easy-going latitudinarianism of religion in Virginia was not unlike the ecclesiastical culture of Jacobean England from which it sprang. The tendency was to tradition rather than reform. In 1647, when the revolutionary regime in England attempted to introduce the Directory of Worship, the Virginia Assembly ordered continuing use of the Book of Common Prayer. By this time, however, the pattern of observances had become a parish option, with strict anglicans and nonconformists each going their way.[7] In any case, economic circumstances, the rigour of the tobacco business, and the harshness of the climate and environment, all worked against the maintenance of old-world liturgical rhythms.

Virginia's ministers were supported by annual tithing that tied together aspects of the economic, social and religious calendar. It is tempting to see here a distinctly Virginian ritual, shaped by tobacco culture, but the evidence is insufficient. By order of the General Assembly in 1632, parishioners had to bring in their 'duty' of ten pounds of tobacco for the minister each 25 October, and a bushel of corn each 19 December. The date of the tobacco contribution was subsequently changed to 20 November.[8] By this time of year planters were prizing or packing their tobacco in hogsheads ready for storage, and this may have been a convenient time to set some aside for the minister. Most likely, however, the tithing involved a paper transaction with a sum set aside on the minister's account. Only detailed diaries or records of disputes would show how the tithing was conducted, and what position it occupied in the early Virginia calendar. Few planters would willingly bring in their tithe or tax until dunned for it, and general laxity worked against the establishment of seasonal fiscal patterns.

England's Protestant holidays – crownation days, Gunpowder Treason day, etc. – left no distinctive mark on seventeenth-century Virginia, but it did not take long for the colony to adopt significant anniversaries of its own. On 22 March 1622, Good Friday, an Indian uprising left about 350 English settlers dead and the survivors severely shaken. The Assembly ordered 'that the 22nd of March be yearly kept holy in commemoration of our deliverance from the Indians at that bloody massacre'. A second Indian rising on 18 April 1644 added another special day to the Virginia calendar. Ministers were required to announce these days on the preceding sabbath, rather as their English counterparts were supposed to bid feasts and fasts. For the survivors at least the March and April anniversaries were days of significant commemoration, invested with special status. Like the church feast days (few of which were strictly observed) the massacre holidays were days free from work. Nor could sheriffs or court officers serve writs or warrants on these occasions. The discovery in 1664 of 'a desperate conspiracy' among indentured servants prompted the Assembly to dedicate 13 September as yet another day of thanksgiving to be kept 'in a perpetual commemoration'.[9]

Through what sectors of Virginia society these days were recognized, and for how long after the events they were observed, is a matter of conjecture. There may be a shallow generational depth to the memory of momentous occurences unless they continue to occupy a niche in the culture. Commemoration only endures so long as one or other group finds it useful for ideological or religious purposes, or for entertainment. Certainly by the eighteenth century these early colonial anniversaries were forgotten, even if the injunction to observe them in perpetuity had not been repealed.

After the Restoration, Virginia added the Stuart commemorative fast of 30 January and the feast of 29 May to its official holiday roster. The General Assembly ordered in 1662 that 30 January 'be annually solemnized with fasting and prayers, that our sorrows may expiate our crimes and our tears wash away our guilt' for the execution of Charles I. In honour of Charles II they ordered that 29 May, 'the day of his majesty's birth and happy restitution, be annually celebrated as an holy day'. These dynastic observances brought the public calendar of Virginia into closer conformity with that of metropolitan England, but in practice the demands of the tobacco culture kept labourers at work. Gunpowder Treason day left little trace in the records of seventeenth-century Virginia, but was well known later in the Williamsburg era when it may have been reintroduced from England.[10]

It is difficult to go deeper into the calendrical experience of seventeenth-century Virginia since diaries and letters from that period are so rare. It is even harder to discern the pattern in the neighbouring Chesapeake colony of Maryland. Catholics worked with conforming anglicans in the founding of Maryland, and their devotion shows in their choice of place names – St Mary's city, county and river, St George's river, St Clement's hundred. Maryland was a Christian colony, but one with a unique concern 'for the suppressing of all such disputes tending to the cherishing of a faction in religion'. By the 1670s there were Presbyterians, Independents, Baptists, and Quakers in Maryland, as well as adherents of the Church of England and Roman Catholics. The colony had laws for sanctifying the sabbath (not always enforced), but did not adopt the Book of Common Prayer until forced to in 1696.[11] Marylanders most likely observed the principal occasions of the Christian year, in accord with their opportunities and inclinations, but not in a way to draw attention to their activities or to leave useful historical records.

★

The ritual calendar of seventeenth-century New England was spare and austere compared with that of the old country, but popular customs developed around harvests and thanksgiving days. Celebration and commemoration were constrained by the dominance of puritan religion, which in its American form looked critically on the pattern of the year. A distinctive puritan culture developed in Plymouth Colony, Massachusetts and Connecticut because there the godly held power. Ministers and magistrates gave legal and political endorsement to reforms that were but briefly adopted in revolutionary England. Out went episcopacy, vestments, altars, and the prayer book, along with other popish and superstitious elements that had, in their eyes, contaminated the English church. There were no Candlemas illuminations, no Rogationtide perambulations, no church ales. Massachusetts substituted an austere perambulation of the bounds of each town, to be conducted 'in the first or second month' every three years.

New England sabbatarianism was antithetical to traditional religious observances, and averse to the distinction of commemorative days. The Christological year fell into decay, with nothing to mark the liturgical seasons of Advent, Epiphany, Lent and Easter. Marriages could be entered at any time of the year without regard for the traditional prohibited periods. Christmas observances were banned in Plymouth and Massachusetts long before the crackdown on Christmas began in England in the 1640s. The year was shorn of its ritual dressing. Thomas Lechford, a New Englander who was out of sympathy with these developments, explained 'there are days of fasting, thanksgiving and prayers upon occasions, but no holy days except the Sunday'. A Massachusetts law required attendance at church on these days, but no others.[12]

In New England as in Virginia, official legal and political business followed an annual cycle similar to the one back home, with quarterly courts and annual elections. In Massachusetts the magistrates met in March, June, September and December, approximating the English law terms. Elections were scheduled for 'the last Wednesday of every Easter term'. This was a rare official mention of Easter in New England records. The year was also marked by musters and training days, and at Cambridge by the Harvard commencement. Fasts and humiliations were called according to the needs of the moment, and had no regularity or periodicity. However, of twenty-nine thanksgivings called by the General Court of Massachusetts between 1632 and 1686 seventeen fell in November, and had some of the flavour of traditional harvest festivals. A similar pattern prevailed in Connecticut, where annual thanksgiving days in October in the 1650s had shifted to November by the 1670s.[13]

By October the harvest was complete, and larders were beginning to fill with fresh-killed animals. A Massachusetts almanac greeted November, 'One day this month each fruitful year/Give thanks to God and eat good cheer.' The spiritual purpose of the thanksgiving was sometimes overwhelmed by the popular pleasures of the post-harvest season. Ned Ward, an English writer who visited Boston in 1682, observed, 'husking of indian corn is as good a sport for the amorous wagtails in New England as Maying amongst us is for our forward youths and wenches. For 'tis observed, there are more bastards got in that season than all the year beside, which occasions some of the looser saints to call it rutting time.'[14]

Beginning in the mid-1630s, the godly in New England attempted to popularize an entirely secular calendar, purged of all pagan and superstitious associations. They adopted a new dating system substituting numbers for the offensive names of the days and months. As Thomas Lechford observed in 1642, somewhat derisively, 'they call the days of the week, beginning at the first, second, third, fourth, fifth, sixth, and seventh, which is Saturday; the months begin in March, by the names of the first, second, and so forth to the twelfth, which is February; because they would avoid all memory of heathenish and idols' names'.[15]

The General Court of Massachusetts began using this system in the spring of 1636, but without consistency or assurance. Business was recorded on 'the 13th day of the 2nd month', on 'September 8th, 1636', and on '8th month, the 25th'. For several years the new and the old dating systems coexisted, with the pagan monthly names being entered in the margin. Plaintiffs were bound over to appear in court in 1637 'the first Tuesday in March', not 'the 3rd day of the 1st month' which might have confused them. The same year the court agreed 'that there should be a general fast the 19th of the 11th month, being the fifth day of the week Thursday come month'. And in 1638 'the court desired that the 12th day of the 2nd month, called April, being the 5th day of the week, should be kept a day of humiliation'. For legal, didactic and communications purposes it was necessary to explain that 'the 4th month' in fact meant June. By the 1640s the court had reverted to the traditional pagan usage. The court records of New Haven also mixed pagan names and puritan numbers, but Connecticut and Plymouth retained the conventional dating.[16]

New England's fairs were regulated by the calendar of numbers. The fairs at Boston, for example, were scheduled 'on the first third day of the third month, and on the first third day of the eighth month' (i.e. first Tuesdays in May and October, spring and autumn). Similar wording regulated the fairs at Salem, Watertown and Dorchester.[17]

Such a confusing reform had few consistent followers. The numerological usage was at its height in the late 1630s and early 1640s, and was thereafter little more than an affectation of the most fastidious. Some will-makers of the 1640s adopted the reformed dating but by the time they came to probate the old months were back in fashion. George Alcock of Roxbury, Massachusetts, dated his will '22 day 11th, called December, Anno Domini 1640,' although December was the tenth month in this scheme. Thomas Nelson of Rowley, Massachusetts, who had returned to England on business, amended his will on 'the sixth day of persextilis, here called August, 1648'. The anti-pagan dating system had already begun to decline in New England by the time a petitioner suggested it to Parliament in England in 1648. The Boston magistrate Samuel Sewall attempted to revive the use of numbers and to cleanse the week of pagan names, but without success.[18]

It is difficult to discover how much of the old religious calendar survived in popular consciousness and popular culture. At least a few New Englanders of the 1630s yearned for the beauty and regularity of the Church of England's traditional religious practices. Others missed the leisure and enjoyment of the old holidays. A minority observed Shrove Tuesday, May day and Christmas, especially after the Restoration.[19] The low intensity of disputes about Christmas from the 1620s to the 1650s suggests that the first generation of settlers was generally in harmony on the suppression of the ancient festival, but this view may be an illusion created by the surviving records.

Early Plymouth Colony was plagued with 'malcontented persons and turbulent spirits' who were likely to be attached to 'barbarous' customs and the unreformed calendar. Some of them gravitated to Thomas Morton's outpost at Merry-Mount where every day was May day and a maypole in 1627 symbolized liberty and good cheer. Morton's maypole, 'a goodly pine tree of eighty foot long . . . with a pair of buck's horns nailed on somewhat near unto the top of it', lasted until John Endecott descended from Salem and cut it down.[20] The reprobates and traditionalists of Massachusetts were never so well organized, but their presence reminds us that not all New Englanders were puritans. Newcomers who were not so fully acculturated to the godly Commonwealth helped to sustain or reintroduce old customs and to restore familiarity with the English festive calendar.

Like their co-religionists Henry Burton and William Prynne, the leaders of New England frowned on May day and regarded May frolics as the devil's work. Without community support the May day custom withered. Nonetheless some individuals made merry on this traditional spring occasion, and a few paid for it before the courts. Offenders were mostly marginal people, servants, sailors, new-comers, rather than solid householders. Paul Wilson, a servant at Charlestown, was rebuked for larking on May day in 1658, awakening neighbours with music, dancing, and early-morning revelry. The puritan magistrate Samuel Sewall cracked down on the equally ignorant observance of April Fool's day a few years later.[21]

More persistent was the keeping of Christmas. The Plymouth separatists ostentatiously ignored the occasion, but the less godly settlers observed Christ's birthday with traditional pastimes. Governor Bradford led his people to work on 25 December 1621 but a party of newcomers declared 'it went against their consciences to work on that day'. At mid-day Bradford found them 'at play openly, some pitching the bar, and some at stool ball and such like sports'. The governor confiscated their playthings, 'and told them that was against *his* conscience that they should play and others work. If they made the keeping of it a matter of devotion, let them keep their houses, but there should be no gaming or revelling in the streets.'[22]

The puritans of Massachusetts Bay followed Plymouth's lead. There would be no official countenance of Christmas, no public festivity on 25 December, no decoration with bays and holly. But Christmas was a winter occasion, traditionally observed indoors over dinner; it was hard to prevent individuals from keeping a private Christmas provided they did it with decorum.

In their revision of the laws in 1658 (published in 1660) the leaders of Massachusetts declared, 'for preventing disorders arising in several places within this jurisdiction, by reason of some still observing such festivals as were superstitiously kept in other countries, to the great dishonour of God and offence of others, it is therefore ordered . . . that whosoever shall be found observing any such day as Christmas or the like, either by forbearing labour, feasting, or any other way upon any such account as aforesaid, every such person so offending shall pay five shillings as a fine to the county'.[23] This resolve may have been prompted as much by the campaign against Christmas in Crom-wellian England as by a resurgence of unreformed practices in the Bay Colony.

Resurgent Christmas customs were among the abuses that were said to mark New England's declension in the second half of the seventeenth century. The puritan grip on New England weakened as a less resolute generation came of age and as the colony became part of the post-Restoration Atlantic world. Anglican practices revived. The royal agent Edward Randolph was offended in 1676 by the Massachusetts prohibition of Christmas and other holidays. In 1682 the laws restricting Christmas were repealed. Anglican traditionalists worshipped and played seasonal games, most notably in Boston, while puritans worked and frowned. Judge Samuel Sewall used his powers as a magistrate to impede Christmas celebrations.[24]

The observance of Christmas divided puritans from anglicans, and saints from sinners. In effect this meant a division between masters and servants, and perhaps between seaport towns and the more conservative hinterland. For Peter Thacher, a young minister at Barnstable in Plymouth Colony, 25 December 1679 was a day like any other (excepting sabbaths), but to his servant Mary Claghorne it was a day of jollification. Thacher promptly dismissed her with the warning, 'if she endeavoured to stifle conviction by running into merry company she would find it bitterness in the latter end'.[25]

Increase Mather, in his *Testimony against several prophane and superstitious customs, now practiced by some in New-England*, charged that the keeping of Christmas was pagan, papist, irreligious, erroneous, and profane. Mather marshalled the arguments that others had used against Christmas during the English revolution. But, he concluded, 'such vanities . . . are good no where; but in New England they are a thousand times worse'. There was nothing he could do, however, to prevent the return of old English customs, especially in a pluralist community like later-Stuart Boston. Increase's son Cotton Mather wrote with disgust about the Christmas revels in 1711.[26]

English almanacs enjoyed a limited circulation in the colonies in the early years. Henry Dunster, president of Harvard College, imported two dozen almanacs from England in 1641. Although their astrological projections were calculated for different latitudes, their calendars and other apparatus still had some value, not least as models for the colonial production. Almanacs were among the first publications produced by the printing presses established in Massachusetts in the late 1630s. New England almanacs presented an eviscerated version of the English calendar. Reflecting the advanced puritan style, some early American almanacs set aside pagan names and substituted 'the first month', 'the eighth month', etc. Urian Oakes combined both systems in his almanac for 1650, and freely used the pagan names when discussing astronomy. Samuel Cheever's almanac for 1661 began the year with 'the first month called March', but later almanacs reverted completely to the traditional terms. Samuel Danforth apologized in his almanac for 1686, 'if that I the names imposed by old idolatry on months and planets still retain, because I'm forced thereto by cruel custom's laws'.[27]

Cambridge and Boston almanacs indicated sabbath days, election days, court days, artillery days, fairs, tides, and a rich range of astronomical information. But they were silent or reticent about traditional holidays. Red-letter printing was unknown in New England almanacs before 1692, and then was not used to mark red-letter days. Most American almanacs ignored 5 November. Not until the anglican revival of the 1680s did New England almanac-makers risk offending the puritan elite by listing the Christian holy days and national remembrances that were commonplace in old England. Under James II they became even bolder. John Tulley's Boston almanac for 1687 was the first in the colonies to begin the year with January, and the first to list the feast and fast days of the English church. Tulley was a supporter of James II and a toady of Sir Edmund Andros and the Dominion of New England. It must have pained the puritan elders to read Tulley's calendar of significant days which was tailored to the taste of the newly ascendant regime. The almanac featured New Year, Twelfth day, Valentine's, Shrove Sunday and Tuesday, Ash Wednesday, St Matthias, Lady day, Easter, St George, Saints Philip and James, Whitsunday, St John the Baptist, St Swithin, St James, Lammas, St Bartholomew, St Matthew, Michaelmas, St Luke, Saints Simon and Jude, Powder Plot day, 'Martlemas' (St Martin), St Andrew, St Thomas, Christmas, St Stephen, St John the Evangelist, and Holy Innocents. To these Tulley's 1689 almanac added Candlemas and St Crispin, and the anniversaries of the 'murder' of Charles I and the birth of James II, in a holy calendar that exceeded the usual recognition of feasts and fasts in England. Tulley continued to produce almanacs after the revolution, but the wind had gone from his sails. His publication of the 1690s were austere to the extreme. No day in 1692 gained special recognition; in 1697 he drew attention only to 4 and 5 November, the birthday of William III and the anniversary of the Gunpowder Plot.[28]

★

Gunpowder Treason day was not an annual observance in the New England colonies, but autumn thanksgiving days sometimes coincided with 5 November. Days of public thanksgiving in Connecticut in the 1680s were usually held on the first Wednesday in November, and from time to time this happened to be the fifth. Unlike their English counterparts, New England ministers did not take to their pulpits on 5 November to reflect on the history of England's deliverances and to urge closer walking with God. (Though some of them, including Thomas Hooker and John Wilson, had delivered Gunpowder Treason sermons in England.) Instead they reserved their remarks for fast-day and election sermons with a purely local compass. There was no echoing tintinnabulation, no Gunpowder Treason day beer for the bellringers, because early American churches had no bells to ring.

Although strenuous Protestants in England saw the Gunpowder deliverance as a signal of God's interest in 'true religion', New Englanders had other evidence of providence, and regarded the popular November commemoration as a sign of unreformed superstition. The godly in Massachusetts separated themselves from the celebrations of Gunpowder Treason day, just as their predecessors withdrew from the culture of licence back home. There are, however, hints and indications that some of the English customs were transmitted or re-imported across the Atlantic where their observance sometimes caused friction between the godly and the less devout.

Carousing sailors built a fire at Plymouth Plantation in 1623 that flamed out of control and destroyed three or four houses. William Bradford records that 'this fire was occasioned by some of the seamen that were roystering in a house where it first began, making a great fire in very cold weather, which broke out of the chimney into the thatch'. Bradford naturally saw this as symptomatic of the clash in culture and discipline between the saints and the reprobate masses. Emmanuel Altham, who was visiting Plymouth at the time, adds the significant information that this incident occurred on 5 November.[29] It seems that the sailors were hosting a Gunpowder Treason day party.

The next recorded incident took place a generation later. The silence of the records may be construed to mean that England's central Protestant anniversary had little part in New England's folk life until it was reintroduced after the Restoration. In 1662, the royalist Samuel Maverick complained, 'divers youths [were] lately prosecuted at Boston for making bonfires on Gunpowder Treason day at night, it being kept as a thanksgiving for the return of the New England agents, the youths being willing to conform to the practice that such a time affords in old England; for this the parents of the youths were fined, but the children of the church members who were guilty as much as others scraped all scot-free'.[30]

The Middlesex County court records of 1662 tell more of the story. Two servants, Thomas Facy and Paul Wilson (who had earlier been reprimanded for Maying), were 'convicted of disorderly carriage on the fifth of November last, being a day of public thanksgiving, in abetting sundry young persons and others gathering themselves into companies and kindling fires in the evening, and absenting themselves from their masters' houses and lodgings after nine at night to the disquiet of the inhabitants, sundry men having their fences by that occasion pulled up and burnt, and one house tumbled into a cove, and sundry guns shot of whereof Paul Wilson confesses he shot one of them'.[31] With its mixture of liberty, noise, fire, and danger, this drew its inspiration from popular Gunpowder observances in London.

The unlicensed celebration on 5 November continued through the rest of the seventeenth century, and became more elaborate in the eighteenth. Puritan ministers averted their eyes or gnashed their teeth, while the magistrates worked to prevent things from getting out of hand. Increase Mather wrote in his diary on 5 November 1664, 'at night much troubled to see the bonfires'.[32] As they were at Plymouth in 1623, the celebrants were malignants, mariners and young people outside the dominant stream of devout New England culture.

In 1665 a group of anglicans, Samuel Maverick among them, petitioned the General Court of Massachusetts to make the laws of the colony conform more closely with those of England. 'There ought to be inserted and ordained to be kept the fifth of November, and the nine and twentieth of May, as days of thanksgiving; the first for the miraculous preservation of our king and country from the Gunpowder Treason; the second for his majesty's birth [and] miraculous and happy restoration to his crowns upon the same day; as also the thirtieth of January as a day of fasting and praying, that God would please to avert his judgment from our nations for that most barbarous and execrable murder of our late sovereign, Charles the first.' This loyal proposal was rejected, but 5 November 1667 was declared 'a day of thanksgiving unto God for the continuance of our peace and liberties'.[33] This was one of the annual thanksgivings, whose day varied from year to year, and it may have served to co-opt or deflect the Gunpowder Treason festivities.

Other evidence testifies to the revived vitality of the memory of the Gunpowder Plot in Restoration New England. In 1669 Thomas Bailey, a resident of Massachusetts, wrote a four-page poem entitled 'In Quintum Novembris'. Bailey recited the history of the plot and praised Jehovah, 'Who sav'd us on 5th day of November/Which may us cause God still to remember.'[34]

In America as in Stuart England, the fear of a Catholic succession in the 1670s gave new life to the Gunpowder commemoration. News of the mock pope burnings in London circulated in New England, perhaps prompting emulation. John Wilson's *Song of deliverance for the lasting remembrance of God's wonderful works*, written in England in the 1620s, was reprinted at Boston in 1680. Wilson himself had moved from Sudbury, Suffolk, to become a minister in Massachusetts. Now his verse on the 'the hellish Powder-Plot' made the same transit. The rising generation in New England could marvel, 'Never since world began was thought plot more abominable./Never deliverance was wrought more strange and admirable.' If solid puritans had once recommended commemoration 'by sermons, prayers, or loud songs, bells, bonfires, or by feast', who could gainsay such celebrations?[35]

New England preachers sometimes invoked the memory of Gunpowder Treason, although they did not observe the special day of prayer and thanksgiving that was part of the seasonal cycle in England. Puritans could countenance the day as part of a pattern of providences while dissociating themselves from disorderly festivity. Samuel Sewall was disappointed on 5 November 1685, noting in his diary, 'Mr Allin preached . . . mentioned not a word in prayer or preaching that I took notice of with respect to Gunpowder Treason.' The next year things were more to his liking when Mr Morton, preaching at Charlestown, 'took occasion to speak of the 5th of November very pithily'.[36]

While the godly were at services, the rowdies were in the streets. In November 1682 Benjamin James and others were brought before the Suffolk County Court for gathering people together to start a bonfire in Boston. On 5 November 1685, 'although it rained hard, yet there was a bonfire made on the common. About fifty people attended it.' On the following night the weather improved and 'about two hundred hallowed about a fire on the common'. Merchants and magistrates were apprehensive that the celebrations might lead to disturbances, but for most years in the late seventeenth century the night passed without violence. At Marblehead in 1702 the day was enlivened with a bull-baiting, to be followed by distribution of the meat to the poor.[37]

With the accession of William III the Gunpowder Treason anniversary became merged with celebration of the king's birthday on 4 November and with the annual autumn thanksgiving. Puritan fastidiousness gave way to English Protestant patriotism. At Boston in 1697, 'guns fired with respect to the king's birthday. At night great illuminations made in the Town House, governor and council and many gentlemen there. About eight Mr. Brattle and Newman let fly their fireworks from Cotton Hill. Governor and Council went thither with a trumpet sounding.'[38]

This organized civic commemoration was soon to be overwhelmed by popular celebration. Over the next half century the 5 November observance developed into an annual carnival and fire-festival which culminated with the ritual burning of an effigy of the pope. A full account of the evolution of Gunpowder Treason day in North America is beyond the scope of this study, but two episodes from eighteenth-century Boston are well worth recording. The Boston almanac for November 1735 year noted, 'Gunpowder Plot/We ha'n't forgot.' Just in case the memory was cold the *Boston Evening Post* recited the story of Guy Fawkes and the conspiracy of 1605, 'for the information of such of our readers as are not furnished with the history of this surprising attempt'. On 10 November 1735 the paper reported, 'Wednesday last, being the 5th of this instant November, the guns were fired at Castle William, in token of joy for the happy deliverance of our nation from one of the most horrid and damnable conspiracies that ever was contrived by hell and Rome . . . In the evening there was a bonfire on Dorchester neck, and several in this town; and there were a variety of fireworks played off upon this occasion, both on the land and on the water.' Apprentices went out in boats to watch the spectacle, and four of them were drowned on their way home.[39]

A generation later the celebration involved competitive processions, effigies and bonfires. In 1764 there was death and destruction as the rival north end and south end gangs of Boston paraded their popes. The annual outbreaks of violent rejoicing had more to do with the social strains of Hanoverian Boston than with distant events in Jacobean England. The calendar provided the occasion for current anxieties to fuse with custom and tradition. The evening had noise, light, licence, festivity, and danger, essential ingredients in this anti-Catholic and anti-authoritarian catharsis. Colonial officials attempted to maintain order as Gunpowder Treason mutated into Pope day and was eventually overshadowed and ended by the American revolution. In 1774 imported tea and an effigy of Lord North were consigned with the pope and the devil to the 5 November fires at Newport, in a politicized adaption of the old vocabulary of celebration.[40]

*

As in the England of an earlier generation, calendrical observances were harnessed by competing ideological traditions. As always, they were capable of bearing multiple meanings. Bonfires and bells accompanied the partisan fracturing of Anglo-American political culture, but here too they served the forces of social and cultural cohesion. Public practices that began in the Elizabethan era in the service of the Tudor state were adapted in the seventeenth century to criticize the ruling regime. By the end of the Stuart era the sensitized calendar marked a battery of occasions, royal, dynastic, religious, providential, and political. The versatility of the vocabulary of celebration proved itself in its eighteenth-century florescence and in its transfer to other parts of the English world.

NOTES

1 Patterns of Time – the Tudor Calendar

1. For the traditional calendar see Martin P. Nilsson, *Primitive Time-Reckoning* (Lund, 1920); J. A. MacCulloch, *The Celtic and Scandinavian Religions* (London, 1948); Kenneth Harrison, *The Framework of Anglo-Saxon History* (Cambridge, 1976); R. T. Hampson, *Medii Aevi Kalendarium, or Dates, Charters and Customs of the Middle Ages* (London, 1841); E. O. James, *Seasonal Feasts and Festivals* (London, 1961); George Caspar Homans, *English Villagers of the Thirteenth Century* (Cambridge, Mass., 1941; New York, 1960), pp. 353–81; A. R. Wright, *British Calendar Customs. England* (3 vols., London, 1936–40). For recent historical treatments see Charles Phythian-Adams, *Local History and Folklore: A New Framework* (London, 1975), and Bob Bushaway, *By Rite: Custom, Ceremony and Community in England 1700–1880* (London, 1982). For a theoretical discussion see Pierre Bourdieu, *Outline of a Theory of Practice* (Cambridge, 1977), esp. pp. 105–7. The quote is from Jeffrey Burton Russell, *Witchcraft in the Middle Ages* (Ithaca and London, 1972), pp. 50–1.
2. Keith Thomas, *Religion and the Decline of Magic* (London, 1971), pp. 47–8; Joshua Stopford, *Pagano-Papismus: Or, an Exact Parallel Betweene Rome-Pagan, and Rome-Christian, in their Doctrines and Ceremonies* (London, 1675), pp. 231–59.
3. For the reformation of manners see Marjorie K. McIntosh, 'Local change and community control in England, 1465–1500', *Huntington Library Quarterly*, 49 (1986), pp. 219–42; Margaret Spufford, 'Puritanism and social control?', in Anthony Fletcher and John Stevenson (eds.), *Order and Disorder in Early Modern England* (Cambridge, 1985), pp. 41–57; Keith Wrightson, *English Society 1580–1680* (London, 1982), pp. 168–215; Keith Wrightson, 'The puritan reformation of manners with special reference to the counties of Lancashire and Essex, 1640–1660', Cambridge University Ph.D. Thesis, 1974.
4. 'The King's Injunctions, restricting the number of holy days', in Stephen Reed Cattley (ed.), *The Acts and Monuments of John Foxe*, vol. 5 (London, 1838), pp. 164–5.
5. William Keating Clay (ed.), *Liturgical Services. Liturgies and Occasional Forms of Prayer Set Forth in the Reign of Queen Elizabeth* (Cambridge, 1847), p. 30; Edward Cardwell (ed.), *Documentary Annals of the Reformed Church of England* (Oxford, 1844), vol. 1, pp. 220–1.

6. 'Injunctions, restricting the number of holy days', p. 164.

7. ibid., p. 165.

8. H. M. C., *Ninth Report*, (London, 1883) vol. 1, pp. 149, 153, 155, 156; David Hugh Farmer (ed.), *The Oxford Dictionary of Saints* (Oxford, 1978), p. 378. On the tenacity of old practices see J. J. Scarisbrick, *The Reformation and the English People* (Oxford, 1984), pp. 109–88; D. M. Palliser, 'Popular reactions to the Reformation during the years of uncertainty 1530–70', Ronald Hutton, 'The local impact of the Tudor Reformations', and Christopher Haigh, 'The continuity of Catholicism in the English Reformation', in Christopher Haigh (ed.), *The English Reformation Revised* (Cambridge, 1987), pp. 94–138, 176–208.

9. Frederic William Russell, *Kett's Rebellion in Norfolk* (London, 1859), p. 25; Joyce Youings, *Sixteenth-Century England* (Harmondsworth, 1984), pp. 96, 213–14.

10. 5 & 6. Edward VI, c. 3.

11. 1. Eliz., c. 2; Clay (ed.), *Liturgical Services*, pp. 47–52, 443–55; Edward Cardwell, *A History of Conferences*, 3rd edn (Oxford, 1849), p. 40.

12. William Harrison, *The Description of England*, ed. Georges Edelen (Ithaca, 1968), p. 36.

13. Robert Charles Hope (ed.), *The Popish Kingdome or Reign of Antichrist Written in Latin Verse by Thomas Naogeorgus and Englyshed by Barnabe Googe* [1570] (London, 1880), f. 44; William Keth, *A Sermon Made at Blanford Forum* (London, 1572), f. 20.

14. 'An Admonition to the Parliament' [1572], in W. H. Frere and C. E. Douglas (eds.), *Puritan Manifestoes* (London, 1954), pp. 21, 24; John Northbrooke, *Spiritus est Vicarius Christi in Terra. A Treatise wherein Dicing, Dauncing, Vaine Playes or Enterludes with other idle pastimes etc. commonly used on the Sabboth day are reproved* (London, 1577), p. 23.

15. William Vaughan, *The Golden-Grove, Moralized in Three Bookes* (London, 1600), sig. O6v.

16. Youings, *Sixteenth-Century England*, p. 214.

17. Grindal's articles for Canterbury, 1576, in Cardwell, *Documentary Annals*, vol. 1, pp. 399–400; Barnes's injunctions for Durham, 1577, in W. P. M. Kennedy, *Elizabethan Episcopal Administration* (Oxford, 1924), p. 72; see also Sandys' articles for York, 1578, and Wickham's articles for Lincoln, 1588, in ibid., pp. 93, 245; Ralph Houlbrooke, *Church Courts and the People During the English Reformation 1520–1570* (Oxford, 1979), p. 249.

18. Richard Carew, *The Survey of Cornwall* (London, 1602), p. 69; Thomas Westcote, *A View of Devonshire in MDCXXX*, ed. George Oliver and Pitman Jones (Exeter, 1845), p. 54; Cardwell, *Documentary Annals*, vol. 2, pp. 243–6.

19. 'Injunctions, restricting the number of holy days', p. 165; Clay (ed.), *Liturgical Services*, pp. 45, 443.

20. Harrison, *Description*, pp. 176–7; Arthur Hopton, *A Concordancy of Yeares* (London, 1612), pp. 242–50.

21. Harrison, *Description*, pp. 178–80.

22. Harrison, *Description*, pp. 178, 180; Brian P. Levack, *The Civil Lawyers in England, 1603–1641: A Political Study* (Oxford, 1973), pp. 158–95.
23. Almanac for 1578 in Clay (ed.), *Liturgical Services*, pp. 444–55; *A Manuall of Praiers* (Douai?, 1595).

2 The Rhythm of the Year in Early Modern England

1. The classic accounts are Henry Bourne, *Antiquitates Vulgares or the Antiquities of the Common People* (Newcastle, 1725), and John Brand, *Observations on Popular Antiquities*, ed. Henry Ellis (London, 1813). See also William Hone, *The Every-Day Book; or, Everlasting Calendar of Popular Amusements* (London, 1826), and T. F. Thiselton Dyer, *British Popular Customs Present and Past* (London, 1900). For a modern critical interpretation see Charles Phythian-Adams, *Local History and Folklore: A New Framework* (London, 1975), and the essays in Eric Hobsbawm and Terence Ranger (eds.), *The Invention of Tradition* (Cambridge, 1984).
2. Lucy Toulmin Smith (ed.), *The Maire of Bristow is Kalendar* (London, 1872), p. 59; C. H. Josten (ed.), *Elias Ashmole (1617–1692) His Autobiographical and Historical Notes*, vol. 2 (Oxford, 1966), p. 317; George Ornsby (ed.), *The Correspondence of John Cosin* (Durham, 1869), pp. 19, 53, 66; Thomas Birch, *The Court and Times of James the First* (London, 1849), vol. 1, p. 165; Thomas Birch, *The Court and Times of Charles the First* (London, 1848), vol. 1, p. 114.
3. New College, Oxford, MS., 'Robert Woodford's diary'. (Extracts in H. M. C., *Ninth Report* (London, 1884) vol. 2, pp. 496–9.)
4. J. E. Foster (ed.), *The Diary of Samuel Newton, Alderman of Cambridge (1662–1717)* (Cambridge, 1890); Alan Macfarlane (ed.), *The Diary of Ralph Josselin 1616–1683* (London, 1976); Robert Latham and William Matthews (eds.), *The Diary of Samuel Pepys* (Berkeley and Los Angeles, 1970–83).
5. Thomas Tusser, *Five Hundred Points of Good Husbandry* (London, 1614), p. 84; Thomas, *Religion and the Decline of Magic*, p. 618; John Aubrey, 'Remaines of Gentilisme and Judaism', in John Buchanan-Brown (ed.), *John Aubrey: Three Prose Works* (Carbondale, Illinois, 1972), pp. 433, 137. See also the seasonal advice in M. Stevenson, *The Twelve Moneths* (London, 1661).
6. Examples abound in the churchwardens' accounts of eighty parishes from twenty-two counties, listed in the bibliography.
7. Thomas, *Religion and the Decline of Magic*, p. 618.
8. Carew, *Survey of Cornwall*, p. 54; 'Robert Woodford's diary'; J. S. W. Gibson and E. R. C. Brinkworth (eds.), *Banbury Corporation Records: Tudor and Stuart* (Banbury, 1977), p. 101.
9. Stevenson, *Twelve Moneths*, pp. 20, 25, 30, 35, 40, 44–5, 49, 54; See Hopton, *Concordancy of Yeares*, pp. 169–80, for a similar list of fairs in 1612.
10. H.M.C., *Ninth Report*, vol. 1, pp. 157, 162; *Banbury Corporation Records*, p. 132; Dorothy M. Meads (ed.), *The Diary of Lady Margaret Hoby 1599–1605* (London, 1930), p. 160; *Vox Graculi, or Iacke Dawes Prognostication*

(London, 1623), p. 50; John Day, *Day's Festivals or, Twelve of His Sermons* (Oxford, 1615), p. 12.

11. Birch, *Court and Times of James the First*, vol. 1, pp. 69, 71; Hope (ed.), *Popish Kingdom*, ff. 44–5; Stevenson, *Twelve Moneths*, p. 4; Aubrey, 'Remains', p. 138; Brand, *Observations on Popular Antiquities*, vol. 1, pp. 27–9.

12. Wright, *British Calendar Customs*, vol. 2, p. 102.

13. Edward Cardwell (ed.), *Documentary Annals of the Reformed Church of England* (Oxford, 1844), vol. 1, p. 46; Keth, *Sermon made at Blanford Forum*, ff. 18v, 20; Hope (ed.) *Popish Kingdome*, f. 47v; Peter Smart, *The Vanitie & Downefall of Superstitious Popish Ceremonies* (Edinburgh, 1628), f. 2v.

14. *Correspondence of John Cosin*, p. 60; Josten (ed.), *Elias Ashmole*, vol. 2, p. 428; Latham and Matthews (eds.), *Diary of Samuel Pepys*, vol. 7, p. 42, vol. 8, pp. 62, 65.

15. James A. Picton (ed.), *Selections from the Municipal Archives* (Liverpool, 1883), p. 35.

16. Michael D. Bristol, *Carnival and Theater: Plebian Culture and the Structure of Authority in Renaissance England* (New York, 1985), pp. 22–39, drawing on the ideas of Emile Durkheim, Arnold van Gennep, and Mikhail Bakhtin.

17. Brand, *Observations on Popular Antiquities*, vol. 1, pp. 72–3, 78; William Fennor, *Pasquils Palinodia, and his Progress to the Taverne* (London, 1619); Hope (ed.), *Popish Kingdome*, ff. 47v–49; Charles Lethbridge Kingsford (ed.), *A Survey of London by John Stow* (Oxford, 1908), p. 92; Keth, *Sermon made at Blanford Forum*, f. 18v; *Vox Graculi*, p. 55.

18. Brand, *Observations on Popular Antiquities*, vol. 1, pp. 74–8; Birch, *Court and Times of James the First*, vol. 1, pp. 138, 464. See also Peter Burke, 'Popular culture in seventeenth-century London', in Barry Reay (ed.), *Popular Culture in Seventeenth-Century England* (London, 1985), pp. 35–6; Tim Harris, *London Crowds in the Reign of Charles II: Propaganda and Politics from the Restoration until the Exclusion Crisis* (Cambridge, 1987), p. 14.

19. Frederick S. Boas (ed.), *The Diary of Thomas Crosfield* (Oxford, 1935), p. 63; *C.S.P.D., 1637*, p. 508; Brand, *Observations on Popular Antiquities*, vol. 1, pp. 63–71; W. Symonds, 'Winterslow church reckonings, 1542–1661', *The Wiltshire Archaeological and Natural History Magazine*, 36 (1909–10), pp. 42–9; Tusser, *Five Hundred Points of Good Husbandry*, p. 135.

20. Cardwell, *Documentary Annals*, vol. 1, p. 53; E. A. Wrigley and R. S. Schofield, *The Population History of England, 1541–1871* (Cambridge, Mass., 1981), pp. 298–305; David Cressy, 'The seasonality of marriage in old and New England', *Journal of Interdisciplinary History*, 16 (1985), pp. 1–21; Henry Mason, *Christian Humiliation, or, A Treatise of Fasting* (London, 1625), pp. 12–48; Daniel Featly, *Ancilla Pietatis: or, The Hand-Maid to Private Devotion* (London, 1626), p. 264; John Cosin, *A Collection of Private Devotions* (London, 1627), preface. Cf. Richard Baxter, *A*

Christian Directory (London, 1673), pt. 3, pp. 152–3. For the significance of Lent on the Jacobean stage, see Gerald Edes Bentley, *The Jacobean and Caroline Stage* (Oxford, 1941–68), vol. 7, pp. 1–9; R. Chris Hassel, Jr., *Renaissance Drama and the English Church Year* (Lincoln, Nebraska, 1979), pp. 112–39; and Bristol, *Carnival and Theater, passim.*

21. Churchwardens' accounts of St Nicholas, Great Yarmouth, described in the bibliography.

22. Cardwell, *Documentary Annals*, vol. 1, p. 56; Brand, *Observations on Popular Antiquities*, vol. 1, pp. 124–55; Keth, *Sermon Made at Blanford Forum*, f. 18v; David Underdown, *Revel, Riot and Rebellion: Popular Politics and Culture in England 1603–1660* (Oxford, 1985), p. 53; churchwardens' accounts of Clifton, Bedfordshire.

23. *Oxford English Dictionary*; Sir Henry Spelman, *Archaeologus. In Modem Glossarii ad Rem Antiquam Posteriorem* (London, 1626), p. 355; Underdown, *Revel, Riot, and Rebellion*, p. 92n; Wright, *British Calendar Customs*, vol. 1, pp. 124–5; Brand, *Observations on Popular Antiquities*, p. 163.

24. Clay (ed.), *Liturgical Services*, p. 441; C. R. Cheney, *Handbook of Dates for Students of English History* (London, 1945), pp. 4–5. Cf. the Roman explanation for the beginning of the year in March, in Ovid, *Fasti*, iii, 135–56.

25. Tusser, *Five Hundred Points of Good Husbandry*, p. 28; various churchwardens' accounts, including St Thomas, Salisbury, in 1609, and Holy Trinity, Cambridge, in 1625.

26. For an exposition of the feats of St George, with a comprehensive calendrical hagiography, see J. Mirk, *The Festyuall* (London, 1532), pp. 95–7; Brand, *Observations on Popular Antiquities*, vol. 1, pp. 165–6. William Hinde, *A Faithfull Remonstrance of the Holy Life and Happy Death of Iohn Bruen of Bruen-Stapleford* (London, 1641), p. 93, included St George among the 'saints that never were'; Daniel Featly was disciplined by Archbishop Laud for doubting the historicity of St George, (D.N.B.). Birch, *Court and Times of James the First*, vol. 1, pp. 96, 398; Birch, *Court and Times of Charles the First*, vol. 1, p. 406, vol. 2, p. 260; Albert J. Loomie, *Ceremonies of Charles I: the Note Books of John Finet 1628–1641* (New York, 1987), pp. 59, 90, 304.

27. Alexandra F. Johnston and Margaret Rogerson (eds.), *Records of Early English Drama: York* (Toronto, 1979), p. 327; David Galloway (ed.), *Records of Early English Drama: Norwich 1540–1642* (Toronto, 1984), pp. 47, 163, 178, 195; Lawrence M. Clopper (ed.), *Records of Early English Drama: Chester* (Toronto, 1979), pp. 258–9.

28. See below, Chapter 11.

29. Wright, *British Calendar Customs*, vol. 2, p. 190; Cardwell, *Documentary Annals*, vol. 1, p. 54.

30. Aubrey, 'Remaines', p. 133; Stopford, *Pagano-Papismus*, pp. 256–9; Kingsford (ed.), *Survey of London*, p. 99; *Vox Graculi*, p. 62; Stevenson, *Twelve Moneths*, p. 22; Stubbes, *Anatomie of Abuses*, p. 109; Wrigley and Schofield, *Population History*, pp. 286–93.

31. Joseph Strutt, *The Sports and Pastimes of the People of England*, ed. W. Hone (London, 1830), p. 353; churchwardens' accounts, including Eltham, Surrey in 1562, and Northill, Bedfordshire in 1560; Underdown, *Revel, Riot and Rebellion*, pp. 54, 56, 68, 85, 86–7, 92.

32. Fennor, *Pasquil's Palinodia*, sig. B3–3v; Audrey Douglas and Peter Greenfield (eds.), *Records of Early English Drama: Cumberland, Westmoreland, Gloucestershire* (Toronto, 1986), pp. 285–7; Percy Maning, 'Collectanea', *Folk-Lore*, 14 (1903), p. 174.

33. Brand, *Observations on Popular Antiquities*, vol. 1, p. 194; Wright, *British Calendar Customs*, vol. 2, p. 209; Kingsford (ed.), *Survey of London*, p. 99; C. H. Firth and R. S. Rait (eds.), *Acts and Ordinances of the Interregnum* (London, 1911), vol. 1, p. 420.

34. Cardwell, *Documentary Annals*, vol. 2, pp. 243–4; Henry Burton, *A Divine Tragedie Lately Acted* (London?, 1636), pp. 4, 6, 7, 9, 16, 25, 27; Boas (ed.), *Diary of Thomas Crosfield*, pp. 14, 63.

35. 'Robert Woodford's diary'.

36. Brand, *Observations on Popular Antiquities*, vol. 1, pp. 4–6; Stevenson, *Twelve Moneths*, p. 25.

37. H.M.C., *Calendar of Cecil MSS. at Hatfield House* (London, 1899), vol. 8, p. 201.

38. Kennedy, *Elizabethan Episcopal Administration*, p. 216; Keth, *Sermon Made at Blanford Forum*, f. 19.

39. Hope (ed.), *Popish Kingdome*, f. 53; H.M.C., *Ninth Report*, pp. 157, 160, 162; Norfolk Record Office, 'Norwich chamberlains' accounts, 1602–1648'.

40. Underdown, *Revel, Riot and Rebellion*, pp. 80–1, 91; churchwardens' accounts of St Matthew Friday Street, St Botolph without Bishopsgate, St Katherine Coleman Street, St Botolph, Cambridge, etc.

41. Carew, *Survey of Cornwall*, pp. 68–9; Stubbes, *Anatomie of Abuses*, pp. 110–13; Brand, *Observations on Popular Antiquities*, pp. 226–32; Underdown, *Revel, Riot and Rebellion*, pp. 50, 60, 93; Patrick Cowley, *The Church Houses. Their Religious and Social Significance* (London, 1970), pp. 73–4.

42. Johnston and Rogerson (eds.) *Records of Early English Drama: York*, pp. 327, 331–3, 340, 341, 390, 392; churchwardens' accounts; Mervyn James, *Society, Politics and Culture: Studies in Early Modern England* (Cambridge, 1986), pp. 16–47.

43. Brand, *Observations on Popular Antiquities*, vol. 1, pp. 238–68; Wright, *British Calendar Customs*, vol. 3, pp. 6–12.

44. 'Extracts from the Privy purse expenses of King Henry the Seventh', in Samuel Bentley (ed.), *Excerpta Historica, or, Illustrations of English History* (London, 1833), pp. 94, 103, 108, 112, 118, 133.

45. Hope (ed.), *Popish Kingdome*, f. 54v; Kingsford (ed.), *Survey of London*, pp. 101–2.

46. Aubrey, 'Remaines', p. 143; Sir James G. Frazer, *Balder the Beautiful: The Fire-Festivals of Europe and the Doctrine of the External Soul*, (London, 1923), vol. 1, pp. 198–9.

47. Frazer, *Balder*, vol. 2, pp. 36–7; Clopper (ed.), *Records of Early English Drama: Chester*, pp. 159–61; George Puttenham, *The Arte of English Poesie* (London, 1589), p. 128.

48. Clopper (ed.), *Records of Early English Drama: Chester*, pp. 197–8, 252–3; Johnston and Rogerson (ed.), *Records of Early English Drama: York*, pp. 337, 396; Underdown, *Revel, Riot and Rebellion*, p. 46.

49. Kingsford (ed.), *Survey of London*, p. 103; H.M.C., *Ninth Report*, vol. 1, pp. 148–55, 277.

50. *Records of the Borough of Nottingham . . . 1547–1625* (London and Nottingham, 1889), pp. 151, 159, 286, 342; *Records of the Borough of Nottingham . . . 1625–1702* (London and Nottingham, 1900), p. 190.

51. Underdown, *Revel, Riot and Rebellion*, pp. 59, 66, 95; F. R. Raines (ed.), *The Journal of Nicholas Assheton* (Manchester, 1848), p. 16; church-wardens' accounts including St Nicholas, Great Yarmouth, and St Botolph without Bishopsgate.

52. Kingsford (ed.), *Survey of London*, p. 104. St Bartholomew's day took on new significance for nonconformist preachers after 1662 as the day of their ejection; see J. Horsfall Turner (ed.), *The Rev. Oliver Heywood, B.A. 1630–1702; His Autobiography, Diaries, Anecdote and Event Books* (Brighouse, 1882–5), vol. 1, p. 281.

53. Hinde, *Faithfull Remonstrance of . . . Iohn Bruen*, pp. 89–91; Raines (ed.), *Journal of Nicholas Assheton*, pp. 19, 29–30, 67–8, 100; Meads (ed.), *Diary of Lady Margaret Hoby*, p. 205.

54. Churchwardens' accounts of St Pancras Soper Lane and St Bartholomew Exchange, London, St Botolph, Cambridge, etc.

55. Brand, *Observations on Popular Antiquities*, vol. 1, pp. 271–2; Macfarlane (ed.), *Diary of Ralph Josselin*, pp. 490, 560.

56. Homans, *English Villagers*, p. 370–1; Wright , *British Calendar Customs*, vol. 3, p. 43; Ornsby (ed.), *Correspondence of John Cosin*, p. 82; R. W. Ingram, *Records of Early English Drama: Coventry* (Toronto, 1981), p. 426.

57. Tusser, *Five Hundred Points of Good Husbandry*, p. 28; Stevenson, *Twelve Moneths*, p. 45; *Banbury Corporation Records*, p. 58; Smith (ed.), *The Maire of Bristow is Kalendar*, pp. 71, 77; H.M.C., *Ninth Report*, vol. 1, pp. 161, 163.

58. Brand, *Observations on Popular Antiquities*, vol. 1, p. 311; Houlbrooke, *Church Courts and the People*, p. 249; Cardwell, *Documentary Annals*, vol. 1, p. 400; Halesowen churchwardens' accounts.

59. Brand, *Observations on Popular Antiquities*, vol. 1, pp. 300–12. A royalist broadsheet of 1647 included All Saints' and All Souls' among the special days of November, Thomason collection, 669 f. 11/93.

60. Smith (ed.), *The Maire of Bristow is Kalendar*, p. 79; churchwardens' accounts of St Andrew by the Wardrobe.

61. Churchwardens' accounts of March, Cambridgeshire; 'Robert Woodford's diary'.

62. David Harris Sacks, 'The demise of the martyrs: the feasts of St Clement and St Katherine in Bristol, 1400–1600', *Social History*, 11 (1986), pp.

141–69; Strutt, *Sports and Pastimes*, p. 362; Clay (ed.), *Liturgical Services*, p. 454.

63. Tusser, *Five Hundred Points of Good Husbandry*, pp. 53–6; Johnston and Rogerson (ed.), *Records of Early Drama: York*, pp. 369–70.
64. Churchwardens' accounts of St Martin in the Fields, Middlesex.
65. Stevenson, *Twelve Moneths*, p. 59; Birch, *Court and Times of James the First*, vol. 1, p. 24; Meads (ed.), *Diary of Lady Margaret Hoby*, p. 91; 'The diary of Samuel Ward', in M. M. Knappen (ed.), *Two Elizabethan Puritan Diaries* (Chicago, 1933; Gloucester, Mass., 1966), p. 116; Andrew Browning (ed.), *Memoirs of Sir John Reresby* (Glasgow, 1936), pp. 74, 95, 103, 285–6.
66. Churchwardens' accounts, including St Stephen Coleman Street, London.
67. Chris Durston, 'Lords of misrule: the puritan war on Christmas 1642–1660', *History Today*, 35 (1985), pp. 7–14. See below, Chapter 3.
68. Underdown, *Revel, Riot and Rebellion*, pp. 54, 86–7.

3 The Politics of the Calendar, 1600–1660

1. Cardwell, *Documentary Annals*, vol. 2, 243–6.
2. Richard Hooker, *Of the Lawes of Ecclesiastical Politie* (London, 1723), pp. 250, 249–59.
3. John Day, *Day's Festivals or, Twelve of His Sermons* (Oxford, 1615), pp. 81–5, 108. See also John Howson, *A Sermon Preached at St Maries in Oxford the 17 Day of November* (Oxford, 1602), sigs. A2, B; John Boys, *An Exposition of the Festiuall Epistles and Gospels* (London, 1615), dedication.
4. Lancelot Andrewes, *XCVI Sermons*, 3rd edn. (London, 1635).
5. ibid., p. 204.
6. ibid., p. 148.
7. ibid., pp. 1, 53, 119.
8. ibid., p. 209.
9. ibid., pp. 459, 608, 596.
10. George Ornsby (ed.), *The Correspondence of John Cosin* (Durham, 1869), pt. 1, pp. 107–10.
11. Henry Mason, *Christian Humiliation, or, A treatise of Fasting* (London, 1625), pp. 148, 147.
12. Mason, *Christian Humiliation*, pp. 129, 139, 123, 134.
13. John Cosin, *A Collection of Private Devotions* (London, 1627).
14. Peter Smart, *The Vanitie & Downefall of Superstitious Popish Ceremonies* (Edinburgh, 1628), ff. 2–2v. See also Smart's 'Articles against the Durham innovators', in Ornsby (ed.), *Correspondence of John Cosin*, pt. 1, pp. 161–99; and Peter Smart, *The Humble Petition of Peter Smart* (London, 1640).
15. Cardwell, *Documentary Annals*, vol. 1, pp. 220–1, 359, 399–400; vol. 2, pp. 179, 253; Ornsby (ed.), *Correspondence of John Cosin*, pt. 1, pp. 110, 113, 118; William Laud, *Articles to be Inquired of in the Metropolitical Visitation . . . for the Diocese of London* (London, 1636), sigs. A3v, A4.;

Keith Wrightson and David Levine, *Poverty and Piety in an English Village: Terling, 1525–1700* (New York, 1979), p. 160.

16. *C.S.P.D., 1634–35*, pp. 263, 319, 26; *C.S.P.D., 1635*, pp. 185, 189.

17. Daniel Featly, *Ancilla Pietatis: or, the Hand-Maid to Private Devotion* (London, 1626), preface, pp. 167, 257.

18. Daniel Featly, *Ancilla Pietatis: or, the Hand-maid to private Devotion*, 6th edn (London, 1639), pp. 381–3, 391–5; *D.N.B.*

19. New College, Oxford, MS., 'Robert Woodford's diary.'

20. Horton Davies, *Worship and Theology in England* (Princeton, New Jersey, 1970), vol. 1, pp. 68, 70, 74, 215–52, 288.

21. Henry Burton, *A Tryall of Private Devotions. or, A Diall for the Houres of Prayer* (London, 1628), sigs. Av, A2, E4, F2. Cf. 'An admonition to the Parliament', in Frere and Douglas (eds.), *Puritan Manifestoes*, pp. 21, 24.

22. Burton, *Tryall of Private Devotions*, sigs. I3, F2, H4, F3v.

23. William Prynne, *Histrio-Mastix. The Players Scourge* (London, 1633), pp. 3, 20, 197, 580, 751, 757–60, 744.

24. ibid., pp. 743–4; William Lamont, *Marginal Prynne 1600–1669* (London, 1963), p. 35.

25. Underdown, *Revel, Riot and Rebellion*, pp. 66–8, 85–6; Leah S. Marcus, *The Politics of Mirth: Jonson, Herrick, Milton, Marvell, and the Defense of Old Holiday Pastimes* (Chicago, 1986), pp. 16–18, 140–68; Ralph Knevet, *Rhodon and Iris. A Pastorall, As it was Presented at the Florists Feast in Norwich, May 3, 1631* (London, 1631), sigs. Av, A2v, Bv.

26. 'Root and Branch Petition', in S. R. Gardiner (ed.), *The Constitutional Documents of the Puritan Revolution 1625–1660*, 3rd edn (Oxford, 1906), pp. 141–2; Anthony Fletcher, *The Outbreak of the English Civil War* (London, 1981), pp. 91–7; William Hinde, *A Faithfull Remonstrance of the Holy Life and Happy Death of Iohn Bruen* (London, 1641), p. 91.

27. *The Orders from the House of Commons for the Abolishing of Superstition, and Innovation, in the Regulating of Church Affairs* (London, 1641); Chris Durston, 'Lords of misrule: the puritan war on Christmas 1642–60', *History Today*, 35 (1985), pp. 7–14; John Syms, 'Journal of the Civil war 1642–1649', British Library, Add. MS. 35,297, f. 67v.

28. *The Scholars Petition for Play-dayes instead of Holy-daies* (London, 1644); Edward Fisher, *The Feast of Feasts. Or, The Celebration of the Sacred Nativity* (Oxford, 1644), pp. 1–3.

29. 'Directory for Public Worship', in Firth and Rait (eds.), *Acts and Ordinances*, vol. 1, p. 607; Macfarlane (ed.), *Diary of Ralph Josselin*, p. 47; Hinde, *Faithfull Remonstrance*, p. 90.

30. 'An Ordinance of Parliament forbidding the observance of the usual Church Festivals as holidays,' Thomason collection, 669.f.11 (18).

31. *Calendar-Reformation. Or, An Humble Addresse to the Right Honorable the Lords and Commons Assembled in Parliament, Touching Dayes and Moneths, that they may be taught to speake such a language as may become the mouth of a Christian.* For the New England usage see below, Chapter 12.

32. John Taylor, *The Complaint of Christmas* (London, 1646), pp. 1–4; Macfarlane (ed.), *Diary of Ralph Josselin*, pp. 81, 108. See also *The*

Arraignment, Conviction, and Imprisoning of Christmas (London, 1646); T. H., *A Ha! Christmas* (London, 1647); and *Women Will Have their Will: or, Give Christmas his Due* (London, 1648).

33. L. M., *A Perfect Relation of the Horrible Plot . . . at Edmondsbury* (London, 1647); *Canterbury Christmas* (London, 1648); *The Declaration of many thousands of the City of Canterbury* (London, 1647).

34. Joseph Heming, *Certain Quaeries Touching the Rise and Observation of Christmas* (London, 1648); George Palmer, *The Lawfulness of the Celebration of Christ's Birthday* (London, 1649); Robert Skinner, *Christs Birth Misse-timed* (London, 1649); *Christs Birth Not Mis-Timed* (London, 1649); Edward Fisher, *A Christian Caveat to the Old and New Sabbatarians. Or, A vindication of our Gospel-Festivals* (London, 1650); Thomas Mocket, *Christmas, The Christians grand Feast* (London, 1650); Allan Blayney (Pastor Fido), *Festorum Metropolis. The Metropolis Feast* (London, 1650); John Collinges, *Responsoria ad Erratica Piscatoris. Or, A Caveat for Old and New Prophanenesse* (London, 1653); *The Vindication of Christmas* (1653). See also Durston, 'Lords of misrule', pp. 7–14.

35. Churchwardens' accounts, including St Peter Mancroft, Norwich, Gt Staughton, Huntingdonshire, Great St Mary's, Cambridge, St Botolph without Bishopsgate, London, and St Martin in the Fields, Middlesex.

36. Edward Sparke, *Scintillula Altaris. Or, A Pious Reflection on Primitive Devotion* (London, 1652), pp. 1, 5.

37. 'A Resolution of Parliament', 24 December 1652, Thomason collection, 669. f. 16 (77); John Taylor, *Christmas in & out* (London, 1653); Hezekiah Woodward, *Christmas Day, The Old Heathens Feasting Day* (London, 1656), preface, pp. 6, 13, 19.

38. *C.S.P.D., 1657–8*, p. 226; *Calendar of State Papers, Venice, 1657–9*, pp. 150, 152.

39. Thomas Hall, *Funebria Florae, The Downfall of May-Games* (London, 1660), p. 13.

40. Macfarlane (ed.), *Diary of Ralph Josselin*, pp. 581, 588.

4 *Crownation Day and the Royal Honour*

1. Unless otherwise noted, the sources for this chapter are churchwardens' accounts from eighty parishes selected from twenty-two counties, listed in the bibliography.

2. J. E. Neale, *Essays in Elizabethan History* (London, 1958), pp. 9–20; Roy Strong, 'The popular celebration of the accession day of Queen Elizabeth I', *Journal of the Warburg and Courtauld Institutes*, 21 (1959), pp. 88–91.

3. Strong, 'Popular celebration', p. 88. For the cult of St Hugh see Henry Mayr-Harting (ed.), *St Hugh of Lincoln* (Oxford, 1987).

4. Thomas Holland, Πανήγυρις *D. Elizabethae . . . A sermon preached at Pauls in London the 17 of November Ann. Dom. 1599* (Oxford, 1601), sig. N4; John Howson, *A Sermon Preached at St Maries in Oxford the 17 Day of November, 1602* (Oxford, 1602), dedication.

5. Quoted in Neale, *Essays in Elizabethan History*, p. 10.

6. Churchwardens' accounts; Strong, 'Popular celebration', pp. 89–91.

7. Maurice Kyffin, *The Blessednes of Brytaine, or A Celebration of the Queenes Holy Day* (London, 1588), sig. B3v.

8. Holland, Πανήγυρις *D. Elizabethae*, sig. A2v; Thomas White, *A Sermon Preached at Paules Cross the 17 of November A. 1589* (London, 1589), p. 63.

9. William Keating Clay (ed.), *Liturgies and Occasional Forms of Prayer Set Forth in the Reign of Queen Elizabeth* (Cambridge, 1847), pp. 548–61; Strong, 'Popular celebration', p. 94.

10. Edmund Bunny, in Clay (ed.), *Liturgies and Occasional Forms*, p. 467.

11. John Foxe, *Actes and Monuments of these latter and perillous days* (London, 1563), dedication.

12. Isaac Colfe, *A Sermon Preached on the Queenes Day being the 17 of November. 1587 at the towne of Lidd in Kent* (London, 1588), sigs. C8–C8v; Holland, Πανήγμυις *D. Elizabethae*, sig. K2.

13. Howson, *Sermon Preached at St Maries*, sigs. A2, C2. Maurice Kyffin thought 17 November 'more fit to be solemnized than many other days in the calendar', *Blessednes of Brytaine*, sig. B3v.

14. James A. Picton (ed.), *Selections From the Municipal Archives and records from the 13th to the 17th Century* (Liverpool, 1883), p. 48.

15. H.M.C., *Ninth Report* (London, 1883), vol. 1, p. 251; Strong, 'Popular celebration', pp. 88, 91–3. Charles Henry Cooper (ed.), *Annals of Cambridge* (Cambridge, 1843), vol. 2, p. 359; David Galloway (ed.), *Records of Early English Drama: Norwich 1540–1642* (Toronto, 1984), pp. 95, 101, 106; Audrey Douglas and Peter Greenfield (eds.), *Records of Early English Drama: Cumberland, Westmoreland, Gloucestershire* (Toronto, 1986), pp. 21–2, 176, 179.

16. Strong, 'Popular celebration', p. 87.

17. Picton (ed.), *Selections from the Municipal Archives*, p. 48.

18. See also Holland, Πανήγυρις *D. Elizabethae*, sigs. A2v, H3, O4v; and the anonymous 'prayer for the queen on her birthday' in Clay (ed.), *Liturgies and Occasional forms*, pp. 556–7.

19. D. M. Livock (ed.), *City Chamberlains' Accounts in the Sixteenth and Seventeenth Centuries* (Bristol, 1966), p. 116.

20. John Cosin, *A Collection of Private Devotions*, 4th edn (London, 1635), calendar, pp. 382–3.

21. Thomas Birch, *The Court and Times of Charles the First* (London, 1848), vol. 2, pp. 82, 145.

22. New College Oxford, MS, 'Robert Woodford's diary.'

23. *C.S.P.D., 1640*, pp. 232–3; 'Constitutions and Canons Ecclesiastical . . . 1640', in William Laud, *Works* (Oxford, 1853), vol. 5, pp. 615–16; *Englands Complaint to Jesus Christ Against the Bishops Canons of the late sinful synod* (Amsterdam, 1640), np. I am grateful to Judith Richards for this reference. See also the loyal verse 'for the king's day' in George Wither, *Halelviah or, Britans Second Remembrancer* (London, 1641), pp. 254–7.

24. J. Horsfall Turner (ed.), *The Rev. Oliver Heywood, B.A. 1630–1702; His Autobiography, Diaries, Anecdote and Event Books* (Brighouse, 1882–5), vol. 1, p. 241; J. E. Foster (ed.), *The Diary of Samuel Newton, Alderman of*

Cambridge (1662–1717) (Cambridge, 1890), pp. 46–7; Andrew Browning (ed.), *Memoirs of Sir John Reresby* (Glasgow, 1936), p. 303. See also Richard Latham and William Matthews (eds.), *The Diary of Samuel Pepys* (Berkeley, 1970–83), vol. 4, p. 163, vol. 5, pp. 159, 162, vol. 6, p. 111, vol. 7, pp. 135–6, vol. 9, p. 217; and Austin Dobson (ed.), *The Diary of John Evelyn* (London, 1906), vol. 2, p. 170, vol. 3, pp. 204–5, 295–6.

5 Bonfires and Bells – the Vocabulary of Celebration

1. Sydney Anglo, 'An early Tudor programme for plays and other demonstrations against the Pope', *Journal of the Warburg and Courtauld Institute*, 20 (1957), pp. 176–9.

2. Isaac Colfe, *A Sermon Preached on the Queenes Day being the 17 of November. 1587* (London, 1588), sig. C5v; Thomas Holland, Πανήγυρις *D. Elizabethae* (Oxford, 1601), sigs. A2v, Bv, H3.

3. Churchwardens' accounts referred to throughout this chapter are listed in the bibliography; Henry Burton, *A Divine Tragedie lately Acted* (London?, 1636), pp. 9, 18; *C.S.P.D.*, *1634*, p. 410.

4. Cf. Mervyn James, *Society, Politics and Culture: Studies in Early Modern England* (Cambridge, 1986), pp. 17–31; Robert W. Malcolmson, *Popular Recreations in English Society 1700–1850* (Cambridge, 1973), p. 12.

5. Margaret Baker, *Wedding Customs and Folklore* (Newton Abbot, 1977), p. 106; Natalie Zemon Davis, 'Charivari, honor, and community in seventeenth-century Lyon and Geneva', in John J. MacAloon (ed.), *Rite, Drama, Festival, Spectacle* (Philadelphia, 1984), pp. 42, 47; Thomas Birch, *The Court and Times of James the First* (London, 1849), vol. 2, p. 360.

6. Maurice Kyffin,, *The Blessednes of Brytaine, or A Celebration of the Queenes Holy day* (London, 1588), sig. B3v.

7. Holland, Πανήγυρις *D. Elizabethae*, sig. P; William Shakespeare, *Troilus and Cressida*, Act 1, scene 3; Ian Donaldson (ed.), *Ben Jonson* (Oxford, 1985), p. 399, 'To the king on his birthday, 19 November 1632'.

8. George Elwes Corrie (ed.) *Sermons by Hugh Latimer* (Cambridge, 1844), p. 498.

9. Ernest Morris, *The History and Art of Change Ringing* (1931, reprinted Wakefield, 1976), pp. 23, 74. See also Jean Sanderson (ed.), *Change Ringing: The History of an English Art* (Guildford, Surrey, 1987), and the classic works of Richard Duckworth and Fabian Stedman, *Tintinnalogia* (1668), and Fabian Stedman, *Campanalogia* (1677).

10. Keith Thomas, *Religion and the Decline of Magic* (London and New York, 1971), pp. 31, 49, 52; J. J. Raven, *Bells of England* (1906), pp. 26, 110–11, 280; Percival Price, *Bells and Man* (New York, 1983), pp. 83–5, 107–29.

11. Valerie Pearl, *London and the Outbreak of the Puritan Revolution* (Oxford, 1961), p. 163. *Mercurius Elencticus*, 5–12 November 1647, the proposal attributed to Henry Marten.

12. William Leigh, *Queen Elizabeth, Paraleld in her Princely vertues, with David, Iosua, and Hezekia* (London, 1612), p. 49.

13. John Gough Nichols (ed.), *The Diary of Henry Machyn, citizen and merchant-taylor of london . . . 1550–1563* (London, 1848), p. 310.

14. Sources are churchwardens' accounts, and H.M.C., *Ninth Report*, vol. 1, p. 261.
15. Thomas Pettit, ' "Here Comes I, Jack Straw:" English Folk Drama and Social Revolt', *Folklore*, 95 (1984), p. 7; *C.S.P.D., Addenda 1566–1579*, pp. 101, 128, 172; Mary Anne Everett Green (ed.), *Diary of John Rous, Incumbent of Santon Downham, Suffolk from 1625 to 1642* (London, 1856), p. 23; Burton, *Divine Tragedie*, p. 27; Ann Hughes, *Politics, Society and Civil War in Warwickshire, 1620–1660* (Cambridge, 1987), p. 153. On the role of church bells in the St Bartholomew's Day Massacre in France, see Denis Richet, 'Sociocultural aspects of religious conflicts in Paris during the second half of the sixteenth century', in Robert Forster and Orest Ranum (eds.), *Ritual, Religion, and the Sacred* (Baltimore, 1982), p. 193.
16. *C.S.P.D., 1629–31*, p. 277.
17. Ronald Hutton, *The Restoration: A Political and Religious History of England and Wales 1658–1667* (Oxford, 1985), pp. 125–6.
18. Anthony Hewitson (ed.), *Diary of Thomas Bellingham, An Officer under William III* (Preston, 1908), p. 23.
19. Price, *Bells and Man*, p. 156.
20. H.M.C., *Ninth Report* (London, 1883), vol. 1, p. 201; H.M.C., *Calendar of the Manuscripts of the Dean and Chapter of Wells* (London, 1914), vol. 2, pp. 376, 380, 431, 446; J. Charles Cox, (ed.), *The Records of the Borough of Northampton . . . 1550 to 1835* (London and Northampton, 1898), p. 478; Lois G. Schwoerer, 'The Glorious Revolution as spectacle; a new perspective', in Stephen B. Baxter (ed.), *England's Rise to Greatness, 1660–1763* (Berkeley and Los Angeles, 1983), pp. 116–17, 143.
21. Sydney Anglo, 'The court festivals of Henry VII', *Bulletin of the John Rylands Library*, 43 (1960–1), pp. 28–43; Burton, *Divine Tragedie*, pp. 6, 7.
22. Elias Canetti, *Crowds and Power* (New York, 1962), p. 50; Joseph Strutt, *The Sports and Pastimes of the People of England*, ed. W. Hone (London, 1830), pp. 360, 372; R. T. Hampson, *Medii Aevi Kalendarium, or Dates, Charters and Customs of the Middle Ages* (London, 1841), vol. 1, p. 299; Alan Gailey, 'The bonfire in north Irish tradition', *Folk-Lore* 88 (1977), pp. 3–38; G. B. Adams, 'European words for "Bonfire" ', *Folk-Lore* 88 (1977), pp. 34–8. Cf. Charles Phythian-Adams, *Local History and Folklore: A New Framework* (London, 1975), pp. 22–4, 29, 31–3.
23. Mabel Peacock, Charlotte S. Burne, and W. Henry Jewitt, 'Correspondence', *Folk-Lore* 14 (1903), pp. 89–91, 185–6; *Folk-Lore* 18 (1907), p. 450; Charlotte S. Burne, 'Guy Fawkes Day', *Folk-Lore* 23 (1912), pp. 406–26; Jeffrey Burton Russell, *Witchcraft in the Middle Ages* (Ithaca, New York, 1972), p. 51. See also John A. MacCulloch, *The Celtic and Scandinavian Religions* (London, 1948), and James G. Frazer, *Balder the Beautiful: The Fire-Festivals of Europe and the Doctrine of the External Soul* (London, 1923).
24. C. L. Kingsford (ed.), 'Two London Chronicles,' in *Camden Miscellany*, 12 (1910), p. 41.
25. Holland, Πανήγυρις *D. Elizabethae*, sigs. O4v, P, P2; Francis Osborne, *Works*, 7th edn (London, 1673), p. 461.

26. Charles Lethbridge Kingsford (ed.), *A Survey of London by John Stow* (Oxford, 1908), pp. 101, 283. The most accessible discussions of 'liminality' and 'communitas' are Victor Turner, *Dramas, Fields, and Metaphors: Symbolic Action in Human Society* (Ithaca, New York, 1974), esp. pp. 47, 231–71, and Victor Turner, *The Ritual Process: Structure and Anti-Structure* (Harmondsworth, 1969), pp. 82 ff.

27. H. M. C., *Ninth Report*, vol. 1, p. 278; Birch (ed.), *Court and Times of Charles the First*, vol. 1, pp. 18, 20, 30; Mary Ann Everett Green (ed.), *Diary of John Rous* (London, 1856), pp. 56, 81; George Roberts (ed.), *Diary of Walter Yonge* (London, 1848), p. 77.

28. *Acts of the Privy Council, 1623–1625*, pp. 369–70.

29. Albert J. Loomie (ed.), *Ceremonies of Charles I: the Note Books of John Finet 1628–1641* (New York, 1987), p. 95.

30. *C.S.P.D., 1628–9*, pp. 156, 172, 175; Birch (ed.), *Court and Times of Charles the First*, vol. 1, p. 362; Greene (ed.), *Diary of John Rous*, p. 16.

31. New College, Oxford, MS., 'Robert Woodford's diary'; *C.S.P.D., 1640–1*, p. 462; Harold Smith, *The Ecclesiastical History of Essex* (Colchester, nd), pp. 176–7; Paul Hardacre, *The Royalists During the Puritan Revolution* (The Hague, 1956), p. 43.

32. British Library, Add. MS. 35,297, f.37; Harl. MS. 2125; I am grateful to Barbara Donagan for providing these references.

33. Hutton, *The Restoration*, pp. 93–4, 97, 126; G. E. Lee (ed.), 'Notebook of P. LeRoy', *Publications of the Guernsey Historical and Antiquarian Society* (1893), p. 25; J. E. Foster (ed.), *The Diary of Samuel Newton, Alderman of Cambridge (1662–1717)* (Cambridge, 1890), p. 1.

34. *The Burning of the Whore of Babylon, As it was Acted, with great Applause, in the Poultrey, London, on Wednesday Night, being the Fifth of November last* (London, 1673), pp. 1–3.

35. H.M.C., *Ormonde* (London, 1906), vol. 4, pp. 470, 561; Margaret M. Verney (ed.), *Memoirs of the Verney Family from the Restoration to the Revolution 1660 to 1696* (London, 1899), vol. 4, p. 259; H.M.C., *Seventh Report* (London, 1879), appendix, p. 477. For further discussion of this period see below, Chapter 11.

36. Andrew Browning (ed.), *Memoirs of Sir John Reresby* (Glasgow, 1936), pp. 237, 502.

37. Anthony Hewitson (ed.), *Diary of Thomas Bellingham* (Preston, 1908), pp. 52, 78, 124, 125, 133; J. Charles Cox (ed.), *The Records of the Borough of Northampton* (London and Northampton, 1898), vol. 2, pp. 471, 479, 482–3; Nicholas Rogers, 'Popular protest in early Hanoverian London', *Past and Present*, 79 (1978), pp. 70–100.

38. John Nichols, *The Progresses, Processions, and Magnificent Festivities of King James the First* (London, 1828), vol. 1, pp. 123, 125; Greene (ed.), *Diary of John Rous*, p. 54; *C.S.P.D., 1629–31*, pp. 336, 346, 397.

39. Birch (ed.), *Court and Times of James the First*, vol. 1, pp. 66–7; *Court and Times of Charles the First*, vol. 1, pp. 29–30; Norman Egbert McClure (ed.), *The Letters of John Chamberlain* (Philadelphia, 1939), vol. 2, p. 588.

40. Foster (ed.), *Diary of Samuel Newton*, p. 1; James Heath, *The Glories and*

Magnificent Triumphs of . . . Charles II (London, 1662), 30–1. See also Alan Macfarlane (ed.), *The Diary of Ralph Josselin 1616–1683* (London, 1976), p. 478.

41. Browning (ed.), *Memoirs of Sir John Reresby*, pp. 352, 519; Foster (ed.), *Diary of Samuel Newton*, pp. 94, 100.
42. Birch (ed.), *Court and Times of James the First*, vol. 1, pp. 67, 144, 224.
43. Francis Blomefield, *An Essay Towards a Topographical History of the County of Norfolk*, vol. 3 (London, 1806), p. 364; Lord Mayor's proclamations against fireworks, 1673–1714, Corporation of London Record Office, PD 10, nos. 72, 74, 86, 88, 99, 100.
44. Francis Malthus, *A Treatise of Artificial Fire-Works, both for Warres and Recreation* (London, 1629); Nathaniel Nye, *The Art of Gunnery* (London, 1670); John White, *A Rich Cabinet, with Variety of Inventions . . . Whereunto is added variety of Recreative Fire-Works, both for Land, Aire, and Water* (London, 1651), Thomason Collection E.1295 (2).
45. Browning (ed.), *Memoirs of Sir John Reresby*, p. 503; Schwoerer, 'The Glorious Revolution as spectacle', p. 117.
46. Audrey Douglas and Peter Greenfield (eds.), *Records of Early English Drama: Cumberland, Westmoreland, Gloucestershire* (Toronto, 1986), p. 170; Alexandra F. Johnston and Margaret Rogerson (eds.), *Records of Early English Drama: York* (Toronto, 1979), p. 410; *Records of the Borough of Nottingham . . . 1625–1702* (London and Nottingham, 1900), pp. 170, 174, 285; Edward Chamberlayne, *Angliae Notitia: or the Present State of England* (London, 1702), p. 168; George Parker, *Mercurius Anglicanus; or the English Mercury: Being a complete Diary for the year of our Lord 1695* (London, 1695).
47. Paul S. Seaver, *The Puritan Lectureships* (Stanford, 1970), p. 347; Ralph Knevet, *Rhodon and Iris. A Pastorall, as it was presented at the Florists Feast in Norwich, May 3, 1631* (Norwich, 1631); *Records of the Borough of Nottingham . . . 1625–1702*, p. 190. Cf. John Brand, *Observations on Popular Antiquities*, ed. Henry Ellis (London, 1813), vol. 2, pp. 203–12; Keith Thomas, *Man and the Natural World: A History of the Modern Sensibility* (New York, 1983), pp. 78, 229; Matthew Henry Lee (ed.), *Diaries and letters of Philip Henry* (London, 1882), p. 53.
48. Loomie (ed.), *Ceremonies of Charles I*, p. 262.

6 *Affectionate Gladness – the Return of Prince Charles*

1. Charles Carlton, *Charles I the Personal Monarch* (London, 1983), pp. 34–46; Pauline Gregg, *King Charles I* (London, 1981), pp. 72–89; J. P. Kenyon, *Stuart England*, 2nd edn, (Harmondsworth, 1985), p. 97. Cf. Barry Coward, *The Stuart Age: A History of England 1603–1714* (London, 1980), p. 135; Derek Hirst, *Authority and Conflict: England 1603–1658* (London, 1986), p. 133.
2. Elisabeth Bourcier (ed.), *The Diary of Sir Simonds D'Ewes 1622–1624* (Paris, 1974), pp. 161–3.
3. Bourcier (ed.), *Diary of Sir Simonds D'Ewes*, pp. 163–4.
4. Thomas Reeve, *Mephibosheths Hearts-Ioy Vpon his Soveraignes Safetie. To*

be imitated by the Subjects of this Land upon the happy Returne of our Prince Charles (London, 1624), pp. 1, 27, 28, 34.

5. Stephen Jerome, *Irelands Iubilee, or Oyes Io-Paean, for Prince Charles his welcome home* (Dublin, 1624), p. 212.

6. John Hacket, *Scrinia Reserata: A Memorial of John Williams* (London, 1693), pt. 1, p. 114.

7. Anti-Catholic publications include *The Abuses of the Romish church anatomised* (London, 1623), and John Mico, *A Pill to Purge out Poperie* (London, 1623). Thomas Scott, *Vox Dei* (Amsterdam? 1624), p. 59; Norman Egbert McClure (ed.), *The Letters of John Chamberlain* (Philadelphia, 1939), vol. 2, p. 488.

8. *The Ioyfull Returne of the most illustrious Prince, Charles . . . from the Court of Spaine* (London, 1623), p. 5. John Taylor, 'Prince Charles his Welcome from Spaine', in Walter Scot (ed.), *A Collection of Scarce and Valuable Tracts (Somers Tracts)*, 2nd edn, (London, 1809), vol. 2, p. 551. Reeve, *Mephibosheths Hearts-Ioy*, p. 35; cf. William Laud to John Scudamore, 2 August 1623: 'We begin to hope again to see the prince's highness well in England. God grant it; and then I shall the more contentedly rest'. Public Record Office, C 115/M24/7775.

9. For the power of these associations see Roy Strong, *Henry Prince of Wales and England's Lost Renaissance* (London, 1986), and William Hunt, 'The spectral origins of the English revolution: legitimation crisis in Early Stuart England', in Geoff Eley and William Hunt (eds.), *Reviving the English Revolution: Reflections and Elaborations on the Work of Christopher Hill* (London, 1988), pp. 305–32.

10. Hacket, *Scrinia Reserata*, pp. 124–5.

11. H.M.C., *Report on the Manuscripts of Lord Montagu of Beaulieu* (London, 1900), p. 105.

12. John Nichols, *The Progresses, Processions, and Magnificent Festivities of King James the First* (London, 1828), vol. 4, p. 927n, quoting Wood's *Annals of Oxford; C.S.P.D., 1623–1625*, p. 89. Cf. *Acts of the Privy Council, 1623–1625*, p. 95. 'Diary of Sir Richard Hutton', Cambridge University Library, Add. MS. 6863; Laud's 'Diary', in *The Works of . . . William Laud* (Oxford, 1853), vol. 3, p. 143. See also Clarendon, *History of the Rebellion*, ed. W. Dunn Macray (Oxford, 1888), vol. 1, p. 22.

13. *Letters of John Chamberlain*, vol. 2, pp. 515–16. *C.S.P.D., 1623–1625*, p. 93, refers to *forty* loads of wood on this occasion. A load of wood comprises 50 cubic feet.

14. Taylor, 'Prince Charles his Welcome', p. 552. Edward Arber (ed.), *A Transcript of the Registers of the Company of Stationers of London, 1554–1640* (London, 1877), vol. 4, p. 67.

15. ibid., p. 552.

16. ibid., p. 552–3.

17. ibid., p. 553.

18. *Ioyfull Returne*, pp. 37–8. This was registered with the stationers on 13 October, Arber (ed.), *Transcript*, vol. 4, p. 68. Much the same story is

told by the Venetian ambassador, *Calendar of State Papers, Venice, 1623–1625*, p. 135.

19. John Speed, *The Theatre of the Empire of Great Britaine* (London, 1611), vol. 2, p. 863; John Stow, *Annales, or A Generall Chronicle of England* (London, 1631), p. 750.

20. Annabel Patterson, *Censorship and Interpretation: the Conditions of Writing and Reading in Early Modern England* (Madison, 1984), p. 78; W. W. Greg (ed.), *A Bibliography of the English Printed Drama to the Restoration*, vol. 2 (London, 1951), pp. 558–64; Alfred Harbage *Annals of English Drama 975–1700*, revised by S. Schoenbaum (London, 1964), pp. 118–21. See Thomas Cogswell, 'Thomas Middleton and the court, 1624: *A Game at Chess* in context', *Huntington Library Quarterly*, 47 (1984), pp. 273–88.

21. Clarendon, *History of the Rebellion*, vol. 1, p. 433. This was barely a week after the passage of the Grand Remonstrance. See also John Taylor, *Englands Comfort and Londons Joy* (London, 1641), pp. 5, 7; Carlton, *Charles I*, p. 230; Gregg, *King Charles I*, p. 340.

22. Cf. David M. Bergeron, *English Civic Pageantry 1558–1642* (London, 1971), pp. 260–5. Malcolm Smuts, 'The political failure of Stuart cultural patronage', in Guy Fitch Lytle and Stephen Orgel (eds.), *Patronage in the Renaissance* (Princeton, 1981), pp. 173–4; Judith Richards, '"His Nowe Majestie" and the English Monarchy: The kingship of Charles I before 1640', *Past and Present*, 113 (1986), pp. 70–96.

23. Corporation of London Record Office, 'Journal, vol. 32 (1622–24)', f.222, dated 6 October 1623.

24. Churchwardens' accounts are listed in the bibliography.

25. Nichols, *Progresses*, vol. 4, pp. 929n–930n; 'Chester chronicles', British Library, Harl. MS. 2125, f. 56; R. W. Ingram (ed.), *Records of Early English Drama: Coventry* (Toronto, 1981), p. 417.

26. Meade to Stuteville, 11 October 1623, quoted in Nichols, *Progresses*, vol. 4, p. 929n. Cambridge University offered *Gratulatio de principis reditu ex Hispaniis* (Cambridge, 1623), to be matched by Oxford's *Carolus redux* (Oxford, 1623).

27. Reeve, *Mephibosheths Hearts-Ioy*, pp. 2, 36, 37, 41.

28. Norfolk Record Office, Norwich Chamberlain's Accounts, 1603–25, f. 399v.

29. ibid., ff. 399v, 401; David Galloway (ed.), *Records of Early English Drama: Norwich* (Toronto, 1984), pp. 179–80.

30. Bourcier (ed.), *Diary of Sir Simonds D'Ewes*, p. 164; *Ioyfull Returne*, p. 37.

31. Suggestive explorations include Denis Richet, 'Sociocultural aspects of religious conflicts in Paris during the second half of the sixteenth century', in Robert Forster and Orest Ranum (eds.), *Ritual, Religion, and the Sacred* (London, 1982), pp 182–94; Natalie Zemon Davis, 'Charivari, honor, and community in seventeenth-century Lyon and Geneva,' in John J. MacAloon (ed.), *Rite, Drama, Festival, Spectacle* (Philadelphia, 1984), pp. 42–7; and Emmanuel Le Roy Ladurie, *Carnival in Romans* (New York, 1979). See also Frank E. Manning, *The Celebration of Society: Perspectives on Contemporary Cultural Performance* (Bowling

Green, Ohio, 1983); Clifford Geertz, *Local Knowledge: Further Essays in Interpretive Anthropology* (New York, 1983), pp. 125–9; Victor Turner, *The Ritual Process: Structure and Anti-Structure* (Chicago, 1969), and *Dramas, Fields and Metaphors: Symbolic Action in Human Society* (Ithaca, NY, 1974); Michael D. Bristol, *Carnival and Theatre: Plebeian Culture and the Structure of Authority in Renaissance England* (London, 1985).

32. Burning wood piles and wood carts was made a felony by 37. Henry VIII, c. 6.
33. Hacket, *Scrinia Reserata*, p. 165.
34. *Luke*, 15: 23, 32. I am grateful to Leland Estes for reminding me of these verses. *Certaine Sermons or Homilies appointed to be read in Churches, in the time of the late Queene Elizabeth of famous memory. And now thought fit to be reprinted* (London, 1623), p. 10; Alfred Harbage, *Annals of English Drama 975–1700*, revised by S. Schoenbaum (London, 1964), p. 206; Richard Brathwaite, *The Prodigals Teares* (London, 1614, repr. 1619). See also Richard Helgerson, *The Elizabethan Prodigals* (Berkeley and Los Angeles, 1976).
35. Thomas Scott, *Vox Dei* (Amsterdam?, 1624), pp. 74–86. Thomas Scott, *Englands Ioy, For Suppressing the Papists* (London?, 1624), pp. 2, 4, 16. Robert E. Ruigh, *The Parliament of 1624: Politics and Foreign Policy* (Cambridge, Mass., 1971), pp. 16–19; Cogswell, 'Thomas Middleton and the court, 1624'.
36. British Library, Add. MS. 21,935. See also Paul Seaver, *Wallington's World: A Puritan Artisan in Seventeenth-Century London* (Stanford, 1985), pp. 8, 10, 51, 157.
37. *The Ioyfull Returne* (London, 1623), p. 42.
38. Stephen Jerome, *Irelands Iubilee, or Oyes Io-Paean, for Prince Charles his welcome home* (Dublin, 1624), p. 213.
39. Jonathan Dove, *An Almanacke for the Yeare of our Lord God 1641* (Cambridge, 1641). Richard Allestree, *A New Almanacke and Prognostication, for this yeare of our Lord God 1628* (London, 1628).

7 The Spanish Armada – Anxiety, Deliverance and Commemoration

1. *Acts of the Privy Council, 1588*, pp. 16–17, 19–21, 31–5; C.S.P.D., *1581– 1590*, pp. 471, 475, 494–7; H.M.C., *Cowper (Twelfth Report)* (London, 1888), appendix, pt. 1, pp. 8–11. See also Joyce Youings, 'Bowmen, billmen and hackbutters: the Elizabethan militia in the south west', in Robert Higham (ed.), *Security and Defence in South-West England before 1800* (Exeter, 1987), pp. 62–5; and Lindsay Boynton, *The Elizabethan Militia, 1558–1638* (London, 1967). For more on the inadequacy of England's defences, see Colin Martin and Geoffrey Parker, *The Spanish Armada* (London, 1988), pp. 271–6.
2. C.S.P.D., *Addenda 1580–1625*, p. 250; C.S.P.D., *1581–1590*, pp. 485, 488, 490; Martin and Parker, *Spanish Armada*, p. 275; John Strype, *Annals of the Reformation*, vol. 3, pt. 2 (Oxford, 1824), pp. 15–17, 533–5.
3. Robert Greene, *The Spanish Masquerado* (London, 1589), sig. B4.
4. Parker and Martin, *Spanish Armada*, pp. 196–200.

5. *Acts of the Privy Council, 1588*, pp. 145, 168; *C.S.P.D., 1581–1590*, p. 509.
6. J. Goring and J. Wake (eds.), *Northamptonshire Lieutenancy papers and Other Documents, 1580–1614* (Northampton, Northants. Record Society, 1975), vol. 27, p. 53.
7. ibid., pp. 19–20; Joan Wake (ed.), *A Copy of Papers Relating to Musters, Beacons, Subsidies, etc. in the County of Northampton* A.D. *1586–1623* (Northampton, Northants. Record Society, 1926), vol. 3, pp. 7–8; H.M.C., *Cowper*, p. 11; T. C. Noble (ed.), *The Names of those Persons who Subscribed towards the Defence of this Country at the Time of the Spanish Armada* (London, 1886), p. xviii. See *C.S.P.D., 1581–1590*, p. 339, for a plot in July to fire the Southampton beacons prematurely and to rob provisions in the ensuing confusion.
8. Garrett Mattingly, *The Armada* (New York, 1959), p. 273; *C.S.P.D., 1581–1590*, p. 510; Youings, 'Bowmen, billmen and hackbutters', p. 65; Felix Barker, 'If Parma had Landed', *History Today*, 38 (May 1988), p. 38.
9. *Acts of the Privy Council, 1588*, p. 172; Edward Arber (ed.), *A Transcript of the Registers of the Company of Stationers of London; 1554–1640* (London, 1875), vol. 2, f. 231; Strype, *Annals of the Reformation*, vol. 3, pt. 2, pp. 15–17.
10. 'Diary of Richard Rogers', in M. M. Knappen (ed.), *Two Elizabethan Puritan Diaries* (1933, repr. Gloucester, Mass., 1966), pp. 76, 79, 80.
11. Oliver Pigge, *Meditations Concerning praiers to Almightie God, for the safetie of England* (London, 1589), pp. 11–14, 22.
12. Strype, *Annals of the Reformation*, pp. 15–17, 546; John Foxe, *Actes and Monuments of matters most speciall and memorable* (London, 1583), preface.
13. *C.S.P.D., 1581–1590*, p. 526; Mattingly, *Armada*, pp. 336, 351; Martin and Parker, *Spanish Armada*, pp. 14, 251.
14. John Speed, *The Theatre of the Empire of Great Britaine* (London, 1611), p. 862. There is some doubt whether the speech was ever delivered as reported; the first text of Elizabeth's words comes from the seventeenth century, and may be a product of Elizabethan nostalgia; Barker, 'If Parma had Landed', pp. 38–9.
15. Thomas Deloney, 'A joyful new Ballad declaring the happy obtaining of the great Galleazzo' and 'The Queen's visiting the Camp at Tilbury, with her entertainment there', in Edward Arber (ed.), *An English Garner*, vol. 7, (Birmingham, 1883), pp. 39–51.
16. Leicester to Shrewsbury, in Edmund Lodge, *Illustrations of British History* (London, 1791), vol. 2, p. 376; *Acts of the Privy Council, 1588*, pp. 234, 239.
17. Arber (ed.), *Transcript of the Stationers' Registers*, vol. 2, f. 231v; *Acts of the Privy Council, 1588*, p. 257; *C.S.P.D., 1581–1590*, pp. 553, 557.
18. Pigge, *Meditations*, sig. A5v; Anthony Marten, *An Exhortation, To stirre up the mindes of all her Maiesties faithfull subiects* (London, 1588), sigs. C2v. D4.
19. John Stow, *Annales, or, A Generall Chronicle of England* (London, 1631),

p. 750; Speed, *Theatre of the Empire*, p. 863; Greene, *Spanish Masquerado*, sig. D4v; *C.S.P.D., 1581–1590*, p. 536; *Calendar of Letters and Papers . . . Simancas, 1587–1603*, p. 438.

20. Arber (ed.), *Transcript of the Stationers' Registers*, vol. 2, ff. 234, 234v, 236, 237v; James Aske, *Elizabetha Triumphans* (London, 1588).

21. *Acts of the Privy Council, 1588*, pp. 297, 334.

22. Strype, *Annals of the Reformation*, vol. 3, pt. 2, pp. 27–29; *Calendar . . . Simancas, 1587–1603*, pp. 488, 494; Stow, *Annales*, p. 751.

23. Strype, *Annals of the Reformation*, p. 28; John Nichols, *The Progresses and Public Processions of Queen Elizabeth* (London, 1823), vol. 2, pp. 537–40; Roy Strong, 'The popular celebration of the accession day of Queen Elizabeth I', *Journal of the Warburg and Courtauld Institute*, 21 (1959), pp. 90, 92n; Noble (ed.), *Names of those Persons who Subscribed*, p. xxvi.

24. Churchwardens' accounts are listed in the bibliography.

25. Francis Blomefield, *An Essay Towards a Topographical History of the County of Norfolk* (London, 1806), vol. 3, pp. 256, 355–6; David Galloway (ed.), *Records of Early English Drama: Norwich 1540–1642* (Toronto, 1984), pp. 95, 101, 105, 117, 350; Strong, 'Popular celebration', pp. 90, 93; J. Charles Cox, *The Records of the Borough of Northampton, vol. II 1550 to 1835* (London and Northampton, 1898), pp. 472–3.

26. Robert Humston, *A Sermon Preached at Reyfham* (London, 1589), ff. 20v, 24.

27. 'Diary of Richard Rogers', p. 81.

28. Pigge, *Meditations*, pp. 24–31, 36, 41.

29. *A Psalme and Collect of thankesgiving, not vnmeet for this present time* (London, 1588); Strype, *Annals of the Reformation*, vol. 3, pt. 2, p. 29.

30. Marten, *An Exhortation*, sig. C2; Maurice Kyffin, *The Blessednes of Brytaine* (London, 1588), sig. C4. See also the Armada portraits and medals, in M. J. Rodriguez-Salgado *et al.*, *Armada 1588–1988* (London, 1988), pp. 274, 276–82.

31. Strype, *Annals of the Reformation*, vol. 3, pt. 2, pp. 28–9; Pigge, *Meditations*, p. 36; Sir Simonds D'Ewes, *The Journals of all the Parliaments During the Reign of Queen Elizabeth* (London, 1682), pp. 471–2.

32. Humston, *Sermon*, ff. 24–24v; Strype, *Annals of the Reformation*, vol. 3, pt. 2, p. 29; *Psalme and Collect of Thanksgiving*; Thomas Deloney, 'A new Ballet of the strange and most cruel whips which the Spaniards had prepared to whip and torment English men and women', in Arber (ed.), *English Garner*, vol. 7, pp. 52–6.

33. Pigge, *Meditations*, p. 30; Greene, *Spanish Masquerado*, sig. B3.

34. Greene, *Spanish Masquerado; A Skeltonicall Salutation* (London, 1589). See also Thomas Nashe, *Pierce Penniless His Supplication to the Divell* (London, 1592), p. 46.

35. See, for example, Richard Allestree, *A New Almanacke and Prognostication for this yeare of our Lord God 1628* (London, 1628); Jonathan Dove, *An Almanack for the yeare of our Lord God 1636* (Cambridge, 1636); Jonathan Dove, *Speculum Anni, or an Almanack for . . . 1695* (Cambridge, 1695).

36. Paul S. Seaver, *Wallington's World: A Puritan Artisan in Seventeenth-century*

London (Stanford, 1985), p. 157; British Library, Add. MS. 21,935, ff. 5r–7r.

37. William Leigh, *Queen Elizabeth Paraleld in her Princely vertues, with David, Iosua, and Hezekia* (London, 1612), pp. 93–7.

38. William Leigh, *Great Britaines Great Deliverance, from the great danger of Popish Powder* (London, 1606), sig. Dv. Leigh remained at court as Prince Henry's chaplain, and became an advisor to Princess Elizabeth after the Prince's untimely death.

39. 'A copie of such matters and things as doe concerne the parish of St Pancrace in Soper Lane in London conteyned in the last will and Testament of Thomas Chapman', Guildhall Library, MS. 5020.

40. Michael Sparke, *Thankfull Remembrances of Gods Wonderful Deliverances of this Land*, 7th edn (London, 1628), sig. A6v.

41. George Carleton, *A Thankfull Remembrance of Gods Mercy* (London, 1624), pp. 119–47, quoting Psalms 111 and 145.

42. 'The Church's Deliverances', in George H. Williams, Norman Pettit, Winifried Herget and Sargent Bush, Jr. (eds.), *Thomas Hooker. Writings in England and Holland, 1626–1633* (Cambridge, Mass., 1975), pp. 67–71. See also Alexander Leighton, *Speculum Bellisaeri: or the looking-glasse of the holy war* (Amsterdam, 1628); and references to the Armada in Paul Christianson, *Reformers and Babylon: English Apocalyptic Visions from the Reformation to the Eve of the Civil War* (Toronto, 1978), pp. 108, 116, 224.

43. Henry King, *A Sermon of Deliverance. Preached at the Spittle* (London, 1626), pp. 69–70, with references to Jeremiah 46.8 and Ezekiel 32.2.

44. idem; Rodriguez-Salgado *et al.*, *Armada*, pp. 281–3.

45. Thomas Gataker, *An Anniuersarie Memoriall of Englands Delivery from the Spanish Invasion* (London, 1626; repr. 1637), preface, pp. 1, 18, 20, 24.

46. John Vicars, *Englands Hallelu-jah; or, Great Britaines Retribution* (London, 1631), sigs. Bv, B3v); John Rhodes, *The Countrie Mans Comfort* (London, 1637), 'to the reader'.

47. John Taylor, 'God's Manifold Mercies in these miraculous deliverances of our Church of England', in *All the works of Iohn Taylor* (London, 1630), vol. 2, pp. 144–5.

48. Thomas Morton, *Ezekiel's Wheels: A Treatise Concerning Divine Providence* (London, 1653), p. 92; Thomas Horton, *The Pillar and Pattern of Englands Deliverances* (London, 1655), p. 40; Wilbur Cortez Abbot (ed.), *The Writings and Speeches of Oliver Cromwell* (Cambridge, Mass., 1945–7), vol. 3, p. 890, vol. 4, pp. 261–79.

49. Samuel Clarke, *A True and Full Narrative of Those two never to be forgotten deliverances: the one from the Spanish invasion in 88. The other from the Hellish Powder Plot* (London, 1671), sigs. A3v–A4.

8 Queen Elizabeth of Famous Memory

1. J. P. Kenyon, 'Queen Elizabeth and the Historians', in Simon Adams (ed.), *Queen Elizabeth. Most Politick Princess* (1984), pp. 52–5; J. E. Neale, *Essays in Elizabethan History* (London, 1958), pp. 9–20; D. R. Woolf, 'Two Elizabeths? James I and the late queen's famous memory',

Canadian Journal of History, 20 (1985), pp. 167–91; Anne Barton, *Ben Jonson, Dramatist* (Cambridge, 1984), pp. 300–20. See also H. R. Trevor-Roper, 'Oliver Cromwell and his parliaments', in his *Religion, the Reformation and Social Change* (London, 1967), pp. 345–91, and C. V. Wedgwood, 'Oliver Cromwell and the Elizabethan Inheritance', in her *History and Hope* (London, 1987), pp. 317–35.

2. Roy Strong, 'The popular celebration of the accession day of Queen Elizabeth I', *Journal of the Warburg and Courtauld Institutes*, 21 (1958), pp. 86–103; Roy Strong, *The Cult of Elizabeth: Elizabethan Portraiture and Pageantry* (London, 1977).

3. Anthony Nixon, *Elizaes memoriall; King Iames his arriuall; and Romes downefall* (London, 1603), sigs. B4v, D3. See also H.S., *Queene Elizabeths Losse and King Iames his Welcome* (London, 1603).

4. Christopher Lever, *Queene Elizabeths Teares* (London, 1607), dedication and preface.

5. William Leigh, *Queen Elizabeth Paraleled in her Princely vertues, with David, Iosua, and Hezekia* (London, 1612).

6. ibid., title page, sig. 5v., pp. 46–8, 60, 104.

7. Samuel Garey, *Great Brittans little Calendar: or, Triple Diarie, in remembrance of three daies* (London, 1618), pp. 2, 63, 95–6.

8. Godfrey Goodman, *Memoirs of the Court of King James*, qu. in Neale, *Essays in Elizabethan History*, p. 14.

9. Thomas Brightman, *Apocalypsis apocalypseos. A Revelation* (Leyden, 1616), pp. 155, 159, 161, 199, 491, 502.

10. George Carleton, *A Thankfull Remembrance of Gods Mercy. In an Historical Collection of the great and mercifull Deliverances of the Church and State of England, since the Gospel began here to flourish, from the beginning of Quene Elizabeth* (London, 1624), sig. A2v., pp. 5, 54, 79.

11. Thomas Morton, *Ezekiel's Wheels: A Treatise Concerning Divine Providence* (London, 1653), p. 92.

12. John Taylor, 'Memorial of all the English Monarchs', in *All the Works of Iohn Taylor* (London, 1630), p. 319.

13. John Stow, *Annales, or A Generall Chronicle of England, continued and augmented . . . by Edmund Howes* (London, 1631), pp. 635–815; John Speed, *Theatre of the Empire of Great Britaine* (London, 1611), vol. 2, pp. 862–3; William Camden, *Annales: The True and Royal History of Elizabeth, Queen of England* (London, 1625); Frederick S. Boas (ed.), *The Diary of Thomas Crosfield* (Oxford, 1935), p. 90.

14. Thomas Gataker, *An Anniversarie Memoriall of Englands Delivery from the Spanish Invasion* (London, 1626). Chapman's will was made in 1616 and proved in 1620; the endowment for the anniversary sermons was augmented by his son in 1626: Guildhall Library MS. 5020.

15. Neale, *Essays in Elizabethan History*, p. 14; Chamberlain to Carleton, 25 June 1625, in *The Court and Times of Charles the First* (London, 1848), vol. 1, p. 36.

16. Gataker, *Anniuersarie Memoriall*, preface. This was reprinted in 1637.

17. Henry King, *A Sermon of Deliverance. Preached at the Spittle on Easter Monday, 1626* (London, 1626), p. 3.
18. Quoted in Kenyon, 'Queen Elizabeth and the Historians', p. 52.
19. Diana Primrose, *A Chaine of Pearle. Or A Memoriall of the peerles Graces and Heroick Vertues of Queene Elizabeth of Glorious Memory* (London, 1630), introduction.
20. Thomas Heywood, *Englands Elisabeth: Her life and troubles, during her minoritie, from the Cradle to the Crown* (Cambridge, 1641), pp. 188, 190, preface.
21. Henry Alleyn, *Alleyns Almanack, Or, A Double diarie & prognostication* (London, 1608); Richard Allestree, *A New Almanacke and prognostication for this yeare of our Lord God* (London, 1628).
22. Birch, *Court and Times of Charles the First*, vol. 1, p. 171, vol. 2, p. 80.
23. ibid., vol. 2, p. 145. See also Ben Jonson, 'To the king, on his birthday 19 November 1632, an epigram anniversary', in Ian Donaldson (ed.), *Ben Johnson* (Oxford, 1985), pp. 399–400; and entries in many church-wardens' books.
24. *Diary of Thomas Crosfield*, p. 74.
25. *Queene Elizabeths Speeche to her last Parliament* (London, 1642, 1648), Thomason collection, E. 199 (41); E. 432 (15). Robert Naunton, *Fragmenta Regalia, or Observations on the late Q. Elizabeth, her times and her favorites* (London, 1641).
26. Stephen Marshall, *A Sermon Preached before the Honourable House of Commons . . . November 17. 1640* (London, 1641), p. 47; Cornelius Burgess, *A Sermon Preached to the Honourable House of Commons . . . Novem. 17. 1640* (London, 1641), p. 39.
27. Burgess, *Sermon . . . Novem. 17*, p. 38; Matthew Newcomen, *The Craft and Cruelty of the Churches Adversaries* (London, 1643), epistle dedicatory; Nathaniel Hardy, *Justice Triumphing, or The Spoylers Spoiled. Laid forth in a Gratulatory Sermon for the Miraculous Discovery of, and Our Glorious Delivery from the Barbarous Powder-Plot* (London, 1647), p. 2.
28. John Dryden, *Astraea Redux: A Poem On the happy Restoration and Return Of His Sacred Majesty Charles the Second* (London, 1660); *The Impartial Protestant Mercury*, 17 November 1681. See below, Chapter 11, for the calendrical politics of exclusion.

9 Remembering the Fifth of November

1. See, for example, Charlotte S. Burne, 'Guy Fawkes' Day', *Folk-Lore*, 23 (1912), pp. 409–26; Ervin Beck, 'Rhymes and songs for Halloween and Bonfire Night', *Lore and Language*, 4 (1985), pp. 1–17; T. F. Thiselton Dyer, *British Popular Customs Present and Past* (London, 1900), pp. 410–416; Enid Porter, *Cambridgeshire Customs and Folklore* (London, 1969), pp. 125–6.
2. 'An acte for a publique thanckesgivingto almightie God everie yeere on the fifte day of November', 3 Jac. I. c. 1. Compare John Williams, *The History of the Gunpowder-Treason, Collected from Approved Authors, As Well Popish as Protestant* (London, 1678); S. R. Gardiner, *What Gunpowder*

Plot Was (London, 1897); and Joel Hurstfield, 'A retrospect: Gunpowder Plot and the politics of dissent', in his *Freedom, Corruption and Government in Elizabethan England* (Cambridge, Mass., 1973), pp. 327–51.

3. *A Form of Prayer with Thanksgiving to be used yearly upon the Fifth day of November; For the happy Deliuerance of the King, and the Three Estates of the Realm, from the most Traiterous and bloody intended Massacre by Gun-powder* (London, 1606).

4. Ten of Andrewes's Gunpowder-Treason sermons were published in 1629, with further editions in 1631 and 1635: 'Sermons preached upon the V of November', in Lancelot Andrewes, *XCVI Sermons*, 3rd edn (London, 1635), pp. 889, 890, 900–1008.

5. William Leigh, *Great Britaines Great Deliverance from the Great Danger of Popish Powder* (London, 1606), sig. Bv.

6. Guildhall Library, MSS. 959/1, 5018/1, 5020.

7. John Rhodes, *A Brief Summe of the Treason intended against the King & State, when they should have been assembled in Parliament, November 5. 1605. Fit for to instruct the simple and ignorant heerein: that they be not seduced any longer by Papists* (London, 1606). See also Denakol (pseud.), *No Parliament Powder. But Shot and Powder for the Pope* (London, 1609).

8. Francis Herring, *Popish Pietie, or the first part of the Historie of that horrible and barbarous conspiracie, commonly called the Powder-treason* (London, 1610), sigs. A3v–A4. See also John Vicars, *Mischeefes Mysterie: or, Treasons Master-peece. The Powder Plot* (London, 1617), which is based on Herring.

9. Edward Pond, *New Almanacke for this Present Yeare of our Lord 1608* (London, 1608); Henry Alleyn, *Alleyns Almanacke, or, a Double diarie & prognostication* (London, 1608); Richard Allestree, *A New Almanacke and Prognostication for this yeare of our Lord God* (London, 1628, 1632, 1640); John Booker, *Telescopium Uranicum: an Ephemeris . . . MDCLXV* (London, 1665); 'Poor Robin', *An Almanack After the Old and New Fashion* (London, 1695).

10. F. R. Raines (ed.), *The Journal of Nicholas Assheton* (Chetham Society, 1848), p. 67. Assheton was a friend of William Leigh, author of the 1606 sermon on Gunpowder Treason. See also George Roberts (ed.), *Diary of Walter Yonge* (Camden Society, 1848), pp. 1–2; Elisabeth Bourcier (ed.), *The Diary of Sir Simonds D'Ewes 1622–1624* (Paris, 1974), pp. 104, 169.

11. Michael Sparke, *Thankfull Remembrance of Gods Wonderfull Deliverances of this Land* (London, 1628), sigs. A6–A6v (bound with his *Crums of Comfort*, 7th edn (London, 1628).

12. Christopher Hill, *Society and Puritanism in Pre-Revolutionary England* (London, 1964), p. 267; William S. Powell, *John Pory, 1572–1636. The Life and Letters of a Man of Many Parts* (Chapel Hill, 1977), microfiche supplement, p. 34.

13. Churchwardens' accounts referred to in this chapter are listed in the bibliography. Henry Burton, *For God, and the King. The Summe of Two Sermons Preached on the fifth of November last in St Mathewes Friday Street. 1636* (London?, 1636), pp. 130–2.

14. Norfolk Record Office, 'City Chamberlain's accounts, 1626–1648', f. 22. v.

15. Norfolk Record Office, 'City Chamberlain's accounts, 1603–1625', ff. 397v, 398v, 415v; '1626–1648', ff. 12v, 13, 73v, 263; Audrey Douglas and Peter Greenfield (eds.), *Records of Early English Drama: Cumberland, Westmoreland, Gloucestershire* (Toronto, 1986), pp. 25, 95; *Records of the Borough of Nottingham . . . 1625–1702* (London and Nottingham, 1900), p. 170; H.M.C., *Calendar of the Manuscripts of the Dean and Chapter of Wells* (London, 1914), vol. 2, p. 373.

16. H.M.C., *Ninth Report* (London, 1883), vol. 1, p. 160.

17. Samuel Garey, *Amphitheatrum Scelerum: or the Transcendent of Treason: For the Fifth of November* (London, 1618), p. 184; Herring, *Popish Pietie*, sig. A4.

18. Samuel Garey, *Great Brittans little Calendar: or, Triple Diarie, in remembrance of three daies* (London, 1618), pp. 185, title page, 184; Garey, *Amphitheatrum Scelerum*, title page. See also John Vicars, *Mischeefs Mysterie*, pp. 3, 100.

19. Garey, *Amphitheatrum Scelerum*, pp. 185–239.

20. George Carleton, *A Thankfull Remembrance of Gods Mercy. In an Historical Collection of the great and mercifull Deliverances of the Church and State of England* (London, 1624), p. 217.

21. Thomas Hooker, 'The Church's Deliverances', in George H. Williams, Norman Pettit, Winifried Herget, and Sargent Bush, Jr. (eds.), *Thomas Hooker, Writings in England and Holland, 1626–1633* (Cambridge, Mass., 1975), pp. 68, 69.

22. Thomas Gataker, *An Anniuersarie Memoriall* (London, 1626), 'to the reader'; Henry King, *A Sermon of Deliverance* (London, 1626), p. 70.

23. John Cope, *A Religious Inquisition* (London, 1629), pp. 14–15; Stella P. Revard, 'Milton's gunpowder poems and Satan's conspiracy', *Milton Studies*, 4 (1972), pp. 63–77.

24. *A Song or Psalm of thanksgiving in remembrance of our deliverance from the Gunpowder Treason* (London, 1625); John Wilson, *A song or story, for the lasting remembrance of divers famous works, which god hath done in our time* (London, 1626), f. 55v.

25. John Taylor, 'Gods Manifold Mercies', in *All the works of Iohn Taylor* (London, 1630), vol. 2, p. 145. Cf. George Wither, *Halelviah or, Britans Second Remembrancer* (London, 1641), pp. 252–4.

26. John Vicars, *Englands hallelu-jah; or, Great Britaines retribution* (London, 1631), stanzas 7, 64, 92, 127.

27. *The Parliamentary Scout*, 5 November 1644. No 'black book' has been found.

28. William Laud, 'Diary', in *The Works of William Laud* (Oxford, 1853), vol. 3, pp. 220, 213, 232; Jeremy Taylor, *A Sermon preached in Saint Maries Church in Oxford Vpon the Anniversary of the Gunpowder-Treason* (Oxford, 1638). See also William Sclater, *Papisto-Mastix, or Deborah's Prayer against God's Enemies* (London, 1642). Henry Burton inveighs against 'these days of lukewarmness and apostacy' in *For God, and the King*, p. 28.

29. Matthew Newcomen, *The Craft and Cruelty of the Churches Adversaries* (London, 1643), p. 32.

30. Public Record Office, SP 16/278/65, ff. 146–7.

31. John Goodwin, *The Saints Interest in God* (London, 1640), pp. 2, 5; Christopher Hill, *Reformation to Industrial Revolution* (Harmondsworth, 1974), p. 114. The quote apparently refers to John Vicars, *Mischeefes Mysterie*, based on Francis Herring. Less objection was raised to the printing of John Rhodes, *The Countrie Mans Comfort* (London, 1637), which included verses on many of England's deliverances.

32. Henry Jacie to John Winthrop, Jr., *The Winthrop Papers* (Massachusetts Historical Society, Boston, 1943), vol. 3, p. 485; Burton, *For God, and the King*, pp. 130–2.

33. Burton, *For God, and the King*, dedication, pp. 1, 100, 54, 101–2.

34. New College, Oxford, MS., 'Robert Woodford's diary'.

10 *History and Providence in the English Revolution*

1. Paul S. Seaver, *Wallington's World: A Puritan Artisan in Seventeenth-Century London* (Stanford, 1985), pp. 51, 157; British Library, Add. MS. 21,935.

2. John Goodwin, *The Saints Interest in God* (London, 1640), 'to the reader'.

3. *Calendar of State Papers, Domestic 1640–41*, p. 247.

4. *The Muses Fire-Works Upon the Fifth of November: or, The Protestants Remembrancer of the Bloody Designs of the Papists in the Never-to-be-forgotten Powder Plot* (London, 1640).

5. John Vicars, *The Quintessence of Cruelty, or Master-peice of Treachery, the Popish Powder-Plot* (London, 1641), sig. A2; Bruno Ryves, *Mercurius Rusticus; Or, The Countries Complaint of the Barbarous Out-Rages Committed by the Sectaries of this Late Flourishing Kingdom* (London, 1646); William Hunt, *The Puritan Moment. The Coming of Revolution in an English County* (Cambridge, Mass., 1983), p. 292.

6. Cornelius Burgess, *Another Sermon Preached to the Honorable House of Commons* (London, 1641), pp. 54, 19, 60, 63.

7. *A Perfect Diurnall of the Passages in Parliament: from October 31 to November 7, 1642*.

8. Matthew Newcomen, *The Craft and Cruelty of the Churches Adversaries* (London, 1642), pp. 20, 31, 33.

9. *A Perfect Diurnall of the Passages in Parliament: from October 31 to November 7, 1642*; Thomason collection, E. 128. (1); *A Transcript of the Registers of the . . . Stationers . . . 1640–1708* (London, 1913), vol. 1, p. 53.

10. *The Parliamentary Scout: Communicating His Intelligence to the Kingdome*, 31 Oct.–7 Nov. 1644.

11. William Spurstowe, *Englands Eminent Judgements Caus'd by the Abuse of Gods Eminent Mercies* (London, 1644), pp. 2, 21, 10, 22, 24–6.

12. John Strickland, *Immanuel, or The Church Triumphing* (London, 1644), pp. 16, 2, 25, 20.

13. Anthony Burgess, *Romes Cruelty and Apostacie Declared* (London, 1645), pp. 11, 21.

14. Charles Herle, *Davids Reserve, and Rescue* (London, 1645), pp. 11, 12, 13, 16. See also William Strong, *The Commemoration and Exaltation of Mercy* (London, 1647); and Nathaniel Hardy, *Justice Triumphing, or The Spoylers Spoiled, Laid forth in a Gratulatory Sermon for the Miraculous Discovery of, and Our Glorious Delivery from the Barbarous Powder-Plot* (London, 1647).
15. William Sclater, *Papisto-Mastix, or Deborah's Prayer against God's Enemies* (London, 1642), pp. 13, 53.
16. *The Fifth of November, or The Popish and Schismatical Rebells. With Their Horrid Plots, Fair Pretences, and Bloudy Practices, Weighed One Against Another* (Oxford, 1644).
17. *November* (London, 1647), Thomason collection, 669. f.11/93, collected 6 November 1647.
18. *Mercurius Elencticus*, 5–12 Nov. 1647.
19. *Mercurius Elencticus*, 5–12 Nov. 1647; *The Kingdomes Weekly Intelligencer*, 2–9 Nov. 1647; *The Perfect Weekly Account*, 2–10 Nov. 1647.
20. William Bridge, *England Saved with a Notwithstanding* (London, 1648), pp. 8, 29.
21. *A Modell of the Fire-Works to be presented in Lincolnes-Inne Fields on the 5th of Novemb. 1647.* (London, 1647). For the technicalities of such a production see Francis Malthus, *A Treatise of Artificial Fire-Works, both for Warres and Recreation* (London, 1629); and John White, *A rich Cabinet, with Variety of Inventions . . . Whereunto is added variety of Recreative Fire-works, both for Land, Aire, and water* (London, 1651).
22. *Mercurius Elencticus*, 5–12 Nov. 1647.
23. Churchwardens' accounts cited in this chapter are listed in the bibliography. For an alternative calendar consciousness, see Nathaniel Hardy, *Justice Triumphing, or The Spoylers Spoiled. Laid forth in a Gratulatory Sermon for the Miraculous Discovery of, and Our Glorious delivery from the Barbarous Powder-Plot* (London, 1647), p. 2: 'This month of November is memorable among other for two days, the seventeenth and the fifth; on the one the purity of the gospels broke forth; on the other the treachery of the gospel's enemies brake out: the one the initiation of as gracious a queen, the other the continuation of as wise a king as England ever enjoyed.' Hardy had been a leading presbyterian, but by 1647 he was moving towards episcopalianism and royalism.
24. 'England alas almost hath quite forgot/The great deliverance from the Powder-plot,' rhymed John Turner, *A commemoration, or a calling to minde of the great and eminent deliverance from the Powder-Plot, A mercie never to be forgotten by the people of God* (London, 1654), p. 1. The master of Jesus College, Cambridge, fell victim to a firework attack on 5 November 1657: James Crossley (ed.), *The Diary and Correspondence of Dr John Worthington* (Manchester, 1847), p. 90.
25. J. Sanderson, *Change Ringing: The History of an English Art* (Guildford, 1987), pp. 38, 48, 73.
26. Peter Sterry, *England's Deliverance from the Northern Presbytery, Compared with its Deliverance from the Roman Papacy* (London, 1652), epistle dedicatory, p. 17. See also William Ames, *The Saints Security Against*

Seducing Spirits (London, 1652); and William Jenkins, *A Sermon Preached at Mary Aldermanbury, on the 5th Day of November, 1651* (London, 1652).

27. Jeffrey Corbet, *The Protestant's Warning-Piece* (London, 1656); Thomason collection, E. 669.f.20 (37).
28. John Turner, *A Commemoration, or a Calling to Minde of the Great and Eminent Deliverance from the Powder-Plot* (London, 1654), pp. 1, 5; Thomason collection, E. 813 (10).
29. *The Weekly Intelligencer of the Commonwealth*, 31 Oct.–7 Nov. 1654; Thomas Horton, *The Pillar and Pattern of Englands Deliverances* (London, 1655), pp. 2, preface, 40.
30. ibid., pp. 20–22.
31. ibid., pp. 23–4, 42; Ralph Venning, *Mercies Memorial: or, Israel's Thankful Remembrance of God* (London, 1657), p. 23.
32. Samuel Clarke, *Englands Remembrancer, Containing a True and Full Narrative of those Two Never to be Forgotten Deliverances: The One from the Spanish Invasion in Eighty Eight; the Other from the Hellish Powder Plot: November 5. 1605* (London, 1657), sig. Av.
33. Clarke, *Englands Remembrancer* (1671 edn), pt. 2, title page, to the reader.
34. Thomas Spencer, *Englands Warning-Peece: or The History of the Gunpowder Treason* (London, 1659), sig. A.
35. Ralph Brownrigg, *A sermon on the 5th of November* (London, 1660), pp. 1, 48, 75. George Thomason had his copy by December 1659, Thomason collection, E. 2107 (3).

11 The Politics of Memory in Later Stuart England

1. John Booker, *Telescopium Uranicum, or an Almanack and Prognostication* (London, 1662); John Booker, *Telescopium Uranicum: an Ephemeris* (London, 1665); 12. Car. II. c. 14, 'An Act for a Perpetuall Anniversary Thanksgiving on the nine and twentyth day of May'; *A form of common prayer, to be used upon the thirtieth of January* (London, 1661); *A form of prayer, with thanksgiving, to be used . . . the 29th of May yearly* (London, 1661).
2. 14. Car. II. c. 4; J. Horsfall Turner (ed.), *The Rev. Oliver Heywood, B.A., 1630–1702* (Brighouse, 1882–5), vol. 1, p. 281, vol. 2, p. 41; 16. Car. II. c. 4; 17. Car. II. c. 2.
3. Matthew Henry Lee (ed.), *Diaries and Letters of Philip Henry* (London, 1882), p. 232.
4. Alan Macfarlane (ed.), *The Diary of Ralph Josselin, 1616–1683* (London, 1976), pp. 502, 513, 525, 538, 571. See also Richard Parkinson (ed.), *The Autobiography of Henry Newcome* (Manchester, 1852), pp. 144, 245–6.
5. Austin Dobson (ed.), *The Diary of John Evelyn* (London, 1906), vol. 2, p. 207; Library of Congress, 'London Newsletter Collection, 1665–85', vol. 1, f. 128.
6. Robert Latham and William Matthews (eds.), *The Diary of Samuel Pepys* (London, 1970–83), vol. 2, p. 208, vol. 5, p. 314; *Calendar of State Papers, Venice, 1666–68*, p. 321; Corporation of London Record Office, PD 10/72, 74, 86, 88, 99.

7. Churchwardens' accounts cited in this chapter are listed in the bibliography. Latham and Matthews (eds.), *Diary of Samuel Pepys*, vol. 7, p. 358; Michael McKeon, *Politics and Poetry in Restoration England* (Cambridge, Mass., 1975), pp. 138–46.

8. 25. Car. II. c. 2; *The Burning of the Whore of Babylon, As it was Acted, with great Applause, in the Poultrey, London, on Wednesday Night, being the Fifth of November last* (London, 1673), p. 2.

9. Macfarlane (ed.), *Diary of Ralph Josselin*, pp. 571, 588.

10. Library of Congress, 'London Newsletter Collection', vol. 4, f. 129.

11. *The Burning of the Whore of Babylon*, pp. 1–3; *Calendar of State Papers, Domestic 1673–75*, pp. 40, 44.

12. *Calendarium Catholicum: Or, An Universal Almanack, 1662*, cited in Thomas Barlow, *The Gunpowder Treason: With a Discourse of the Manner of its Discovery* (London, 1679), p. 9; Tillotson's sermon, 5 November 1678, cited in E. S. de Beer (ed.), *The Diary of John Evelyn* (Oxford, 1955), vol. 3, p. 25.

13. Edward Stephens, *A Discourse concerning the Original of the Powder-Plot: Together with a relation of the Conspiracies against Queen Elizabeth, and the Persecutions of the Protestants in France* (London, 1674); Jacobus Augustus Thuanus (De Thou), *Popish Policies and Practices Represented in the Histories of the Parisian massacre; Gun-powder Treason; Conspiracies Against Queen Elizabeth* (London, 1674); idem, *A Narration of that Horrible Conspiracy Against King James and the Whole Parliament of England, Commonly called the Gun-Powder Treason* (London, 1674); Barlow, *Gunpowder Treason*.

14. *The Gunpowder Treason: With a Discourse of its Discovery* (London, 1609, 1679); John Williams, *A History of the Gunpowder Treason* (London, 1678, 1679); John Wilson, *A Song or story for the lasting remembrance of divers famous works which God hath done in our time* (London, 1680); Samuel Clarke, *Englands Remembrancer, containing a true and full narrative of those two never to be forgotten deliverances: the one from the Spanish invasion in eighty eight: the other from the hellish Powder Plot, November 5. 1605* (London, 1657, 1671, 1679).

15. *Archaeological Journal*, 11 (1854), p. 180. The cards are reproduced in J. R. S. Whiting, *A Handful of History* (London, 1978). *Faux's Ghost: or, Advice to Papists* (London, 1680); *The Domestick Intelligence*, 3–7 November 1681.

16. *London Gazette*, no. 1249, 5–8 November 1677; *Calendar of State Papers, Domestic 1677–78*, p. 446.

17. Edward Maude Thompson (ed.), *Correspondence of the Family of Hatton . . . 1601–1704* (London, 1878), p. 157.

18. For the Popish Plot and the Exclusion crisis see J. P. Kenyon, *The Popish Plot* (London, 1972); John Miller, *Popery and Politics in England 1660–1688* (Cambridge, 1973); and Tim Harris, *London Crowds in the Reign of Charles II: Propaganda and Politics from the Restoration to the Exclusion Crisis* (Cambridge, 1987).

19. William Lloyd, *A Sermon Preached at St Martin in the Fields, on November the Fifth, 1678* (London, 1679), p. 26; idem, *A Sermon Preached before the*

House of Lords on November 5, 1680 (London, 1680), p. 37.

20. Thomas Wilson, *A Sermon on the Gunpowder Treason with Reflections on the Late Plot* (London, 1679), pp. 1, 10, 11, 18. See also John Chetwynd, *Eben-Ezer. A Thankful Memorial of God's Mercy in Preserving England from the Gunpowder-Treason* (London, 1682).

21. *The True Protestant Mercury*, 12–16 November 1681; Miller, *Popery and Politics*, p. 186; Harris, *London Crowds*, pp. 93, 104, 121.

22. *The Manner of the Burning of the Pope in Effigies in London on the 5th of November, 1678* (London, 1678). See also *The Solemn Mock Procession of the Pope, Cardinalls Iesuits, Fryers, etc. through ye City of London, Nouember ye 17th. 1679* (London, 1679); and *London's Defiance to Rome. A Perfect Narrative of the magnificent procession and solemn burning of the Pope* (London, 1679). Similar accounts, some illustrated, accompanied the processions of 1680 and 1681: Sheila Williams, 'The pope-burning processions of 1679, 1680 and 1681', *Journal of the Warburg and Courtauld Institutes*, 21 (1958), p. 106.

23. *The Solemn Mock-Procession* (London, 1680), pp. 1, 2; Miller, *Popery and Politics*, pp. 182–7; R. J. Allen, *The Clubs of Augustan London* (London, 1967), p. 21; H.M.C., *Seventh Report* (London, 1879), appendix, p. 477; Margaret M. Verney, *Memoirs of the Verney Family from the Restoration to the Revolution 1660 to 1696* (London, 1899), vol. 4, pp. 259–60; H.M.C., *Ormonde*, (London, 1906), vol. 4, pp. 472, 561.

24. Turner (ed.), *Oliver Heywood*, vol. 2, p. 218.

25. Williams, 'Pope-burning processions', p. 116; *The Solemn Mock-Procession* (1680), p. 6; Miller, *Popery and Politics*, p. 185; Harris, *London Crowds*, pp. 104, 120–1. See also *The Domestick Intelligence*, 14–17 November 1681; *The Impartial Protestant Mercury*, 17 November 1681; Library of Congress, 'London Newsletter Collection', vol. 7, f. 264; and the churchwardens' accounts listed in the bibliography.

26. Library of Congress, 'London Newsletter Collection', nos. 858–9; Harris, *London Crowds*, pp. 26, 104, 160.

27. Williams, 'Pope-burning processions', pp. 108–13.

28. Library of Congress, 'London Newsletter Collection', vol. 7, f. 264; Martin Ingram, 'Ridings, rough music and the "reform of popular culture" in early modern England', *Past and Present*, 105 (1984), pp. 79–113.

29. 'Order in Council', in *London Gazette*, no. 1772, 10 November 1682; repeated in No. 2084, 5–9 November 1685; *The Loyal Protestant, and True Domestick Intelligence*, 9 November 1682; Harris, *London Crowds*, pp. 185–7.

30. Library of Congress, 'London Newsletter Collection', vol. 9, loose folio.

31. ibid.

32. Library of Congress, 'London Newsletter Collection', vol. 8, f. 257; ibid., nos. 1298, 1299; Miller, *Popery and Politics*, p. 186.

33. Library of Congress, 'London Newsletter Collection', nos. 1459, 1612, 1614; Corporation of London Record Office, PD 10/86,88.

34. Library of Congress, 'London Newsletter Collection', no. 1730; Dobson (ed.), *Diary of John Evelyn*, vol. 3, pp. 191, 212.
35. Library of Congress, 'London Newsletter Collection', nos. 1730, 1733; Corporation of London Record Office, REP.93, f.2.
36. *A form of prayer, with thanksgiving . . . fifth day of November* (London, 1690); A. C. Edwards (ed.), *English History from Essex Sources 1550–1750* (Chelmsford, 1952), p. 120.
37. Dobson (ed.), *Diary of John Evelyn*, vol. 3, 269; William Lloyd, *A Sermon Preached before Their Majesties At Whitehall. On the Fifth day of November, 1689. Being the Anniversary-day of Thanksgiving For that Great Deliverance From the Gunpowder-Treason, And also the Day of His Majesties Happy Landing in England* (London, 1689), pp. 1, 32; Gilbert Burnet, *A Sermon Preached before the House of Peers* (London, 1689), p. 27; Samuel Freeman, *A Sermon Preached before the Honourable House of Commons* (London, 1690); John Sharp, *A Sermon Preached before the Lords* (London, 1691), p. 24. See also William Fleetwood, *A Sermon Preached before the Honourable House of Commons* (London, 1691).
38. See above, Chapter 5; J. Charles Cox, *The Records of the Borough of Northampton . . . 1550 to 1835* (London and Northampton, 1898), pp. 479, 481.
39. William Lloyd, *A Sermon preached before the Queen at Whitehall. January the 30th* (London, 1691), pp. 27–9; idem., *A Sermon Preach'd before the House of Lords . . . 30th of January* (London, 1697); idem., *A Sermon Preached before her majesty, On May 29* (London, 1692), pp. 10–19.
40. Henry Sacheverell, *The Perils of False Brethren both in Church and State* (London, 1709); Geoffrey Holmes, 'The Sacheverell riots: the crowd and the church in early eighteenth-century London', *Past and Present* 72 (1976), 55–85.
41. Abel Boyer, *History of the Reign of Queen Anne digested into Annals . . . 1711* (London, 1711), p. 270; J. J. Cartwright, *The Wentworth Papers* (London, 1883), p. 210. I am grateful to Robert Bucholz for these references.
42. Boyer, *Reign of Queen Anne . . . 1712* (London, 1712), p. 291.
43. Nicholas Rogers, 'Popular protest in early Hanoverian London', *Past and Present* 79 (1978), 70–100. A forthcoming study by Kathleen Wilson discusses popular calendrical politics in the reign of George I.

12 The English Calendar in Colonial America

1. Thomas Minor, *The Diary of Thomas Minor, Stonington, Connecticut* (New London, 1899); Samuel Clough, *The New-England Almanack for 1701* (Boston, 1701); Richard P. Gildrie, 'The ceremonial puritan: days of humiliation and thanksgiving', *New England Historical and Genealogical Register*, 136 (1982), pp. 3–16.
2. Rhys Isaac, *The Transformation of Virginia 1740–1790* (Chapel Hill, 1982), esp. pp. 22–30; T. H. Breen, *Tobacco Culture: The Mentality of the Great Tidewater Planters on the Eve of Revolution* (Princeton, NJ, 1985), esp. pp. 45–55. For more on this displaced English community see Gloria L.

Main, *Tobacco Colony: Life in Early Maryland, 1650–1720* (Princeton, 1983), Darrett and Anita Rutman, *A Place in Time: Middlesex County, Virginia, 1650–1760* (New York, 1984), and the work of Lorena Walsh for the Colonial Williamsburg Foundation.

3. William Waller Hening (ed.), *The Statutes at Large: Being a Collection of all the Laws of Virginia* (New York, 1823), vol. 2, p. 566; George Maclaren Brydon, *Virginia's Mother Church and the Political Conditions under which it Grew* (Richmond, Virginia, 1947), p. 440; 'Decisions of Virginia General Court, 1626–1628', in *Virginia Magazine of History and Biography*, 3 (1896), p. 367; 'Council Papers, 1698–1702', in *Virginia Magazine of History and Biography*, 24 (1916), p. 395.

4. William, J. Van Schreeven and George H. Reese (eds.), *Proceedings of the General Assembly of Virginia July 30–August 4, 1619* (Jamestown, Virginia, 1969), pp. 59–61; Brydon, *Virginia's Mother Church*, p. 83.

5. ibid., pp. 427, 430.

6. Van Schreeven and Reese (eds.), *Proceedings of the General Assembly*, p. 59; Brydon, *Virginia's Mother Church*, pp. 24, 85, 90, 426.

7. ibid., pp. 121, 131.

8. ibid., pp. 432, 438–9.

9. ibid., pp. 85, 144, 434, 447, 462.

10. ibid., pp. 461–2. For eighteenth-century recognition of Gunpowder Treason see *The Virginia Gazette*, 4–11 February 1736–7; ibid., 1 December 1774; and *The Virginia Almanack* (Williamsburg, 1743, 1764, 1774).

11. *Archives of Maryland* (Annapolis, 1883–99), vol. 4, p. 38; vol. 5, p. 133; vol. 1, p. 343; vol. 19, pp. 436–7.

12. Winton U. Solberg, *Redeem the Time: The Puritan Sabbath in New England* (Cambridge, Mass., 1977), pp. 47, 114; Thomas Lechford, *New-Englands Advice to Old England* (London, 1644), pp. 56–8. For another perspective on calendrical inhibitions and cultural transfer see David Cressy, 'The seasonality of marriage in old and New England', *Journal of Interdisciplinary History*, 16 (1985), pp. 1–21.

13. *The Book of the General Lawes and Libertyes . . . Massachusetts* (Cambridge, Mass., 1648), p. 14; Nathaniel B. Shurtleff (ed.), *Records of the Governor and Company of the Massachusetts Bay* (Boston, 1853–4), vol. 1, p. 277; Massachusetts Historical Society, microfilm, 'Diary of Francis Borland', 1682 and 1683; W. DeLoss Love, *The Fast and Thanksgiving Days of New England* (New York, 1895), pp. 241–8; Gildrie, 'Ceremonial puritan', pp. 3–16.; J. Hammond Trumball (ed.), *The Public Records of the Colony of Connecticut* (Hartford, 1850), vol. 1, *passim*.

14. *Diary of Thomas Minor*; Samuel Clough, *The New-England Almanack for the Year of our Lord, MDCCIII* (Boston, 1703); Ned Ward, 'A Trip to New England', in George P. Winship (ed.), *Boston in 1682 and 1699* (Providence, Rhode Island, 1905), p. 55.

15. Thomas Lechford, *Plain Dealing or News from New England* [1642], ed. Darrett B. Rutman (London, 1969), p. 54.

16. Shurtleff (ed.), *Records . . . Massachusetts*, vol. 1, pp. 143, 173, 176, 177,

181, 184, 187, 200, 226, etc.; Charles J. Hoadly (ed.), *Records of the Colony and Plantation of New Haven, 1638–49* (Hartford, 1857), pp. 40, 46; *New-Haven's Settling in New England* (London, 1656; Hartford, 1858), p. 14.

17. *General Lawes and Libertyes . . . Massachusetts*, pp. 21–2.

18. *Suffolk County Wills* (Baltimore, 1984), p. 3; *The Probate Records of Essex County, Massachusetts* (Salem, 1916–20), vol. 1, p. 110; M. Halsey Thomas (ed.), *The Diary of Samuel Sewall 1674–1729* (New York, 1973) vol. 1, p. 351; David D. Hall, 'The mental world of Samuel Sewall', in David D. Hall, John M. Murrin, and Thad W. Tate (eds.), *Saints and Revolutionaries: Essays on Early American History* (New York, 1984), p. 84.

19. Lechford, *New-Englands Advice*, pp. 56–8; Increase Mather, *A testimony against several prophane and superstitious customs, now practised by some in New-England* (London, 1687), p. 38.

20. Letter from James Sherley in William Bradford, *Of Plymouth Plantation 1620–1647*, ed. Samuel Eliot Morison (New York, 1963), p. 372; William Bradford, *History of Plymouth Plantation 1620–1647* (Boston, 1912), vol. 2, p. 54; Thomas Morton, *New English Canaan . . . an Abstract of New England*, ed. Charles Francis Adams, Jr (Boston, 1883), pp. 276–282: 'of the revels of New Canaan'.

21. Deloraine Pendre Corey, *The History of Malden Massachusetts 1633–1785* (Malden, 1899), p. 124; Roger Thompson, 'Adolescent culture in colonial Massachusetts', *Journal of Family History*, 9 (1984), p. 131.

22. William Bradford, *Bradford's History 'Of Plimoth Plantation'* (Boston, 1898), p. 135.

23. Record Commissioners of the City of Boston, *The Colonial Laws of Massachusetts . . . 1660 . . . to 1672* (Boston, 1889), p. 153; *The Colonial Laws of Massachusetts . . . 1672 . . . through 1686* (Boston, 1890), pp. 57–58.

24. Robert Noxon Tappan (ed.), *Edward Randolph; Including His Letters and Papers . . . 1676–1703* (Boston, 1898), vol. 2, pp. 198–201; *Colonial Laws . . . Through 1686*, p. 291; Hall, 'Mental world of Samuel Sewall', p. 84.

25. Massachusetts Historical Society, microfilm, 'Journal of Peter Thacher 1679–99'.

26. Mather, *Testimony against several prophane and superstitious customs*, pp. 18, 22, 35, 40; 'Diary of Cotton Mather 1709–1724', *Massachusetts Historical Society Collections*, ser. 7, vol. 8 (1912), p. 146. Cf. William Waldron to Richard Waldron Jr.: 'Christmas which used to be a time of wickedness in some of the towns is now arrived to such a regulation as that all disorders are banished and instead thereof a serious sermon is preached and collections made for the poor', Massachusetts Historical Society, 'Dana MSS.' 1725.

27. 'The Dunster Papers', *Massachusetts Historical Society Collections*, ser. 4., vol. 2 (1854), p. 191; Urian Oakes, *An Almanacke for . . . 1650* (Cambridge, Mass., 1650); Samuel Cheever, *An Almanack for . . . 1661* (Cambridge, Mass., 1661); Samuel Danforth, *The New-England Almanack for . . . 1686*.

28. Benjamin Harris, *Boston Almanack for . . . 1692* (Boston, 1692); John Tulley, *An Almanack for . . . 1687* (Boston, 1687), also 1689, 1692, 1697; Marion Barber Stowell, *Early American Almanacs: The Colonial Weekday Bible* (New York, 1977), pp. 40–62.

29. Bradford, *Bradford's History*, p. 182; Sydney V. James, Jr. (ed.), *Three Visitors to Early Plymouth* (Plymouth, Mass., 1963), p. 37; Morton, *New English Canaan*, p. 260.

30. Maverick to the Earl of Clarendon, in *Collections of the New York Historical Society* (New York, 1870), p. 47.

31. Thompson, 'Adolescent culture in colonial Massachusetts', p. 132.

32. American Antiquarian Society, 'Increase Mather's Diary'. At New London on 5 November 1711, 'the sailors made a bonfire in the evening', *Diary of Joshua Hempstead of New London, Connecticut* (New London, 1901), p. 3.

33. Shurtleff (ed.), *Records . . . Massachusetts*, vol. 4, pt. 2, p. 212; Record Commissioners of the City of Boston (eds.), *Sixth Report* (Boston, 1881), 'Roxbury land and court records', p. 206.

34. Massachusetts Historical Society, MSS. Miscellaneous bound, 1657–1671.

35. John Pynchon to John Winthrop, Jr., 1674, in Carl Bridenbaugh (ed.), *The Pynchon Papers* (Boston, 1982), p. 126; John Wilson, *A Song of deliverance from the lasting remembrance of Gods wonderful works* (Boston, 1680).

36. *Diary of Samuel Sewall*, vol. 1, pp. 81, 124.

37. *Abstract and Index of the Inferior Court of Pleas (Suffolk County Court) held at Boston 1680–1698* (Boston, 1940), p. 116; *Diary of Samuel Sewall*, vol. 1, pp. 82, 300, vol. 2, p. 627; Josiah Cotton to Rowland Cotton, in *Massachusetts Historical Society Collections*, 80 (1972), p. 271, 'Saltonstall Papers'.

38. *Diary of Samuel Sewall*, vol. 1, pp. 380, 416.

39. A start is made in Alfred F. Young, 'English plebian culture and eighteenth-century American radicalism', in Margaret Jacob and James Jacob (eds.), *The Origins of Anglo-American Radicalism* (London, 1984), pp. 185–212. Nathaniel Ames, *The Almanack for 1735* (Boston, 1735; *Boston Evening Post*, no. 13, 10 November 1735; Henry W. Cunningham (ed.), 'Diary of Rev. Samuel Checkley, 1735', *Publications of the Colonial Society of Massachusetts*, 12 (1908–9), p. 288.

40. Anne Rowe Cunningham (ed.) *Letters and Diary of John Rowe* (New York, 1969), pp. 67–8, 76, 114, 145, 194, 254, 287; Cunningham (ed.), 'Diary of Samuel Checkley', pp. 288–95; *Virginia Gazette*, 1 December 1774. See also Hiller B. Zobel, *The Boston Massacre* (New York, 1970), pp. 27, 37–8, 65; and Gary B. Nash, *The Urban Crucible: Social Change, Political Consciousness and the Origins of the American Revolution* (Cambridge, Mass., 1979), pp. 260–1, 299; 'Report of the Journey of Francis Louis Michel', *Virginia Magazine of History and Biography*, 24 (1916), pp. 127–8.

BIBLIOGRAPHY

Primary Sources

ALMANACS

Allestree, Richard, *A New Almanacke and Prognostication, for this yeare of our Lord God* (London, 1619; also 1626, 1628, 1629, 1632, 1640).

Alleyn, Henry, *Alleyns Almanacke, or, A Double diarie & prognostication* (London, 1608).

Ames, Nathaniel, *The Almanack for 1735* (Boston, 1735).

An astronomical diary, or, an Almanack for . . . 1760 . . . calculated for the Meridian of Boston, in New England (Boston, 1760).

An episcopal Almanack for . . . 1678 (London, 1678).

Andrews, William, *News from the Stars: or, an Ephemeris for the Year 1695* (London, 1695).

Booker, John, *Coelestiall Observations: or an Ephemeris* (London, 1656).

Booker, John, *Telescopium Uranicum, or an Almanack and Prognostication for . . . MDCLXII* (London, 1662).

Booker, John, *Telescopium Uranicum: an Ephemeris . . . MDCLXV* (London, 1665).

Bowker, James, *An Almanack for the year of our Lord God, MDCLXXVII* (London, 1677).

Brattle, William, *An Almanack . . . for . . . 1694* (Boston, 1694).

Buckminster, Thomas, *An Almanacke and Prognostication for . . . MDXCVIII* (London, 1598).

Cheever, Samuel, *An Almanack for . . . 1661* (Cambridge, Mass., 1661).

Clough, Samuel, *The New-England Almanack for the Year of our Lord MDCCI* (Boston, 1700; also 1701 and 1703).

Clough, Samuel, *Kalendarius Nov-Anglicanum, or an Almanack . . . for 1706* (Boston, 1705; also 1707).

Clough, Samuel, *An Almanack for . . . 1708* (Boston, 1708).

Coelson, Lancelot, *Speculum perspicuum Uranicum: or, an Almanack for . . . 1684* (London, 1684).

Coley, Henry, *Merlinus Anglicus Junior: or the Starry Messenger* (London, 1695).

Dade, William, *A New Almanacke . . . 1632* (London, 1632).

Dade, William, *A New Almanacke . . . 1633* (London, 1633).

Danforth, Samuel, *The New-England Almanack For the year of our Lord, 1686* (Cambridge, Mass., 1685).

Dove, Jonathan, *An Almanacke for the yeare of our Lord God 1636* (Cambridge, 1636; also 1641).

Dove, Jonathan, *Speculum Anni, or an Almanacke* (Cambridge, 1695; also 1696).

Gadbury, John, *Ephemeris, or a Diary – astronomical, astrological, meteorological, for the year of Grace, 1695* (London, 1695).

Harris, Benjamin, *Boston Almanack for . . . 1692* (Boston, 1692).

Lakes, Thomas, *The Countrey-Mans Kalender: with a plain Prognostication for the yeare of our Lord MDCXXVII* (Cambrige, 1627).

Lily, William, *Merlini Anglici Ephemeris. Astrological Predictions for the Year 1656* (London, 1656).

Oakes, Urian, *An Almanack for . . . 1650* (Cambridge, Mass., 1650).

Parker, George, *Mercurius Anglicanus, or the English Mercury: being a complete Diary for the year of our Lord 1695* (London, 1695).

Partridge, John, *Merlinus Liberatus. Being an Almanack for . . . 1697* (London, 1697).

'Philoprotest', *The Protestant Almanack, for the year 1697* (London, 1697).

Pond, Edward, *A new Almanacke for this Present Yeare of our Lord. 1608* (London, 1608).

'Poor Robin', *An Almanack After the Old and New Fashion* (London, 1695).

Richardson, John, *An Almanack . . . for . . . 1670* (Cambridge, Mass., 1670).

Sherman, John, *An Almanacke . . . for . . . 1676* (Cambridge, Mass., 1676).

Sherman, Roger, *An Almanack for the year of our Lord Christ, 1750 . . . for the meridien of the City of New York* (New York, 1750).

Tulley, John, *An Almanack for . . . 1687* (Boston, 1687; also 1689, 1692, 1697).

The Virginia Almanack (Williamsburg, 1743; also 1747, 1750, 1764, 1771, 1774, 1776).

Woodhouse, William, *An Almanacke and Prognostication for . . . 1608* (London, 1608).

CHURCHWARDENS' ACCOUNTS

Bedfordshire
Farmiloe, J. E. and Nixseaman, Rosita (eds.), *Elizabethan Churchwardens' Accounts* (Bedfordshire Historical Record Society, Bedford, 1953) [Clifton, Northill, and Shillington, 1561–1612].

Cambridgeshire
Cambridge Record Office, 'Cambridge, Holy Trinity accounts, 1569–1690'.
Cambridge Records Office, 'Cambridge, St Botolph accounts, 1600–1702'.
Cambridge Record Office, 'Cambridge, St Mary the Great accounts, 1570–1700'.
Cambridge Record Office, 'Coton accounts, 1576–1715'.
Cambridge Record Office, 'March accounts, 1541–1679'.
Foster, J. E. (ed.), *Churchwardens' Accounts of St Mary the Great, Cambridge, from 1504 to 1635* (Cambridge, 1905).

Bibliography

Derbyshire
Cox, J. Charles, 'The registers, and churchwardens' and constables' accounts of the parish of Repton', *Journal of the Derbyshire Archaeological and Natural History Society*, 1 (1879), pp. 27–41.
Cox, J. Charles, and Hope, W. H. St John (eds.), *The Chronicles of the Collegiate Church or Free Chapel of All Saints, Derby* (London, 1881).

Devon
Devon Record Office, 'Bere Ferrers accounts'.
Devon Record Office, 'Exeter, St Mary Major accounts, 1536–1743'.
Devon Record Office, 'Exeter, St Petrock accounts'.
Devon Record Office, 'Morebath accounts'.
Devon Record Office, 'Tavistock accounts'.
Devon Record Office, 'Westbury accounts, 1537–1792'.
Gregory, Ivon L. (ed.), *Hartland Church Accounts, 1597–1706* (London, 1950).

Dorset
Dorset Record Office, 'Bere Regis accounts, 1607–42'.
Dorset Record Office, 'Dorchester, All Saints' accounts, 1649–1738'.
Dorset Record Office, 'Dorchester, Holy Trinity accounts, 1613–41'.
Dorset Record Office, 'Sherborne accounts, 1560–1710'.

Durham
Durham Record Office, 'Darlington, St Cuthbert accounts, 1630–92'.
Durham Record Office, 'Durham, St Nicholas accounts, 1666–1703'.
Durham Record Office, 'Gateshead, St Mary accounts, 1626–78'.

Gloucestershire
Bruce, John (ed.), 'Extracts from accounts of the churchwardens of Minchinhampton in the county of Gloucester', *Archaeologia*, 35 (1853), pp. 409–52.

Hertfordshire
Palmer, Anthony (ed.), *Tudor Churchwardens' Accounts* [Ashwell, Baldock, St Peter's] (Hertfordshire Record Society, Braughing, Herts, 1985).

Huntingdonshire
Huntingdon Record Office, 'Great Staughton accounts, 1637–1744'.

Kent
Plomer, Henry R. (ed.), *Kent Records. The Churchwardens' Accounts of St Nicholas, Strood, 1555–1662* (Kent Archaeological Society, 1927).

Lancashire
Bailey, F. A. (ed.), *The Churchwardens' Accounts of Prescot, Lancashire 1523–1607* (Preston, 1953).

London
Freshfield, Edwin, *Accomptes of the Churchwardens of the Paryshe of St Christofer's in London. 1575 to 1662* (London, 1885).
Freshfield, Edwin, *The Account Book of the Parish of St Christopher le Stocks in the City of London 1662–1685* (London, 1895).

243

Freshfield, Edwin, *The Accounts Books of the Parish of St Bartholomew Exchange in the City of London 1596–1698* (London, 1895).

Guildhall Library, 'St Andrew by the Wardrobe accounts, 1570–1704'.

Guildhall Library, 'St Antholin accounts, 1574–1708'.

Guildhall Library, 'St Botolph Billingsgate accounts, 1603–74'.

Guildhall Library, 'St Botolph without Bishopsgate, accounts, 1567–1661'.

Guildhall Library, 'St Katherine Coleman Street accounts, 1609–71'.

Guildhall Library, 'St Mary Aldermanbury accounts, 1570–1695'.

Guildhall Library, 'St Matthew Friday Street accounts, 1547–1678'.

Guildhall Library, 'St Michael Cornhill accounts, 1608–1702'.

Guildhall Library, 'St Pancras Soper Lane accounts, 1616–1700'; 'The Great Book of the Parish'.

Guildhall Library, 'St Paul's Cathedral, chamberlains' accounts, 1631–44'.

Guildhall Library, 'St Stephen Coleman Street accounts, 1586–1685'.

Overall, William Henry (ed.), *The Accounts of the Churchwardens of the Parish of St Michael, Cornhill, in the City of London, from 1456 to 1608* (London, 1868).

Middlesex

Hammersmith and Fulham Archives, 'Fulham accounts, 1637–79'.

Hounslow Public Library, 'Isleworth accounts, 1649–90'.

Kitto, John V. (ed.), *St Martin-in-the-Fields. The Accounts of the Churchwardens 1525–1605* (London, 1901).

Lysons, Daniel, *The Environs of London: Being an Historical Account*, vol. 2 (London, 1795) [extract accounts of Brentford, Chelsea, Fulham].

Westminster Archives, 'St Clement Danes accounts, 1609–1685'.

Westminster Archives, 'St Margaret Westminster accounts, 1550–1700'.

Westminster Archives, 'St Mary le Strand accounts, 1586–1698'.

Westminster Archives, 'St Martin in the Fields acounts, 1601–80'.

Norfolk

Hillen, Henry J., *History of the Borough of Kings Lynn* (Norwich, *c.* 1907) [St Margaret accounts, extracts].

Norfolk Record Office, 'Fersfield accounts'.

Norfolk Record Office, 'Great Yarmouth, St Nicholas accounts, 1575–1682'.

Norfolk Record Office, 'Norwich, St Gregory accounts, 1574–1771'.

Norfolk Record Office, 'Norwich, St Margaret Coslany accounts, 1586–1697'.

Norfolk Record Office, 'Norwich, St Peter Mancroft, accounts 1580–1700'.

Norfolk Record Office, 'Norwich, St Saviour's accounts'.

Norfolk Record Office, 'Reymerston accounts'.

Norfolk Record Office, 'Swaffham accounts'.

Stallard, A. D. (ed.), *The Transcript of the Churchwardens' Accounts of the Parish of Tilney All Saints', Norfolk, 1443 to 1589* (London, 1922).

Northamptonshire

Cox, J. Charles, and Serjeantson, R. M., *A History of the Church of the Holy Sepulchre, Northampton* (Northampton, 1897).

Bibliography

Oxfordshire
Brinkworth, E. R. C. (ed.), *South Newington Churchwardens' Accounts 1553–1684* (Banbury Historical Society, Banbury, 1964).
New College, Oxford, MS. Long Books, 1617–1673.

Shropshire
Wright, Thomas (ed.), *Churchwardens' Accounts for the Town of Ludlow, in Shropshire, from 1540 to the end of the reign of Queen Elizabeth* (Camden Society, London, 1869).

Somerset
Pearson, C. B. (ed.), *The Churchwardens' Accounts of the Church and Parish of St Michael without the North Gate, Bath, 1349–1575* (Taunton, 1878).
Historical Manuscripts Commission, *Calendar of the Manuscripts of the Dean and Chapter of Wells*, vol. 2 (London, 1914).

Surrey
Davis, C. T. (ed.), 'Early churchwardens' accounts of Wandsworth [1545–1639]', *Surrey Archaeological Collections*, 15 (1900), pp. 80–127; 17 (1902), pp. 135–75; 18 (1903), pp. 96–152; 19 (1906), pp. 145–94; 20 (1907), pp. 169–222; 24 (1911), pp. 92–161.
Drew, Charles (ed.), *Lambeth Churchwardens' Accounts 1504–1645* (Surrey Record Society, 1941, 1950).
Kirby, J. W., 'The churchwardens' accounts of the parish of St Alfege, East Greenwich, 1630–1640', *Transactions of the Greenwich and Lewisham Antiquarian Society*, 4 (1954), pp. 270–84.
Lysons, Daniel, *The Environs of London: Being an Historical Account*, vol. 1 (London, 1792) [extract accounts of Kingston upon Thames, Wandsworth].

Wiltshire
Baker, T. H., 'The churchwardens' accounts of Mere', *The Wiltshire Archaeological and Natural History Magazine*, 108 (1907), pp. 23–92.
Swayne, Henry James Fowle (ed.), *Churchwardens' Accounts of S. Edmund & S. Thomas, Sarum 1443–1702* (Wiltshire Record Society, Salisbury, 1896).
Symonds, W. (ed.), 'Winterslow church reckonings, 1542–1661', *The Wiltshire Archaeological and Natural History Magazine*, 36 (1909–10), pp. 27–49.

Worcestershire
Amphlett, John (ed.), *The Churchwardens' Accounts of St Michael's in Bedwardine, Worcester, from 1539 to 1603* (Oxford, 1896).
Somers, Frank (ed.), *Halesowen Churchwardens' Accounts (1487–1582)* (Worcester Historical Society, Worcester, 1957).

Yorkshire
Borthwick Institute, 'York, Holy Trinity, Goodramgate accounts, 1559–1712'.
Borthwick Institute, 'York, St John Ousebridge accounts, 1585–1668'.
Borthwick Institute, 'York, St Martin cum Gregory accounts, 1569–1700'.

Bibliography

Borthwick Institute, 'York, St Michael Spurriergate accounts, 1626–1710'.

TOWN RECORDS

Blomefield, Francis, *An Essay Towards a Topographical History of the County of Norfolk*, vol. 3 (London, 1806) [Norwich records].

'Cambridge Treasurers' Accounts, 1611–28', Downing College, Bowtell MSS.

'Chester Chronicles', British Library, Harleian MS. 2125.

Clopper, Lawrence M. (ed.), *Records of Early English Drama: Chester* (Toronto, 1979).

Corporation of London Record Office, 'Lord Mayors' Journals, Repertories, and Proclamations'.

Cox, J. Charles (ed.), *The Records of the Borough of Northampton . . . 1550 to 1835* (London and Northampton, 1898).

Douglas, Audrey, and Greenfield, Peter (eds.), *Records of Early English Drama: Cumberland, Westmoreland, Gloucestershire* (Toronto, 1986).

Galloway, David (ed.), *Records of Early English Drama: Norwich 1540–1642* (Toronto, 1984).

Gibson, J. S. W. and Brinkworth, E. R. C. (eds.), *Banbury Corporation Records: Tudor and Stuart* (Banbury Historical Society, Banbury, 1977).

Historical Manuscripts Commission, *Ninth Report* (London, 1883) [Canterbury chamberlains' accounts, Plymouth borough annals, Carlise corporation records, Ipswich chamberlains' accounts].

Ingram, R. W. (ed.), *Records of Early English Drama: Coventry* (Toronto, 1981).

Johnston, Alexandra F. and Rogerson, Margaret, *Records of Early English Drama: York* (Toronto, 1979).

Livock, D. M. (ed.), *City Chamberlains' Accounts in the Sixteenth and Seventeenth Centuries* (Bristol Record Society, Bristol, 1966).

'Norwich chamberlains' accounts, 1580–1700', Norfolk Record Office.

Overall, W. H. and H. C. (eds.), *Analytical Index to the Series of Records Known as Remembrancia . . . 1579–1664* (London, 1887).

Picton, James A. (ed.), *Selections from the Municipal Archives and Records from the 13th to the 17th Century* (Liverpool, 1883).

Records of the Borough of Nottingham . . . 1547–1625 (London and Nottingham, 1889).

Records of the Borough of Nottingham . . . 1625–1702 (London and Nottingham, 1900).

Smith, Lucy Toulmin (ed.), *The Maire of Bristow is Kalendar by Robert Ricart* (Camden Society, London, 1872).

Twemlow, J. A. (ed.), *Liverpool Town Books . . . 1571–1603* (Liverpool, 1935).

DIARIES

[Ashmole], *Elias Ashmole (1617–1692) His Autobiographical and Historical Notes*, ed. C. H. Josten (Oxford, 1966).

Bibliography

[Assheton], *The Journal of Nicholas Assheton*, ed. F. R. Raines (Chetham Society, Manchester, 1848).

[Bellingham], *Diary of Thomas Bellingham, An Officer under William III*, ed. Anthony Hewitson (Preston, 1908).

[Borland], 'Diary of Francis Borland', Massachusetts Historical Society, microfilm.

[Cartwright], *The Diary of Dr Thomas Cartwright*, ed. Joseph Hunter (Camden Society, London, 1843).

[Checkley], 'Diary of Rev. Samuel Checkley, 1735', *Publications of the Colonial Society of Massachusetts*, 12 (1908–9).

[Crosfield], *The Diary of Thomas Crosfield*, ed. Frederick S. Boas (Oxford, 1935).

[D'Ewes], *The Diary of Sir Simonds D'Ewes 1622–1624*, ed. Elisabeth Bourcier (Paris, 1974).

[Evelyn], *The Diary of John Evelyn*, ed. Austin Dobson (London, 1906).

[Hempstead], *Diary of Joshua Hempstead of New London, Connecticut* (New London Historical Society, New London, 1901).

[Henry], *Diaries and Letters of Philip Henry*, ed. Matthew Henry Lee (London, 1882).

[Heywood], *The Rev. Oliver Heywood, B.A. 1630–1702; His Autobiography, Diaries, Anecdote and Event Books* (Brighouse, 1882–5).

[Hoby], *The Diary of Lady Margaret Hoby 1599–1605*, ed. Dorothy M. Meads (London, 1930).

[Hutton], 'Diary of Sir Richard Hutton', Cambridge University Library, Add. MS. 6863.

[Isham], *The Diary of Thomas Isham of Lamport (1658–81)*, ed. Norman Marlow (Farnborough, 1971).

[Josselin], *The Diary of Ralph Josselin 1616–1683*, ed. Alan Macfarlane (London, 1976).

[Laud], 'Diary', in *The Works of William Laud*, vol. 3 (Oxford, 1853).

[Le Roy], *Notebook of P. Le Roy*, ed. G. E. Lee (Publications of the Guernsey Historical and Antiquarian Society, 1893).

[Machyn], *The Diary of Henry Machyn, Citizen and Merchant-Taylor of London . . . 1550–1563*, ed. John Gough Nichols (Camden Society, London, 1848).

[Mather], 'Diary of Cotton Mather 1709–1724', *Massachusetts Historical Society Collections*, ser. 7, vol. 8 (1912).

[Minor], *The Diary of Thomas Minor, Stonington, Connecticut* (New London, 1899).

[Newcome], *The Diary of the Rev. Henry Newcome . . . 1661 to 1663*, ed. Thomas Heywood (Chetham Society, Manchester, 1849).

[Newcome], *The Autobiography of Henry Newcome*, ed. Richard Parkinson (Chetham Society, Manchester, 1852).

[Newton], *The Diary of Samuel Newton. Alderman of Cambridge (1662–1717)*, ed. J. E. Foster (Cambridge, 1890).

[Pepys], *The Diary of Samuel Pepys*, ed. Robert Latham and William Matthews (Berkeley and Los Angeles, 1970–83).

[Reresby], *Memoirs of Sir John Reresby*, ed. Andrew Browning (Glasgow, 1936).

[Rogers], 'The Diary of Richard Rogers', in *Two Elizabethan Puritan Diaries*, ed. M. M. Knappen (Chicago, 1933; repr. Gloucester, Mass., 1966).

[Rous], *Diary of John Rous, Incumbent of Santon Downham, Suffolk, from 1625 to 1642*, ed. Mary Anne Everett Green (Camden Society, London, 1856).

[Rowe], *Letters and Diary of John Rowe*, ed. Anne Rowe Cunningham (Boston, 1903; repr. New York, 1969).

[Sampson], 'Diary of William Sampson', in *The Rector's Book of Clayworth, Notts*, ed. Harry Gill and Everard L. Guilford (Nottingham, 1910).

[Sewall], *The Diary of Samuel Sewall 1674–1729* (New York, 1973).

[Thacher], 'Journal of Peter Thacher', Massachusetts Historical Society, microfilm.

[Ward], 'The Diary of Samuel Ward', in *Two Elizabethan Puritan Diaries*, ed. M. M. Knappen (Chicago, 1933; repr. Gloucester, Mass., 1966).

[Woodford], 'Robert Woodforde's diary, 1637–1641', New College, Oxford, MS.

[Woodford], 'The Diary of Robert Woodford, Steward of Northampton', in Historical Manuscripts Commission, *Ninth Report*, vol. 2 (London, 1884), pp. 496–9.

[Woodford], 'Diary of Samuel Woodford, 1662', Yale University, Beineke Library, Osborne MSS.

[Worthington], *The Diary and Correspondence of Dr John Worthington*, ed. James Crossley (Chetham Society, Manchester, 1847).

[Yonge], *Diary of Walter Yonge . . . from 1604 to 1628*, ed. George Roberts (Camden Society, London, 1848).

OTHER PRIMARY SOURCES

Abbot, George, *Articles to be inquired of, in the first Metropoliticall visitation* (London, 1616).

The Abuses of the Romish church anatomised (London, 1623).

Acts of the Privy Council of England.

'An Admonition to the Parliament' [1572], in W. H. Frere and C. E. Douglas (eds.), *Puritan Manifestoes* (London, 1954).

Ames, William, *The Saints Security against Seducing Spirits* (London, 1652).

Andrewes, Lancelot, *A sermon preached the fifth of November, 1617* (London, 1618).

Andrewes, Lancelot, *Ninety-six Sermons* (Oxford, 1856).

Andrewes, Lancelot, *XCVI Sermons*, 3rd edn ((London, 1635).

Arber, Edward (ed.), *A Transcript of the Registers of the Company of Stationers of London, 1554–1640* (London, 1877–94).

Archives of Maryland (Annapolis, 1883–99).

The Arraignment, Conviction, and Imprisoning, of Christmas (London, 1646).

Aske, James, *Elizabetha Triumphans. Conteyning The Damned practizes, that the divelish Popes of Rome have used ever sithence her Highnesse first comming to the Crowne* (London, 1588).

Aubrey, John, 'Remaines of Gentilisme and Judaisme', in John Buchanan-

Bibliography

Brown (ed.), *John Aubrey: Three Prose Works* (Carbondale, Illinois, 1972).

B., I., *Calendar-Reformation. Or, An Humble Addresse To the Right Honorable the Lords and Commons Assembled in Parliament* (London, 1648).

Barlow, Thomas, *The Gunpowder-Treason: With a Discourse of the Manner of its Discovery* (London, 1679).

Baro, Peter, *A Speciall Treatise of Gods Prouidence* (London?, 1588).

Basley, Thomas, 'In Quintum Novembris', Massachusetts Historical Society, MS. Miscellaneous bound, 1659–1671.

Baxter, Richard, *A Christian Directory* (London, 1677).

Bayley, Lewis, *The Practice of Pietie*, 35th edn (London, 1635).

Bentley, Samuel (ed.), *Excerpta Historica, or, Illustrations of English History* (London, 1833).

Birch, Thomas (ed.), *The Court and Times of Charles the First* (London, 1848).

Birch, Thomas (ed.), *The Court and Times of James the First* (London, 1849).

Blayney, Allan (Pastor Fido), *Festorum Metropolis. The Metropolitan Feast* (London, 1652).

Blayney, Allan, *Festorum Metropolis*, 2nd edn (London, 1654).

The Book of the General Lawes and Libertyes . . . Massachusetts (Cambridge, Mass., 1648).

The Boston Evening Post, 10 November 1735.

Boyer, Abel, *History of the Reign of Queen Anne Digested into Annals* (London, 1711–12).

Boys, John, *An Exposition of the Festivall Epistles and Gospels* (London, 1615).

Boys, John, *The Autumne Part from the Twelfth Sunday after Trinity to the last in the whole yeare* (London, 1616).

Bradford, William, *Of Plymouth Plantation 1620–1647*, ed. Samuel Eliot Morison (New York, 1963).

Brathwait, Richard, *The Prodigals Teares: or His Fare-well to Vanity* (London, 1614; repr. 1619).

Bridge, William, *England Saved with a Notwithstanding: Represented in a sermon to the Honorable House of Commons, assembled in Parliament, Novemb. 5. 1647. The Day of Thanksgiving for Deliverance from the Powder-Plot* (London, 1648).

Brightman, Thomas, *Apocalypsis apocalypseos. A Revelation* (Leyden, 1616).

Brownrigg, Ralph, *A Sermon on the 5th of November* (London, 1660).

Burgess, Anthony, *Romes Cruelty & Apostacie: Declared in a Sermon Preached on the fifth of November, 1644* (London, 1645).

Burgess, Cornelius, *A Sermon Preached to the Honourable House of Commons . . . Novemb. 17. 1640* (London, 1641).

Burgess, Cornelius, *Another sermon Preached to the Honorable House of Commons . . . November the fifth, 1641* (London, 1641).

Burnet, Gilbert, *A Sermon Preached . . . On the Fifth of November, 1684* (London, 1684).

Burnet, Gilbert, *A sermon preached before the House of Peers . . . On the 5th of November 1689* (London, 1689).

The Burning of the Whore of Babylon, As it was Acted, with great Applause, in the Poultrey, London, on Wednesday Night, being the Fifth of November last. (London, 1673).

Burton, Henry, *A Divine Tragedie Lately Acted, or A Collection of sundry memorable examples of Gods judgements upon Sabbath-breakers* (London?, 1636).

Burton, Henry, *For God, and the King. The Summe of Two Sermons Preached on the fifth of November last* (London?, 1636).

Burton, Henry, *A Tryall of Private Devotions. Or, A Diall for the Houres of Prayer* (London, 1628).

C., G.B., *Plots, Conspiracies and Attempts of Domestick and Forraigne Enemies . . . beginning with the Reformation of Religion under Queene Elizabeth* (London, 1642).

Calendar of Letters and Papers . . . Simancas.

Calendar of State Papers, Domestic.

Calendar of State Papers, Foreign.

Calendar of State Papers . . . Venice.

Canterbury Christmas (London, 1648).

Cardwell, Edward (ed.), *Documentary Annals of the Reformed Church of England* (Oxford, 1844).

Cardwell, Edward (ed.), *Synodalia. A Collection of Articles of religion, canons, and Proceedings of Convocations* (Oxford, 1842).

Carew, Richard, *The Survey of Cornwall* (London, 1602).

Carleton, George, *A Thankfull Remembrance of Gods Mercy. In an Historicall Collection of the great and mercifull Deliverances of the Church and State of England* (London, 1624; also 1625, 1627, 1630).

Carolus Redux (Oxford, 1623).

Certaine Sermons and Homilies appointed to be read in Churches, in the time of the late Queene Elizabeth of famous memory. And now thought fit to be reprinted (London, 1623).

[Chamberlain], *The Letters of John Chamberlain*, ed. Norman Egbert McClure (Philadelphia, 1939).

Chamberlayne, Edward, *Angliae Notitia: or, the Present State of England* (London, 1669; also 1702).

Chapman, George, *May-Day. A Witty Comedie* (London, 1611).

Chetwynd, John, *Eben-ezer. A Thankfull Memorial of God's Mercy in Preserving England from the Gunpowder-Treason* (London, 1682).

Clarendon, *The History of the Rebellion*, ed. W. Dunn Macray (Oxford, 1888).

Clarke, Samuel, *Englands Remembrancer, containing A true and full Narrative of those two never to be forgotten deliverances: The one from the Spanish Invasion in Eighty eight: The other from the Hellish Powder Plot* (London, 1657).

Clarke, Samuel, *The Gun-Powder Treason: Being a Remembrance to England, of that Ancient Deliverance from the Horrid Plot* (London, 1671).

Clarke, Samuel, *A True and Full Narrative of Those two never to be forgotten deliverances* (London, 1671).

Clay, William Keating (ed.), *Liturgical Services. Liturgies and Occasional Forms of Prayer Set Forth in the Reign of Queen Elizabeth* (Parker Society, Cambridge, 1847).

Colfe, Isaac, *A Sermon Preached on the Queenes Day Being the 17 of November. 1587 at the towne of Lidd in Kent* (London, 1588).

Collinges, John, *Responsoria ad Erratica Piscatoris. Or, A Caveat for Old and New Prophanenesse* (London, 1653).

Cope, John, *A Religious Inquisition* (London, 1629).

Corbet, Jeffrey, *The Protestant's Warning-Piece: Or, the humble Remonstrance of Jeffrey Corbet* (London, 1656).

Cosin, John, *A Collection of Private Devotions* (London, 1627).

Cosin, John, *A Collection of Private Devotions*, 4th edn (London, 1635).

[Cosin], *The Correspondence of John Cosin*, ed. George Ornsby (Surtees Society, Durham, pt. 1, 1869; pt. 2, 1872).

[Cromwell], *The Writings and Speeches of Oliver Cromwell*, ed. Wilbur Cortez Abbott, vols. 3 & 4 (Cambridge, Mass., 1945–7).

[Davenant], *Sir William Davenant. The Shorter Poems, and Songs from the Plays and Masques*, ed. A. M. Gibbs (Oxford, 1972).

Day, John, *Day's Festivals or, Twelve of His Sermons* (Oxford, 1615).

'Decisions of Virginia General Court, 1626–1628', in *Virginia Magazine of History and Biography*, 3 (1896).

The Declaration of many thousands of the City of Canterbury (London, 1647).

Deloney, Thomas, 'Three ballads on the Armada fight', in Edward Arber (ed.), *An English Garner*, vol. 7 (Birmingham, 1883).

Denakol (pseud.), *No Parliament Powder. But Shot and Powder for the Pope* (London, 1609).

Denton, William, *The Burnt Child dreads the Fire: or an Examination of the Merits of the Papists, relating to England* (London, 1675).

The Domestick Intelligence, 3–17 November 1681.

Duckworth, Richard, and Stedman, Fabian, *Tintinnalogia: or, The Art of Ringing* (London, 1671).

Edwards, A. C. (ed.), *English History from Essex Sources 1550–1750* (Chelmsford, 1952).

Eleutherius, N. (pseud.), *Trivmphalia De Victoriis Elisabethae . . . Contra Instrvctissimam Philippi Hispaniarum Regis* (London, 1589).

Englands Complaint to Jesus Christ Against the Bishops Canons of the late sinfull synod (Amsterdam, 1640).

Englands Miraculous Preservation Emblematically Described (London, 1646).

An Exhortation to all English Subiects, to ioine for the defence of Queene Elizabeth, and their native country (London, 1588).

Faux's Ghost: Or, Advice to Papists (London, 1680).

Featly, Daniel, *Ancilla Pietatis: or, The Hand-Maid to Private Devotion* (London, 1626; 6th edn, 1639).

Fennor, William, *Pasquils Palinodia, or his progresse to the taverne* (London, 1619).

The fifth of November, or The Popish and Schismaticall Rebells. With their horrid Plots, fair pretences, & bloudy Practices, weighed one against another (Oxford, 1644).

[Finet], *Ceremonies of Charles I: The Note Books of John Finet 1628–1641*, ed. Albert J. Loomie (New York, 1987).

Firth, C. H., and Rait, R. S. (eds.), *Acts and Ordinances of the Interregnum, 1642–1660* (London, 1911).

Fisher, Edward, *A Christian Caveat To the Old and New Sabbatarians. Or, A Vindication of our Gospel-Festivals* (London, 1650).

Fisher, Edward, *The Feast of Feasts. Or, The Celebration of the Sacred Nativity* (Oxford, 1644).

Fitz-Geffry, Charles, *The Blessed Birthday* (London, 1654).

Fleetwood, William, *A Sermon Preached before the Honourable House of Commons . . . 5th of November, 1691* (London, 1691).

A Form of Common prayer, to be used upon the thirtieth of January (London, 1661).

A Form of prayer, with thanksgiving, to be used . . . the 29th of May yearly (London, 1661).

A Form of Prayer with Thanksgiving to be used yearly upon the Fifth day of November; For the happy Deliverance of the King, and the Three Estates of the realm, from the most Traitorous and bloody intended Massacre by Gun-powder (London, 1606).

A Form of prayer, with thanksgiving . . . fifth day of November (London, 1690).

Foxe, John, *Actes and Monuments of these latter and perillous dayes* (London, 1653).

Foxe, John, *Actes and Monuments of Matters most speciall and memorable* (London, 1583; also 1632, 1641, and 1684 edns.).

[Foxe], *The Acts and Monuments of John Foxe*, ed. Stephen Reed Cattley and George Townsend (London, 1838).

Freeman, Samuel, *A Sermon Preached before the Honourable House of Commons . . . Fifth of November* (London, 1690).

Frere, W. H. and Douglas, C. E. (eds.), *Puritan Manifestoes* (London, 1954).

Frere, W. H. (ed.), *Visitation Articles and Injunctions of the Period of the Reformation* (London, 1910).

Gainsford, Thomas, *The Glory of England* (London, 1618).

Garey, Samuel, *Amphitheatrum Scelerum: or the Transcendent of Treason: For the fift of Nouember* (London, 1618).

Garey, Samuel, *Great Brittans little Calendar: or, Triple Diarie, in remembrance of three days* (London, 1618).

Gardiner, S. R. (ed.), *The Constitutional Documents of the Puritan Revolution 1625–1660*, 3rd edn (Oxford, 1906).

Gataker, Thomas, *An Anniversarie Memoriall of Englands Delivery from the Spanish Invasion* (London, 1626).

Gataker, Thomas, *Certaine Sermons* (London, 1637).

Gilbey, Anthony, *A Pleasaunt Dialogue* (London, 1581).

Goodwin, John, *The Saints Interest in God* (London, 1640).

Googe, Barnaby, *The Popish Kingdome or reigne of Antichrist written in Latin Verse by Thomas Naogeorgus and Englyshed by Barnabe Googe* [1570], ed. Robert Charles Hope (London, 1880).

Goring, J., and Wake, J. (eds.), *Northamptonshire Lieutenancy Papers and Other Documents, 1580–1614* (Northants Record Society, Northampton, 1975).

Gratulatio de principis reditu ex Hispaniis (Cambridge, 1623).

Greene, Robert, *The Spanish Masquerado* (London, 1589).

H., T., *A Ha! Christmas . . . a sound and good perswasion for Gentlemen, and all wealthy men, to keepe a good Christmas* (London, 1647).

252

Hacket, John, *Scrinia Reserata: A Memorial . . . of John Williams* (London, 1693).

Hall, Thomas, *Funebria Florae, The Downfall of May-Games* (London, 1660).

Hardy, Nathaniel, *Justice Triumphing or the Spoylers Spoyled. Laid forth in a Gratulatory Sermon for the Miraculous Discovery of, and our Glorious Delivery from The Barbarous Powder-Plot* (London, 1647).

Harrison, William, *The Description of England*, ed. Georges Edelen (Ithaca, New York, 1968).

[Hatton], *Correspondence of the Family of Hatton . . . 1601–1704*, ed. Edward Maude Thompson (Camden Society, London, 1878).

Heath, James, *The Glories and Magnificant Triumphs of the Blessed Restitution of His Sacred Majesty K. Charles II* (London, 1662).

Heming, Joseph, *Certaine Quaeries Touching the Rise and Observation of Christmas* (London, 1648).

Hening, William Waller (ed.), *The Statutes at Large: Being a Collection of all the Laws of Virginia* (New York, 1823).

Herle, Charles, *Davids Reserve, and Rescue, in a Sermon preached Before the Honourable, the House of Commons, On the Fifth of November. 1644* (London, 1645).

Herring, Francis, *Popish Pietie, or The first part of the Historie of that horrible and barbarous conspiracie, commonly called the Powder-treason* (London, 1610).

Heywood, Thomas, *Englands Elisabeth: Her life and troubles, during her minoritie, from the cradle to the crown* (Cambridge, 1641).

Hinde, William, *A Faithfull Remonstrance of the Holy Life and Happy Death of Iohn Bruen of Bruen-Stapleford, in the County of Chester, Esquire* (London, 1641).

Historical Manuscripts Commission, *Seventh Report* (London, 1879).

Historical Manuscripts Commission, *Ninth Report* (London, 1883).

Historical Manuscripts Commission, *Cowper* (London, 1888).

Historical Manuscripts Commission, *Cecil* (London, 1899).

Historical Manuscripts Commission, *Montague of Beaulieu* (London, 1900).

Historical Manuscripts Commission, *Ormonde* (London, 1906).

Holingworth, Richard, *A Sermon Preached before the Right Honourable the Lord mayor, Aldermen and Citizens of London . . . November the 5th 1682* (London, 1682).

Holland, Thomas, Πανήγυρις D. *Elizabethae . . . A sermon preached at Pauls in London the 17 of November Ann. Dom. 1599* (Oxford, 1601).

Hooker, Richard, *Of the Lawes of Ecclesiastical Politie* (London, 1723).

Hooker, Thomas, 'The Church's Deliverances', in George H. Williams, Norman Pettit, Winifried Herget, and Sargent Bush, Jr., (eds.), *Thomas Hooker. Writings in England and Holland, 1626–1633* (Cambridge, Mass., 1975).

Hopton, Arthur, *A Concordancy of Yeares* (London, 1612).

Horton, Thomas, *The Pillar and Pattern of Englands Deliverances* (London, 1655).

Howson, John, *A Sermon Preached at St Maries in Oxford the 17 Day of Novemb. 1602* (Oxford, 1602).

The humble petition of the communaltie to their most renowned and gracious Soveraigne, the Ladie Elizabeth (London, 1588).

Humston, Robert, *A Sermon Preached at Reyfham in the Countie of Norff.* (London, 1588).

The Impartial Protestant Mercury, 15–18 November 1681.

Jenkins, William, *A Sermon Preached at Mary Aldermanbury, on the 5th day of November, 1651* (London, 1652).

Jerome, Stephen, *Irelands Iubilee, or Ioyes Io-Paean, for Prince Charles his welcome home. With the Blessings of Great Brittaine, her Dangers, Deliverances, Dignities from God, and Duties to God, pressed and expressed* (Dublin, 1624).

[Jonson], *Ben Jonson*, ed. Ian Donaldson (Oxford, 1985).

The Ioyfull Returne of the most illustrious Prince, Charles . . . from the court of Spaine (London, 1623).

Kennedy, W. P. M. (ed.), *Elizabethan Episcopal Administration* (Oxford, 1924).

Keth, William, *A Sermon made at Blanford Forum* (London, 1572).

King, Henry, *A Sermon of Deliverance. Preached at the Spittle on Easter Monday* (London, 1626).

The Kingdomes Weekly Intelligencer, Sent Abroad to Prevent Misinformation, 2–9 November 1647.

Knevet, Ralph, *Rhodon and Iris. A Pastorall, As it was Presented at the Florists Feast in Norwich, May 3, 1631* (London, 1631).

Kyffin, Maurice, *The Blessednes of Brytaine, or A celebration of the Queenes Holy day* (London, 1588).

[Latimer], *Sermons by Hugh Latimer*, ed. George Elwes Corrie (Parker Society, Cambridge, 1844).

Laud, William, *Articles to be Enquired of within the Dioces of London, in the First General Visitation* (London, 1628).

Laud, William, *Articles to be Inquired of in the Metropolitical Visitation . . . for the Dioces of London* (London, 1636).

[Laud], *The Works of . . . William Luad, D.D.* (Oxford, 1853).

Lechford, Thomas, *New-Englands Advice to Old England* (London, 1644).

Lechford, Thomas, *Plain Dealing or News from New England* [1642], ed. Darrett B. Rutman, (London, 1969).

Leigh, Richard, *The Copie of A Letter Sent out of England* (London, 1601).

Leigh, William, *Great Britaines Great Deliverance, from the great danger of Popish Powder, By way of Meditation, upon the late intended Treason* (London, 1606).

Leigh, William, *Queene Elizabeth, Paraleld in her Princely vertues, with David, Iosua, and Hezekia* (London, 1612).

Leighton, Alexander, *Speculum Bellisaeri: or the looking-glasse to the holy war* (Amsterdam, 1628).

Lever, Christopher, *Queene Elizabeths Teares* (London, 1607).

Lloyd, Ludowick, *Hilaria: or The Triumphant Feast for the fift of August* (London, 1607).

Lloyd, William, *A Sermon Preached at St Martin in the Fields, on November the Fifth, 1678* (London, 1679).

Lloyd, William, *A Sermon Preached before the House of Lords on November 5, 1680* (London, 1680).

Lloyd, William, *A Sermon Preached before Their Majesties at Whitehall, on the Fifth day of November, 1689* (London, 1689).

Lloyd, William, *A Sermon Preached before the Queen at Whitehall. January the 30th. being the day of the Martyrdom of King Charles the First* (London, 1691).

Lloyd, William, *A Sermon Preached before Her Majesty on May 29, being the Anniversary of the Restauration of the King and royal Family* (London, 1692).

Lloyd, William, *A Sermon Preach'd before the House of Lords . . . 30th of January 1696/7* (London, 1697).

Lodge, Edmund (ed.), *Illustrations of British History* (London, 1791).

The London Gazette, 1665–85.

'London Newsletter Collection, 1665–85', Library of Congress.

The Loyal Protestant, and True Domestick Intelligence, 9 November 1682.

M., L., *A Perfect Relation of the Horrible Plot . . . at Edmondsbury* (London, 1647).

The Magnificent Princely, and most Royall Entertainments given to the High and Mightie Prince, and Princesse, Frederick . . . and Elizabeth (London, 1613).

Malthus, Francis, *A Treatise of Artificial Fire-Works, both for Warres and Recreation* (London, 1629).

The Manner of the Burning the Pope in Effigies in London On the 5th of November, 1678 (London, 1678).

A Manuall of Praiers . . . whereunto is added a newe Callendar (Douai?, 1595).

The Marriage of the two great Princes, Fredericke Count Palatine etc., and the Lady Elizabeth . . . with the showes and Fire-workes upon the water (London, 1613).

Marshall, Stephen, *A Sermon Preached before the Honourable House of Commons . . . November 17. 1640* (London, 1641).

Marten, Anthony, *An Exhortation, To stirre up the mindes of all her Maiesties faithfull subiects* (London, 1588).

Mason, Henry, *Christian Humiliation, or, A Treatise of Fasting* (London, 1625).

Mather, Increase, *A testimony against several prophane and superstitious customs, now practiced by some in New-England* (London, 1687).

Maxwell, James, *Queene Elizabeths Looking-glasse of Grace and Glory* (London, 1612).

Mercurius Elencticus, 5–12 November 1647.

Mercurius Politicus, 3–10 November 1653.

[Michel], 'Report of the Journey of Francis Louis Michel', *Virginia Magazine of History and Biography*, 24 (1916), pp. 113–41.

Mico, John, *A Pill to Purge out Poperie* (London, 1623).

Mirk, J., *The Festyuall* (London, 1532).

Mocket, Thomas, *Christmas, The Christians grand Feast . . . Also of Easter, Whitsuntide, and other Holydayes* (London, 1650).

A Modell of the Fire-workes to be presented in Lincolnes-Inne Fields on the 5th of Novemb. 1647. Before the Lords and Commons of Parliament, and the Militia of London, in commemoration of Gods great Mercy in delivering this kingdome from the hellish Plots of Papists, acted in the damnable Gunpowder-treason (London, 1647).

Morton, Thomas (Duresme), *Ezekiel's Wheels: A Treatise concerning Divine Providence* (London, 1653).

Morton, Thomas, *New English Canaan . . . An Abstract of New England*, ed. Charles Francis Adams (Boston, 1883).

The Muses Fire-Works Upon the Fifth of November: or, The Protestants Remembrancer of the Bloody Designs of the Papists (London, 1640).

Nashe, Thomas, *Pierce Penniless His Supplication to the Divell* (London, 1592).

Naunton, Sir Robert, *Fragmentalia Regalia or Observations on Queen Elizabeth, Her Times & Favorites* [1641], ed. John S. Cerovski (Washington, D.C., 1985).

Nelson, Robert, *A Companion for the Festivals and Fasts of the Church of England* (London, 1704).

Newcomen, Matthew, *The Craft and Cruelty of the Churches Adversaries* (London, 1643).

'Newsletters, 1674–1715, addressed to the Newdigate family', Folger Shakespeare Library.

Nichols, John (ed.), *The Progresses and Public Processions of Queen Elizabeth* (London, 1823).

Nichols, John (ed.), *The Progresses, Processions, and Magnificent Festivities of King James the First* (London, 1828).

Nixon, Anthony, *Elizaes memoriall; King Iames his arriuall; and Romes downefall* (London, 1603).

Northbrooke, John, *Spiritus est vicarius Christi in terra. A Treatise wherein Dicing, Dauncing, Vaine playes or Enterluds with other idle pastimes etc. commonly used on the sabboth day are reproved* (London, 1577).

November . . . Red in its Inke, Redder in Wine (London, 1647).

Osborne, Francis, 'Historical Memoires of the Reigns of Q. Elizabeth and King Iames', in *Works*, 7th edn (London, 1673).

Palmer, George, *The Lawfulness of the Celebration of Christs Birthday* (London, 1649).

The Parliament Scout: Communicating His Intelligence to the Kingdome, 31 October–7 November, 1644.

A Perfect & exact account of all the Holy-Daies in the Year, Together with the Reasons why they were set apart as Festivals by the Church (London, 1661).

A Perfect Diurnall of the Passages in Parliament, 31 October–7 November, 1642.

The Perfect Weekly Account, 2–10 November 1647.

Perkins, William, *A Golden Chaine: or, the description of Theologie, containing the order of the causes of Salvation and Damnation* (Cambridge, 1600).

Pigge, Oliver, *Meditations Concerning praiers to Almightie God, for the safetie of England, when the Spaniards were come into the narrow seas. August 1588. As also other Meditations concerning thanksgiuing, for deliuering England from the crueltie of the Spaniards, and for their meruellous confusion and overthrow.* (London, 1589).

Pilkington, James, 'A Godlie Exposition upon certaine chapters of Nehemiah' [1585], in James Schofield (ed.), *The Works of James Pilkington* (Cambridge, 1842).

Prime, John, *A Sermon Briefly comparing the Estate of King Salomon And his*

Subiectes togither with the condition of Queene Elizabeth and her people (Oxford, 1585).

Primrose, Diana, *A Chaine of Pearle. Or A Memoriall of the peerles Graces, and heroick Vertues of queene Elizabeth of Glorious Memory* (London, 1630).

Prynne, William, *Histrio-Mastix. The Players Scourge* (London, 1633).

A Psalme and Collect of thankesgiuing, not vnmeet for this present time (London, 1588).

[Pynchon], *The Pynchon Papers. Letters of John Pynchon 1654–1700*, ed. Carl Bridenbaugh (Boston, 1982).

Puttenham, George, *The Arte of English Poesie* (London, 1589).

Reading, John, *Christmas Revived: or an Answer to Certain Objections* (London, 1660).

Reeve, Thomas, *Mephibosheths Hearts-Ioy Upon his Soveraignes Safetie . . . upon the happy Returne of our Prince Charles* (London, 1624).

Rhodes, John, *A Brief Summe of The Treason intended against the King & State, when they should have been assembled in Parliament. November 5. 1605. Fit for to instruct the simple and ignorant heerein* (London, 1606).

Rhodes, John, *The Countrie mans Comfort* (London, 1637).

Ryves, Bruno, *Mercurius Rusticus: Or, The Countries Complaint of the barbarous Out-rages committed by the Sectaries of this late flourishing kingdome* (London, 1646).

S., H., *Queene Elizabeths Losse and King Iames his Welcome* (London, 1603).

The Scholars Petition for Play-dayes instead of Holy-daies (London, 1644).

Sclater, William, *Papisto-Mastix, or Deborah's Prayer against God's Enemies* (London, 1642).

Scott, Thomas, *Englands Ioy, For Suppressing the Papists* (London?, 1624).

Scott, Thomas, *Vox Dei* (Amsterdam? 1624).

Seldon, John, *Table-Talk*, ed. Edward Arber (London, 1869).

Sharp, John, *A Sermon Preached before the Lords . . . Fifth of November, 1691* (London, 1691).

Shurtleff, Nathaniel B., *Records of the Governor and Company of the Massachusetts Bay* (Boston, 1853–4).

A Skeltonicall Salutation Or condigne gratulation, And iust vexation Of the Spanish Nation (London, 1589).

Small, Peter, *Mans May or a Moneth's minde* (London, 1615).

Smart, Peter, *The Humble Petition of Peter Smart* (London, 1640).

Smart, Peter, *The Vanitie & Downefall of Superstitious Popish Ceremonies* (Edinburgh, 1628).

The Solemn Mock-Procession: or the Tryal & Execution of the Pope and his Ministers, On the 17 of Nov. at Temple-Bar (London, 1680).

Sparke, Edward, *Scintillula Altaris. or, A Pious Reflection on Primitive Devotion: as to the Feasts and Fasts of the Christian Church* (London, 1652).

Sparke, Michael, *Thankfull Remembrances of Gods Wonderfull Deliverances of this Land* (London, 1628).

Sparke, Michael, *To the glory of God in thankefull remembrance of our three great deliverances* (London, 1627).

Speed, John, *The Theatre of the Empire of Great Britiane* (London, 1611).

Spelman, Sir Henry, *Archaeologus. In Modum Glossarii ad rem antiquam posteriorem* (London, 1626).

Spencer, Thomas, *Englands Warning-Peece: or the History of the Gun-powder Treason* (London, 1659).

Spurstowe, William, *Englands Eminent Judgements Caus'd By the Abuse of Gods Eminent Mercies* (London, 1644).

Statutes of the Realm.

Stedman, Fabian, *Campanalogia* (London, 1677).

Stephens, Edward, *A Discourse concerning the original of the Powder-Plot: together with a Relation of the Conspiracies against Queen Elizabeth, and the Persecutions of the Protestants in France* (London, 1674).

Sterry, Peter, *Englands Deliverance from the Northern Presbytery, Compared with its Deliverance from the Roman Papacy: or a Thanksgiving sermon preached on Nov. 5. 1651* (London, 1652).

Stevenson, M., *The Twelve Moneths* (London, 1661).

Stopford, Joshua, *Pagano-Papismus: Or, an Exact Parallel Betweene Rome-Pagan, and Rome-Christian, In their Doctrines and Ceremonies* (London, 1675).

Stow, John, *Annales, or, A Generall Chronicle of England* (London, 1631).

[Stow], *A Survey of London by John Stow*, ed. Charles Lethbridge Kingsford (Oxford, 1908).

[Stow], 'Two London chronicles from the collections of John Stow', ed. C. L. Kingsford (Camden Miscellany, London, 1910).

Strickland, John, *Immanuel, or The Church Triumphing in God with us* (London, 1644).

Strong, William, *The Commemoration and Exaltation of Mercy* (London, 1647).

Strype, John, *Annals of the Reformation*, vol. 3 (Oxford, 1824).

Stubbes, Philip, *The Anatomie of Abuses* (London, 1595).

Taylor, Jeremy, *A Sermon Preached in Saint Maries Church in Oxford Vpon the Anniversary of the Gunpowder-Treason* (Oxford, 1638).

Taylor, John, *All the works of Iohn Taylor* (London, 1630).

Taylor, John, *Christmas in & out* (London, 1653).

Taylor, John, *The Complaint of Christmas* (London, 1646).

Taylor, John, *Englands Comfort and Londons Joy* (London, 1641).

Taylor, John, 'Gods Manifold Mercies in These miraculous deliverances of our Church of England, from the yeare 1565 untill this present, 1630', in *Workes* (London, 1630).

Taylor, John, *A Memorial of all the English Monarchs . . . in heroicall verse* (London, 1622).

Taylor, John, 'Prince Charles his Welcome from Spaine', in Walter Scot (ed.), *A Collection of Scarce and Valuable Tracts* [Somers Tracts], 2nd edn (London, 1809).

Thou, Jacques Auguste, *A Narration of that Horrible Conspiracy Against King James and the Whole Parliament of England, Commonly called the Gun-Powder Treason* (London, 1674).

Thou, Jacques Auguste, *Popish Policies and Practices Represented in the Histories of the Parisian Massacre; Gun-powder Treason; Conspiracies Against Queen Elizabeth* (London, 1674).

Turner, John, *A Commemoration, or A calling to minde of the great and Eminent Deliverance from the Powder-Plot* (London, 1654).

Tusser, Thomas, *Five Hundred Points of Good Husbandry* (London, 1614).

Valentine, Henry, *God save the King. A Sermon Preached in St Pauls Church the 27th of March 1639. Being the Day of His Maiesties Most Happy Inauguration, and of His Northerne Expedition* (London, 1639).

Van Schreeven, William J., and Reese, George H., *Proceedings of the General Assembly of Virginia . . . 1619* (Jamestown, 1969).

Vaughan, William, *The Golden-grove, moralized in three Bookes* (London, 1600).

Venning, Ralph, *Mercies Memorial; or, Israel's thankful Remembrance of God* (London, 1657).

Verney, Margaret M., *Memoirs of the Verney Family from the Restoration to the Revolution 1660 to 1696* (London, 1899).

Verus Pater, or, A bundell of Truths (London, 1611).

Vicars, John, *Englands hallelu-jah; or, Great Britaines retribution* (London, 1631).

Vicars, John, *Mischeefes Mysterie: or, Treasons Master-peece, the Powder Plot* (London, 1617).

Vicars, John, *November the 5. 1605. The Quintessence of Cruelty, or Master-peice of treachery* (London, 1641).

The Vindication of Christmas (London, 1653).

The Virginia Gazette, 1736–1774.

Vox Graculi, or Iacke Dawes Prognostication (London, 1623).

Wake, Joan (ed.), *A Copy of Papers relating to Musters, Beacons, Subsidies, etc. in the County of Northampton AD. 1586–1623* (Northants Record Society, Northampton, 1926).

Ward, Ned, 'A trip to New England', in George P. Winship (ed.), *Boston in 1682 and 1699* (Providence, Rhode Island, 1905).

Webb, George, *Catalogue protestantium: Or, The Protestants Kalender* (London, 1624).

The Weekly Intelligencer of the Common-wealth 31 October–7 November 1654.

Westcote, Thomas, *A view of Devonshire in MDCXXX*, ed. George Oliver and Pitman Jones (Exeter, 1845).

White, John, *A Rich Cabinet, with Variety of Inventions . . . Whereunto is added variety of Recreative Fire-works, both for Land, Aire, and Water* (London, 1651).

White, Thomas, *A sermon preached at Paules Cross the 17 of November A. 1589* (London, 1589).

Williams, John, *The History of the Gunpowder-treason, Collected from Approved authors, As well Popish as Protestant* (London, 1678; 2nd edn 1679).

Williams, John, *A Vindication of the History of the Gunpowder-Treason . . . To which is added A parallel betwixt That and the Present Popish Plot* (London, 1681).

Wilson, John, *A Song of deliverance for the lasting remembrance of Gods wonderful works* (Boston, 1680).

Wilson, John, *A Song or Story, for the lasting remembrance of divers famous works, which God hath done in our time* (London, 1626).

Bibliography

Wilson, Thomas, *A Sermon on the Gunpowder Treason with Reflections on the Late Plot* (London, 1679).

[Winthrop], *The Winthrop Papers . . . 1623–49* (Boston, 1931–47).

Wither, George, *Britain's Remembrancer* (London, 1628).

Wither, George, *Halelviah or, Britans Second Remembrancer* (London, 1641).

Women Will have their Will: or, Give Christmas his Due (London, 1648).

Woodward, Hezekiah, *Christmas Day, The old Heathens feasting Day, in honour to Saturn their Idol God. The Papists Massing Day. The Prophane mans Ranting Day. The Superstitious Mans Idol Day. The Multitudes Idle Day* (London, 1656).

Select Secondary Sources

Anglo, Sydney, 'The court festivals of Henry VII', *Bulletin of the John Rylands Library*, 43 (1960–1), pp. 12–45.

Anglo, Sydney, 'An early Tudor programme for plays and other demonstrations against the Pope', *Journal of the Warburg and Courtauld Institutes*, 20 (1957), pp. 176–9.

Ashton, Robert, 'Popular entertainment and social control in later Elizabethan and Stuart London', *The London Journal*, 9 (1983), pp. 3–19.

Barton, Anne, *Ben Jonson, Dramatist* (Cambridge, 1984).

Beard, I. M., 'A complex of times: no more sheep on Romulus' birthday', *Proceedings of the Cambridge Philological Society*, 213 (1987), pp. 1–15.

Beck, Ervin, 'Rhymes and songs for Halloween and bonfire night', *Lore and language*, 4 (1985), pp. 1–17.

Bergerson, David M., *English Civic Pageantry 1558–1642* (London, 1971).

Bourdieu, Pierre, *Outline of a Theory of Practice* (Cambridge, 1977).

Bourne, Henry, *Antiquitates Vulgares or the Antiquities of the Common People* (Newcastle, 1725).

Brand, John, *Observations on Popular Antiquities*, ed. Henry Ellis (London, 1813).

Breen, T. H., *Tobacco Culture: The Mentality of the Great Tidewater Planters on the Eve of Revolution* (Princeton, 1985).

Bristol, Michael D., *Carnival and Theatre: Plebian Culture and the Structure of Authority in Renaissance England* (New York, 1985).

Brydon, George Maclaren, *Virginia's Mother Church and the Political Conditions under Which it Grew* (Richmond, Virginia, 1947).

Burke, Peter, 'Popular culture in seventeeth-century London', *The London Journal*, 3 (1977), pp. 143–62.

Burne, Charlotte S., 'Guy Fawkes' day', *Folk-Lore*, 23 (1912), pp. 409–26.

Bushaway, Bob, *By Rite: Custom, Ceremony and Community in England 1700–1880* (London, 1982).

Canetti, Elias, *Crowds and Power* (New York, 1962).

Capp, Bernard, *Astrology and the Popular Press: English Almanacs 1500–1800* (London, 1979).

Cardwell, Edward, *A History of Conferences . . . Connected with the Revision of the Book of Common Prayer*, 3rd edn (Oxford, 1849).

Christianson, Paul, *Reformers and Babylon: English Apocalyptic Visions from the*

Reformation to the Eve of the Civil War (Toronto, 1978).

Cogswell, Thomas, 'Thomas Middleton and the court, 1624: *A Game at Chess* in context', *Huntington Library Quarterly*, 47 (1984), pp. 273–88.

Cowley, Patrick, *The Church Houses. Their Religious and Social Significance* (London, 1970).

Cox, J. Charles, *Churchwardens' Accounts from the Fourteenth Century to the Close of the Seventeenth Century* (London, 1913).

Davies, Horton, *Worship and Theology in England . . . from Cranmer to Hooker* (Princeton, 1970).

Durston, Chris, 'Lords of misrule: the puritan war on Christmas 1642–60', *History Today*, 35 (1985), pp. 7–14.

Dyer, T. F. Thisleton, *British Popular Customs Present and Past* (London, 1900).

Frazer, J. G., *Balder the Beautiful: the Fire-Festivals of Europe and the Doctrine of the External Soul* (London, 1923).

Furley, O. W., 'The Pope-burning processions of the late seventeenth century', *History*, 44 (1959), pp. 16–23.

Gailey, Alan, 'The bonfire in north Irish tradition', *Folk-Lore*, 88 (1977), pp. 3–38.

Geertz, Clifford, *Local Knowledge: Further Essays in Interpretive Anthropology* (New York, 1983).

Gildrie, Richard P., 'The ceremonial puritan: days of humiliation and thanksgiving', *New England Historical and Genealogical Register*, 136 (1982), pp. 3–16.

Hampson, R. T., *Medii Aevi Kalendarium or Dates, Charters and Customs of the Middle Ages* (London, 1841).

Harris, Tim, *London Crowds in the Reign of Charles II: Propaganda and Politics from the Restoration until the Exclusion Crisis* (Cambridge, 1987).

Hassel, R. Chris Jr., *Renaissance Drama & the English Church Year* (Lincoln, Nebraska, 1979).

Hill, Christopher, 'God and the English Revolution', *History Workshop Journal*, 17 (1984), pp. 19–31.

Hill, Christopher, *Society and Puritanism in Pre-Revolutionary England* (London, 1964).

Hobsbawm, Eric, and Ranger, Terence (eds.), *The Invention of Tradition* (Cambridge, 1984).

Holmes, Geoffrey, 'The Sacheverell riots: the crowd and the church in early eighteenth-century London', *Past and Present*, 72 (1976), pp. 55–85.

Homans, George Caspar, *English Villagers of the Thirteenth Century* (Cambridge, Mass., 1941).

Houlbrooke, Ralph, *Church Courts and the People During the English Reformation 1520–1570* (Oxford, 1979).

Hughes, Ann, *Politics, Society and Civil War in Warwickshire, 1620–1660* (Cambridge, 1987).

Hunt, William, *The Puritan Moment. The Coming of Revolution in an English County* (Cambridge, Mass., 1983).

Hutton, Ronald, 'The local impact of the Tudor reformation', in Christopher

Bibliography

Haigh (ed.), *The English Reformation Revised* (Cambrige, 1987), pp. 114–38.

Hutton, Ronald, *The Restoration: A Political and Religious History of England and Wales 1658–1667* (Oxford, 1985).

Isaac, Rhys, *The Transformation of Virginia 1740–1790* (Chapel Hill, 1982).

James, E. O., *Seasonal Feasts and Festivals* (London, 1961).

Johnston, Ron, *Bell-ringing: The English Art of Change-ringing* (Harmondsworth, 1986).

Lamont, William M., *Marginal Prynne 1600–1669* (London, 1963).

Legg, J. Wickham, *English Church Life from the Restoration to the Tractarian Movement* (London, 1914).

Love, W. DeLoss, *The Fast and Thanksgiving Days of New England* (New York, 1895).

MacAloon, John J. (ed.), *Rite, Drama, Festival, Spectacle* (Philadelphia, 1984).

Main, Gloria, L., *Tobacco Colony: Life in Early Maryland, 1650–1720* (Princeton, 1983).

Malcolmson, Robert W., *Popular Recreations in English Society 1700–1850* (Cambridge, 1973).

Maltby, William S., *The Black Legend in England: The Development of Anti-Spanish Sentiment, 1558–1660* (Durham, North Carolina, 1971).

Marcus, Leah S., *The Politics of Mirth: Jonson, Herrick, Milton, Marvell, and the Defense of Old Holiday Pastimes* (Chicago, 1986).

Martin, Colin, and Parker, Geoffrey, *The Spanish Armada* (London, 1988).

Mattingly, Garrett, *The Armada* (Boston, 1959).

Miller, John, *Popery and Politics in England 1660–1688* (Cambridge, 1973).

Morris, Ernest, *The History and Art of Change Ringing* (Wakefield, 1976).

Nash, Gary B., *The Urban Crucible: Social Change, Political Consciousness, and the Origins of the American Revolution* (Cambridge, Mass., 1979).

Neale, J. E., 'November 17th', in *Essays in Elizabethan History* (London, 1958), pp. 9–20.

Nilsson, Martin P., *Primitive Time-Reckoning* (Lund, 1920).

Noble, T. C. (ed.), *The Names of those Persons who Subscribed towards the defence of this Country at the Time of the Spanish Armada* (London, 1886).

Patterson, Annabel, *Censorship and Interpretation: The Conditions of Writing and Reading in Early Modern England* (Madison, Wisconsin, 1984).

Pettit, Thomas, '"Here comes I, Jack Straw": English folk drama and social revolt', *Folklore*, 95 (1984), pp. 3–20.

Phythian-Adams, Charles, *Local History and Folklore: A New Framework* (London, 1975).

Powell, William, S., *John Pory, 1572–1636. The Life and Letters of a Man of Many Parts* (Chapel Hill, 1977).

Price, Percival, *Bells and Man* (New York, 1983).

Raven, J. J., *The Bells of England* (London, 1906).

Reay, Barry (ed.), *Popular Culture in Seventeenth-Century England* (London, 1985).

Revard, Stella P., 'Milton's gunpowder poems and Satan's conspiracy', *Milton Studies*, 4 (1972), pp. 63–77.

Rodriguez-Salgado, M. J., et al., Armada 1588–1988 (London, 1988).

Rogers, Nicholas, 'Popular protest in early Hanoverian London', Past and Present, 79 (1978), pp. 70–100.

Rutman, Darrett and Rutman, Anita, A Place in Time: Middlesex County, Virginia, 1650–1760 (New York, 1984).

Sacks, David Harris, 'The demise of the martyrs: the feasts of St Clement and St Katherine in Bristol, 1400–1600', Social History, 11 (1986), pp. 141–69.

Sanderson, J. (ed.), Change Ringing: The History of an English Art (Guildford, 1987).

Seaver, Paul, S., Wallington's World: A Puritan Artisan in Seventeenth-Century London (Stanford, 1985).

Schwoerer, Lois G., 'The Glorious Revolution as spectacle: a new perspective', in Stephen B. Baxter (ed.), England's Rise to Greatness (Berkeley and Los Angeles, 1983), pp. 109–149.

Schwoerer, Lois G., 'Propaganda in the Revolution of 1688–89', American Historical Review, 82 (1977), pp. 843–74.

Solberg, Winton, U., Redeem the Time: The Puritan Sabbath in Early America (Cambridge, Mass., 1977).

Stowell, Marion Barber, Early American Almanacs: The Colonial Weekday Bible (New York, 1977).

Strong, Roy, The Cult of Elizabeth: Elizabethan Portraiture and Pageantry (London, 1977).

Strong, Roy C., 'The popular celebration of the accession day of Queen Elizabeth I', Journal of the Warburg and Courtauld Institutes, 21 (1958), pp. 86–103.

Strutt, Joseph, The Sports and Pastimes of the People of England, ed. W. Hone (London, 1830).

Tilley, H. T., and Walters, H. B., The Church Bells of Warwickshire: Their Founders, Inscriptions, Traditions, and Uses (Birmingham, 1910).

Thomas, Keith, Religion and the Decline of Magic (London and New York, 1971).

Turner, Victor, Dramas, Fields, and Metaphors: Symbolic Action in Human Society (Ithaca, New York, 1974).

Turner, Victor, The Ritual Process: Structure and Anti-Structure (Harmondsworth, 1969).

Underdown, David, Revel, Riot and Rebellion: Popular Politics and Culture in England 1603–1660 (Oxford, 1985).

Wedgwood, C. V., 'Oliver Cromwell and the Elizabethan inheritance', in History and Hope (London, 1987), pp. 317–35.

Williams, Sheila, 'The Pope-burning processions of 1679, 1680 and 1681', Journal of the Warburg and Courtauld Institutes, 21 (1958), pp. 104–18.

Woolf, D. R., 'Two Elizabeths? James I and the late queen's famous memory', Canadian Journal of History, 20 (1985), pp. 167–91.

Wright, A. R., British Calendar Customs, ed. T. E. Lones (London, 1936–40).

Wrightson, Keith, 'The puritan reformation of manners with special reference to the counties of Lancashire and Essex, 1640–1660', Cambridge University, Ph.D. thesis, 1974.

Bibliography

Youings, Joyce, *Sixteenth-Century England* (London, 1984).

Young, Alfred F., 'English plebian culture and eighteenth-century American radicalism', in Margaret Jacob and James Jacob (eds.), *The Origins of Anglo-American Radicalism* (London, 1984), pp. 185–212.

Zerubauel, Evitar, *Hidden Rhythms: Schedules and Calendars in Social Life* (Chicago, 1981).

Zobel, Hiller B., *The Boston Massacre* (New York, 1970).

INDEX

265